Books, Libraries, Reading, and Publishing in the Cold War

Edited by
Hermina G.B. Anghelescu
and Martine Poulain

LIBRARY OF CONGRESS
THE CENTER FOR THE BOOK
WASHINGTON, D.C., 2001

Books, Libraries, Reading, and Publishing in the Cold War
Copyright ©2001 by the University of Texas Press
Published by special arrangement with the University of Texas Press
Based on the conference Books, Libraries, Reading, and Publishing in the Cold War, organized by the IFLA Round Table on Library History École nationale superiéure des sciences de l'information et des bibliothèques (ENSSIB), Villeurbanne Centre de Formation aux Carrières de Bibliothèques (Médiadix) Paris assisted by the IFLA Section on Reading.

No part of this book may be reproduced in any form or by any means, electronic or mechanical, including photocopying, recording or by any information storage and retrieval system without permission in writing.

Inquiries should be addressed to
Library of Congress
Center for the Book
101 Independence Avenue SE
Washington D.C. 20540-4920

First printing by *Libraries & Culture,* Graduate School of Library and Information Science, University of Texas at Austin, 2001.

Library of Congress Cataloging-in-Publication Data

Books, libraries, reading, and publishing in the Cold War / edited by Hermina G. B. Anghelescu and Martine Poulain.
   p. cm.
"Based on the conference Books, Libraries, Reading, and Publishing in the Cold War, organized by the IFLA Round Table on Library History, Ecole nationale supérieure des sciences de l'information et des bibliothèques (ENSSIB), Villeurbanne centre de formation aux carrières de bibliothèques (Médiadix) Paris assisted by the IFLA Section on Reading"–T.p. verso
   Originally published as Libraries & Culture, v. 36, no. 1, winter 2001.
   Includes bibliographical references and Index.
   ISBN 0-8444-1056-X (alk. paper)
   1. Books and reading–Communist countries–Congresses. 2. Censorship–Communist countries–Congresses 3. Cold War–Influence–Congresses. 4. Libraries and communism–Congresses. I. Anghelescu, Hermina G.B. II. Poulain, Martine. III. IFLA Round Table on Library History. IV. Ecole nationale supérieure des sciences de l'information et des bibliothèques (France) V. Villeurbanne centre de formation aux carrières de bibliothèques. VI. International Federation of Library Associations and Institutions. Section on Reading. VII. Libraries & culture.

Z1003.5.C725 B66 2001
027'.009'045–dc21   2001041208

∞ The paper used in this publication meets the minimum requirements of American National Standard for Information Sciences–Permanence of Paper for Printed Library Materials, ANSI Z39.48-1984.

✿ This book is printed on recycled paper.

Printed in the United States of America
at Morgan Printing in Austin, Texas

Contents

vii Foreword
    John Y. Cole

Pamela Spence Richards (1941–1999)

xi A Biographical Sketch
    Betty Turock
xviii A Tribute from the United States
    Donald G. Davis, Jr.
xx A Tribute from Russia
    Valeria D. Stelmakh

Books, Reading, and Publishing in the Cold War

xxi Preface
    Martine Poulain
xxiii Editorial Note
    Donald G. Davis, Jr.

Articles

Session 1: Books during the Cold War

1 "With malice toward none": IFLA and the Cold War
    Donald G. Davis, Jr. (U.S.A.), assisted by Nathaniel Feis
16 A Soviet Research Library Remembered
    Edward Kasinec (U.S.A.)
27 The Overseas Libraries Controversy and the Freedom to Read: U.S. Librarians and Publishers Confront Joseph McCarthy
    Louise S. Robbins (U.S.A.)
40 The Effect of the Cold War on Librarianship in China
    Cheng Huanwen (China)
51 Political Censorship in Finnish Libraries from 1944 to 1946
    Kai Ekholm (Finland)
58 Books and Libraries as Instruments of Cultural Diplomacy in Francophone Africa during the Cold War
    Mary Niles Maack (U.S.A.)

Session 2: Publishing during the Cold War

87 Censors and Their Readers: Selling, Silencing, and Reading Czech Books
   Jiřina Šmejkalová (Czech Republic)
104 Control of Literary Communication in the 1945–1956 Period in Poland
   Oskar Stanislaw Czarnik (Poland)
116 International Harmony: Threat or Menace? U.S. Youth Services Librarians and Cold War Censorship, 1946–1955
   Christine Jenkins (U.S.A.)
131 Le Comité de Défense de la Littérature et de la Presse pour la Jeunesse: The Communists and the Press for Children during the Cold War
   Thierry Crépin (France)

Session 3: Reading during the Cold War

143 Reading in the Context of Censorship in the Soviet Union
   Valeria D. Stelmakh (Russia)
152 Symbolic Censorship and Control of Appropriations: The French Communist Party Facing "Heretical" Texts during the Cold War
   Bernard Pudal (France)
162 American Literature in Cold War Germany
   Martin Meyer (Germany)
172 A Cold War Best-Seller: The Reaction to Arthur Koestler's *Darkness at Noon* in France from 1945 to 1950
   Martine Poulain (France)
185 Library Secret Fonds and the Competition of Societies
   István Király (Romania)

Session 4: Libraries during the Cold War

193 Cold War Librarianship: Soviet and American Library Activities in Support of National Foreign Policy, 1946–1991
   Pamela Spence Richards (U.S.A.)
204 Foreign Libraries in the Mirror of Soviet Library Science during the Cold War
   Boris Volodin (Russia)
211 Finland Pays Its Debts and Gets Books in Return: ASLA Grants to the Finnish Academic Libraries, 1950–1967
   Ilkka Mäkinen (Finland)

233 Romanian Libraries Recover after the Cold War: The Communist Legacy and the Road Ahead
    Hermina G.B. Anghelescu (U.S.A.)
253 Leaning to One Side: The Impact of the Cold War on Chinese Library Collections
    Priscilla C. Yu (U.S.A.)

267 The Bookplate
    Martin Manning
275 Contributors
287 Index

Foreword

The Center for the Book in the Library of Congress was established by Librarian of Congress Daniel J. Boorstin in 1977 as a public-private sector partnership to stimulate public interest in books, reading, and libraries. This mission, which encompasses the historical study of books, reading, and print culture, has been an important activity since the Center's earliest years.

This book, *Books, Libraries, Reading and Publishing in the Cold War*, presents papers presented at a stimulating international conference in Paris, France on June 11–12, 1998. Donald G. Davis, Jr. provides further information about the conference in his Editorial Note. The papers were edited by Hermina G.B. Anghelescu and Martine Poulain, one of the conference organizers, and published in the Winter 2001 issue (Volume 36/1) of *Libraries & Culture: A Journal of Library History*, which is published by the University of Texas Press.

As part of its publishing program, Center for the Book is pleased to sponsor this volume, which is dedicated to Pamela Spence Richards (1941-1999) of Rutgers University. Along with Martine Poulain and Marie-Noelle Frachon, Pam organized the 1998 conference documented in these pages.

Due to illness, Pam was unable to attend the conference she spent so much time and effort organizing. She died fifteen months later, in September 1999. Her unique contribution to library history, particularly its international dimension, is addressed through special contributions to this volume from Martine Poulain, Don Davis, Betty Turock, and Valeria Stelmakh. I join my library history colleagues in paying tribute to Pam's devotion to our field and to her many personal achievements.

In particular, I remember how skillfully she persuaded me that the Center for the Book should provide financial support for a 1996 conference on "Reading in Times of Cultural Change," held in Vologda, Russia. This meeting was organized by Pam and her friend Valeria Stelmakh, a colleague in the International Federation of Library Associations and Institutions (IFLA). By 1998 I was chair of IFLA's Section on Reading, and Pam enlisted my help for the Paris conference, where I was privileged to chair one of the sessions.

Our book is enhanced, not only by the tributes to Pamela Spence Richards, but also by an index prepared by students in the Indexing and Abstracting class LIS 8230, Library and Information Science Program, Wayne State University, Detroit, Michigan, under the supervision of co-editor Hermina G.B. Anghelescu.

This publication is made possible by a financial contribution to the Center for the Book by its founder, historian Daniel J. Boorstin, who served as Librarian of Congress from 1975 to 1987. The Daniel J. and Ruth F. Boorstin Fund, established when Dr. Boorstin retired in 1987, supports several key Center for the Book activities.

Finally, the volume continues previous Center for the Book projects and publications in book, library, and publishing history. Recent publications include: *A Handbook for the Study of Book History in the United States*, by Ronald J. Zboray and Mary Saracino Zboray (2000); *Library History Research in America: Essays Commemorating the Fiftieth Anniversary of the Library History Roundtable* (2000, published by special arrangement with the University of Texas Press); and *The Rivers of America: A Descriptive Bibliography* (2001, copublished with the Oak Knoll Press). For further information, consult the Center for the Book's Web site: www.loc.gov/cfbook.

The Center for the Book in the Library of Congress is pleased to present, to a wide public, these papers about the intriguing Cold War relationships among books, reading, libraries and publishing.

John Y. Cole
Director, The Center for the Book
in the Library of Congress

Pamela Spence Richards (1941–1999)

Pamela Spence Richards (1941-1999)
A Biographical Sketch

Betty Turock
Professor, School of Communication, Information & Library Studies, Rutgers University

Pamela Spence Richards was born in New York City on June 2, 1941. Her mother, Mary Frances Lavine, moved from Georgia to New York during the Depression to pursue a career in acting. Her father, Guy Richards, was a descendant of the Dutch Verplanck family, among the first settlers of New Amsterdam. He became a journalist whose career culminated as City Editor for the *New York Herald Tribune*. During World War II he was a Marine colonel, and afterwards undertook a history of the Marine Corps in the war. His interests influenced her own pursuits, both professionally and personally; throughout her life she read about World War II with "never-flagging interest."

Richards's elementary education was completed at the premier Brearley School in New York City. Upon graduating from the Masters School at Dobbs Ferry, New York, in 1959, she entered Radcliffe College at Harvard University, where, in 1963, she was awarded the B.A. degree magna cum laude in Germanic literature. Shortly after receiving her bachelor's degree, she married James Barzun, a medical doctor and the son of cultural historian Jacques Barzun. The union ended in divorce 1968. In 1969 she wed the Dutch social historian, J. Wilhelmus Smit, holder of the Queen Wilhelmina Chair in History at Columbia University and known to all as Wim. They were married for more than 30 years.

To begin her graduate education, Richards enrolled at Columbia University and continued there on and off over the next 13 years. After earning her first master's degree in Germanic languages in 1966 and through her two pregnancies, Richards pursued a master's degree in library service (MLS), which she completed in 1971. While working full-time as a research associate at Columbia Business School, and later as an instructional services librarian at Westchester Community College in Valhalla, she began work toward her doctoral degree in library service. In 1979, two years after launching her teaching career at Rutgers University's

School of Library Service, she received her D.L.S. from Columbia. Consistent with her ongoing interest in history, her dissertation entailed a comprehensive review of the New York Historical Society Library from 1804 to 1979. The work was later published as a book, *Scholars and Gentlemen: The Library of the New York Historical Society* (Hamden, CN: Archon Books, 1984).

In her biography for the 25th Anniversary Report of Harvard and Radcliffe's Class of 1963, Richards wrote frankly about the American upper-middle class mentality that had shaped her thinking in the years leading up to her graduate work, and of her own process of "unlearning" that mentality. She described her original vision for her life as revolving around marriage, children, and social life, and showing her ability to direct her wry wit at herself, she added, "enhanced, naturally, by the requisite patina of *Kultur*."

The turbulence of the 1960s at Columbia made Richards come to view her values and prejudices as "irrelevant, even obscene," in the context of the newly emerging society. She credited her husband Wim with helping her to shed her social and racial bias and the "social snobbism" that had limited her growth during the earlier years of her life.

In the same biography, Richards celebrated the fact that her children had grown up with such different mindsets from her own at their age, and that they would never have to unlearn the fallacies that loomed supreme throughout her youth: "that the American upper-middle class sits at the right hand of God; that non-Americans are at least to be pitied if not despised; that it's a (white) man's world; and that a woman is only as good as her looks." Her life's work serves as a lasting testament to her success in freeing herself of these views. Issues such as freedom of information for all people in both American and global contexts became passionate points of interest throughout her distinguished career. She took great personal interest in issues of equality as well.

A professor at Rutgers for over twenty years, Richards was a proponent of the merger of the Graduate School of Library Service with the undergraduate Departments of Communication and Journalism and Mass Media to form the School of Communication, Information and Library Studies (SCILS). She was a dynamic classroom presence, who taught in the undergraduate Communication program as well as at the master's and doctoral level in Library and Information Studies (LIS). Over the years her specialties were the reference process, international librarianship, library history, and scholarly communication. Librarianship "enormously excited" Richards, and she claimed to practice it with "a missionary fervor." She was a role model for the academic life thoroughly enjoyed and well lived, who not only found a home for her scholarship, but also for her avid advocacy of good teaching. Recalling her entry into the ranks of the professorate with no tutelage as a teacher, she organized special workshops for new faculty and Ph.D. students serving as teaching assistants and enlisted the SCILS faculty in their presentation.

Richards was a citizen of the world who traveled to remote places here at home and also in obscure areas of Siberia and Kamchatka. In her travels she recruited students from around the globe to the SCILS. She made her international interests known to her university colleagues in symposia with such presentations as "Library Education in Europe: Lost Opportunities, Future Promise." She was a principled advocate of faculty governance, who for many years was elected as the SCILS representative to the Rutgers Faculty Council, ultimately serving on the Council's Executive Board.

A prodigious author, Richards was among the most widely published faculty members in her discipline in the United States, according to "Productivity of U.S. Library and Information Science Faculty: The Hayes Study Revisited," *(Library Quarterly* 66:1-20 [January 1996]). At the close of her career in 1999, her scholarly contributions were recognized with Rutgers University's Award for Excellence in Research and the Jesse Shera Research Award from the American Library Association (ALA). Earlier honors included the Harold Lancour Scholarship from Beta Phi Mu and the Justin Winsor Award for excellence in library history research from the ALA's Library History Round Table. Richards's recognition as a scholar was further attested to by her invitations to membership on the editorial boards of *Library History,* published in the United Kingdom, and *Bibliografija,* published in Lithuania. In the United States, she served in a similar capacity for the *International Library Review* and as Contributing International Editor for the *Bulletin of the American Society for Information Science.* For more than a decade she was also a member of the editorial board of *Library Quarterly* and Editor-in-Chief of the *Journal of the Rutgers University Libraries.*

Her research was frequently supported by grants. Awards came from the American Council of Learned Societies, the American Philosophical Society, the Association for Library and Information Science Education (ALISE), the Council on Library Resources, the Library Council of the Union of the Soviet Socialist Republics (USSR), the H. W. Wilson Company, the International Research and Exchange Board (IREX), the National Endowment for the Humanities (NEH), the Soros Foundation's Open Society Institute, and the United States Information Agency (USIA), a remarkable record for a humanities scholar.

Richards's research focused on three major streams, which sometimes overlapped throughout her professional life. She was meticulous in the presentation of her research, but seldom veered far from the facts. Her work would have benefited from more interpretation and speculation.

As a scholar, her love of people and their stories became the raw material for her first and enduring passion, history. Her research into the history of American libraries as social institutions continued throughout her career in studies of Carnegie libraries and of library service to black populations, even as she developed and pursued other areas of interest. Her early work, starting with her dissertation in 1979, focused primarily on American library history.

More than fifteen years later, in 1995, she brought the history of American library service into a global perspective by publishing "Library Services for African-Americans in the Twentieth Century," in the South African journal *Cape Librarian/Kaapse Bibiotekaris*. In that same year, she lectured on this topic at the Russian Ministry of Culture's Conference on Library Services to Culturally Isolated Populations. Her message of library service for all people, communicated through the medium of history, struck a chord with these very different societies, which nonetheless faced the same challenge of reaching all their diverse members with the power of information.

The second theme of her research was scientific information exchange during times of war. An early article, "Information Science in Wartime: Pioneer Documentation Activities during World War II," won inclusion in *The Best of Library Literature 1988,* (Metuchen, NJ: Scarecrow Press, 1989, 59-72). This period of research also included an article entitled "The Movement of Scientific Knowledge to and from Germany under National Socialism," (*Minerva* 28:401-426 [Winter 1991) of which she was especially proud, and culminated in the publication of her book *Scientific Information in Wartime* (Westport CT: Greenwood Press, 1994).

Richards lectured tirelessly in this realm of her research interests. "Gathering Enemy Scientific Information in World War II," "The Government Role in American Scientific and Technical Information: A Model of Reluctant Support," and "The Transformation of Information into Intelligence: The Historical Background," were among her many presentations. Although this work concentrated on the Allied-German rivalry, 1939-1945, she determined that "no study of wartime information would be complete without including the Soviet role in the game of scientific spying." With typical vivacity, she took on the challenge of learning Russian. Though an accomplished linguist who published chapters and articles in English, Dutch, German, French, and ultimately in Russian, she later described this undertaking as "a truly humbling mid-life experience."

In the early 1990s, Richards' investigations into Russia's wartime history spurred the third stream of scholarship, Russian librarianship and library education. It led to her publishing articles on Soviet librarianship, from the purely scientific to the relation between Soviet library institutions and Soviet society. Some of her finest publications in this area include the chapter "Education and Training for Information Science in the Soviet Union" *(Annual Review of Information Science and Technology* 1992, 267-290) and the article "Soviet-American Library Relations in the 1920s and '30s" *(Library Quarterly* 68:390-405 [October 1998]). She served as guest editor for a special issue of *Libraries & Culture* focusing on "The History of Reading and Libraries in the United States and Russia" (Vol. 33, No.1, Winter 1998). Richards' final presentation, "The Soviet Overseas Information Empire and the Implications of Its Disintegration," given at the 1998 Conference on the History and Heritage of Science Information Systems, was delivered with her usual vigor, although by this time she was engaged in a valiant battle with the malignant brain tumor that would end her life. The lecture was added to her personal list of best works.

Richards's devotion to Russia and Russian librarianship, was cemented in August, 1991. While lecturing at the conference of the International Federation of Library Associations (IFLA) in Moscow on reading and reader research, the coup against Gorbachev and Perestroika broke out. Immediately, she went the center of the confrontation to join the demonstration for democracy. Pictures of her leaning against a Russian tank quickly circulated among the Americans who had not fled the conference. As she revisited the scene over the years, her only regret was that she could not get to the top of the tank to join the troops because "her mini-skirt was too tight to make the climb."

A lasting relationship with the Russian Ministry of Culture led to invitations to lecture at conferences. It was in the 1995 Kamchatka conference that Richards became a vibrant life force for Russian librarianship. Throughout the next year, she used her abundant charm and tenacity to pursue funding from the Soros Foundation and the ALA to organize, with Ghenya Kuzmin, Russian Minister of Culture for Libraries, the conference, *Libraries and Reading in Times of Cultural Change.* In June 1996, scholars from around the world gathered in Vologda, Russia. Richards went back to early roots to bring the history of the United States to bear on the current Russian transition, when she spoke about "Library Services for the African-American Intelligentsia before 1960."

Richards traveled to her beloved Russia for the last time as a Fulbright Scholar in 1997. Upon returning home her repeated remark to her Rutgers colleagues was, "my fortunes will be tied to Russia and Russian librarianship for the rest of my life." The women of the LIS had eagerly awaited her return. After a fallow decade, Richards was the first woman to become a full professor in their department. Now there were four, Carol Kuhlthau, Betty Turock, Kay Vandergrift, and Pamela Richards, enough to form a caucus and make certain their views were heard. They met frequently with Richards' feminist core electrifying their discussions and plans for the future of the department.

Richards' professional affiliations reflected her commitment to library history, scientific and technical information studies, and freedom of access to information. She was chair of the Round Table on Library History of the IFLA and an active member of the ALA's counterpart. A leader in the American Society for Information Science (ASIS), whose mission she saw as "raising the nation's consciousness to its responsibility to share its scientific and technical information riches with the underdeveloped world," Richards was chair of the Special Interest Group for International Information Interests and a nominee for president in 1992.

But life was not all work for Richards. She took part in the annual ASIS conference effort to spoof the discipline and profession. Her starring role came in 1991, when she gave an unforgettable performance as a stuffy German professor, complete with appropriate attire, make-up and accent. Her comedic presentation of the pompous in the professorate brought the house down. She was an enthusiastic dancer whose beauty and grace made her a highly sought partner; she often led the pace far into the night at the ASIS conference celebrations.

Richards and her family made their home in New York City's Morningside Heights ten months of the year, while she taught at Rutgers and her husband taught at Columbia. She embraced running, fast walking, and fitness with her usual intensity and completed many New York marathons. The family spent their summers in Smit's native Netherlands at their country home outside of Arnhem. She shared her husband's passion for the Netherlands and Dutch culture, and together they authored two books on the subject: *The Dutch in America* (Dobbs Ferry, NY: Oceana Publications, 1972) and *The Netherlands: A Chronology and Factbook,* (Dobbs Ferry, N.Y., Oceana Publications, 1973). She enjoyed doing yard work around their summer home, which she jokingly referred to as "mudwork," due to the rainy Dutch climate.

Richards and Smit had two children. Their daughter, Marijka, holds a master's degree in Urban Planning from Columbia University and is employed by the New York Development Corporation. She worked on the restoration of Grand Central Station and is now involved in planning for the new Pennsylvania Station in New York City. Their son, Guy, is a Rutgers-educated artist whose painting and video work has commanded the attention of the press; he has had exhibitions throughout the United States and Europe.

Her family and friends have established the Pamela Richards Memorial Fellowship in her honor at the Rutgers University Foundation to support the graduate studies of international students, with special emphasis on students from Russia and the countries of the former USSR. A message from Vladimir Zaitsev, president of the Russian Library Association and director of the Russian National Library, read at the Memorial services for Richards held at Rutgers' Kirkpatrick Chapel and in New York City's Riverside Chapel, confirmed that her deep and abiding affection for Russia was not unilateral. Sent on behalf of Russian librarians, he said, "Pamela Richards was a scholar who used her influence to improve the lives of the Russian people through their libraries. She loved Russia and Russian libraries and Russia returned that love."

Richards died in New York on September 28, 1999. She was fifty-eight years old. Her fascination with wartime history combined with her intent focus on the social mission of libraries, sparked interest among students and colleagues alike in studying information as a global resource. Her concern with the social implications of the application of technology to information became irresistible to those with whom she worked. As an international scholar long before international issues had any cachet in academia, Richards struggled to make global interests the university's interest. Her legacy at Rutgers was a curriculum strongly attuned to the international concerns and the development of students who considered the world their professional domain.

Biographical Listings and Obituaries–[Obituary]. Turock, Betty J. and Tefko Saracevic. "Celebrating the Life and Works of Pamela Richards, 1991–1999." *Bulletin of the American Society for Information Science* 26:9 (December/January 2000). [Obituary]. *American Libraries* 30:69 (November 1999). [Obituary] Davis, Donald G., Jr. "Pamela Spence Richards (1941–1999)" *Library History Round Table Newsletter* 4/3:10 (Fall 1999) [Obituary]. Vodosek, Peter. "Pamela Spence Richards." *Wolfenbütteler Notizen zur Buchgeschichte.* (August, 2000) (in German). [Obituary]. "In Memoriam of Pamela Spence Richards." *Newsletter of the Russian IFLA Committee* 23-24, Point 8 (September/October 1999) (in Russian). [Obituary]. Zaitsev, Vladimir. Memorial to Pamela Richards in *Biblioteka* (forthcoming) (in Russian). Richards, Pamela Spence. Biography for the Harvard and Radcliffe Class of 1963 *25th Anniversary Report* (1988). *Who's Who in American Women,* 19th ed. (1995-1996).

Primary Sources and Archival Materials–Material by and about Pamela Spence Richards is held in the special collections division of the Archibald Stevens Alexander Library at Rutgers University in New Brunswick, New Jersey.

This sketch was prepared for the forthcoming *Dictionary of American Library Biography*, 2d Supplement (Libraries Unlimited, Englewood, Colorado).

A Tribute from the United States

Donald G. Davis, Jr.
Professor, Graduate School of Library & Information Science,
The University of Texas at Austin

My first encounter with Pam Richards was twenty years ago, when she proposed a paper for Library History Seminar VI, "Libraries & Culture," that convened in Spring 1980 in Austin. I had begun editing the *JLH/L&C* three years before and was caught up on directing the first Seminar under the aegis of the Journal and the Texas LIS school. Her proposed paper dealing with enemy information in wartime seemed an interesting one and I pushed for its acceptance with the steering committee. When I actually met Pam at the Seminar and joined her and other for dinner one evening, I began to realize what a remarkable woman and scholar she was. Her paper was indeed an early step in what would be her special angle on scholarly and scientific communication that would be, with some exceptions, her unfolding theme for next two decades. Taking full advantage of her language gifts and her frequent summer travel in Europe, Pam progressively researched the role of information first in the period of the Second World War and then in the Cold War, making colleagues of many kindred spirits in Western and Eastern Europe. Her published work on these topics was coupled with the boundless spirit she imparted to colleagues, young and old, in her associations. Her recent tenure as chair of the IFLA Round Table on Library History was a crowning recognition of her role in the international profession. As her successor in that position, I am very conscious of the legacy that she leaves. The conferences that she planned–"The History of Reading and Libraries in the United States and Russia," (Vologda, Russia, June 1996) and "Books, Libraries, Reading and Publishing in the Cold War" (Paris, June 1998)–drew together a spectrum of scholars from West and East in a fruitful exchange of ideas and intellectual dialogue. I am grateful that they will be preserved in the pages of *Libraries & Culture*. These experiences will be long remembered by Pam's colleagues, especially those who worked with her on the programs. In addition to her scholarly contributions, I also want to acknowledge the *joie de vivre*, sense of style, and enthusiastic encouragement that she brought to every venture that she touched. Her attractive persona reflected the beauty of her inner character and was infectious. She brought unique luster and respect to the study of library history and to her profession. Alas, I cannot envision her baton passing to another. But her memory will inspire us all for a very long time.

This tribute has appeared in the ALA *Library History Round Table Newsletter* 4/3 (Fall 1999): 10 and *RTLH: Newsletter of the IFLA Round Table on Library History*, no. 13 (Winter 2000): 1.

A Tribute from Russia

Valeria D. Stelmakh
Senior Researcher,
Russian State Library, Moscow

The world of librarianship lost Pamela Spence Richards more than two years ago. I had the privilege and pleasure of being her friend and of working with her on several cooperative Russian-American and International Federation of Library Associations and Institutions (IFLA) projects.

Pamela Richards was a powerful, bright and talented historian. Her enthusiasm for library history was obvious, but her professional interests reached into many fields. When she became chairperson of the IFLA Round Table on Library History, she initiated several cooperative projects with the IFLA Section on Reading, which I chaired. The first was the conference "Libraries and Reading in Times of Cultural Change," which in 1996 provided the opportunity for distinguished American and Russian librarians, scholars, and educators to meet in the northern Russian city of Vologda to exchange ideas about reading studies and the history of reading.

This wonderful woman was known to many in Russia, either personally or through her lectures, articles, or books. She did much for Russian librarianship. She gave a course of lectures on librarianship at the St. Petersburg Academy of Culture that was extended to include different Russian cities, from Kamchatka to Moscow. Furthermore, she helped initiate many opportunities for young and gifted Russian and Ukrainian librarians to study at American universities. Even in the middle of times of great change, Pam never forgot the importance of tradition and the great heritage of our libraries.

The conference "Books, Libraries, Reading, and Publishing in the Cold War," initiated by Pam, was the last joint project of the IFLA Round Table on Library History and the IFLA Section on Reading. Together with our French colleagues she put brilliant ideas and unbelievable energy into the conference's preparation. But she was felled by her grave disease just before the conference, and she could not travel to Paris. Our colleague Martine Poulain carried on brilliantly in her absence. These proceedings are a token of gratitude, love, and deep respect for Pamela Spence Richards. Thank you Pam!

Books, Reading, and Publishing in the Cold War
Preface

Martine Poulain
General Conservator of the Libraries and Director of Médiadix, University of Paris

One monumental night in June 1996 we were on a train somewhere between Vologda and Moscow. The colloquium "Reading and Libraries in Times of Cultural Changes" had just recently concluded. The American and Russian participants, especially, had just demonstrated their desire to establish new collaborative relationships based on free intellectual exchange and research ("recherche de la compréhension"). We all shared a common interest in the complexity of the history of book ("appropriation"). It was a year to celebrate, given the fact that Russian researchers were, for the first time, able to reveal their opinions regarding the tremendous denial of the freedom to write and to read that had previously overwhelmed their culture during the Communist-led Soviet regime. Two visionaries who were not only talented but also extremely competent, Pamela Spence Richards and Valeria Stelmakh, longtime affiliates of IFLA, had been the coordinators of this long overdue meeting.

Without taking a moment for a deep breath and after organizing an international meeting, Pam Richards began, with a communicative and generous intellectual enthusiasm, to consciously think aloud and to express her concerns about the extreme importance of reading and writing in the recent world of political history. Pam Richards belonged to a school of researchers who, far from cultivating an aesthetic history of the book, are not afraid to confront the crucial, sometimes controversial issues present within the field. She was interested in the history of the book to the extent that it serves as a vehicle to document the retrospective record of individuals giving evidence to the world's history. This issue had been, as we all know, the main topic of concern for many of her past concentrated studies, and, in addition, she had always had an immense interest in the utility of the use of writing during World War II. Within a few brief moments, the die had been cast. Our discussion aboard that night train led to the decision to hold a colloquium in Paris pertaining to the essential role of the book during the Cold War.

The essays that follow attest to the importance of the book at a time when the ability to write freely had been at stake throughout the confrontation between the Eastern and Western blocs of the Cold War. To be able to dominate writings meant to dominate the mind and spirit of a nation; it meant that one would be able to lay the course for the manipulation of the political scenarios that were to unfold. The Cold War was also a war of words. Since weapons could not express political agendas, each bloc wanted to ensure its supremacy by conquering mentalities and the free expression of ideas. How else to guarantee and solidify the domination of an ideology, if not by a very elaborate strategy aimed at disseminating and sharing it, sometimes unwillingly, sometimes forcefully.

The free world, decimated by war, was seeking the rebirth of new ideals and the emergence of freedom of intellect. Many hoped that new cultural utopias would protect them forever from surrendering their freedoms, once again, as during the dark years of Nazism that had just ended. Once these powers were established, however, the utopias turned into dictatorships. Far from liberating the book, they reduced it to the servitude of delivering propagandist material. They experienced nervous trepidation, equally, from external forces and internal enemies. The democracies themselves had feared their own allotted freedoms, and some of them, testing the integrity of the propaganda of social equality, became tempted to keep publications under surveillance and punish the apostate writing.

We now present an investigation and exploration into the history of the place of the book within the context of this ideological rivalry. This volume is dedicated to one whose vision and dedication we shall all sorely miss—Pam Richards.

Editorial Note

Donald G. Davis, Jr.

My delight in introducing these essays is a special one, not just because I am the editor of the journal in which they appear for the first time in published form for a wider community, but also because I was a participant in the extraordinary conference that they document. The conference–"Books, Libraries, Reading, and Publishing in the Cold War/Livre, Edition, Bibliothèques, Lecture durant la Guerre Froide"– took place during early summer, 11–12 June 1998, at Centre Sèvres in central Paris, where we shared Paris streets with visitors to the first round of the Coupe du Monde.

A unique conference like this one does not materialize without the efforts of many people. The planning committee for the conference included Martine Poulain of Médiadix–Université de Paris and the IFLA Section on Reading; Pamela Spence Richards of Rutgers University and the IFLA Round Table on Library History; and Marie-Noëlle Frachon of the École nationale supérieure des sciences de l'information et des bibliothèques (ENSSIB), the local sponsor. Between fifty and sixty people heard presentations of great diversity from about two dozen speakers from numerous countries in Eastern and Western Europe as well as China and the United States of America. Scholars from Russia, Poland, Romania, and the Czech Republic complemented those from Finland, France, and the former East and West regions of Germany. Many had personal experience with the events they had studied. Though the papers were delivered in either English or French, they were available in both languages through the conference packet given to participants. The four sessions in two days allowed for presentations and frank, spirited discussion as well as ample breaks for coffee and lunch.

As reported in the American Library Association's *Library History Round Table Newsletter*:

> The conference brought together a remarkable group of scholars who, many for the first time, were able to share their research and insights and to discuss with their colleagues the implications of the many

facets of the Cold War era. All were grateful for the opportunity to be present and to benefit from the spirited interchange that followed the paper sessions. Though the breaks did not seem nearly long enough, the conference organizers encouraged further dialogue by arranging for lunches for the speakers nearby in the dining room of Le Bon Marché and by arranging for a pleasant reception on the first evening at the American Library in Paris, hosted by the director and staff.[1]

Despite a number of obstacles, some foreseen and others not, the essays in this volume are now available for the benefit of a larger audience. The untimely passing of Pamela Spence Richards in September 1999 notwithstanding, Hermina Anghelescu, a trilingual conference participant who was completing her doctoral dissertation at the same time as she began her graduate teaching career at Wayne State University in Detroit, was able to edit the papers with the help of Martine Poulain and to prepare the abstracts and the index them with the assistance of her indexing and abstracting class. Readers of these essays owe these colleagues a great deal of thanks.

The essays are arranged in the configuration in which they appeared in the conference program under four broad headings. A glance at the table of contents indicates that the first and last relate to libraries in the Cold War; the other two relate to publishing and reading. They reflect some national variance in research emphasis, scholarly communication, and documentation. The editors omitted from this collection three papers originally delivered at the Paris conference—those by Peter Borchardt, Christine Martin, and Jürgen Freytag—that could not be included because of a complex set of circumstances; their papers may appear elsewhere.

Libraries & Culture is an appropriate medium for the initial public appearance of these essays. The editors are grateful to the contributors, who complied with the requirements of this project, and they hope that the published papers will stimulate more thinking, more analysis, and more scholarship on one of the defining phenomena of the last half of the twentieth century—the Cold War.

Note

1. *Library History Round Table Newsletter* 4:1, n.s. (Fall 1998): 9–10.

"With malice toward none": IFLA and the Cold War

Donald G. Davis, Jr., assisted by Nathaniel Feis

The International Federation of Library Associations (IFLA) strengthened its international character and maintained its political neutrality throughout the tense years of the Cold War. Literature dealing with this period in history describes an atmosphere of intercultural understanding, characterized not merely by tolerance but also by appreciation of regional differences. However, two global political movements created suspicion and resentment among members within the organization. First, the Western members criticized the lack of freedom and openness in the Soviet Union. At the time of the 1970 IFLA conference in Moscow, the Western countries accused the Soviet Union of suppressing its literature and of denying visas to members. Second, IFLA members of the Third World who felt threatened by Western cultural imperialism expressed feelings of resentment toward the West. They felt that they were denied equal opportunity to participate, particularly at international conferences, all of which were held in Europe. Now, after the collapse of Communism and the Eastern European bloc, some of these feelings of conflict have been resolved. In particular, IFLA members from the Soviet Union enjoy more freedom to access information.

He returned to the cellar, selected one of the volumes at random, opened it to be certain that it was one of the dangerous books. He glanced at the page and saw the word Communist. Then he ripped the back cover off. The pages were thick and heavy, and while they ripped quite easily page by page they would not come loose in handfuls... So patiently he ripped the pages out, a few at a time... Hare opened the iron door and stuffed the paper bundle inside. The free edges caught fire and curled back in flame from the smoldering ashy remains of the morning's trash.
           Abraham Polonsky, *A Season of Fear*

  This passage from the about-to-be-blacklisted Hollywood Ten writer Abraham Polonsky's novel *A Season of Fear* (1956) delves into the crippling fear of infiltration by the ideological Other that seized the world as the Cold War intensified. As stern-faced presidents and commissars confronted each other, a kind of bomb-shelter mentality enveloped citizens across the world. Naturally, as fear and suspicion spread into many occupations and discourses, librarianship was not spared, and neither was the International Federation of Library Associations (IFLA), the prime international organization of librarianship. Claiming, and for the most part maintaining, a stand of neutrality, IFLA still suffered from the verbal darts and political skirmishes of an international community undergoing tremendous postwar changes as well as the restricting pressures of the Cold War.

From the 1917 October Revolution until the demise of the totalitarian manifestation of Communism at the end of the 1980s, the main struggle engaging the political powers of the twentieth century was the conflict between capitalism and Communism. There was a brief interlude during World War II in which these natural enemies formed an uneasy alliance to defeat the common enemy of Axis fascism. Almost immediately after the war, however, the primary struggle resumed with greater energy and purpose. By the time Winston Churchill fired what was, in effect, the starting gun for the Cold War (his Iron Curtain speech, delivered on 6 March 1946), the world powers were already lined up in opposition to each other.[1] In 1948 in London, IFLA president W. Munthe addressed this new political animosity. He stated: "The ideals we fought for seem farther away than ever. Shall our most urgent concern be to prepare bigger evacuation premises, to dig deeper anti-air raid—nay anti-atomic bomb shelters in which we can bury the intellectual treasures we have in our custody? Shall we, the torchbearers of enlightenment, end as gravediggers of science and scholarship?"[2] By the time Munthe voiced these sentiments, IFLA had already weathered the storms of international depression, the rise of fascism, and the devastation of World War II. Now it was preparing to face another era of uneasiness and calamity. In order to accomplish its goals and to create an international community of librarians, IFLA, under the leadership of Munthe, strove to "support all beneficial forces in shaping new modes of thought in accordance with Abraham Lincoln's famous words: 'with malice towards none, with charity for all.'"[3] With this ideal as a beacon, IFLA entered the Cold War era.

The International Federation of Library Associations came into being at the fiftieth-anniversary celebrations of the (British) Library Association in Edinburgh on 30 September 1927. The initiating members included groups from the United Kingdom, Germany, Switzerland, France, and the United States. By the outbreak of World War II, IFLA comprised member organizations from thirty-one countries, including such non-European nations as China, Japan, Mexico, the Philippines, and India. Reminiscing about the organization, ex-president Preban Kirkegaard stated that IFLA's "establishment and its internationalism is the cultural effort of men and women of good will after World War I to recreate what had been for hundreds of years the tradition for the scientific and scholarly layer of society. After the peace, cultural people, who appreciated their national situation, were open minded and could see that their nations could not master all things and needed cooperation and inspiration. This is the background on which IFLA grew."[4]

After surviving the destruction of the war in Bern, Switzerland, IFLA reorganized and began assisting damaged and decimated libraries around the world. It is appropriate that IFLA spent the war years headquartered in a neutral land, because during the Cold War IFLA itself became a kind of organizational Switzerland. It ignored the politics of its member states and allowed Britons to work with Russians to work with Germans to work with Czechs–and eventually to work with Nigerians and Cambodians. As IFLA president Frank Francis later said at the 1968 Frankfurt conference:

> First, IFLA is an international association in which all members have equal rights to participate in the discussions and to influence the conclusions. Second, its power stems from its ability to facilitate and organize fruitful discussion of subjects of current interest in the world of librarianship. IFLA believes that the best service it can perform is to bring together periodically a world-wide variety of authoritative practitioners of the arts of library service; to provide them with the opportunity for comparing practices and experiences with each other; and on the basis of informed and matured discussion to make recommendations for action.[5]

This front of professionalism remained intact, for the most part. IFLA held conferences at which committees met and reports were issued, and, overall, much good and useful work was accomplished. However, throughout the association's survival during the Cold War, not surprisingly, there were disagreements among the various factions that threatened the foundations of the federation.

The geopolitical structure of the world was transformed, in theory, when the ailing Roosevelt, Churchill, and Stalin divided up the world at the Yalta Conference and, in fact, when Berlin and Tokyo surrendered. The Yalta Conference set the stage for future disagreements that led to the Cold War. Soon thereafter, library organizations from nations under Soviet influence began queuing up to join the ranks of

IFLA. Actually, Poland and Czechoslovakia boasted members from as early as 1929.[6] These neo-Communist organizations were joined by groups from Yugoslavia, Romania, the German Democratic Republic, and Hungary. Gradually, the Soviet satellite nations formed a strong presence in the ranks of IFLA.[7] By 1957, and since that time, Soviet (and later Russian) members have held a vice presidency on the executive board.[8] In 1959 the Union of Soviet Socialist Republics Library Council joined IFLA.[9] Now the two dominant ideologies of the world, capitalism and Communism, were head to head in the prime international library organization. This inclusion of the feuding superpowers and their minion nations even affected the structure of the IFLA governing organization. In a 1972 conference report, Victor Britannicus asked: "Why does an Executive Board opinion (added to the IFLA Statutes) specify that of six Vice Presidents there be a Vice President for North America, a Vice President for the socialist countries of Eastern Europe, and a Vice President for Western Europe? Why does international politics blow into the rules of this federation of library associations?"[10] He then appended the territorial question, "Why do all the associations have a voice in electing a Vice President who represents one region, such as North America?"[11] By this inclusion, the whole line of questioning does not seem to be one of altruism but one of geography and maybe even of one group suspicious of infiltration by another. This is not surprising, as John Berry wrote after the 1985 Chicago conference: "Many Americans were uneasy with the overt way 'we' pursued political goals at IFLA. While much lip service is given to the notion that 'there are no national delegations to IFLA,' the reality is that the delegates from most nations vote *en bloc* and there is substantial politicking."[12] Though the clashes and disagreements between the two primary sides would not escalate to the severity of the conflicts taking place in the world theater, there were conflicts nonetheless.

The differences in governing philosophies trickled down to the differences in library philosophies. Upon induction into IFLA, V. I. Shunkow, president of the U.S.S.R.'s Library Council, explained that organization's library philosophy. "In our country libraries carry on a work of enlightenment among the people, disseminate knowledge, help raise the qualifications and social consciousness of the Soviet people. They participate actively in every political, economic or cultural campaign."[13] At the 1971 Liverpool conference, a Soviet delegate further explained that the mission of Soviet libraries was the "advance of ideology, culture and science."[14] At that same conference, an ALA representative defined the main concerns of American libraries as "social responsibility, intellectual freedom and the freedom to read."[15]

This ALA representative, in a none-too-stealthy example of American cultural imperialism, also offered to help other libraries around the world to achieve the same goals.[16] All was not tension, however: at the thirtieth IFLA conference in Sofia, eleven librarians from the United States and an equal number from the Soviet delegation met to explain and debate the advantages and disadvantages of their library systems. Although the attendees of the meeting walked away secure in the knowledge that their system was superior, Karl A. Baer, reporting on the gathering, commented that "this was a useful get together[,] and follow-up in the future should, gradually, prove even more helpful."[17] This early meeting led to many instances of Soviet and American librarians working closely and, for the most part, amicably together. Upon visiting a smaller committee conference in Moscow, Penny Biggs contrasted the two governing ideologies as follows: "In the West we tend to think in terms of provision of materials the users want, and of making what the reader chooses as available as possible.... In Eastern Europe the library has a primary responsibility for educating people and guiding users' reading. The word propaganda is used frequently in its original sense of to propagate, disseminate, which we have lost sight of since World War II and Goebbels."[18] Reporting on a separate conference, P. Harvard-Williams noted that the "Russians have a great deal to show other nations in the organization of their libraries."[19] Preban Kirkegaard stated that the Soviets were "very positive and active."[20] Yet even when the global foes were getting along admirably, there was still a shadow of the great conflict hanging over them. Discussing Soviet librarian Margarita Rudomino, Frank Francis remembered her as "very friendly, modest, [and] shy, partly because she was apprehensive that she might say more than she should."[21]

IFLA grew from the most powerful imperialist nations of Western Europe and North America. Just as the nation-states of the Cold War era used the countries of the Third World to further their own game, so did the international cold warriors/librarians treat the libraries of the Third World as backward and in need of a caretaker. In his brave and damning indictment of the treatment the so-called developing world had received in IFLA, Indian library leader S. R. Ranganathan suggested that "the old view that 'international' in IFLA is exhausted by Western Europe and Northern America persists. It may be unconscious and even unmeant on their part. But to us outsiders, it is clear as day light in the tropics."[22] One example of this influence is U.S. policies in Japan during its post–World War II occupation. Japan, Ranganathan stated, had made illustrious progress in the realm of librarianship on its own, but Japan's further progress as a nation of libraries was hampered by the policies and direction of the U.S.

occupying forces.²³ Both before and after the war, IFLA had failed to attract representatives from the nations of Africa, Asia, and Latin America.²⁴ This was largely due to the limited "international" focus Ranganathan mentioned and the financial strain these poorer nations would feel in attending meetings as well as the other costs incurred by being part of such an organization. The financial burden for the European majority of IFLA kept these early meetings in Europe. When China and India requested that the 1936 meeting be held in Asia, the "financial structures" of the organization forced IFLA to decline.²⁵ President Frank Francis even noted, "If [IFLA] had a weakness, it was that it did not manage to project itself as a spokesman for libraries in general but much more for European libraries and European points of view."²⁶ Eventually, these views of the international library world changed, and IFLA developed healthy programs to foster and encourage librarianship throughout the developing nations. However, even by the 1985 conference, only representatives from a quarter of the nations held seats on standing committees, and twelve nations occupied 79 percent of the committee placements.²⁷

The literature and publications produced under the auspices of IFLA present a calm, united portrait. The little controversies and disputes are quietly ignored. Most of the reports focus on the accomplishments and the dry details of meetings and discussions. The reports note advances and agreements, and, indubitably, there were and are legions of valid and useful decisions and discussions amongst IFLA personal members and committees. The disagreements and disputes leak out mostly in reports on the various conferences published in an array of library journals. As I. F. Stone said, "[E]very people has committed its sins."²⁸ Yet the judge always measures sins, and the sins of the Other are always greater than those committed by the self. The Other is always the threat, never the self, especially in the conflict between the supporting ideologies of capitalist and Communist nations. The Soviet menace, in terms of IFLA, was one of propaganda, both in its "original sense" and in a post-Goebbels sense. Internationally, Soviet librarians presented an exquisite version of their official doctrines. This came out most clearly at the conferences held behind the Iron Curtain. The United States, saturated with the doctrines of the Marshall Plan and fearing the threat of Communist infiltration, saw itself as the policeman and big brother to all the other peoples of the world. Americans, as citizens of a democracy, were more vociferous about their beliefs and more arrogantly straightforward in their propagandizing. For example, the ALA representative generously offered to help all the libraries of the world "follow suit," a "suit" tailor-made after the pattern of America's own outfit. The *Library Journal* reported on a similar example of America's cultural attitude: "When *LJ* asked a number of U.S. leaders what our goals [in IFLA] were, the response was almost always a version of: 'We pay a big share of the IFLA budget, don't you think we should have some voice in how it is run?'"[29] This sort of confident, postimperialist attitude has led many of the world's citizens to express disdain for "America." It has also provoked cultural responses such as that of Ranganathan mentioned above.

In 1957, as fear of the Communist menace permeated U.S. society, Lucile M. Morsch addressed the American Library Association. Noting existing programs dedicated to furthering U.S. foreign policy, she stressed that "[t]here is every reason to believe that initiatives on the part of the ALA would be welcome by the Department of State in its search for the best ways to carry out this part of the government's program."[30] This comment followed her description of the minor role the library profession played in the cultural imperialism initiated by the federal government through such agencies as the Office on International Projects Abroad of the American Council on Education's International Cooperation Administration. These initiatives had featured many representatives in other educational fields but only a minuscule number of librarians. She urged the American Library Association and its members to take action, as did two librarians who approached the State Department to suggest a program of bringing certain international librarians to the United States for a year. Morsch encouraged librarians to assist the government, which "recognizes its own limitations in carrying out its foreign policy, particularly in the fields of cultural affairs."[31] In a June 1956 White House conference, President Eisenhower, rallying the cold warriors as he had once rallied soldiers, said, "[T]here will never be enough diplomats and information officers at work in the world to get the job done without the help of the rest of us. Indeed, if our American ideology is eventually to win out . . . it must have the active support of thousands of independent private groups and institutions and of millions of Americans."[32] Morsch also called for librarians to take an active part in fostering foreign librarians, because "[r]elatively few of them have had the experience of seeing a good public library, or a school library, or have any conception at all of the qualifications required for a professional librarian."[33] This seemingly smug attitude of national superiority was not always appreciated in other parts of the world, needless to say.

The first major ideological controversy to spring up at an IFLA conference occurred during the 1968 conference at Frankfurt when

Soviet troops invaded Czechoslovakia. Elizabeth Welch reported the way this news gripped conference-goers: "The meetings continued after the news of the invasion, but at every break groups gathered around transistor radios."[34] The events of the Prague Spring caused "feelings of sympathy, of fear for the future, and the instability of world relations made it clear to everyone that we must have communication and friendship with all countries."[35] IFLA president Sir Frank Francis later commented, "We were frightened of the potentialities."[36] Herman Liebaers, who attempted to calm Soviet and Czechoslovakian participants, spent his time "running back and forth between the hotels where the Soviet delegation and the Czechoslovak librarians stayed. The two groups were sad, silent, and bewildered. They could not make up their minds whether to stay or leave."[37] Eventually, all parties chose to stay at the conference. The next IFLA conference was scheduled for Moscow, which might have caused an impasse had not the IFLA president responded in a diplomatic manner. "The members of the eastern bloc countries could not vote against Moscow; those from the West could not approve it."[38] President Francis proposed that the voting on this matter be decided by the executive committee once tempers had cooled. Thus, by an act of very able diplomacy, Francis was able to keep within the principles for IFLA he had stated at the opening of the conference: that IFLA is "an organization formed without consideration of political beliefs, bias or prejudice."[39]

As it turned out, the next conference was not held in Moscow but in Copenhagen. By this time the outrage that followed the oppression of Czechoslovakia had faded. Outgoing president Francis even praised the "firm adherence of Canada, the United States of America and the USSR during recent years and . . . these countries as well as the European countries have been a significant factor in the establishment of IFLA as a recognized international forum for the discussion of matters affecting the effectiveness of library services."[40]

The 1970 IFLA conference was held in Moscow. It is the policy of IFLA to hold meetings only in nations that will admit all delegates. Questioning whether the Soviet government would adhere to this policy, the United States was more than ready to withdraw from the Moscow conference. One week before the conference, the Israeli delegates were still without visas and withdrew from the conference on the same date that U.S.S.R. officials contacted UNESCO to inform it that the Israelis' passports were on the way.[41] Preban Kirkegaard remembered working closely with the Israelis to obtain the needed visas: "The visas were denied until the day before the meeting was to open. Two Israelis waited in the airport in Vienna but were not able to attend IFLA."[42] Many other participants in the conference did not receive their visas until days before or sometimes during their trip to the conference.[43] IFLA president Herman Liebaers interpreted the tardiness of his visa's arrival as harassment by the Soviet government. All of this occurred too late for any group or nation to withdraw, so the conference proceeded with all delegations except for Israel's. The IFLA board translated this action as "part of Soviet policy and it was therefore difficult for the board to interpret whether entrance had been denied to the Israeli delegate."[44]

Other conflicts and tensions developed as the Moscow conference progressed. The theme of the conference was "Lenin and Libraries." Librarians from around the world spoke on Lenin's contributions to library development; even Americans described the Lenin collections held in the United States. Although most of the speeches were laudatory and even propagandistic, U.S. delegate Foster Mohrhardt's presentation on Lenin's relationship to censorship provoked "sharp commentary" from the Swiss delegation.[45] Conference participants each received a kit of printed material, as they did at every IFLA conference. In Moscow, delegates found that "no material in the kit was produced outside the USSR, a striking contrast with other meetings of IFLA, where much material is available from many countries."[46] Attempting to discover why copies of the *Wilson Library Bulletin* (which had been sent to Moscow several weeks earlier) were not distributed with the kits, U.S. delegate William R. Eshelman ran into an insurmountable bureaucratic wall. He tried to trace the shipment of journals through the Office of Foreign Literature, then through Pan American Airlines. Here he found a receiving record dated weeks before the actual conference. When confronted with the receipt, Mme. Rudomino, director of the Office of Foreign Literature, replied, "It couldn't be," but she acknowledged having received six copies of the magazine.[47] Eshelman then asked, "Why wasn't one of these copies used in an extensive IFLA exhibit opened with great fanfare instead of the outdated materials in the case labeled 'Soviet Librarianship in the Foreign Press'?"[48] In his report on the conference, Eshelman subtly hinted that Soviet suppression accounted for the absence of international materials, including the *Wilson Library Bulletin*. However, he did not let the mask of amiability drop too far and quickly returned to an upbeat chronicle of the conference's events.

More tension flared at the 1974 conference in Washington, D.C. Under the strong influence of UNESCO, IFLA dropped members that were viewed as troublesome for the entire international community. This action enraged President Liebaers. In a speech he blasted UNESCO for this action: "When we had to force resignation upon our members in South Africa and in Formosa—perhaps tomorrow in

Israel—UNESCO was ruining the very purpose it stands for."[49] In discussing the banishment of South Africa, Liebaers commented: "The argument that was used in the discussions in UNESCO was that this was not a political question but a humanitarian one, a respect for human dignity. That was probably true, but it opened the door to the dangers of political acts. Six months later there was the question of Taiwan and Mainland China. That was purely political."[50] By questioning the exclusion of South Africa, Liebaers exemplified just how apolitical IFLA hoped to remain.

But with every speech and every comment, the political differences became apparent. Contrasting the opening statements of Frederick Burkhardt, the chairman of the U.S. National Commission on Libraries and Information Science, and N. M. Sikorsky of Moscow's All-Union Book Chamber reveals some of the practical realities coming from these divergent politics. Sikorsky stated that "[i]n the Socialist state, the libraries' activity is organically bound up with the economic, political, and educational tasks facing their country . . . The activity of Soviet libraries is based on clearest ideological and organizational principles."[51] He emphasized that the 360,000 libraries in the country reach "every community and family."[52] Conversely, Burkhardt said, "The quality of library and information services in different states [of the United States] and localities is very uneven—excellent in some areas and in others extremely poor."[53] He also stressed the various paths of legislation, committees, and voting a national library initiative must traverse. He summed up the U.S. situation by saying that "[i]t begins and ends with the people."[54] Shirley Elder, comparing these two speeches, wrote, "[T]he United States has problems the Soviets never could imagine; they are the problems of an open society unknown to a closed one."[55]

The intensity of Cold War animosity and tension waned throughout the 1970s. With the unilateral reduction in nuclear arms and the U.S. withdrawal from Vietnam, the superpowers became less antagonistic. In fact, the international public enemy of the United States became the non-Soviet-aligned Iran. This development allowed the Soviets and Americans slowly, warily to progress in their relations. With the exception of the conflict in Afghanistan, all ideological fronts were relatively quiet. This all changed, however, with the dawning of the Reagan years. With Reagan's conservatism and comments on outlawing the "Evil Empire," the Cold War escalated once again, though not to the level of two decades earlier. It was during the Reagan years, at the 1985 IFLA conference in Chicago, that the ideological conflicts within the association became most pronounced.

At the Chicago conference, former ALA president E. J. Josey openly protested the inclusion of South African delegates whose hands were "dripping with the blood of thousands of innocent people" and snidely added, "We know that the [conference] theme of Universal Availability of Information is meaningless in that troubled land."[56] John Brademas of New York University then broke an IFLA taboo by criticizing his own nation's government. He blasted the Reagan administration for reducing funding for the National Archives, restricting information, and starting a "systematic assault" on aid for library programs.[57] The most significant incident, in terms of Cold War tension, was Librarian of Congress Daniel J. Boorstin's speech entitled "The Indivisible World: Libraries and the Myth of Cultural Exchange." In his address, Boorstin noted that "all librarians must be saddened that a new Russian word recently entered our desk dictionary: '*samizdat* . . . The secret publication and distribution of government-banned literature in the U.S.S.R. . . . The literature produced by this system.' How happy we could be someday to see this word disappear from our dictionaries and to learn that the word had become obsolete!"[58] He ended by saying, "We can hope and must try everywhere to make the world of books more open—so that men and women everywhere may breathe freely the uncensored open air of ideas."[59] This speech caused such an immediate outrage that an IFLA staffer attempted to halt the distribution of Boorstin's paper at the conference itself.[60] On the defensive, Valentina S. Lesokhina, head of the Soviet Ministry of Culture Chief Library Directorate, answered Boorstin's words by turning the other cheek. She said that she envisioned IFLA conference as a place "offer[ing] a great possibility for exchange of experiences and constructive discussion of progress . . . only an atmosphere of mutual trust and good will among us—who represent one of the most humanitarian of professions—will allow us to unite and solve our common problems."[61] More officially, the Soviet delegation protested Boorstin's "provocative" words to the IFLA executive board and referred to his remarks as an "unfriendly act."[62] Harold Granheim said that the executive board understood the Soviets' position and "resolved to prevent such actions in the future."[63] More criticism came from the home front. A letter sent to the *Library Journal* declared, "[B]oth the talks by Daniel Boorstin and John Brademas [were] totally inappropriate for this kind of meeting. Boorstin did not say much, but what he said clearly insulted the Russians. I don't mind insulting them in the appropriate setting, but this was not it."[64] For some the comments were a matter of principle, for others they were merely etiquette.

In another speech at the same conference, Stefan Kubow reported on the misfortune of the Polish Librarians Association. After having suffered its way through the horrors of World War II, the association had finally seen national library legislation pass and had been able to establish a network of libraries. However, these advances lapsed under volatile postwar social conditions. In 1968 the State Library Council–subordinate to the Ministry of Culture and Art–began to ineffectively and nonchalantly manage the nation's libraries. After joining the Patriotic Movement for National Revival and the Polish United Worker Party, the association lost autonomy and was unable to achieve much more than small victories as it struggled on.[65] This saga illustrated the trials a dedicated organization must face under the pressure of its government bureaucracy.

As the 1980s continued, Soviet Communism weakened. Finally, the system collapsed under the policies of Gorbachev, and though the memory of the Cold War still lingers, the actual struggles and conflicts brought about by the global stand-off have mostly evaporated. Now, our profession does well to remember and document the struggle and pain of the second half of the twentieth century.

At the 1970 conference for the International Federation of Library Associations held in Moscow, Hans Peter Geh asked a member of the Soviet coalition if publications were universally available in the Soviet Union. The fellow replied that the universal availability of publications "existed to a certain extent, but some books [are available] only for certain people."[66] Twenty-one years later, at the 1991 IFLA conference held again in Moscow, Geh found that "information is easily accessible now."[67]

Delegates at the 1991 IFLA conference witnessed more than just a society with more accessible information. They witnessed the final unraveling of the Union of Soviet Socialist Republics. While the conference was under way, the Communist hard-liners attempted to overturn Gorbachev's *glasnost* initiatives, but they failed in their attempt.[68] Not only did *glasnost* policies close a chapter in Eurasian history, they ended an epoch for IFLA as well. With the collapse of the Soviet Union and the demise of the Soviet bloc, IFLA was finally able to acknowledge the elephant at the dinner table. This conference continued the explication of a painful period in human history: the second half of the twentieth century.[69]

Notes

I would like to acknowledge the influence of Paul Kaegbein, formerly of the University of Cologne, who inspired me to think about emphasizing the art of the possible within an international organization such as IFLA. I further thank my colleague Bette Oliver for her helpful suggestions for textual revision.

1. Paul Brodeur, *Secrets: A Writer in the Cold War* (Boston: Faber and Faber, 1997), 3. Current surveys abound, such as James E. Cronin, *The World the Cold War Made: Order, Chaos, and the Return of History* (New York: Routledge, 1996); Brian Crozier, *Free Agent: The Unseen War, 1941–1991* (London: HarperCollins, 1993); Abbott Gleason, *Totalitarianism: The History of the Cold War* (New York: Oxford University Press, 1995); John W. Young, *Cold War Europe, 1945–1991: A Political History* (New York: Doubleday, 1996), as well as Thomas G. Paterson, *On Every Front: The Making of the Cold War* (New York: W. W. Norton, 1979).

2. Joachim Wieder, "An Outline of IFLA's History," in Willem R. H. Koops and Joachim Wieder, eds., *IFLA's First Fifty Years* (Munich: Verlag Dokumentation, 1977), 28.

3. Ibid., 28.

4. Laverne Frances Carroll, "Former Presidents of IFLA 1963–1979," *International Library Review* 18:2 (April 1986): 149. For the best current brief survey of IFLA history, see Carol Henry, "International Federation of Library Associations and Institutions," in Robert Wedgeworth, ed., *World Encyclopedia of Library and Information Services*, 3rd ed. (Chicago: American Library Association, 1993), 378–82, as well as W. Boyd Rayward's coverage in "Library Associations, International," in *Encyclopedia of Library History* (New York: Garland Publishing, 1994), 342–47.

5. Elizabeth Welch, "IFLA's International Importance," *Wilson Library Bulletin* 43:5 (January 1969): 428.

6. Lev I. Vladimirov, "The Socialist Countries of Europe in IFLA," in Koops and Wieder, eds., *IFLA's First Fifty Years*, 101.

7. Ibid., 102.

8. Carroll, "Former Presidents," 151.

9. Edith Scott, "IFLA and FID–History and Programs," *Library Quarterly* 32:1 (January 1962): 12.

10. Victor Britannicus, "International Federation of Library Associations: 1971 IFLA General Council–37th Annual Session," *Special Libraries* 63:1 (January 1972): 44.

11. Ibid.

12. John Berry, "The U.S. at IFLA," *Library Journal*, 1 October 1985: 5.

13. Scott, "IFLA and FID," 12.

14. Michael P. Barnett, "IFLA in Liverpool: Return of the Native," *Wilson Library Bulletin* 46:5 (January 1972): 469.

15. Ibid.

16. Ibid.

17. Karl A. Baer, "A World-Wide Future," *Special Libraries* 56:2 (February 1965): 91.

18. Penny Biggs, "Impressions of a Moscow Conference," *Library Association Record* 86:9 (September 1984): 351.

19. P. Harvard-Williams, "The IFLA Conference–As I Saw It," *Library World* 66:774 (December 1964): 146.

20. Carroll, "Former Presidents," 151.

21. Ibid.

22. S. R. Ranganathan, "IFLA–What It Should Be and Do," *Libri* 5:2 (1954): 183.

23. Ibid., 187.

24. Morris A. Gelfand, "The Organization of the Library Profession: 37th IFLA," *Wilson Library Bulletin* 46:5 (January 1972): 471.

25. Wieder, "An Outline," 15–16.

26. Carroll, "Former Presidents," 151.
27. Edith Dyer, "The Body Politic: IFLA Meets in Chicago," *Wilson Library Bulletin* 60:4 (December 1985): 27–28.
28. I. F. Stone, speech, Ford Hall Forum, National Public Radio, 12 April 1983.
29. Berry, "The U.S. at IFLA," 5.
30. Lucile M. Morsch, "Promoting Library Interests throughout the World," *ALA Bulletin* 51:8 (September 1957): 581.
31. Ibid.
32. Ibid.
33. Ibid.
34. Welch, "IFLA's International Importance," 428.
35. Ibid., 429.
36. Carroll, "Former Presidents," 150.
37. Ibid.
38. Welch, "IFLA's International Importance," 428.
39. Ibid.
40. Rudolph C. Ellsworth, "IFLA–1969 in Copenhagen," *Wilson Library Bulletin* 44:3 (November 1969): 346.
41. William R. Eshelman, "Libraries as a Force of Education," *Wilson Library Bulletin* 45:3 (November 1969): 218.
42. Carroll, "Former Presidents," 151.
43. Eshelman, "Libraries as a Force of Education," 218.
44. "Of Note," *American Libraries* 1:11 (December 1970): 1011.
45. Ibid.
46. Eshelman, "Libraries as a Force of Education," 220.
47. Ibid., 222.
48. Ibid.
49. Shirley Elder, "IFLA Comes to the United States," *American Libraries* 6:2 (February 1975): 76.
50. Ibid.
51. Ibid.
52. Ibid.
53. Ibid.
54. Ibid.
55. Ibid. Eight years later, at the IFLA annual conference in Montreal in 1982, I had my first encounter with the Soviet delegation and was intrigued with its isolationist composition and behavior patterns. One example of an individual who fostered international relations was Paul Kaegbein, who served the IFLA Round Table on Library History and the Round Table on Reading from the 1960s through the 1980s and who was instrumental in providing contacts between library historians in the Western and Eastern bloc countries, primarily by arranging small international conferences.
56. "Sleep No More at IFLA," *American Libraries* 16:9 (October 1985): 610.
57. Ibid.
58. Daniel J. Boorstin, "The Indivisible World: Libraries and the Myth of Cultural Exchange," in *The Republic of Letters* (Washington, D.C.: Library of Congress, 1989), 82.
59. Ibid., 83.
60. "Notes and Asides at an International Conference," *American Libraries* 16:9 (October 1985): 615.
61. "Sleep No More at IFLA," 614.

62. Ibid.
63. Ibid.
64. Berry, "The U.S. at IFLA," 5. Despite the slightly chilling effect of Boorstin's address, I remember well a bus tour of Chicago Public Library branches with the Soviet delegation and a very fruitful exchange about the nature of American and Soviet public libraries.
65. "Sleep No More at IFLA," 617.
66. Esther Dyer, "IFLA in Moscow: Libraries and Culture Meet Politics," *Wilson Library Bulletin* 66:4 (December 1991): 50.
67. Ibid. For another view, see *Information in Eastern and Central Europe: Coming in from the Cold* (Washington, D.C.: Special Libraries Association, 1991).
68. Dyer, "IFLA in Moscow," 50. Those who were in Moscow will always remember the general reception held in the great ballroom of the Kremlin's Palace of Congresses on Wednesday night, 21 August 1991. They will never forget the euphoric celebration of unity and freedom that took place. See Donald G. Davis Jr., "Caught in the Coup: IFLA in Moscow, 1991," *Libraries & Culture* 27:2 (Spring 1992): 192–97. A collection of reminiscences and memorabilia is deposited in the American Library Association Archives housed at the library of the University of Illinois at Urbana-Champaign.
69. For an adumbration of this spirit, see special journal issue *The History of Reading and Libraries in the United States and Russia: Proceedings of an International Conference, 19–21 June 1996, Vologda, Russia*, ed. Pamela Spence Richards, *Libraries & Culture* 33:1 (Winter 1998): 1–140.

A Soviet Research Library Remembered

Edward Kasinec

The author, curator of the Slavic and Baltic Division at the New York Public Library, reflects on his first experience with libraries and archives during a year of research in the former Soviet Union in 1971–72. Kasinec experienced both the positives and negatives of research work under the Soviet regime. He had the opportunity to work closely with some of Russia's finest historians, bibliographers, librarians, and archivists, benefiting from their considerable erudition and gaining a degree of familiarity with collections at some of the greatest libraries in the world. Much of Kasinec's research was conducted at the Lenin State Library in Moscow, renamed the Russian State Library in 1992.

However, as a foreigner studying Filaret (Drozdov, d. 1867), a hierarch of the Russian Orthodox Church and a figure distasteful to the Communist regime, Kasinec encountered skepticism toward his research. Kasinec notes the Marxist-Leninist organization of those catalogs that were publicly accessible, versus those to which access was limited to staff and the most trusted Soviet scholars. "Specially" trained librarians ultimately determined what it was possible to consult and photocopy. Some older scholars, mindful of the experiences of the Stalin era, were reluctant to even meet with him, and in general, the shadow of Soviet censorship (and the occasional attempted provocation) loomed over his research experience.

Since the collapse of the Soviet Union, suspicions relating to Soviet attempts to shape research–by barring access to special collections (whose existence was largely denied) and through the careful selection of those files that were presented to readers–have been confirmed. It is Kasinec's concern that such manipulation may have, in effect, "tainted" the "knowledge base," resulting in extensive Western holdings of tendentious material upon which researchers have based their own studies. It will take many years before we can fully assess the impact of this censorship on scholarship.

In 1972, the Lenin Library celebrated its 110th anniversary. It is a national library, and has the following functions: state depository for all publications, manuscripts and other materials printed in the country; depository of foreign literature; the leading research institute of the country in the field of library science and theoretical bibliography; scientific, methodological and coordinating center for Soviet libraries. Its stock amounts to more than 26 million items in 201 languages of the peoples of the world. The library contains unique publications of various countries and epochs. It serves nearly 11,000 users every day.[1]

A leading ideological, research and information centre of the country, the Library bases its work on the principles of Party ideology and genuine democracy. These principles underly [sic] the building up of the Library stocks, the reader service, determine scientific information work, the subject-matter of research work and methodological activity. Drawing upon its rich traditions, on the experience of Soviet and foreign library service and scientific information supply, the Library is continuously stepping up the efficacy of its activity for the sake of further scientific, cultural and technical progress.[2]

I first entered the Lenin Library almost thirty years ago, in the summer of 1971. I have since revisited the library many times, most especially over the last decade. Yet whenever I am in Moscow, my thoughts return to my first experiences in that great library and working with many individuals who were among the greatest bibliographers and librarians of their generation. This presentation recounts some of these experiences. These comments are not meant to be all-inclusive, descriptive, or historical, and they represent only a small number of the very many positive and educative hours that I spent at that important world cultural institution. However, I trust that my remarks will suggest at least some of the conditions by which research was undertaken in Russian libraries during the Cold War, and–to my mind, much more significantly–how these characteristics may have profoundly influenced the development of Western collections of Russian materials since the end of the Second World War.

The Context of My Stay

The thirteen months that I spent in Moscow and St. Petersburg (the summer of 1971 through the summer of 1972) were part of the bilateral exchange of young scholars between the Russian Ministry of Culture and Moscow University, on the one hand, and the International Research and Exchanges Board and Columbia University, on the other. By the time I departed for Russia, I had completed my doctoral oral exams in Eastern European and Russian history at Columbia University. In addition, I had gained some library experience by working in the Acquisitions Department of the Columbia University Library, as well as at the New York Public Library and at St. Vladimir's Seminary Library in Crestwood, New York. My goal in Russia was to study the archives, manuscript collections, and printed bibliography of sources relating to the history of the great hierarch of the Russian Orthodox Church in the nineteenth century, Filaret (Drozdov), and his relationship with Moscow society. For much of the Soviet period, Filaret was considered a political retrograde, and anyone wanting to study him was viewed with a dose of skepticism. In traveling to Russia, I fully suspected that many of the sources I would need to consult would be poorly accessible if not proscribed.

Before departure, we were assigned a scholarly advisor from among the faculty of Moscow University. My advisor was Sergei Sergeevich Dmitriev, a historian and docent of the history faculty at Moscow University. Dmitriev was an unusual person in many respects. Born in Iaroslavl', he spent his early years working as a curator in various provincial museums. After his move to Moscow and the history faculty of the university, Dmitriev became interested in the history of the Slavophile movement, a philosophical and cultural movement of the second half of the nineteenth century. The political ambience of the 1930s was inhospitable to Dmitriev's interests, so in order to survive professionally, he turned his concerns to the auxiliary historical disciplines and bibliography. He was also very cautious and what we would term today "politically correct." As the year developed, Professor Dmitriev proved to be a strong supporter of my work. He willingly shared his contacts in the field of Russian historical bibliography, archival, and library collections.

My daily routine was rather straightforward. After breakfast in the university cafeteria, I most often went to the archives located near the Novo-Devichii Convent or to the Manuscript Division of the Lenin Library. I often took lunch at the American Embassy and also availed myself of the free books, records, and tapes that were being distributed by the Cultural Office of the embassy. The more politically sensitive of the books I gave over to the Lenin Library's International Exchanges Division, then headed by the very smart and energetic Boris Petrovich Kanevskii. The second half of the day was most often spent in the Lenin Library and occasionally in the State Historical Library (still at Bohdan Khmelnitsky Street and now celebrating its centenary), the Fundamental Library on the Social Sciences (earlier the Library of the Communist Academy and now the Institute for Scientific Information in the Social Sciences, or INION), and sometimes the old Library of Moscow University, then as now in the center of the city. While Americans were still rare birds in the Moscow of the early 1970s, I was treated well and even cordially in all of these libraries, especially after introductions from colleagues in the Lenin Library and the Foreign Section of the university. Dinner was usually an afterthought, taken at the university's late-night buffet.

Such was the background to my student experiences in Russia. Now for a few observations and, I hope, illustrative anecdotes.

Research and Scholarship—of a Kind

One of the characteristics of research libraries in Europe—as opposed to those in North America—is the fact that they fulfill the function of centers of research and scholarship as well as being curatorial institutions. In the case of Soviet research libraries, however, the scholarship that was practiced was, to a significant degree, motivated by the concrete political and social needs of the regime and its Ministry of Culture and carried on in conditions that were very isolated from comparable activities in Western Europe and the United States. In the early 1970s, entire sections of the Lenin Library were engaged in research, writing, and publishing on topics such as the sociology of readership, methodological guidance on readers' services in public libraries, the theory and practice of international book exchange, and the history of book culture.

In terms of professional staffing, these curatorial and research departments were in their heyday, with distinguished scholars, some of whom had begun their careers in the 1920s. My entrée to these individuals was afforded by my older friend, an important bibliographer and staff member of the Lenin Library, Galina Andreevna Glavatskikh, whose primary duties were in the Reference Department but who also had close connections with the department compiling major reference works in the humanities, especially in Russian history. Through her I became acquainted with a number of the more prominent members of the staff—Sokrat Aleksandrovich Klepikov, Mark Mitrofanovich Klevenskii, Boris Kanevskii, Tatiana Nilovna Kameneva—as well as such prominent professors and bookmen as Petr A. Zaionchkovskii and the late Alexander Ivanovich Rogov.[3]

At one stage in my work, I was frequenting the Manuscript Division on a daily basis. The division was headed by a rather well known literary specialist (still alive and flourishing), Sara Vladimirovna Zhitomirskaia.[4] She reigned forcefully but was widely respected by staff and readers alike. Among the division's dozen or so staff members were such esteemed specialists as Valentina G. Zimina (the deputy), Galina Dovgailo, Nikolai B. Tikhomirov, and the redoubtable Marietta Omarovna Chudakova.[5] The opportunity to meet and, in some cases, work with these individuals was something for which I shall always be thankful. Unfortunately, politics often intruded even into this aspect of my work at the Lenin Library.

A number of bibliographers were reluctant to meet with me. Fear of political and economic retribution was pervasive throughout the society in which they and I lived. These included such important bookmen as Isaak Mikhailovich Kaufman and Ioel Naftal'evich Koblents.[6] Koblents, in particular, was a fascinating figure whose career dated back to the 1920s and the founding of the Library of the Communist Academy by the American-trained Henrietta K. Derman.

Politics intruded into scholarship in even more subtle ways. For example, entire categories of literature were excluded from the bibliographical publications that were sponsored by the Lenin Library, while the content of published works was carefully proscribed. For example, the major bibliography by Glavatskikh and Zaionchkovskii on *Dnevniki i vospominaniia* excludes globally the thousands of relevant publications that were published by the Russian and other emigrations (Ukrainian, Belarusian),[7] while memoirs and writings of the Russian Orthodox religious community published in Imperial Russia were very poorly represented. All the compilers were painfully aware of this omission but optimistically shared hopes that their colleagues in the West would someday fill these gaps.[8]

Other forms of distortion and censorship were still more subtle and involved giving preference in production and distribution to publications dealing with Russian secular, not religious (*slavianskaia*), or foreign culture (*innostrannaia*) in Russia. An important example is the *Svodnyi katalog russkoi knigi grazhdanskoi pechati XVIII veka* in six volumes.[9] The volumes dealing with civil script publications were issued in a print-run of 4,000 copies; by contrast, the volumes by Kameneva of Slavonic (primarily religious) publications were issued in a run of only 350 copies.[10] Other publications spearheaded by the Lenin Library included a multivolume bibliography of publications dealing with the revolutionary movement of the late nineteenth century and a whole host of bibliographies dealing with the history of book culture during the Soviet period.

Unreconciled Accounts

One of the paramount concerns of the administration of the Lenin Library was the protection of the collection from both physical harm and inappropriate use. During the winter months, one went first to the cloakroom, where readers who had already been issued tickets to the first Reading Room did not have to stand in line (*vne ocheredi*) and were guaranteed a peg. One could not enter the library with papers, photocopies, or any other types of printed materials, so these were left in the cloakroom as well. One then passed by the *dejournyi* (a staff member who sits at a desk on each floor and monitors the comings and goings of guests) and militia and was given a small slip of paper to insert in the reader's card. This ticket remained with you throughout the day, and each time you received books, the number of items was noted. On one occasion, the librarian in the Reference Department inadvertently noted on my slip more volumes of the *Pravoslavnaia bogoslovskaia entsiklopediia* (Orthodox theological encyclopedia) than I had actually requested and received. At closing (around 10:00 P.M.), I returned fewer volumes than were indicated on the slip, and the staff fell into consternation. I was ultimately "released," but only after one of the staff members opined that if I had been a Soviet citizen, I would have never been let out of the library.

Security in the library was so intense that some divisions were anonymous, even mythical. This was especially the case with the Military Division and the legendary *spetskhran*, or repository for special collections. As a student, I knew only that the *spetskhran* was behind an unmarked door on the third floor, situated between a smoking area and the men's washroom. In the 1970s, even positing the existence of a *spetskhran* to a Soviet librarian was almost tantamount to a political provocation. Decades later, in the 1990s, I was given a tour of this division by the curator, who informed me that it contained around half a million volumes, many published by the Russian emigrations (in this sense, it was very much like a Hoover Library in miniature), as well as erotica, literature on espionage, and other types of sensitive materials. In recent years, a bibliography published by the Lenin Library—the late Viktor Kharlamov's book on the library's émigré holdings—has in part inventoried these collections.

Mnozhitelnye Apparat

Upon entering the Soviet Union, we were warned that we would have to "register" our typewriters with customs and security officials. As far as I knew, there was only one public photocopying machine for the entire city of Moscow, and that was used primarily for various kinds of legal documents. The few pieces of reprographic and printing equipment that were available at the Lenin Library were strictly controlled in all respects, with public reprographic orders accepted in only one room during designated hours. Two senior members of the staff reviewed materials for suitability as well as to determine the quantity that might be ordered. Certain categories of materials were forbidden to reproduce, including cartographic materials, statistical and economic figures, and even some types of belles lettres. Staff was familiar with the research plans (*nauchnyi plan*) of many of the Western scholars and simply refused to accept materials that they considered out of scope. In the practice of those days, microfilming was used in lieu of photocopying, even to copy individual articles or a small number of pages. This too may have had a political dimension. After all, while photocopies might be easily circulated (and, ultimately, copied again), reading and reproducing microfilm required special machinery.

An Exercise in Penmanship: The Catalogs

During the early 1970s, only individuals with a higher education were registered to use the reading rooms of the Lenin Library. These reading rooms were differentiated not only by format (newspapers and periodicals, reference, etc.) but also by subject interest. High-ranking political, military, and academic figures as well as Western scholars and graduate students were serviced in the formidable Reading Room Number 1, a rather large and pleasant room whose windows looked out over the Kremlin cupolas. There was space in this room for thirty to forty readers, some of whom constituted the academic elite of the city and the nation. No doubt there was some resentment that their space had to be shared with mere foreign graduate students from the *kap strans* (capitalist countries). The *pervyi zal* had a regular staff of librarians that saw to the needs of their readers. They provided what was called "full service" (*polnoe obsluzhivanie*). This included maintaining the reserve shelves for each of the readers and checking the fullness, accuracy, appropriateness, and pertinence (very important) of their requests for literature. It even involved coordinating with the librarians working behind the scenes and directly with the catalogs so that class marks or call numbers could be assigned to each call slip. The full service provided by the staff of Reading Room Number 1 obviated any necessity for any foreign or high-ranking Russian reader to have contact with either the public or, much less, the internal, archival-quality catalogs of the library.

The public catalogs were great in number and rather complex in nature, ranging from catalogs arranged by the Marxist-Leninist classification, to the BBK (*Bibliotechno-bibliograficheskaia klassifikatsiia*) catalogs of English and foreign language books in the collection (a very typical phenomenon for Soviet libraries), to the alphabetical (author-title) catalog. The most comprehensive catalog—the one that reflected the full holdings of the library—was accessible only to library staff. It was termed the "alphabetical official service catalog" (*alfavitnyi sluzhebnyi katalog*) and was kept in a strategic, central area of the Lenin Library. It was strictly off limits to readers and perhaps even to some members of the staff. It was only many years later, and in very different political circumstances, that I was to see this *sanctum sanctorum*.

As I mentioned earlier in my remarks, I was working on a religious cum political figure who was considered then an archreactionary and even odious figure. (He has now been sainted by the Moscow Patriarchate.) In the process of collecting a bibliography, I turned to the scholarly or executive secretary of the library, the formidable T. L. Pastremova, with a request to consult the alphabetical service catalog on the grounds that the public catalog available to me was incomplete and inadequate for my theme. The request to directly consult the card catalog was, of course, denied, but with a very original twist, namely, that the bibliographers of the library would transcribe cards dealing with my person. This in fact was done, and after a reasonable period of time I was presented with a stack of several hundred carefully written cards. Only subsequently did I learn from a friend and colleague how much consternation my request had caused to the individuals who had to carry out this *ukase* (decree).

The Protests of the Optina Elders: A Provocation?

Immediately upon arriving in Moscow, we were apprised by the American Embassy of security risks that we might encounter in Russia. It was well known, for example (and those of us who studied there have ample anecdotal evidence of this), that our rooms were bugged. This was par for the course. However, one morning at the Lenin Library I experienced a possibly more sinister manifestation of Soviet preoccupation with its foreign visitors.

In the early 1970s, the Manuscripts Reading Room, like the divisional collections and staff rooms, was housed in one of the wings of the Pashkov House, the eighteenth-century building of the Lenin Library. It shared this building with one of the other "limited access" (or special access) collections of the Lenin Library, the dissertation collection (dissertations, too, were considered to be manuscripts—*na pravakh rukopisei* [restricted material]). Gaining access to the Manuscripts Reading Room did not necessarily give one access to all the collections the division held, most especially if one were from one of the *kap strans*. Readers from the *kap strans* were not given access to the *opisi* (descriptive registers or finding aids), nor were they given permission to publish from collections that were being researched by Soviet scholars. No researcher–Soviet or Western–was given access to collections that were unworked (*nerazobrannye*). Unfortunately, this accounted for a significant part–at that time and from a Western perspective–of the manuscript collections of the library.

My daily work in the Manuscripts Reading Room was fairly routine and regularized. At the end of the day, those documents on which I had been working were left on a shelf that was designated for my materials. One morning, I called for the materials I had been working on the evening before. After briefly examining these papers, I was surprised (and even mildly frightened) to see that my papers included several folders of documents from the manuscript collections of the Optina Pustyn, the influential monastery of the nineteenth and early twentieth centuries. Among the documents were the protests of the Optina elders to the Soviet government regarding the closing of the monastery in the 1920s. This was clearly strictly forbidden fruit, which I had not plucked, and it was made especially so by the fact that the entire fond was *nerazobrannye* (unpublished). I quickly closed the files and returned them to the young assistant, stating that they were not my materials. I subsequently learned that another reader in the division, an archival researcher for the atelier that was restoring the monastery, had requested that these materials be placed with mine. I subsequently met this young and rather attractive Samaritan, and she even volunteered to accompany me on my various research trips in the Soviet Union. Was this a provocation or enthusiastic goodwill? I never tried to find out.

Some Final Reflections

My choice of anecdotes, as mentioned at the outset, perhaps speaks less to the difficulties facing researchers in the Lenin Library during the Soviet era than to how policies concerning the official Soviet hierarchy of "desirable" research topics, coupled with the various obstacles placed before Western and Soviet researchers, may have adversely shaped the knowledge base there and in the West. This is well illustrated by the structure of the public catalog, the BBK, and other policies mentioned above. The Lenin Library's Marxist-Leninist conceptualization and organization of knowledge in effect created a hierarchy of research topics that relegated humanistic topics–my own included–to the bottom of the barrel. The careful scrutiny of what was requested, provided, and in some cases reproduced, the provocatory incidents, the subtle "censorship" of library publications—all had an effect on objective scholarship. And this requires Western librarians to reexamine the scholarly value of some of what we received during the Soviet period.

Herein may lie the larger significance of some of the anecdotal evidence that I have recounted. Many good people, both in Russia and the world outside, were mandated to work in ways and on topics that proved to be unproductive and without enhancement to learning and scholarship. Now, almost a decade after the implosion of the Communist and Socialist societies of Eastern Europe, we are perhaps beginning to witness and to sense the full and tragic impact of Soviet library practices on the Slavic studies profession, scholarship, publishing, and the development of library collections in Russia and throughout the world.

Notes

1. A. N. Yefinov, V. V. Serov, and O. S. Chubaryan, eds., *Books in the Service of Society (Based on the Experience of Soviet Libraries): Collection of Articles of Soviet Authors* (Moscow: Ministry of Culture, 1974).
2. *The State Lenin Library of the U.S.S.R.* (Moscow: The Library, 1987).
3. Among the many works either authored or edited by Zaionchkovskii, see, for example, *Spravochniki po istorii dorevoliutsionnoi Rossii: bibliograficheskii ukazatel'* (Handbooks on the history of pre-Revolutionary Russia: Bibliographical index) (Moscow: Kniga, 1978); *Ukazatel' vospominanii, dnevnikov i putevykh zapisok XVIII–XIX vv.: iz fondov Otdela rukopisei, Gosudarstvennaia biblioteka SSSR imeni V. I. Lenina* (Index of memoirs, diaries, and travelers' notes of the eighteenth and nineteenth centuries: From the collections of the Manuscripts Department of the Lenin Library) (Moscow: The Library, 1951). For examples of their respective bibliographical work, see Klepikov, *Filigrani i shtempeli na bumage russkogo i inostrannogo proizvodstva xvii–xx veka* (Watermarks and stamps on paper manufactured in Russia and abroad during the eighteenth through twentieth centuries) (Moscow: Vsesoiuznoi Knizhnoi Palaty, 1959); Klevenskii, *Istoriia gosudarstvennaia ordena Lenina biblioteki SSSR imeni V. I. Lenina* (History of the V. I. Lenin State Library) (Moscow: The Library, 1953); Kanevskii, *Mezhdunarodnyi knigoobmen sovetskikh bibliotek* (International book exchange of Soviet libraries) (Moscow: Kniga, 1964); Kameneva, *Ukrainskie knigi kirillovskoi pechati XVI–XVIII vv.: katalog izdanii, khraniashchikhsia v gos. biblioteke SSSR im. V. I. Lenina* (Ukrainian books in Church Slavic printed in the sixteenth and seventeenth centuries: A catalog of books located in the Lenin Library) (Moscow: The Library, 1976–); Rogov, *Svedeniia o nebol'shikh sobraniiakh slavianorusskikh rukopisei* (A report concerning small collections of Slavic Russian manuscripts) (Moscow: Akademiia Nauk SSSR, 1962).
4. For an example of one of her more recent compilations, see *Voprosy sobiraniia, ucheta, khraneniia i ispol'zovaniia dokumental'nykh pamiatnikov istorii i kul'tury* (Questions concerning the collection, numbering, storage, and use of documentary monuments of history and culture), comp. S. V. Zhitomirskaia et al. (Moscow: Arkheograficheskaia Komissiia AN SSSR, 1982–).

5. For examples of works by two of these figures, see *Svodnyi katalog slavianorusskikh rukopisnykh knig, khraniashchikhsia v SSSR, XI–XIII vv* (Union catalog of Slavic-Russian manuscript books of the eleventh through thirteenth centuries, located in the U.S.S.R.), ed. L. P. Zhukovskaia et al. (Moscow: Nauka, 1984); Chudakova, *Masterstvo Iuriia Oleshi* (The craftsmanship of Iurii Olesha) (Moscow: Nauka, 1972), or her *Zhizneopisanie Mikhaila Bulgakova* (A biography of Mikhail Bulgakov) (Moscow: Kniga, 1988).

6. Among Kaufman's works are *Russkie entsiklopedii* (Russian encyclopedias) (Moscow: The Library, 1960–) and *Russkie biograficheskie i bibliograficheskie slovari* (Russian biographical and bibliographical dictionaries) (Moscow: Gos. Izd-vo Kul'turno-prosvetitel'noi Lit-ry, 1955). Koblents produced *Istochniki i deiateli russkoi bibliografii xv–xviii vv* (Sources and practitioners of Russian bibliography of the fifteenth through eighteenth centuries) (Moscow: Nauka, 1991).

7. *Istoriia dorevoliutsionnoi Rossii v dnevnikakh i vospominaniiakh: annotirovannyi ukazatel' knig i publikatsii v zhurnalakh* (The history of pre-Revolutionary Russia in diaries and memoirs: Annotated index to books and publications in journals), comp. G. A. Glavatskikh et al., ed. P. A. Zaionchkovskii, 5 vols. in 13 (Moscow: Izd-vo "Kniga," 1976–89).

8. An ongoing, multiyear project organized by Professor Terence Emmons of Stanford University (an American student of P. A. Zaionchkovskii) seeks to fill these gaps, documenting the output of the Russian emigrations.

9. *Svodnyi katalog russkoi knigi grazhdanskoi pechati XVIII veka, 1725–1800* (Union catalog of Russian books in civil script printed in the eighteenth century), ed. I. P. Kondakov et al., comp. E. I. Katsprzhak et al., 6 vols. (Moscow: Izd-vo "Kniga," 1962–75).

10. *Svodnyi katalog russkoi knigi kirillovskoi pechati XVIII veka* (Union catalog of Russian books printed in Church Slavic during the eighteenth century) (Moscow: Lenin Library, 1968).

Some Additional Bibliographical References

Chubaryan, O. S. *Libraries in the Soviet Union.* Memphis: J. W. Brister Library Monograph Series, 1974.

Geyer, Hans. *Zhit' i uchit'sia v MGU: moskovskie vospominaniia nemetskogo stazhera* (Life and study at Moscow State University: The Moscow memoir of a German special student). Moscow: Izd-vo NIIEM im. N. D. Gamalen, n.d.

Gosudarstvennaia ordena Lenina biblioteka SSSR imeni V. I. Lenina: pamiatka chitateliu (The Lenin State Library: Commemorative booklet of readers). Moscow: The Library, 1985.

Klevenskii, M. M. *Putevoditel' po gosudarstvennoi biblioteke SSSR imeni V. I. Lenina* (Guide to the Lenin State Library). Moscow: The Library, 1959.

The Overseas Libraries Controversy and the Freedom to Read: U.S. Librarians and Publishers Confront Joseph McCarthy

Louise S. Robbins

In the early Cold War years, censorship pressures on libraries led in 1948 to the adoption of a strengthened Library Bill of Rights by the American Library Association (ALA). In 1953 pressures intensified when Senator Joseph McCarthy opened an investigation of the United States Department of State's Overseas Libraries. This essay explores the response of the ALA and the American Book Publishers Council to McCarthy's attacks. Through adoption of *The Freedom to Read* and the Overseas Libraries Statement, librarians and publishers identified librarians as defenders of intellectual freedom. In addition, they helped to restore balance to book selection for U.S. information services abroad and affected the role of books and libraries in cultural diplomacy.

The early years of the Cold War saw increased challenges to library materials in the United States. Both governmental bodies and special interest groups sought to protect citizens from "subversive" or "un-American" perspectives in publications of all kinds. The mounting pressure on libraries to restrict selection of materials representing certain points of view led the American Library Association (ALA) in 1948 to adopt a strengthened Library Bill of Rights. Although this intellectual freedom credo pledged librarians to fight censorship and provide materials that presented all sides of controversial issues, it did not reduce the pressures on libraries.

In fact, challenges increased. From New York to Los Angeles librarians reported demands to remove or label library materials.[1] In 1950 in Bartlesville, Oklahoma, for example, the librarian was fired for circulating subversive materials—the liberal magazines the *Nation* and the *New Republic*.[2] A 1952 congressional report highlighted testimony against paperbacks and comics and advised citizen groups how to limit distribution of publications they disliked.[3] Thus the leadership of the ALA's Intellectual Freedom Committee (IFC) was already concerned with supporting librarians and educating the public about intellectual freedom when Senator Joseph McCarthy (R-Wis.), chairman of the Permanent Subcommittee on Investigations of the Senate Committee on Government Operations, began a series of hearings on the State Department's International Information Administration (IIA), including overseas libraries, in February 1953.

Although the 1952 election of Republican Dwight D. Eisenhower to the presidency had raised hopes that McCarthy's attacks against the State Department—begun in February 1950—would subside, those hopes were soon dashed. Barely a month after the inauguration, Dan Lacy, who had just returned to the Library of Congress after a stint as director of the IIA's Information Centers Service (ICS) (which ran the libraries), received a call from Richard Humphrey, acting ICS chief, that McCarthy had asked for a list of the libraries' holdings. A partial listing had been made available to him. Lacy foresaw "a pretty indiscriminate weeding of the overseas libraries that might well be fatal to their utility as instruments of anti-communist propaganda."[4]

Librarians and publishers had come to accept the role of books and libraries in what President Truman had called the Campaign of Truth. Eisenhower also believed in the utility of information as an instrument in an ideological battle against Communism. During the Truman administration, several prewar and World War II information and cultural exchange agencies, such as the Office of War Information and the Coordinator of Inter-American Affairs, were merged into the IIA, a new agency. The 1948 Smith-Mundt Act gave the IIA legislative authority. The ALA, which had pioneered the use of libraries in cultural diplomacy and turned over libraries it sponsored to the new agency, embraced the idea that libraries should present what Truman called "a full and fair picture of American life and of the aims and policies of the United States Government." The clearest demonstration of the strengths of the United States—pluralism, freedom of inquiry, and faith in the ability of citizens to govern themselves—could be found in libraries that provided a diversity of views, librarians believed.[5]

Congress, on the other hand, was ambivalent about entrusting the administration with a propaganda role. And although Eisenhower was convinced of the importance of cultivating favorable public opinion for the United States, he had not yet established his own priorities in this arena. While McCarthy's subcommittee scrutinized the IIA and a subcommittee of the Senate Committee on Foreign Affairs (the Hickenlooper Committee) also examined the agency, Eisenhower's Jackson Committee was studying ways to revamp the information roles of government. In addition, Eisenhower's appointees in the IIA (like Robert Johnson, who arrived after the McCarthy hearings began) were new, often distrustful of holdover appointees, and–like their boss, Secretary of State John Foster Dulles–little inclined to stand up to McCarthy's challenges.[6]

In February 1953 McCarthy's subcommittee called author Howard Fast, a reputed Communist, for questioning, but McCarthy's real target was a directive on the use of books by "controversial authors" in the IIA's overseas libraries. The directive instructed librarians to judge materials primarily by their content. Works by controversial authors, however, would be used only when they supported "importantly" and effectively a specific IIA objective and when their use would not enhance their producer's prestige. Fast's *Citizen Tom Paine*, for example, which gave a positive picture of the United States, could be retained. This directive had been authored by an advisory committee of respected educators and book men, among them Harvard Libraries director Keyes Metcalf; Robert B. Downs, director of the library and Library School at the University of Illinois and 1953 ALA president; and publishers Cass Canfield of Harper and Brothers and George Brett of the Macmillan Company.[7]

The IIA tried to placate McCarthy by replacing the directive on 19 February, one day after Fast's testimony, with another that banned material by "any controversial persons, Communists, fellow travelers, 'et cetera.'" The new directive, however, merely "opened a Pandora's box of confusion" for ICS personnel and librarians in the 196 libraries in 64 countries who had to translate the directive into workable policy. Chaos ensued; between 19 February and 8 July the State Department issued as many as ten separate confidential directives concerning overseas libraries materials. They ranged from an order to destroy a 1946 issue of the *Annals of the American Academy of Political and Social Science* because it contained an article on the United Nations; to an order to remove individual issues of periodicals that contained material detrimental to U.S. objectives; to an order to remove works by authors who had claimed Fifth Amendment protection in testifying before congressional committees. The flow of books to the overseas libraries slowed to a trickle as ICS personnel tried to gain security clearance for every author and title.[8]

In late March and early April, McCarthy sent chief counsel Roy Cohn and consultant David Schine to ensure that European libraries had purged books of "some seventy-five different communist authors." Librarians and other staff members were unsettled by Cohn and Schine's visits. One officer called their visit "an absolutely obscene show," while another reported pocketing a Dashiell Hammett paperback until an inspection visit ended. On 7 April McCarthy sent an "encouraging" report to Secretary of State Dulles that "works of

Communist authors, which were purchased by the [previous] Acheson administration and stocked in our libraries throughout the world," were being removed. He indicated, however, that despite his lieutenants' best efforts, they were still unable to ascertain who was "directly responsible" for "placing the U.S. stamp of approval on a vast number of well known Communist authors." Dulles expressed hope that McCarthy's committee could help him "pin down the responsibility for these conditions." A 13 May communiqué to the overseas libraries specifically ordered the removal of books by people who had refused to testify before McCarthy's subcommittee. Two days later, in response to reports that some removed books had been burned, a directive cautioned that "books withdrawn . . . will not (repeat: NOT) be destroyed, but stored pending further instructions." Although the directives were supposed to be confidential, press coverage stimulated by the McCarthy hearings made at least partial knowledge of the turmoil inevitable.[9]

The ALA leadership knew of the turmoil through other channels as well. Downs and Metcalf were on the Advisory Committee on Books Abroad. A number of prominent ALA members—such as International Relations Board chairman Douglas Bryant—had been overseas librarians. Bryant, along with president-elect Flora Belle Ludington and Francis R. St. John, testified before the Hickenlooper Committee, the Subcommittee on Overseas Information Programs of the Senate Foreign Relations Committee, on the ALA's behalf in March. Lacy, a member of the ALA's IFC, kept in close touch with Humphrey, his former second-in-command, now under McCarthy's scrutiny.[10]

Lacy, who had rapidly traded his Library of Congress position for a job with the American Book Publishers Council (ABPC), believed that if McCarthy succeeded in his attacks on the overseas libraries, "there was every reason to believe" that he would "go after" domestic libraries. He had spent the early days of the controversy trying to prevent the creation of a blacklist of authors that could be used domestically. But even before the IIA controversy arose, spurred by the "national trend toward the restriction of the free trade in ideas," IFC chairman William S. Dix had suggested an off-the-record conference of national leaders to discuss threats to intellectual freedom. He wanted to bolster librarians "in defending their basic principles" but also "have some effect on public opinion." He felt that an "aroused and determined opposition" had to make its voice heard soon, or the country would experience an "era of book burning such as we have never seen before." Thus the IFC and the ABPC arranged a conference at the Westchester Country Club in Rye, New

York, on 2 and 3 May 1953. Under the chairmanship of Librarian of Congress Luther Evans, twenty-five librarians, publishers, and citizens "representing the public interest" achieved "substantial areas of agreement" on a wide group of concerns. A continuations committee wrote them into a statement for publication, *The Freedom to Read*.[11]

The Westchester Conference had completed but not released its work, and plans for an Intellectual Freedom Conference before the ALA summer conference were nearing fruition when, on 14 June, President Eisenhower addressed graduates at Dartmouth College. Speaking off the cuff, he exhorted, "Don't join the book burners. . . . Don't be afraid to go in your library and read every book, as long as any document does not offend [y]our own ideas of decency. That should be the only censorship." The nation could not defeat Communism, he said, unless citizens knew what it taught and why it had appeal. Concealing ideas critical of the United States, ideas that should be accessible through libraries, could not defeat it. Denying access to ideas was inimical to the American way, he said.[12]

The press interpreted Eisenhower's remarks as directed against McCarthy's attack on the overseas libraries, and ALA president Downs wrote to thank Eisenhower. When Dulles revealed that a few of the banned books had actually been burned (reminiscent of the Nazi book burning of the 1930s), critical editorials, cartoons, and articles abounded. At a press conference a few days later, the president retreated under questioning, evading a confrontation with McCarthy. The sequence of events sparked a bevy of newspaper reports on the overseas libraries, complete with lists of prohibited authors and paraphrases of the numerous directives, accompanied by more critical press.[13]

Opening less than a week after Eisenhower's Dartmouth speech, the Intellectual Freedom Conference (at which ABPC's president, Douglas Black, was a featured speaker) bubbled with intensity. The excitement carried over into the ALA's annual conference. At the first council meeting on 22 June, Downs's customary presidential "stock-taking report" vividly described the "virulent disease" of McCarthyism as it was affecting the overseas libraries. "Censorship directives, issued in the atmosphere of fear, hysteria, and repression now prevailing in Washington[,] threaten to place the entire information library system in jeopardy." Every writer, every contributor to an anthology had to have security clearance, and "if any derogatory information, no matter how irresponsible, exists about a writer, his books cannot be used in the information program." Praising the counterattack led by Dix and IFC secretary Paul Bixler, he promised a report later in the week on the Westchester Conference and hailed the Intellectual Freedom Conference as a success.[14]

Intellectual freedom quickly became the conference watchword. As its authors "held [their] breath a little bit," afraid that librarians' fear might defeat it, the council and the 3,300 librarians present adopted "overwhelmingly by a shouting and enthusiastic vote" the Westchester Conference's statement, *The Freedom to Read*.[15] It enunciated seven basic propositions that placed the defense of the freedom to read uncompromisingly in the public interest. First, publishers and librarians have a responsibility to "make available the widest diversity of views and expressions," including "unorthodox or unpopular" ones. Second, they need not "endorse every idea or presentation contained in the books they make available," nor should they "establish their own political, moral, or aesthetic views as the sole standard for publication or selection." Third, it is "contrary to the public interest" for them to "determine the acceptability of a book solely on the basis of the personal history or political affiliations of the author." Fourth, while obscenity laws "should be vigorously enforced," extralegal activities "to coerce the taste of others, to confine adults to the reading matter deemed suitable for adolescents, or to inhibit the efforts of writers to achieve artistic expression" have no place in our society. Fifth, labeling books or authors as "subversive or dangerous" is not in the public interest. Sixth, publishers and librarians have a responsibility "to contest encroachments" upon the freedom to read by those "seeking to impose their own standards or tastes upon the community at large." And finally, publishers and librarians should "give full meaning to the freedom to read by providing books that enrich the quality of thought and expression." Thus they can demonstrate "that the answer to a bad book is a good one, the answer to a bad idea is a good one." They concluded: "We do not state these propositions in the comfortable belief that what people read is unimportant. We believe, rather, that what people read is deeply important; that ideas can be dangerous but that the suppression of ideas is fatal to a democratic society. Freedom itself is a dangerous way of life, but it is ours."[16]

Somewhat anticlimactically, at its session on 25 June the ALA Council unanimously adopted an International Relations Board resolution. It criticized the "confused and fearful response of the State Department to recent attacks" upon the overseas libraries and applauded the president's statement against book burning. Overseas libraries must embody the "ideas of freedom for which they speak," it asserted, for their usefulness depended "on the assurance of their users that they are places in which to learn the truth." While they should not disseminate material harmful to the United States, "elaborate, irrelevant, and offensive schemes of 'clearance' of authors" were unworkable. The American people were entitled to have overseas libraries "express the finest ideals of responsible freedom."[17]

The ALA worked hard to make sure that the actions of the conference got full press coverage. The controversy surrounding the libraries heightened the press's interest in the conference and especially in *The Freedom to Read* and the resolution concerning the Overseas Libraries Statement. The ALA was not, however, simply the beneficiary of fortunate coincidence as it sought to gain public support for the freedom to read.[18] Rather, careful planning paid off when, the day following the endorsement of *The Freedom to Read*, Downs read a letter from Eisenhower, who praised librarians as preservers of freedom of the mind and decried those who believe freedom can be served "by the devices of the tyrant." Eisenhower wrote: "The libraries of America are and must ever remain the homes of free, inquiring minds. To them, our citizens—of all ages and races, of all creeds and political persuasions—must be ever able to turn with clear confidence that there they can freely seek the whole truth, unwarped by fashion and uncompromised by expediency."[19]

The situation was perfect for maximum publicity. The ALA had secured a ringing endorsement for freedom of inquiry and permission to publicize the president's letter. Each session of the council had kept the focus on librarians' support of intellectual freedom. It was "one event after another," Bixler wrote a colleague after the conference, "and Bill [Dix] and I had to pretend that we hadn't planned it that way." The public relations consultant added, "As you might well imagine, the letter from President Eisenhower was no accident." Douglas Black of Doubleday, president of the ABPC, an attendee of the Westchester Conference, a speaker at the Intellectual Freedom Conference, and "a blazing freedom of speech guy," had been Eisenhower's "close friend" at least since his days as president of Columbia University, where Black was a trustee. It is likely that he arranged for the letter. According to Lacy and Robert Frase, the ABPC's Washington lobbyist, Black may also have prompted the Dartmouth speech. He did speak with Eisenhower a few days before the speech, and the day after he wrote a warm letter of thanks to "Dear Ike," telling him about the upcoming conference and sending along the not-yet-adopted *Freedom to Read*.[20]

The publicity effort was successful; even McCarthy read the newspaper accounts of *The Freedom to Read* and the Overseas Libraries Statement. He wired Downs, asking if the accounts represented Downs's point of view. They did, Downs replied, and heard nothing more.[21] The *New York Times* placed *The Freedom to Read* with "America's outstanding state papers" and printed it in full, as did the *Washington Post*, the *Christian Science Monitor*, the *Baltimore Sun*, and the *Norfolk Virginian-Pilot*. The Associated Press carried the story to most daily papers; both *Time* and *Newsweek* covered the statement. Within two weeks the statement had garnered editorial support in a dozen major newspapers, with unfavorable comment in only four. *Saturday Review*, the *New Republic*, and *School and Society* also gave it favorable coverage.[22]

The *American Library Association Bulletin*'s editor urged librarians to seize the moment. "Since the Eisenhower letter and the Freedom to Read statement hit the headlines," he said, "libraries of this country have never been more within the consciousness of the American public." Numerous congratulatory messages were evidence that many people had "realized for the first time what the library stands for and what it means to them." He encouraged librarians to capitalize on their sudden prominence to work for the national library bill.[23]

Other organizations rushed to endorse *The Freedom to Read*, among them the American Booksellers Association, the National Commission for Defense of Democracy through Education, the American Newspaper Guild, and the American Bar Association. An article in *Connecticut Libraries* reported that librarians were having the "unusual experience of swift public eminence." A year later, a new IFC chairman raved about the statement as "one of the documents of the century." Two years later, a St. Louis librarian wrote Bixler that the manifesto was "the shining peak of all that has grown out of ALA since I have known it." She recounted rushing to the county seat to buy the *New York Times* in order to get the full text of *The Freedom to Read*. "I have never been so excited over anything done by librarians," she recalled with fervor. The Westchester Conference's objectives of bolstering librarians and creating national visibility for the cause of freedom to read in libraries had been achieved.[24]

Neither the Westchester manifesto nor the Overseas Libraries Statement was quite so effective in restoring the ICS libraries. They had, however, encouraged embattled State Department officials. Martin Merson, Administrator Robert Johnson's assistant, later recounted his experience of "the hysterical days" when McCarthy and his aides "intimidated even the President." After months of battering by McCarthy and lack of support from the State Department, Merson welcomed the "clarity" of the Overseas Libraries Statement. The press reaction to the statement was "as heartening as anything that had happened for a very long time," he said.[25]

The horror of the press at the book burnings—though only eleven books were burned, according to reports—and the good press given librarians' and publishers' response to the situation gave IIA personnel the necessary courage to reassert some semblance of sanity in book selection criteria. On 8 July Johnson issued a new policy statement on book selection. The policy—"an attempt to apply common sense and American principles of freedom to the operation of our book program"— had been developed largely by Merson and a committee he had gathered, including George Brett of Macmillan, Norman Cousins of the *Saturday Review*, and Douglas Black. Dulles, whose relief that the IIA would be removed from his jurisdiction when the independent United States Information Agency was formed later that summer was only too evident, backed it. Johnson reasserted that the "yardstick" for book selection should be the usefulness of a title's content in relation to the particular needs of a given area of the world. (The next day he had to clarify when a book by an avowed Communist or a person who had claimed Fifth Amendment protection before an investigating committee could be used.) On 15 July Merson issued on Johnson's behalf a report enumerating the anti-Communist books provided to library and translation programs and the books removed under specific directives between 18 February and 8 July. He also announced a fatigued Johnson's resignation.[26]

While the new directive emphasized that book selection must be based "primarily on content," even librarians and publishers appeared to agree that the special character of the overseas libraries made acceptable the continued proscription of the works both of avowed Communists and those who had refused to testify. As Humphrey pointed out, this proscription was of "questionable legality" and in any event was difficult to carry out, since a book might have been purchased some years before its author refused to testify. In the face of appropriations hearings, however, caution prevailed.[27]

While the July policy statement reaffirming content as the main criterion for book selection had the support of the Advisory Committee on Books Abroad, "fear of inquiry and of reduced appropriations" continued to influence book selection for the overseas libraries at least for a time. Franklin L. Burdette, chief of the Information Service, told librarians at the 1954 annual conference that only 60 remained of the 122 overseas librarians who had been serving in April 1953. Nevertheless, although the evidence is mixed and slight, it appears that—in spite of internal pressures—the policy emphasizing content over author's affiliation and the insistence by librarians and publishers that access to diverse points of view communicated more clearly the strengths of the United States than massive doses of anti-Communist propaganda gradually brought about a return to subtler and slower methods of cultural diplomacy, at least as far as the libraries were concerned. Whether the strong sentiment elicited by ALA and ABPC's stand against McCarthy's tactics changed the role of books and libraries in the United States foreign affairs, however, the librarians and publishers did change their own image. One librarian remembered the episode with great pride: "There developed a fighting profession," he said, "made up of dedicated people who were sure of their direction, certain that full information was the most certain way to preserve the democratic processes." In addition, "the librarian, without any specific political power of his [sic] own, accepted the challenge of twentieth century Know-Nothingism and played a leading role in calling to the attention of the American people some of the seemingly forgotten facts of our heritage." The confrontation with McCarthy gave librarians and publishers a high profile as defenders of an essential democratic freedom, the freedom to read.[28]

Notes

Some portions of this article appear in different form in chapter 3 of my book *Censorship and the American Library: The American Library Association's Response to Threats to Intellectual Freedom, 1939–1969* (Westport, Conn.: Greenwood Press, 1996). I am also indebted to Richard Humphrey, formerly of the Information Centers Service, for the use of his file on this episode, made available to me by Robert Frase.

1. See chapter 2 of Robbins, *Censorship and the American Library,* for the period from 1948 to 1952.

2. Louise S. Robbins, *The Dismissal of Miss Ruth Brown: Civil Rights, Censorship, and the American Library* (Norman: University of Oklahoma Press, 2000).

3. Will Oursler, "Books on Trial," *Library Journal* 78 (1 February 1953): 173–78.

4. Dan Lacy, Daily Diary, 18 February 1953, Record Group ADM 37-1, Box 633, Library of Congress Central File (MacLeish-Evans), Archives and Manuscripts Reading Room, Library of Congress, Washington, D.C. (hereafter cited as LC).

5. A number of books deal with the evolution of the information aspects of foreign affairs, among them Thomas C. Sorenson, *The Word War: The Story of American Propaganda* (New York: Harper and Row, 1968); John W. Henderson, *The United States Information Agency* (New York: Frederick A. Praeger, 1969); Wilson P. Dizard, *Strategy of Truth: The Story of the U.S. Information Service* (Washington, D.C.: Public Affairs Press, 1961); Edward W. Barrett, *Truth Is Our Weapon* (New York: Funk and Wagnalls, 1953). Gary E. Kraske analyzes the role of the American Library Association in the development of cultural diplomacy in *Missionaries of the Book: The American Library Profession and the Origins of United States Cultural Diplomacy* (Westport, Conn.: Greenwood Press, 1985). The "full and fair picture" is attributed to Truman in, for example, William Benton, "A Full and Fair Picture of American Life," *Library Journal* 71 (15 February 1946): 244.

6. Kraske, *Missionaries of the Book*; Shawn J. Perry-Giles, "Propaganda, Effect, and the Cold War: Gauging the Status of America's War of Words," *Political*

Communication 11 (April–June 1994): 203–13; Shawn J. Perry-Giles, "The Eisenhower Administration's Conceptualization of the USIA: The Development of Overt and Covert Propaganda Strategies," *Presidential Studies Quarterly* 24 (Spring 1994): 263–76; Richard A. Humphrey, "Censorship in High Places (The Department of State/U.S. Information Agency, 1953)," manuscript in possession of the author, 5–6.

7. Richard A. Humphrey to Robert Frase, "Memo on Censorship and the ICS Book Program," 10 May 1987, manuscript in author's possession; Salvatore D. Nerboso, "U.S. Libraries," *Library Journal* 79 (1 January 1954): 20–25. See *State Department Information Program—Voice of America: Hearings before the Permanent Subcommittee on Investigations of the Committee on Government Operations, United States Senate, Eighty-third Congress, Second Session, Part 2*, 18 and 19 February 1953 (Washington, D.C.: Government Printing Office, 1953). The text (or paraphrases) of the State Department directive and both earlier and succeeding directives can be found in *Overseas Information Programs of the United States: Hearing before a Subcommittee of the Committee on Foreign Relations, United States Senate, Eighty-third Congress, Second Session, Part 3*, 15 January 1954 (Washington, D.C.: Government Printing Office, 1954), 1600–1622; Downs's and Metcalf's names are listed with the Committee on Books Abroad in an attachment to a letter of concern sent to Secretary of State John Foster Dulles from John L. Morrill, chairman of the Advisory Committee on Educational Exchange, 10 April 1953, Record Group 59/2257, National Archives and Records Administration, Washington, D.C. (hereafter cited as NARA).

8. *State Department Information Program—Voice of America, Part 2*, 126–35; Nerboso, "U.S. Libraries," 21; *Overseas Information Programs of the United States, Part 2*, 90; *Part 3*, 1600–1622.

9. Chester H. Opal, USIA, oral history interview, 10 and 12 January 1989, 76, and David Nalle, oral history interview, 29 March 1960, 9, both in Foreign Affairs Oral History Collection, Georgetown University Library; Senator Joseph R. McCarthy to Secretary of State John Foster Dulles, 7 April 1953, and John Foster Dulles to My dear Senator McCarthy, Document No. 511.0021/4-753 A/20, State Department File, Record Group 59/2257, NARA; Chronology of Pertinent Directives, undated, personal file of Richard Humphrey; Circular Airgram, Disposition of Books, etc., withdrawn from USIC's under Circ. 961 and Circ. 1065, 15 May 1953, Document No. 511.0021/5-1553, State Department File, Record Group 59/2257, NARA.

10. *Overseas Information Programs of the United States, Part 2*, 333–55; Dan M. Lacy, interview with author, 19 February 1993, Irvington-on-Hudson, New York.

11. Lacy, interview with author, 19 February 1993; Paul Bixler, "Freedom to Read," *Newsletter on Intellectual Freedom* 2 (March 1954): 8; William S. Dix, "Report of the ALA Committee on Intellectual Freedom, 1952–1953" (June 1953), 3, Record Group 18/1/26, Box 3, American Library Association Archives, University of Illinois at Urbana-Champaign (hereafter ALA); Robert B. Downs, *Perspectives on the Past: An Autobiography* (Metuchen, N.J.: Scarecrow Press, 1984), 157; Everett T. Moore, "Intellectual Freedom," in *Research Librarianship: Essays in Honor of Robert B. Downs*, ed. Jerrold Orne (New York: R. R. Bowker, 1971), 1–17; "Working Paper. American Library Association/American Book Publishers Council Conference on the Freedom to Read. Westchester Country Club, Rye, New York, May 2–3, 1953," Record Group 18/1/26, Box 3, ALA; "ALA/ABPC Conference on the Freedom to Read" (confidential summary of proceedings), 2 and 3 May 1953; William S. Dix cited in Robert S. Downs to Luther H. Evans, 7 April 1953, Library Cooperation Folder 18, Box 871, LC; American Library Association and American Book Publishers Council, *The Freedom to Read. A*

Statement Prepared by the Westchester Conference of the American Library Association and the American Book Publishers Council, May 2 and 3, 1953 (Chicago: American Library Association, 1953).

12. Dwight D. Eisenhower, "The President Speaks," Library Journal 78 (July 1953): 1206; William S. Dix to Members of the Committee on Intellectual Freedom, 16 June 1953, Box 1, Folder 12, Paul H. Bixler Papers, Antiochiana, Olive Kettering Library, Antioch College, Yellow Springs, Ohio (hereafter cited as Bixler Papers).

13. Nerboso, "U.S. Libraries," 22; Eisenhower, "The President Speaks," 1206; Dix to Bixler, 16 June 1953, Record Group 69/1/5, Box 2, ALA; Downs, *Perspectives on the Past*, 158; "Some Books Literally Burned after Inquiry, Dulles Reports," *New York Times*, 16 June 1953; see, for example, "Making Ourselves Ridiculous," *Washington Post*, 17 June 1953, and the cartoons of Herblock, e.g., "I Don't Smell Anything," *Washington Post*, 16 June 1953, which depicts Dulles standing in front of a pile of burning books and holding a newspaper carrying Eisenhower's Dartmouth speech.

14. Robert B. Downs, "The ALA Today–A 1953 Stocktaking Report to the Council, June 23, 1953, Los Angeles," *American Library Association Bulletin* 47 (October 1953): 397–99.

15. Quotations from Lacy, interview with author, 19 February 1993; "Conference Round-Up," *Library Journal* 78 (August 1953): 1261.

16. ALA and ABPC, *The Freedom to Read*.

17. "For the Record" (column), *American Library Association Bulletin* 47 (September 1953): 362–63; Lacy, interview with author, 19 February 1993; "Overseas Libraries Statement; Adopted by Council June 15, 1953," *American Library Association Bulletin* 47 (November 1953): 487; "Conference Round-Up," 1262.

18. Len Arnold to Paul Bixler, 12 June 1953, Arnold to Berninghausen, 14 July 1953, both Record Group 69/1/5, Box 2, ALA.

19. "Third Council Session of American Library Association; Pacific Ballroom, Hotel Statler, Los Angeles, California, 9:30 A.M., Friday, June 26, 1953," Record Group 1/1/1, ALA; Eisenhower, "The President Speaks."

20. David K. Berninghausen from Bixler (n.d., but after June 1953), Arnold to Berninghausen, 14 July 1953; both Record Group 69/1/5, Box 2, ALA; Lacy, interview with author, 19 February 1993; Robert S. Frase, interview with author, 1 May 1993, Madison, Wisconsin; Humphrey, "Censorship in High Places," 23; telephone logs at the Dwight D. Eisenhower Library, Abilene, Kansas; Dear Ike from Doug, 15 June 1953, Dwight D. Eisenhower Library, Abilene, Kansas.

21. Downs, *Perspectives on the Past*, 158.

22. Ibid., 159; William S. Dix to Paul H. Bixler, 3 July 1953, Box 1, Folder 12, Bixler Papers; Charles G. Bolte to Members of the [American Book Publishers] Council, 10 July 1953, Library Cooperation 18, Record Group 871, LC.

23. Ransom L. Richardson, "Editorial," *American Library Association Bulletin* 47 (September 1953): 337.

24. Clift, "Memo to Members" (column), *American Library Association Bulletin* 47 (September 1953): 338–39; Clift, "Memo to Members" (column), *American Library Association Bulletin* 47 (November 1953): 450–51; Bixler, "Introduction," in Fredric Mosher, ed., *Freedom of Book Selection* (Chicago: American Library Association, 1954), 2; Frederick D. Weinstein, "Of the American Library Association Manifesto on the Freedom to Read," excerpt from article in *Connecticut Librarian* 3 (October 1953), Record Group 69/1/5, Box 2, ALA; Emerson Greenaway, "Report of the American Library Association–Intellectual Freedom

Committee, Given at Minneapolis," 23 June 1954, Record Group 18/1/26, Box 3, ALA; [unknown] to Paul Bixler, 10 May 1955, Box 1, Folder 12, Bixler Papers.

25. Martin Merson, *The Private Diary of a Public Servant* (New York: Macmillan, 1955), 113-15.

26. Ibid., 115; "Policy Statement on Book and Library Program, International Information Administration, Department of State, 8 July 1953," in *Report on the Book and Library Program* (Washington, D.C.: IIA, Department of State, July 1953), 64-73 (mimeographed document from file of Richard Humphrey, in author's possession); Sorenson, *The Word War*, 39; "A Statement to the Press by Dr. Robert L. Johnson, Administrator of the International Information Administration, Read by Mr. Martin Merson, Special Assistant to the Administrator, 15 July 1953," in *Report on the Book and Library Program*, 7; "Department of State: For the Press, 9 July 1953," in *Report on the Book and Library Program*, 74-75; "Instructions for Selection and Retention of Material in Book and Library Program, 15 July 1953," in *Report on the Book and Library Program*, 9-11; "Report on the Operations of the Overseas Book and Library Program, 15 July 1953," in *Report on the Book and Library Program*, 13-62.

27. Humphrey, "Censorship in High Places," 15-17.

28. Ibid., 20-22; "Government and Libraries," *Library Journal* 79 (15 April 1954): 736; "Conference Highlights," *Library Journal* 79 (August 1954): 1343-53; Downs, *Perspectives on the Past*, 159; Kraske, *Missionaries of the Book*, 250-51; Sorenson, *The Word War*, 39; Jerome Cushman, "The Librarian as Citizen," *American Library Association Bulletin* 49 (April 1955): 157.

The Effect of the Cold War on Librarianship in China

Cheng Huanwen

Librarianship in China can be divided into four distinct areas because of the Cold War. The first period covers approximately 1840 to 1949. When Chinese intellectuals realized that Chinese libraries were underdeveloped, they began looking at foreign librarianship, and American practices became dominant within Chinese libraries. In 1949, following the end of World War II and the beginning of the Cold War, the ideological differences between Communist China and the capitalist United States forced Chinese librarians to renounce all American librarianship ideologies, and the ideological pendulum swung toward socialist library ideas dominated by Soviet librarianship. Because of the Cuban Missile Crisis and a three-year ecological disaster in China, relations between the U.S.S.R. and China broke down, and from 1966 to 1976 China was segregated from the two superpowers and underwent the Great Proletarian Culture Revolution. During this time intellectuals suffered political persecution and were re-educated in manual labor camps. Library science came to a standstill, and many books were destroyed because of censorship. The fourth and final phase of Chinese librarianship covers the period from 1977 to 1991, when relations between the United States, the Soviet Union, and China normalized, and library theory and technology from the West began again to exert an influence on Chinese librarianship. Chinese librarianship grew and developed substantially during this time period and allowed Chinese librarians to reenter the international arena.

In general, China was not a part of the opposing ideological camps (e.g., the North Atlantic Treaty Organization and the Warsaw Treaty Organization) during the period of the Cold War because of its long-term policies of maintaining independence and keeping the initiative in its own hands, self-reliance, and the "Five Principles of Peaceful Coexistence."[1] However, the Western world, and especially capitalist countries, usually regarded China as a hostile country. As a large Eastern country with an ancient civilization, China not only had struggled against the Western powers for a long time but also has been one of the great socialist countries of the world since 1949. Examples of pre-Liberation struggles include the Opium War (Britain's invasion of China in 1840-42), the Sino-Japanese War of 1894-95, the Yihetuan Movement in 1900, and the War of Resistance against Japan (1937-45).[2]

No matter what the Western world thought about China and no matter whether or not China was involved in the Cold War, China was unable to escape the turmoil of the world and was unavoidably influenced by the Cold War. In fact, the geopolitical environment from 1945 to 1991 had a profound effect on China and its librarianship. While most studies focus on the effects of the Cold War on librarianship in the United States and the former U.S.S.R., it is essential and of historic significance to analyze the social, cultural, and intellectual impact of the Cold War on librarianship in China.

The history of modern librarianship in China can be divided into four periods: (1) the period of the influence of the United States (before 1949); (2) the period of the influence of the Soviet Union (1949-65); (3) the period of diplomatic segregation from the Western world (1966-76); and (4) the period of the influence of the developed countries (1977-91).[3]

The Influence of American Librarianship on Chinese Librarianship before 1949

After 1840, with the imperialist intrusion, traditional Chinese self-sufficiency and the small-scale peasant economy were shattered, and the conservative and closed Chinese librarianship, carried over from ancient times and established on the basis of that economy, was also shaken.[4] Chinese librarianship experienced the influence of library development in the Western countries, and the most profound influence came from the most advanced American librarianship. As a result, American-type librarianship was established in China before 1949.

Around the time of the Bourgeois Reform Movement of 1898, a large number of Chinese intellectuals were aware of the relatively underdeveloped state of Chinese librarianship, but not everyone understood the development of foreign librarianship in all its complexities. Each person aired his own view of foreign librarianship based on what he read or saw; therefore, the librarianship of Europe, Japan, and America was introduced indiscriminately into China. Using the examples of European, American, and Japanese public libraries, the Public Library Movement was launched between 1905 and 1916. As a result, public libraries in large numbers were established in China on the basis of the feudal library traditions;

that is, the Public Library Movement only engendered public libraries in name and form but not in essence.

As time passed, especially as translated articles about American librarianship gradually increased in various journals and newspapers around 1910, the indiscriminate introduction of world librarianship changed into a special emphasis on American librarianship. Mr. Shen Zhurong and Mr. Hu Qingsheng were sent to the United States to study library science in 1914 and 1917, respectively, under the financial support of Miss Mary Elizabeth Wood. Thereafter, so many Chinese librarians went to America to study library science that by the early 1920s almost all the experts in Chinese librarianship had graduated from American library schools.

Between 1917 and 1925, Miss Wood and a large number of Chinese librarians who had attended American library schools launched the well-known nationwide New Library Movement in China. This movement criticized the feudal library tradition, promoted American librarianship throughout China, introduced American library science and technology into China, and raised the social standing of Chinese librarians. As a result, American-type librarianship was established and developed throughout China.

It is safe to say that, before 1949, almost all aspects of librarianship in China were modeled on those in the United States. For example, all of the modern Chinese classification systems were modeled on the Dewey decimal classification, cataloging rules were based on those of the Library of Congress, and most courses in library science imitated those taught in the United States. The great impact of American librarianship on Chinese librarianship can be illustrated by examining the work of four leading library figures in China.

The first leading library figure is Miss Mary Elizabeth Wood (1861–1931; her Chinese name was Wei Dihua), the "Queen of the Modern Library Movement in China."[5] Giving up the directorship of the Richmond Memorial Library in New York, Miss Wood came to China as a clergywoman of the American Church in 1899. She worked first as an English teacher at Boone College in Wuhan and then as a librarian and library educator until she passed away in China in 1931. Miss Wood dedicated the last half of her life to the development of Chinese librarianship. With funds collected in the United States in 1910, she established Boone Library, one of the earliest public libraries in China. Her support of Shen Zhurong and Hu Qingsheng's study of library science in the United States created a precedent for sending Chinese library staff to study library science overseas. In 1920 she and Shen Zhurong founded Boone Library School, an independent library school unique in China before 1949 that initiated library science education in

China. In 1925 she promoted the establishment of the Library Association of China, which ushered in a new epoch in the development of Chinese librarianship.

The second figure is Shen Zhurong (1884–1977; his English name is Samuel T. Y. Seng), the "Father of Library Science Education in China."[6] His graduation from the New York Public Library School in 1916 started the Chinese practice of studying library science abroad. In 1917 he edited and published "A System of Classification of Chinese Books Based on Dewey's Classification," the first modern classification system in China, and launched the nationwide New Library Movement in China. In 1920 he and Miss Wood founded the Boone Library School. He served as the director of and professor at the school for almost forty years, and as a result, most leading Chinese library professionals are his students or the students of his students.

The last two figures are Mr. Liu Guojun (1899–1980) and Mr. Du Dingyou (1898–1967). Mr. Liu graduated from the School of Library and Information Studies of the University of Wisconsin in 1925, and Mr. Du obtained his B.A. degree in library science from Philippines University in 1921. They devoted their lives to introducing American library theory and technology into China and to developing modern library science in China. It is generally acknowledged in China that they made the greatest contributions to the development of library science in China in the twentieth century; therefore, they are acclaimed as "North Liu and South Du" (the greatest library scientist in northern China is Liu and in southern China is Du).[7]

The Influence of Soviet Librarianship on Chinese Librarianship from 1949 to 1965

With the end of World War II and the beginning of the Cold War, the geopolitical environment in the world changed a great deal, and so did the political environment in China. Following victory in the War of Resistance against Japan (1937–45), China underwent the War of Liberation (1945–49). On 1 October 1949 the Communist party of China founded the People's Republic of China, a completely independent country. Since then, China has been one of the most important socialist countries in the world. Along with the development of the socialist system of China, the internal and external political environment of China greatly changed.

On the one hand, because of its opposing ideology, the United States attempted to contain China in every possible way, even trying to overthrow the political power of the Communist party of China in a military way. For example, from 1950 through the 1960s, the United

States supported the Kuomingtang (KMT) in Taiwan to counterattack Mainland China. Under these circumstances, China not only participated in the War to Resist U.S. Aggression and Aid Korea (1950–53) but also started a new ideological movement against American imperialism. The relationship between the United States and China entered a stage of confrontation.[8]

On the other hand, because of the long-term friendship between the Communist party of the Soviet Union and the Communist party of China, a brotherly relationship between the Soviet Union and China was established after 1949, although some contradictions existed between them. During the 1950s, as the largest socialist country, the Soviet Union gave China much economic and technical assistance; and China began learning from "the elder brother Soviet Union" in the way of "lean-to-one-side," although China refused to accede to "the big socialist family" headed by the Soviet Union.[9] As a result of this new political environment, tremendous changes in Chinese librarianship took place after 1949: China developed a new socialist librarianship according to the model of Soviet librarianship while giving up the original model of American librarianship.

At the time of the War to Resist U.S. Aggression and Aid Korea, an ideological remolding movement was launched in China. The aim of the movement was to imbue the intellectuals with socialist ideas and to eliminate feudal and capitalist ideas. Since the United States and the Western European countries were capitalist countries, their librarianship was regarded as capitalist librarianship, which must be criticized and abandoned in China. Almost all library professionals in China cherished a feeling of great reverence for American librarianship, and their professional ideas basically had come from the United States; therefore, deep in their hearts they were involved in a sharp ideological struggle. They had to criticize American library science, even their own professional ideas, and give up their original ideas of American-type library science completely.

The Anti-Rightist Struggle that occurred in 1957 was a counterattack against the bourgeois Rightists in name but a more ruthless political movement of depriving intellectuals of freedom of speech in reality. Some intellectuals were declared to be bourgeois Rightists, and they suffered political persecution for almost twenty years (1957–76); others did not dare to express their views unreservedly any longer but kept firm in their proletarian stance outwardly.

Meanwhile, in the "lean-to-one-side" movement learned from "the elder brother Soviet Union," library professionals in China had to study Russian and Soviet library science from the very beginning; they eventually replaced their so-called capitalist library ideas with the so-called socialist library ideas. As the Soviet Union sent some library experts to China to disseminate Soviet library ideas, China also sent about ten younger library professionals to the Soviet Union for advanced studies of library science. Therefore, just as American librarianship had in the 1920s, Soviet librarianship began to enjoy the privilege of being the only type of librarianship introduced in China during the 1950s.[10]

In fact, great changes in Chinese librarianship took place in every aspect. For example, the acquisition of English publications decreased to such a low level that there were almost no new English publications in most libraries; meanwhile, Russian publications increased in large numbers. Courses concerning American library theory and technology, such as Dewey decimal classification (even UDC) and Library of Congress classification, Anglo-American bibliography and cataloging, and English reference tools, were replaced by those concerning Soviet library theory and technology at all library education institutions.

However, this situation did not last long. About the time of the 1963 Cuban Missile Crisis, the socialist brotherly relations between the Soviet Union and China broke down. China held that the Soviet Union in the post-Stalin period had transformed from Marxism-Leninism into revisionism and strongly struggled against Soviet hegemonies. Ignoring a three-year-long ecological disaster in China beginning in 1959, the Soviet Union withdrew all its experts from China and compelled China to clear all its debts to the Soviet Union at once. The influence of Soviet librarianship immediately ended.

The Segregation of Chinese Librarianship from Western Librarianship from 1966 to 1976

During this period, the external political environment of China was very adverse. Facing the two superpowers in opposing ideological camps, China underwent an ideological struggle against both capitalism and revisionism. Also, China was indirectly involved in the Vietnam War by supporting Vietnam and had a military conflict with the Soviet Union on the border of northeastern China in 1969.[11] So, to some extent, China was in a state of diplomatic segregation from both of the superpowers, and Chinese librarians had very infrequent relations with those in any of the developed countries.

Much more importantly, during this period China underwent the notorious Great Proletarian Culture Revolution (1966-76), a great, unprecedented catastrophe for culture. With the deepening of the Culture Revolution, large numbers of intellectuals suffered political persecution and were transferred to the countryside to do manual labor, as were many library experts and professors. Library professionals undertook no research, teaching, and professional work but remolded their own ideology through manual labor. Library science education was at a standstill; libraries not only became ideological battlefields but also suffered the destruction of many books.[12] In a word, we cannot bear to look back to the history of Chinese librarianship in this period.

The Influence of Western Librarianship on Chinese Librarianship from 1977 to 1991

With the ending of the Culture Revolution in 1976, China entered a new era of reform and openness. Since then, China has held that peace and development are the two major issues affecting the world. Therefore, in international affairs, China not only improved its relations with the Soviet Union but also accomplished the normalization of its relations with the United States. In internal affairs, China first brought order out of chaos in the ideological field and rehabilitated all intellectuals who suffered political persecution. It then transformed the national focus from political movement into economic reform. Accordingly, Chinese librarianship entered a golden age of diversified development. All of the advanced library theory and technology in the Western countries were introduced into China and exerted a great influence on Chinese librarianship once more.

Similar to the situation before 1949, although all advanced library theory and technology in the Western countries were introduced into China and had a varied impact on Chinese librarianship in this period, the impact of American librarianship has dominated over that of other countries.[13]

It also was Liu Guojun, one of China's four leading library figures, who had a keen insight into the forthcoming great change of society and librarianship in China. He was the first to reintroduce Western librarianship into China after the long-term segregation from the West. Early in 1975, Liu Guojun, dean of and professor in the Department of Library Science at Beijing University, introduced the Library of Congress MARC Format into China and opened a new chapter in the annals of relations between Chinese librarianship and Western librarianship.[14] During the last years of his life (1977–81), he translated and published dozens of papers and works about Western librarianship that advocated advanced Western librarianship, especially American library automation, in China (see, for example, "A

Corpus of Translated Data about the MARC Format," "A Brief Introduction to the Papers of Library Science in the USA and Europe," "Review on the Main Classifications in the Western World," and "The Trends of the Western Classifications").[15] Since then, the study and application of American library automation has been one of the main trends in the development of Chinese librarianship.

In 1979 the China Society for Library Science (CSLS) was founded, ending the state of no national library organization in China for thirty years. According to the charter of the CSLS, one of its major tasks is to conduct academic exchanges between China and foreign countries and to strengthen relations and cooperation with the international library sectors. As we know, China was one of the founders of IFLA. However, after 1949, China suspended its contacts with IFLA for about thirty years due to the above-mentioned political factors. With the resumption of China's membership in UNESCO, the issue concerning China's IFLA membership was also resolved. In April 1981 the CSLS resumed its national association membership in the IFLA. Since then, the CSLS has participated in the activities organized by IFLA and has been playing an active role in international library contacts and academic exchange.[16]

Meanwhile, in the ten years from 1978 to 1988, China signed eighty-five cultural agreements with foreign counterparts to international projects involving libraries and established relationships with over 130 countries around the world. Since 1978, many Chinese libraries have actively developed all forms of international contact. The exchange of librarians has increased every year, and forms of international contact have diversified.[17]

During this period, the Chinese library community also expanded its multilateral exchange with many international library organizations. In 1979 China not only joined the Technical Committee for Documentation Standardization of the International Organization for Standardization (ISO/TC46) but also set up the China Technical Committee for Documentation Standardization and ten subcommittees and then started documentation standardization work compatible with ISO/TC46. The year 1992 witnessed the formation of thirty-nine national standards promulgated for implementation by the State Standard Bureau of China. The implementation of these standards has pushed forward documentation standardization and automation in China. In October 1985 the State Council of China approved the establishment of the National Center for ISDS (International Serials and Data System) in the National Library of China. In addition to the distribution and assignment of ISSN to the journals published in China, the ISSN

TABLE 1
THE TOTAL NUMBER OF PUBLIC AND ACADEMIC LIBRARIES IN CHINA FROM 1949 TO 1990

Year	Public Library	Academic Library	Year	Public Library	Academic Library	Year	Public Library	Academic Library
1949	55	132	1963	490		1977	851	
1950	63		1964	540		1978	1,256	598
1951	66		1965	573		1979	1,651	
1952	83		1966	477		1980	1,732	675
1953	93		1967	399		1981	1,786	
1954	93		1968	375		1982	1,889	
1955	96		1969	335		1983	2,038	
1956	375	225	1970	323		1984	2,217	
1957	400	229	1971	354		1985	2,344	
1958	922		1972	414		1986	2,406	1,053
1959	1,011		1973	469		1987	2,440	
1960	1,093		1974	527		1988	2,485	
1961	873		1975	629		1989	2,512	
1962	541		1976	768		1990	2,527	1,075

Note: Public libraries are those above county level, and the blanks in every column under "Academic Library" show the lack of statistical figures.

China Center is also responsible for sending its record regularly to the ISSN International Center located in Paris.[18]

Great advances have been made in every field of Chinese librarianship. The total number of libraries has increased (see table 1); the number of schools and departments of library and information science grew from two in 1977 to about fifty in 1990; following the founding of the CSLS, thirty-six provincial and special national library societies were founded from 1979 to 1991; the number of library journals increased from two in 1977 to about seventy in 1991; according to incomplete statistics, the number of papers in library science has increased from about 4,600 from 1949 to 1979 to 46,260 from 1980 to 1994.[19] More importantly, because of the effect of American librarianship, library and information services in China are being transformed from traditionally manual services to automated and networked services.

In general, economics is the base, politics is the concentrated expression of economics, and war is the continuation of politics, be it military war (e.g., World War II) or ideological war (e.g., the Cold War). Since librarianship is the inevitable outcome of social development, it is bound to be variously affected by society. Generally, economics decides the development of librarianship. However, politics often plays a decisive role in the development of librarianship, and the Cold War is the best example.

Generally speaking, the impact of politics on librarianship in a country can be divided into two parts: the impact of external politics and that of internal politics. It is safe to say that the impact of internal politics on librarianship in a country is usually greater than that of external politics; however, in many cases, both of them are equally important because they are interrelated and interact with each other. The development of Chinese librarianship in the twentieth century is the best example.

In analyzing the varied effects of the Cold War on Chinese librarianship, it is not difficult to distinguish several phases: before 1949, the major influence was from the United States, from 1949 to 1965 it came from the Soviet Union, and from 1977 to 1991 from the whole Western world (mainly from the United States). Although it may appear that external politics did not affect Chinese librarianship during the Culture Revolution because of diplomatic separation from the two superpowers, in fact, this segregation was a direct result of the Cold War.

Any given culture (surely including librarianship) is a reflection of the politics and economics of a given society, and the politics and economics of any society will inevitably find expression in its librarianship.

Notes

1. The "Five Principles of Peaceful Coexistence" are mutual respect for territorial integrity and sovereignty, mutual nonaggression, noninterference in each other's internal affairs, equality and mutual benefit, and peaceful coexistence.
2. The Yihetuan Movement (also known as the Boxer Uprising) was an antiimperialist armed struggle waged by northern Chinese peasants and handicraftsmen in 1900.
3. Cheng Huanwen, "Glory and Dream: A Look back at Chinese Librarianship in the Twentieth Century" (in Chinese), *Library* 3 (1994): 18–24.
4. Cheng Huanwen, "The Impact of American Librarianship on Chinese Librarianship in Modern Times (1840–1949)," *Libraries and Culture* 26:2 (Spring 1991): 372–87.
5. Samuel T. Y. Seng, "Miss Mary Elizabeth Wood: The Queen of the Modern Library Movement in China," *Quarterly of the Boone Library School* 3:3 (September 1931): 8–13.
6. Cheng Huanwen, *A Biography of Samuel T. Y. Seng: The Father of Library Science Education in China* (in Chinese) (Taibei: Student Book Co., 1997).
7. Cheng Huanwen, "The Great Contributions of Mr. Du Dingyou to Modern Librarianship in China" (in Chinese), in *Selected Works of the Symposium of Du*

Dingyou Scholastic Thoughts (Guangzhou: Library Society of Guangdong Province, 1988), 13–43; Cheng Huanwen, "On the Characteristics of Library Talents: A Study of Four Generations of Librarians" (in Chinese), *Guangdong Library Journal* 3 (1988): 22–29.

8. Roderick MacFarquar and John K. Fairbank, eds., and Li Xiangqian, trans., *The Cambridge History of China*, vol. 15, *The People's Republic of China, 1966–1982* (in Chinese) (Hainan Press, 1992).

9. Ibid.

10. Cheng Huanwen, "Forty Years of Progress: A Review and Outlook of Librarianship in the People's Republic of China" (in Chinese), *Library* 5 (1989): 3–10.

11. MacFarquar and Fairbank, eds., and Li, trans., *The Cambridge History of China*, vol. 15.

12. Cheng, "Forty Years of Progress."

13. Cheng, "Glory and Dream."

14. Liu Guojun, "A Brief Introduction to the Library of Congress MARC" (in Chinese), *Library Work* 1 (1975).

15. Liu Guojun, *Selected Papers of Liu Guojun in Library Science* (in Chinese) (Beijing: Bibliography and Documentary Publishing House, 1983).

16. The Compilation Group, *The General Survey of the China Society for Library Science* (English-Chinese) (Beijing: Bibliography and Documentary Publishing House, 1996), 105.

17. Wu Weici et al., *The Vigorous Advancement of Libraries in China* (English-Chinese) (Beijing: Bibliography and Documentary Publishing House, 1996), 117.

18. Ibid., 117–18.

19. Ibid., 77; Cheng, "Glory and Dream"; Huang Zongzhong, *An Introduction to Library Science* (in Chinese) (Wuhan: Wuhan University Press, 1988), 216.

Political Censorship in Finnish Libraries from 1944 to 1946

Kai Ekholm

Ekholm presents an overview of the forms that library censorship took in postwar Finland when the country was under the auspices of a Soviet Controlling Commission (Valvontakomissio). He demonstrates that censorship of library materials followed patterns long established in the Soviet Union. Most censorship involved the "unshelving" of "politically incorrect" (i.e., anti-Soviet) books. Nazi materials were also removed (292 copies of *Mein Kampf* alone). Ekholm then explores the context of Soviet "omnicensorship," which was the guiding principle for Finnish censorship. The most illuminating aspect of this practice was the formulation of the *spetskhran*, or closed collection. A *spetskhran* was a collection of forbidden books that were nonetheless cataloged and stored. The author postulates that this postwar system was a possible precursor to a long period of self-censorship throughout the 1970s and 1980s. The essay also raises some issues in the theory of censorship in libraries first by discussing a study by Lowenthal of self-censorship at California public libraries and then by looking at a study by Stieg of prewar censorship by the Nazi government in German libraries. Ekholm concludes by raising new questions about the methodology of research on censorship and argues for a Hermeneutic rather than a moralistic perspective on patterns of political and self-censorship.

The postwar period was a dramatic one in Finnish history. The country had lost the war and was controlled by the Allied forces and the so-called Valvontakomissio (Controlling Commission), led by the Soviets and directed by Zhdanov. From 1944 to 1946, the commission gave an order to the Finnish Ministry of Education to unshelve so-called politically incorrect books from public libraries. These consisted mostly of prewar books that contained heavy criticism of and political propaganda against the Soviets.

Bookstores were given two printed catalogs that listed nearly three hundred titles of books to be unshelved. The censoring of books from libraries was a more interesting and complicated process than their removal from bookstores. There were no catalogs or "indexes" sent to libraries. For this reason, the collection of the removed books was a very eclectic one. In most libraries fewer than one hundred titles were removed, but in the biggest libraries hundreds of books were removed. In total, more than 1,700 titles and over 30,000 books were unshelved from 403 communal libraries. (If we estimate 30 books per shelf meter, over 650 shelf meters were removed.) There were many politically incorrect books that were the "right target" to unshelve, but also many mistakes were made because of misleading book titles. Even books dealing with nineteenth-century Russian history were removed. Obviously, the book most often removed was Hitler's *Mein Kampf* (*Taisteluni*), followed by this top twenty list: (1) Adolf Hitler, *Taisteluni*, 292 copies removed, (2) Kirsti Huurre, *Sirpin ja moukarin alla*, 267, (3) Erkki Palolampi, *Kollaa kestää*, 219, (4) Mika Waltari, *Neuvostovakoilun varjossa*, 202, (5) Aleksandra Rahmanova, *Avioelämää punaisessa myrskyssä*, 189, (6) Aleksandra Rahmanova, *Ylioppilaita, rakkautta, kuolemaa*, 174, (7) Aleksandra Rahmanova, *Uusien ihmisten tehdas*, 170, (8) Miihkali Onttoni, *Raatteen tiellä*, 160, (9) Viljo Saraja, *Lunastettu maa*, 159, (10) Hjalmar Siilasvuo, *Suomussalmen taistelut*, 159, (11) Jaan Siiras, *Viro Neuvostokurimuksessa*, 158, (12) Aatami Kuortti, *Pappina, pakkotyössä ja pakolaisena*, 148, (13) Imam Raguza, *Moskovan hirmuvaltias*, 144, (14) Väinö Salminen, *Viena–Aunus, Itä-Karjala sanoin ja kuvin*, 140, (15) Miihkali Onttoni, *Suomussalmen sotatanterilla*, 134, (16) Armas J. Pulla, *Ja Pöh, sanoi sotamies Ryhmy*, 131, (17) Örnulf Tigerstedt, *Vastavakoilu iskee*, 130, (18) Tatjana Tsernavin, *Pako Neuvosto-Venäjältä*, 126, (19) Eino Hosia, *Tuliholvin alla*, 121, and (20) Armas J. Pulla, *Jees, punamultaa, sanoi kersantti Ryhmy*, 117. The removed books were officially returned to the shelves in 1958. Usually they were still in stores and available only for "research purposes." There were not very many interesting books around anymore because many new politically bitter and harsh books had already been published by then. There were still many misconceptions about the role of these Finnish closed collections, even in the 1960s and 1970s.

The Role Model of Soviet Censorship

In the Soviet Union, politics and censorship were never clarified or stagnant, they were always faceless and all-embracing. The so-called omnicensorship concept describes well the situation prevailing in the Soviet Union, where, in addition to the authors' self-censorship, books had to pass through publisher censorship as well as tight library inspection.

The omnicensorship concept also describes the situation that the Soviet Union wanted to create after the Second World War in the countries it had occupied and, unofficially, also in Finland. It describes forms of self-censorship as well as the internally known Finlandization of the 1960s and 1970s. Generally, authors or translators knew their own limits. Publishers knew them even better and, as a rule, obeyed them. In some rare cases, libraries opted not to acquire these types of books either.

From 1944 to 1946, book censorship followed the principle of the *spetskhran*. According to this practice, Finnish librarians were instructed to separate anti-Soviet literature into a special collection of its own. This was the method that had been applied in the Soviet Union for more than twenty years, and its functionality was probably not even questioned by the Soviet leadership of the Controlling Commission. Assigning Finnish librarians the task of increasing and cataloging a forbidden collection also resembles the Soviet practice to some extent.

The director of the *spetskhran* at Lenin's library complained that librarians were sometimes accused of being fascists and sometimes KGB people, although they themselves did not forbid one single book. They only obeyed orders coming from Glavlit, the organization in the U.S.S.R. that controlled censorship. On the other hand, a document dated 1949 indicates that Glavlit delegated some of its tasks to the employees of the *spetskhran* with the intent that they should themselves make lists of politically dangerous literature. A censorship group was also set up, comprised of employees who knew foreign languages, since after the war Glavlit could not cope with the stream of books alone.

The best explanation may be to say that Finnish authorities, while respecting the order given by the Controlling Commission, only followed the Paasikivi-Kekkonen foreign policy line and implemented a new kind of friendship policy. (J. K. Paasikivi and Urho Kekkonen designed the official foreign policy between Finland and the U.S.S.R., the so-called peaceful coexistence that was ultimately referred to as the Paasikivi-Kekkonen foreign policy line.) If we want to be nasty, we could say, for instance, that the fate of forbidden books is a typical example of Finlandization and self-censorship.

We can also speculate a lot about the long-term effects of this process. Was it the cornerstone of a so-called self-censorship era (in the 1970 and 1980s) or just a very short period that left no marks? Although it is not my task to give the final answer, I think it at least started a paradigm of political overcarefulness called "self-censorship" that was controlled by the late president Urho Kekkonen. And as we know, paradigms organize different materials and opinions very effectively that may astound us afterward. Politically and historically, the process was analogous to the reeducation of occupied countries led by the United States and its allies in Japan and by the Soviet Union in Estonia.

Librarians as Censors

Sociologist Marjorie Fiske Lowenthal's *Book Selection and Censorship* (1959), a research study into book selection and censorship in general and school libraries in California, is one of the basic works of research into library censorship. Lowenthal wanted to find out whether some external body poses restrictions on librarians or whether librarians themselves limit their activities so that citizens' rights to versatile collections become threatened. The outcome of the research was that the California librarians themselves acted as the most effective censors of their own library collections. There was not much external pressure to remove or include certain books in the library. Instead, when making acquisitions, librarians themselves estimated what books would probably arouse indignation in clients and school authorities, and these books were not acquired. According to the view of the librarians, the best way to avoid book removals and censorship disputes was not to acquire controversial books in the first place.

According to Theodor Adorno, a person with an authoritarian personality demands absolute obedience. Other characteristics associated with an authoritarian personality include cringing before a person higher up in the hierarchy, contempt of weakness, rigidity, rejection of outside groups, conventionality, and the desire to define everything in an unambiguous way. In her book *Public Libraries in Nazi Germany* (1992), Margaret F. Stieg, professor of library and information studies at the University of Alabama, investigates the development, selection procedures, and censorship of the Nazi zxlibrary system. Stieg notes that there has been only minimal interest in the libraries of wartime Germany. The same phenomenon applies to the Finnish library system. The years of war and their problems have been mentioned only in passing in library histories, perhaps because they are too sensitive an issue.

Public libraries are an institution whose purpose is to collect, maintain, and distribute cultural material. When cultural content is defined politically, the social role of libraries becomes emphasized, and we can even detect some features of a political institution in them. Stieg shows how libraries in Nazi Germany were harnessed to ideological work. Similar development started in the Soviet Union after the 1917 Revolution. After the Second World War, equivalent development took place in overseas libraries financed and directed by the United States. In addition to the section on history, Stieg's study has a great deal of valuable information on general book censorship and librarians' "mental" adjustment to the change. In the 1930s the library system of Nazi Germany was a microcosm of the whole state, where politics became the only standard and where political values controlled the whole moral code, beliefs, attitudes, and social behavior.

Maybe we should just accept the extensive censorship that took place in Finnish libraries as a "political microcosm" and, at the same time, accept the idea that in the end there is no place where libraries could have a completely independent cultural strategy of their own, even though we would like to think so.

It has been noted that the damages caused by indirect censorship have remained effective in some Soviet-controlled countries. People are still evaluating books using ideological rather than artistic criteria, and the invisible boundaries of self-censorship remain in force. Jean Baudrillard goes even further when he states that Soviet censorship exercised its influence by creating a collective unconscious on which art and thinking operated:

> The USSR *perestroika* has been characterized not only by ethnic and political demands, but also, by a surge of accidents and natural catastrophes (including crimes and accidents of the past, now disinterred). A kind of spontaneous terrorism has emerged in response to liberalization and the extension of human rights. All this, we are told, was already there but censored. One of the most deeply felt criticisms directed against the former Stalinist regime is that it deprived us of the many bloody events it censored, thus rendering them useless save as part of a political unconscious to be inherited by future generations; that it froze or deep-froze the titillating and bloodcurdling details of these crimes; and that, like the Nazis in the case of the Holocaust (another almost perfect crime), it flouted the universal law of information. (Baudrillard 1993:109)

Methodological Considerations

I would like to mention some methodological considerations and additions to censorship research.

Censorship should not be researched from a moralistic perspective but, rather, a hermeneutic one. Censorship is always, even when open to interpretation, part of a hermeneutic chain whose conditions change according to the situation. For this very reason, it is possible that the same book is forbidden in the United States, the Soviet Union, and China but for completely different reasons. The problem of censorship research is singularity, because it is difficult to find general patterns or principles that can be researched qualitatively even if one studies a long period of time.

Censorship can be researched using discourse analysis, whereby its various hidden/public strategies become manifest. The censor may justify his or her action with a strategy of no alternatives, whereby censorship is the only sensible alternative. In general, it is impossible to get exact information about the "black box of censorship." We can only draw conclusions afterward from the arguments and solutions that supported it.

The hermeneutics of censorship can be defined as the study of expressed, explicit or unexpressed, tacit rules and the assessment of these general principles used when investigating the procedures, extent, and cultural meanings of censorship. Since self-censorship involves constant self-definition and clarification, I consider hermeneutic scrutiny very fruitful.

Archival Material

Oppikirjojen tarkastustoimikunnan mietintö as. 21.12.1944
Opetusministeriön kirjeet kirjastotoimikunnalle 19.7.1945 ja 7.8.1945
Valtion kirjastotoimiston kiertokirje n:o 24. 20.10.1944
Valtion kirjastotoimiston kiertokirje n:o 26. 13.8.1945
Valtion kirjastotoimiston arkisto 1912–62 *Valtionarkistossa, erityisesti*
Aa 5 *Diaarit* 1939–50
Bb 2 ja 3 *Poliittisista syistä kirjastoista poistetut kirjat*
Ca 1945–49 *Valtion kirjastotoimikunnan pöytäkirjat*
D 3 *Lähteneet kirjeet* 1944–47
Db 6 *Muut konseptit ja taltiot* 1942–63
Ea 6 *Saapuneet kirjeet* 1943–44
Ed 7–9 *Saapuneet asiakirjat* 1943–44, 1945, 1946
Hb 6 *Tilastot Suomen kansankirjastoista* 1941–50

Secondary Sources

Baudrillard, Jean. *The Transparency of Evil* (*La Transparence du Mal,* 1990). London, 1993.
Blanshard, P. *The Right to Read: The Battle against Censorship.* 2nd ed. Boston, 1956.
Choldin, Marianna Tax, and Maurice Friedberg, eds. *The Red Pencil: Artists, Scholars, and Censors in the USSR.* Boston, 1989.
Ekholm, Kai. *Kielletty! 11-osainen artikkelisarja kotimaisesta kirjasensuurista.* Helsingin sanomat helmikuu–maaliskuu, 1991.

———. *Kielletyt kirjat. Kirjasensuurin historiaa ja kirjaluettelo.* Orivesi, 1989.
———, toim. *KIELLETYT. Antologia kirja- ja taidesensuurista.* Orivesi, 1990.
———, toim. *Kielletyt kirjat. Kirjasensuurin historiaa ja kirjaluettelo. Uudistettu ja täydennetty laitos.* Orivesi, 1995. Eduskunnan kirjaston tutkimuksia ja julkaisuja.

Kuusela, Marjo-Riika. "Spetskhran * kirjojen vankileiri." In Kai Ekholm, toim, *Kielletyt kirjat. Kirjasensuurin historiaa ja kirjaluettelo. Uudistettu ja täydennetty laitos.* Orivesi, 1995. Eduskunnan kirjaston tutkimuksia ja julkaisuja.

Neumann, Julek. Shadows on the Stage: Indirect Theatre Censorship in Czechoslovakia, 1969–1989. Ed. E. S. Shaffer. New York, 1994. Interviews with leading directors Pavel Kohout, Lubos Pistorius, Jan Schmid, Jan Kacer, and Jaroslava Siktancova. Comparative criticism. An annual journal. Revolutions and censorship.

Patterson, Annabel. Censorship and Interpretation: The Conditions of Writing and Reading in Early Modern England. London, 1984.

Steig, Margaret F. *Public Libraries in Nazi Germany.* Tuscaloosa AL and London, 1992.

Books and Libraries as Instruments of Cultural Diplomacy in Francophone Africa during the Cold War

Mary Niles Maack

During the period of the Cold War, Britain, France, and the United States employed similar strategies in the cultural efforts they directed toward Francophone Africa; all three countries sponsored language instruction and set up cultural centers with libraries reflecting their national heritage, but the priority that each nation gave to these activities was a result of underlying ideologies that provided the foundation for its cultural diplomacy. Although this essay analyzes and compares British, French, and American book-related programs throughout the region, particular attention is given to Senegal, whose capital city, Dakar, had formerly served as the federal capital for all of French West Africa. The first American book-related program in the region was the United States Information Agency (USIA) library set up in Dakar in 1958; because the objective of the USIA centered on building understanding and support for the U.S. position on international issues, half of the books in its library were French translations of American authors. In contrast, the goal of the French cultural center library, established one year later, was to encourage African authors writing in French to foster cultural exchange. Since its entire collection was in French, this library drew a large number of students and general readers and thus partially filled the gap created by the lack of a municipal public library. In 1965 the British Council also set up a library in Dakar to support its English language instruction program. Although better known for its work in Ghana and Nigeria, the efforts of the British Council in Francophone Africa present a third approach to the use of books in cultural diplomacy. This study examines book donation and translation programs as well as libraries and is based on primary source material collected during research trips to Africa and France; secondary sources include recent historical studies of U.S. public diplomacy as well as publications by and about the British Council and the French aid programs that provide books to Africa.

Book donations, translation and publishing programs, and the creation of cultural center libraries were all means by which foreign governments sought to influence the African elite during the Cold War era. Because of their close economic and political ties with France, the Francophone states in Africa were certainly on the periphery of the ideological struggles between the United States and the Soviet Union. Nonetheless, the region did attract the attention of several foreign embassies that had come to see books as a significant element of their cultural diplomacy. *Cultural diplomacy* is defined here as that aspect of diplomacy that involves a government's efforts to transmit its national culture to foreign publics with the goal of bringing about an understanding for national ideals and institutions as part of a larger attempt to build support for political and economic goals. Although the primary focus of this essay will be on activities with direct government support, attention will also be given to organizations such as the Alliance Française and the British Council that have received both public and private funding along with income from language classes.

Although the broad goals of cultural diplomacy were somewhat similar for all three countries, different justifications, strategies, and outcomes have characterized the book-related activities carried out in Africa on behalf of France, Britain, and the United States. Furthermore, while metropolitan political leaders and staff involved with cultural diplomacy had certain expectations or goals, these were not always completely understood or shared by staff working abroad. Even when those in the field—cultural attachés, information officers, and librarians—were committed to following the guidelines from their home government, the actual outcome of their efforts may have been considerably different from what they expected, recorded, or reported home. This is particularly true of any cultural exchanges involving books and libraries. As Jean-Paul Sartre remarks in *Les Mots*, "La Bibliothèque c'était le Monde pris dans un miroir; elle en avait l'épaisseur infinie, la variété, l'imprévisibilité." [The Library was the World caught in a mirror; it had infinite depth and unanticipated variety.] (quoted in Pauchet 1995:263).

While the use people make of libraries in any country and their personal interpretations of what they read can be far different from what is intended, in a situation where books move across cultural and linguistic borders, the outcome can be even harder to predict. One striking example was reported by an American cultural officer, who noted that during the early postwar years officials in an unnamed Asian country asked that the distribution of free copies of the Declaration of Independence be stopped because the grievances it listed against King George III of England "described too accurately the grievances of present-day opposition groups in this particular country against their own king" (Dizzard 1951:66). Even a selection of books that have become part of the national literary canon will not necessarily be interpreted or used abroad in ways that can be anticipated. For example, historian Richard Pells notes that during the 1950s and 1960s

> it was fashionable . . . for Europeans to reaffirm their prejudices about the United States by relying on the works of America's most disenchanted and acerbic authors. . . . Often passages . . . were used selectively to illustrate the inhumanity of mass production, the claustrophobia of the American small town . . . No novel was more influential than *Babbitt* [and] the name became . . . a handy code word for American blandness and conformity.

Pells also speculates that *Babbitt*'s author, Sinclair Lewis, was given the Nobel Prize in 1930 in part because of "his indictments of American society" (1997:20).

Since the intellectual and cultural impact of book distribution and of library use is difficult to document and almost impossible to measure, this essay will instead focus on the ideological goals of each country, the rhetoric used at home and abroad to justify national investment in cultural diplomacy, and the metaphors used to describe the goals of this work. The first part presents a brief historical overview of the major agencies and organizations involved with cultural diplomacy through books. The second section describes the efforts of these organizations in Francophone Africa from the period just prior to independence through the end of the Cold War. Examples will be drawn from a number of countries, but Senegal, the country that historically has had the closest ties with France, will be presented as a case study where the various elements of cultural exchange, persuasion, and competition are evident. The final section offers a comparative analysis of the rhetoric of cultural diplomacy and compares the British, French, and American efforts in establishing and maintaining cultural programs during the Cold War.

Part 1: Antecedents and Early History

The Alliance Française

The oldest and best-known society for the diffusion of French language and culture is the Alliance Française, a private association founded in Paris in 1883 with the goal of promoting "the propagation of the French language in the colonies and abroad" (Tetu 1988:74). On the occasion of the hundredth anniversary of the Alliance Française, Philip Greffet, the executive secretary of the association, paraphrased the founders' underlying goal as an effort to "save" French culture through the spread of the French language (1983:6). During the 1880s the Alliance Française expanded rapidly, enrolling well-known supporters such as Louis Pasteur and Gen. Louis Léon Faidherbe, the former governor of Senegal, as well as diplomats, politicians, religious leaders, and many noted writers, including several members of the Academie Française. However, along with their devotion to the *mission civilitrice,* the founders of the Alliance also believed that the expansion of the language was a tangible means to reestablish French power and prestige abroad by promoting French "in the battle [for hegemony] among the languages of the world" (Peroncel-Hugoz 1983:2). The historic significance of this struggle for linguistic expansion was illustrated by the remarkable success of one of the earliest African branches of the Alliance Française that recruited 150 members on the British island of Mauritius in 1884; Peroncel-Hugoz notes that this feat could be considered an act of defiance to the English ("véritable défi à l'Albion"), to whom France had ceded the colony in 1814 (1983:2).

Although it remained a private, nonprofit association, the Alliance Française soon began to receive various kinds of governmental aid, and in 1900 the Ministry of Foreign Affairs established a special section to provide funding for French schools and organizations abroad (Deibel and Roberts 1976:37). By 1933 a British Embassy official in Paris remarked that, with a budget of nearly six million francs a year, the Alliance Française had become a "powerful instrument of cultural propaganda" that had financial support from three ministries (foreign affairs, national education, and the colonies) as well as more modest funding from local governments (Donaldson 1984:3). Although the work of the Alliance Française centered on language instruction, the larger centers abroad often established small libraries and sponsored poetry readings, theatrical presentations, and other cultural events. While books were important in supporting these cultural events, the libraries were usually set up and maintained by volunteers.

The British Council

In 1934, over fifty years after the foundation of the Alliance Française, Britain moved to emulate France by creating the British Council. Reflecting on why the United Kingdom waited so long to enter into cultural diplomacy, British statesman Sir Harold Nicolson wrote:

> It pleases us to imagine that we are bad at self-advertisement and even at self-explanation. The Americans, we are assured, are born

with the gift of salesmanship, and go through life lauding the size, the novelty and the excellence of their wares.... The French... being convinced that since the age of Pericles there has existed no type of civility comparable to [theirs] ... have in all sincerity regarded it as their mission to spread latin culture across the globe. Until the twentieth century, the British, having been trained to regard as obnoxious all forms of self-display, were arrogantly reticent. If foreigners failed to notice our gifts then there was nothing that we could or should do. (1955:4)

In the fiftieth-anniversary history of the British Council, Lady Frances Donaldson expressed doubt as to whether "the utilitarian British" would have entered into cultural diplomacy at all had they not believed that in Asia and Latin America the Germans and Italians were creating an atmosphere of hostility toward Britain; by 1929 the Foreign Office estimated that Germany and Italy were spending £300,000 on "cultural propaganda," while the French had invested £500,000 in spreading their language and culture (1984:4, 16). Recommendations from Foreign Office staff that called attention to the need for "cultural propaganda" were supported by the Department of Trade, which, on the basis of several official economic missions, "argued that cultural projection was inseparable from successful commerce and diplomacy" (Coombs 1988:2). While the French regarded it as "crude" to support the Alliance Française out of a belief that "every client of the French language ... [might become] a natural customer for French products," the British did not hesitate to justify cultural expenditures abroad on the grounds that the flow of trade would follow (Peroncel-Hugoz 1983:2). Thus one catalyst that stimulated reconsideration of cultural programs abroad was the 1930 report of a British Economic Mission to South America that criticized the government for not having "sufficiently understood the direct relation between culture and trade" (Donaldson 1984:18).

This conjuncture of political and economic concerns was noted by Reginald Leeper, who, as a staff member at the News Department of the Foreign Office, had been vainly trying to promote the idea of "cultural propaganda." Finally, in November 1934 Leeper succeeded in bringing together a group of businessmen and educational experts who formed a committee to consider "a scheme for furthering the teaching of English abroad and to promote thereby a wider knowledge and understanding of British culture generally" (Nicolson 1955:10). With support from influential political leaders, along with a promise of funding from commercial firms and the patronage of the prince of Wales, the British Council was officially launched in

1935. A sum of £6,000 was granted by the government, but it was decided from the beginning that although general policy must be "under distant supervision" of the Foreign Office, the Council should be governed by a board "accorded the greatest possible autonomy" (Nicolson 1955:10).

Even after the war broke out in 1939 the British Council retained its identity as a cultural organization and refused to become a department of the Ministry of Information. Instead of being involved in propaganda work or in the dissemination of timely war information, the British Council chose "the unhurried continuance of a permanent task which the war will not be allowed to interrupt" (Nicolson 1955:21). Although government support had risen from £330,000 in 1940 to over £2.5 million by 1945 (over three fourths of the Council's total revenue), Sir Harold Nicolson noted with pride that "the initial principle that the Council should not be subjected to direct official control has enabled it to remain independent of parties and politics and acquire continuity and impartiality" (Nicolson 1955:11).

Even though the Council remained above partisan politics, it did engage in commercial activities through its work in negotiating translation rights for British books and through the Book Export Scheme initiated by Sir Stanley Unwin, a prominent publisher who served on the British Council board. This program represented the first official assistance offered to the book export trade; its goal was to stimulate the sale of British periodicals and books by organizing a "sale-and-return operation" for overseas booksellers who were having difficulties with the wartime currency exchange. Although the program ended shortly after the war, it was the first of several efforts to make British books available through book presentation programs and through a "low priced book scheme which subsidizes British publishers to produce and market English textbooks . . . at less than half their normal published price" (Saunders and Broome 1977:13).

During the war the task of developing good relations with neutral countries was given high priority, and the Council extended its representation to the Near East, North Africa, China, and Latin America; by the early 1940s it also began its work in colonial Africa (the Gold Coast, Nigeria, and Sierra Leone, 1943; the Belgian Congo, 1941–44). When the war ended, the Council had over thirty offices overseas and was supporting nearly one hundred institutes (Coombs 1988:11). While the Council's earliest efforts in Southern and Eastern Europe were often carried out in conjunction with a privately founded British Institute or with a local university, in other parts of the world independent centers were often set up with a library as the heart of their operation.

Although no librarian was hired until 1940, by 1937 the British Council board included Lionel McColvin, one of the most distinguished public library leaders in Britain. McColvin provided valuable advice and also served as liaison with the Library Association, where he held the title of honorary secretary. However, Ann Ormrod, a trained librarian who served as head of the Books Department from 1940 to 1946, is credited as the architect of the British Council's library development. Historian Douglas Coombs notes that during this period of rapid wartime expansion, "her forceful advocacy of professional standards and professional supervision for Council libraries provided a base upon which her successors have been able to build" (1988:15–16). By 1944, in response to a memo from McColvin on postwar planning for overseas library service, she urged that the Council establish "a central English library on the best professional model which would serve the specialist needs of readers in the country" (Coombs 1988:30). She further clarified the nature and purpose of the Council libraries in 1945 when she firmly rejected Deputy Secretary Richard Seymour's suggestion that the British Council support the American Library in Paris rather than establishing its own library. In countering this plan, Ann Ormrod unequivocally declared that the library was "an integral part of the Council's work and one of the most cogent expressions of it." She emphasized that it was impossible to "divorce the library from the Council's direct control without distorting or even destroying the fundamental character of . . . the work." She further declared that because the Council's field was "British life, thoughts and culture," its library must be "the reflection of the country of its origin" (Coombs 1988:21–22).

These principles laid out by Ann Ormrod were followed by her successor, John Barnicot, who provided continuity in the Council library program through his twenty-four years of service. During his early years he issued a number of procedural directives designed to guide country librarians and provide consistency in the smaller libraries, which were run by nonprofessionals. By 1952 Barnicot had also codified the Council's book selection policy in a circular that identified certain topics as "integral" to the collection. These included five "cultural subjects" (British drama, fine arts, literature, and music as well as the English language) along with works on British civilization and institutions. Although foreign publications in English were allowable if they dealt with British life and culture, British editions were preferred if available, and "British authorship was normally prerequisite for works of the imagination" (Coombs 1988:49).

In addition to excluding foreign literary works, this document also excluded "political books," a term that Coombs describes as being "very narrowly" defined to include only books dealing with "the current policies and actions of H. M. Government and of other governments" (1988:48-49). The purpose of this later directive was to reinforce the separation of the Council's work from that of the British Information Service, which maintained small, separate reference collections in its posts abroad. Although the definition document issued by the Foreign Office in 1946 sought to "prevent overlap between these Information Services and the Council," joint libraries could be established in certain circumstances; in such instances, books on "cultural subjects" would be chosen by the Council, while books on "political subjects" would be the responsibility of the information officer (Coombs 1988:41). However, the number of joint libraries remained small because priority was usually given to maintaining a separate Council library "as a preferred means of cultural projection by way of the printed word" (Coombs 1988:272).

From the Office of War Information (OWI) to the United States Information Agency (USIA)

In contrast to the clear and consistent separation between information and culture in British overseas libraries, the United States attempted to combine the two functions in the work of the Office of War Information (OWI). The first OWI library opened in London in 1942 and was followed by others in the British Commonwealth and in Europe; by 1945 there were collections in Stockholm, Lisbon, Madrid, Istanbul, Cairo, Moscow, Chung-king, Beirut, Melbourne, Sydney, and Damascus. Although the goal of the OWI was to favorably influence the public in Allied or neutral countries, its library work was begun at a time when President Franklin D. Roosevelt referred to "the growing power of books as weapons," stressing that "a war of ideas can no more be won without books than a naval war can be won without ships" (quoted in Larson 1951:433). When the OWI was disbanded in 1945, a number of its functions were transferred to the Department of State; these included a radio broadcasting service (Voice of America), educational exchange programs, and cultural centers, which often included book collections. In addition to the OWI libraries, the State Department was also responsible for three other kinds of collections: (1) libraries in Latin America established by the American Library Association with contractual support from the State Department; (2) libraries in Amerika Häuser established by the U.S. military government in West Germany; and (3) information centers started under the auspices of U.S. forces in Austria, Japan, and Korea (James 1953:84).

In 1948, as part of an attempt to bring some coherence to these varied U.S. information and cultural activities abroad, Congress passed the Smith-Mundt Act, which authorized the State Department "to promote a better understanding of the United States in other countries and to increase mutual understanding between the people of the United States and the people of other countries" (Henderson 1969:41). A product of mounting Cold War tensions, passage of the Smith-Mundt Act was influenced by a delegation of congressmen, who, after an extended visit to Europe, reported in 1947 that the Continent was a "vast battlefield of ideologies in which words have to a large extent replaced armaments as the active elements of attack and defense." The report continued ominously: "The USSR and its obedient Communist parties throughout Europe have taken the initiative in this war of words against the western democracies. . . . The United States must take positive and aggressive steps to carry the true story of her ideals, motives and objectives" (Henderson 1969:40). In addition, the delegation noted that Great Britain, although heavily in debt, was supporting an information service three times the size of the American program.

Under the provisions of the Smith-Mundt Act, the diverse overseas library programs remained within the Department of State and were administered by the Information Center Service (ICS), which developed book selection guidelines that grouped potential purchases in three broad categories: (1) descriptions of the United States; (2) examples of American achievements in the humanities and the natural and social sciences; and (3) works in accord with U.S. foreign policy. This latter category, which included anti-Communist books, received growing emphasis during the early 1950s, when the administrator of the program declared that "it is more important to provide books that support American aims, whoever the author, than to supply only pleasant commentaries on American life and customs" (James 1953:84). While the majority of books sent abroad were by Americans and were chosen to present a positive image of the United States, Henry James Jr., a State Department staff member, noted that inclusion of magazines critical of the Truman administration and books on racial questions impressed readers abroad with the "credibility of the material." He particularly noted that even though the presence of *An American Dilemma: The Negro Problem and Modern Democracy* (Gunnar Myrdal's extensively documented critique of race relations in America, written in 1944) and copies of the *Reporter* and the *Nation* had "scandalized certain members of Congress," such works in fact enhanced the acceptance of the whole information program (James 1953:87). Although a brief period of hysteria and censorship was brought on by the attacks of Senator McCarthy and his supporters, a public outcry followed, and by July 1953 new directives were issued that allowed books to be chosen on their merits and usefulness without regard to their authors' current or past political affiliations.

When the United States Information Agency was created in August 1953, it inherited a book stock of 1,800,000 volumes dispersed among 196 libraries in 64 different countries. Established as an autonomous agency within the Executive Branch, the USIA also inherited a number of other programs transferred from the State Department, including Voice of America as well as information offices and cultural centers. While the consolidation of these programs under the USIA gave them somewhat greater stability, in 1960 a congressional committee reported: "Since World War II . . . the principal overseas agency of the United States government has been renamed six times and reorganized four times. It has in the past been subjected to great year-to-year variations in its appropriations, much to the disadvantage of long-term programs, effective planning and needed personnel development" (Henderson 1969:57). Yet even during the Kennedy years (1960–63), when the USIA received greater support, its budget for cultural presentations in the performing arts was slashed, leading one scholar to comment: "Culture was a tough sell to Congress, whereas information could more easily be tailored to macho cold war rationales" (Ninkovich 1996:30).

Shortly before President Johnson named him assistant secretary of state for educational and cultural affairs in 1965, Columbia professor Charles Frankel wrote: "Probably of all large countries, the United States, until the last twenty years, has shown the least official interest in . . . cultural competition" (1965:77). Frankel, who entitled his book *The Neglected Aspect of Foreign Affairs,* suggested that in addition to a longstanding tendency toward isolationism, the reasons for this included "the assumption that the advantages of the American way of life were self-evident, [and] an indifference toward many of the activities, such as music, architecture, higher mathematics, in which cultural competition takes place" (1965:77). While Frankel's assessment of American cultural diplomacy echoes the "arrogantly reticent" stance that Nicolson attributed to the British, other scholars have suggested that the U.S. lack of interest in cultural programs was linked to other American beliefs and attitudes, such as an aversion to "official culture," populist anti-intellectualism, a sense of the conceptual incompatibility of culture and power, and "a chronic apprehensiveness about government playing an active role in the promotion of ideas" (Ninkovich 1996:7, 41).

It should also be noted that in the United States, support of culture– including libraries and book culture–has remained the responsibility of the private sector and of state and local governments. At the national level there has never been an American equivalent to a "Ministry of Culture," and thus there has been no agency within the federal government to actively promote cultural programs at home or abroad. Operating in virtual isolation from other federal agencies, the USIA's efforts to promote cultural relations overseas have been characterized by a "pattern of diplomatic marginality and scholarly indifference" (Ninkovich 1981:1). Given the low esteem and lower appropriations allotted to cultural activities, it is not surprising that the majority of the USIA's efforts have focused on the information function.

During its forty-five-year history, USIA leaders have vacillated between insistence on "objective" or balanced portrayals of the United States to acceptance of a propagandistic role in which the "truth" was selectively presented, carefully framed, and aggressively disseminated with the goal of persuading foreign audiences to support U.S. foreign policy aims. The two approaches were succinctly stated in the highly polarized 1964 presidential campaign. Reflecting on the USIA's first decade and its future role, the Democrats declared: "The United States Information Agency has been transformed into a *powerful, effective and respected weapon of the Free World.* The new nations of the world have come to know an America that is not afraid to tell the truth about itself—and so can be believed when it tells the truth about Communist imperialism." That same year the Republican party platform took a more aggressive stance, asserting: "We will take a *cold war offensive* on all fronts, including for example, a reinvigorated USIA. It will broadcast not our weakness but our strength. It will mount a *psychological warfare attack* on behalf of freedom and against communist doctrine and imperialism" (both quotes from Henderson 1969:22, emphasis mine). While the two parties disagreed on the means of winning over foreign audiences, they were in agreement over the goal—that the USIA should gain support for American strategic aims. Furthermore, both Democrats and Republicans participated in the Cold War rhetoric in which words were seen as weapons and books were viewed as instruments in the global struggle "to win the minds of men."

Part 2: Cultural Diplomacy in Francophone Africa

USIA Libraries in Francophone Africa: "Symbols of Our Open Society"

Prior to the acceleration of the African independence movement in the late 1950s, foreign relations and cultural exchanges in Africa were viewed as marginal by U.S. policymakers, who focused on the ideological struggles in the nonaligned nations in Europe and

Asia. However, a few American libraries had been set up in Anglophone Africa in the 1940s (e.g., Liberia, 1947; Kenya, 1949), and in 1955 a USIA library was opened in Accra, just two years before the independence of Ghana. Meanwhile, in 1956 France passed legislation creating a new administrative structure that gave greater autonomy to its territories in sub-Saharan Africa and thus paved their way to independence. By 1960, when these nations became independent states, the USIA had established twenty-seven libraries in Africa, a number that would double by 1964 (Rowan 1964:43). Visited by more than 4 million people in 1964, these newly created African libraries were targeted for further expansion by Carl Rowan, the first black director of the USIA (Rowan 1964:43). However, despite a geographical reorientation from Europe to developing countries, USIA book collections in Africa grew modestly, increasing from 192,000 volumes in 1964 to over 201,000 volumes in 1972. While the individual cultural centers or embassies in Francophone Africa had an average of 3,500 books per library, the collections ranged from 1,000 volumes in Ouagadougou to nearly 5,000 volumes in Dakar (Rowan 1964:43; Dadzie and Strickland 1965).

Created in 1958, the USIA library in Dakar was the first free circulating collection to be set up by a foreign embassy in any of the French West African territories. While administrators such as Carl Rowan saw the USIA libraries as "symbols of our open society and free access to information," cultural officers in Africa also realized that even though the collections were small and somewhat specialized, they nonetheless presented local library leaders with an alternative model to the closed stack libraries then common in the region (Rowan 1964:43). In 1958 no other library in Dakar used the Dewey decimal classification, and almost none offered free access, with books on open shelves. Free loan privileges were also something of an innovation in a city where readers were accustomed to paying a registration fee for library privileges and were often expected to pay an additional guarantee for each book borrowed.

Mindful of the novelty of these practices, Rolf Jacoby, the USIA cultural center director, was happy to accept an invitation to discuss American public libraries at the first library institute held in Dakar in 1959. Jacoby also profited from this opportunity to encourage visits to the USIA library by leading African librarians. Among these was E. W. K. Dadzie, the executive secretary of the newly created inter-African library association; Dadzie, who had studied in Scandinavia and France on a UNESCO scholarship, was so impressed with the USIA library that he described it as a "model library" in terms of its organization and working methods. In a 1961 conference presentation, he further remarked that, despite the library's specialized collection, which focused on the United States, it enjoyed "great success" and could be considered "among the best public libraries that Dakar possesses" (Dadzie 1961:4). Dadzie was not alone in seeing the library's value in future Senegalese library development; in 1963, when the first training program for librarians in Francophone Africa was set up in Dakar by UNESCO, its director, Louis Seguin, brought his students to the USIA library for their practical training sessions. As the school expanded, students were assigned to many other sites for their practice work, but the USIA continued to host a few students each year.

Even though the USIA library collection in Dakar remained at about 6,000 books, it included the entire range of subjects represented by Dewey decimal classes. Following the agency guidelines, all the books dealt with the United States, but from one third to one half of the collection was devoted to French translations of American authors. In evaluating and recommending materials for post libraries, the USIA Bibliographic Services Division in Washington arranged its book lists into four categories: (1) maximum promotion: those books that treat a political subject as the USIA would; (2) normal use: books that have some relevance and concur with or do not directly oppose U.S. foreign policy; (3) conditional use: books that may require some special knowledge for understanding or interpretation, suitable for teachers but not judged satisfactory for general public use; and (4) not suitable: books that deal critically with contemporary American political leaders or strongly advocate a policy line contrary to American foreign policy (adapted from Sussman 1973:9).

Although such selection guidelines would appear to be hopelessly biased and restrictive, in a critique of the USIA Professor Robert Elder estimated that fewer than 1 percent of the books actually fell into category four; he also noted that a book deemed "unsuitable" could be supplied to the library to protect the USIA's "credibility," but only if it had been "properly justified by the post" (Elder 1968:261). However, the post was not limited to choosing only those titles reviewed by the Bibliographic Services Division; instead, the local librarian was free to use standard professional reviewing tools as selection sources. Acquisitions were expected to follow the stated collection development goal, which was for "each collection to have a wide range of viewpoints on topics controversial in American life such as politics, labor, and race" (Henderson 1969:154). Thus, despite the consistency of its Cold War rhetoric, USIA policy generally allowed the posts to "obtain whatever books they choose, regardless of ideological slant" (U.S. Senate 1983:6).

In Dakar the most popular titles were the translations of American novels (especially those by black writers) and works on American business, industry, and technology. Although the collection contained a few children's books, loan privileges were limited to adult residents of Dakar and to students in the last two years of secondary school. Fines were not charged, but borrowing privileges were suspended for readers who failed to return or renew their books at the end of the fifteen-day loan period; only two books could be taken out at a time. By the early 1970s the librarian estimated that 80 percent of the borrowers were Senegalese, 10 percent Americans, and 5 percent Europeans. Even though most Senegalese secondary students took English as a foreign language, the number who read it fluently was quite limited. Nonetheless, many young Senegalese frequented the library and the cultural center, whether drawn to the collection by an interest in America, a need to improve their English, or a desire to skim through popular periodicals like *Time* or *Newsweek.* Its central location also helped to attract some passersby, and an active program of exhibits, films, slide presentations, and guest speakers also served to bring in a clientele of secondary school and university students.

The British Council Libraries: "To Recognize Our Virtues Such as They Are"

The second English language collection in Dakar, that of the British Council, was established in 1965 with a small selection of British books meant to complement the Council's English language teaching program. Like the establishment of a Council library in Paris after World War II (when the American Library in Paris contained nearly 100,000 English language books), the creation of the Council library in Dakar must have been motivated by the desire to establish a British cultural presence in Francophone Africa as well as by the need to make books available to language students, English-speaking Africans, and expatriates from the United Kingdom. Although the number of British users was not available, it should be noted that Council librarians were often ambivalent about serving this group of readers, since many believed that their overseas work should be directed toward the local population (Saunders and Broome 1977:14).

With a collection entirely restricted to English language books, the Council library was far less popular than the USIA collection, even though both libraries were listed as containing 6,000 volumes by 1975 (Zidouemba 1977:230). At that time the British collection was mainly used by the four hundred students taking language courses at the British Institute; however, the library also granted borrowing privileges to outsiders who were willing to pay a registration fee of 1,500 CFA francs each year. It was common practice for Council libraries to charge for registration, and while this fee was not exorbitant, it probably discouraged interest among potential Senegalese readers who could use the USIA library for free. Although several other cultural center libraries did charge fees and may have thus discouraged student use, the British Council library was atypical in its outright decision to bar Senegalese secondary school students from registration—a policy that reduced its potential clientele in a city where the most avid library users were young people.

By the time its library was set up in Senegal, the British Council's mission had become more strongly focused on education; following this pattern, the Dakar center also gave language teaching priority over its role in informing the Senegalese public about Britain. Therefore, the library mainly contained works that concerned linguistics, pedagogy, or teaching English as a foreign language. Although the majority of these books were by British authors, the collection also included some works by authors from Anglophone Africa whose books were used in the English classes. Book selection was guided by book lists from London, but local staff could select other titles they deemed appropriate.

Aside from its Senegalese library and one somewhat smaller collection set up in the Cameroon in 1972, the British Council had no other library facilities in Francophone Africa during the Cold War. However, it would be unfair to end a discussion of the Council's library work without some brief mention of its extensive involvement in Anglophone Africa. The first British Council libraries in colonial West Africa date from 1943, when small collections were set up in Sierra Leone, Nigeria, and the Gold Coast. As a result of the work of Council librarian Evelyn Evans, the Gold Coast became the first African state to set up a national library board and to pass comprehensive library legislation. Historian Douglas Coombs remarks that from the time of her arrival in December 1945, Evans "considered her task not to build up Council libraries as such but rather to develop a national library service. Moreover, she was never in doubt that this was what the Council wanted her to do" (Coombs 1988:101). After skillfully negotiating with the colonial government in the Gold Coast and the town council in Accra, Evans arranged to transfer the British Council collection of 5,000 books to the city, only to find out later that the Colonial Office in London was unwilling to approve the transaction. Eventually, agreement was reached with all parties concerned, and the Accra library became the centerpiece for an extensive public library system.

Coombs notes that the transfer of the Council library in Lagos to local authorities and the situation in Accra exhibited "a curious parallel . . . in that both transactions were carried out without approval from the Council in London, let alone the Colonial Office" (Coombs 1988:101). It also appears that in both cases, strong-willed, independent Council librarians had proceeded without realizing that their actions were far in advance of the Council's general goal of moving into an advisory role as local public libraries came into being. Roy Flood, another experienced British Council librarian, noted that the Council achieved its unique role in African library development because its staff "in the years following the war . . . not only preached the concept of library development but put it into practice and argued with and persuaded overseas governments, British ministries and the Council itself" (quoted in Coombs 1988:73).

Although financial restraints inhibited some of the Council's plans in Africa during the early 1950s, its budget and its library development program got a new wind as a result of recommendations by a review committee chaired by the Earl of Drogheda. This report not only advocated increased government investment in the work of the Council, it also shifted the priority of the work from Europe to developing countries and differentiated between a purely cultural function and an educational role, emphasizing the latter. The Drogheda committee further stated that the value of the Council's work rested on the following factors:

1. The nature and extent of British political and commercial interests.
2. The attitude towards the United Kingdom of the educated classes.
3. The extent to which the educational and cultural leaders and university graduates are likely to have political influence.
4. The extent of the danger of Communism, especially in universities among intellectuals and the degree to which the work of the Council is likely to lessen this danger.
5. The demand for cultural and educational contacts with the United Kingdom (including the desire to learn English) and the extent to which this demand could be filled by private enterprise or required assistance. (Donaldson 1984:183–84)

The committee also stated that it did not believe that "a knowledge of the English language, [and] a taste for British books . . . are likely to make the slightest difference to the average educated European on the subject of Communism" (Donaldson 1984:185). While this statement aptly expressed the inherent skepticism the British held toward the political efficacy of cultural work abroad, it also served to justify the shift from expenditures in Europe to the developing world, where the needs were greater and where Britain might have a greater chance of influencing public opinion.

After the government finally accepted the Drogheda committee's recommendations, funding was significantly increased for overseas programs. Lady Frances Donaldson believed that this was due to the report's more pragmatic approach, "which merely gave form and substance to the prevailing ideas of the time." She continued: "The British proved once more, that unlike the French, the Germans and the Italians, they will not pay for something they understand and regard as little as the projection of the national culture. The Council could hardly have survived much longer in the idealistic form envisioned by Rex Leeper" (Donaldson 1984:193).

With increased funding available, the Council again turned its attention to British Africa, where the colonies were rapidly moving toward independence. In 1959 the Council launched an ambitious Public Library Development Scheme (PLDS), which began in cooperation with the Colonial Office but was subsequently funded by the Overseas Development Ministry. The half million pounds spent by the Council between 1959 and 1969 aided in the creation of national public library services in Kenya, Tanzania, Uganda, Sierra Leone, Malawi, Botswana, and Swaziland and provided assistance in the expansion and development of services in Nigeria (Coombs 1988:157). By the early 1970s, when Britain anticipated entry into the European Community, the British Council began to expand its work on the Continent. Meanwhile, in Africa Council libraries were thriving; these included "second growth libraries" that the Council had reestablished in cities such as Accra and Lagos, where the original collection had been given to newly created public library boards. Council libraries containing collections of 10,000 to 25,000 books were located in cities such as Banjul, Kumasai, Kaduna, Ibadan, Kimusu, Mombassa, and Dar es Salaam. Although the Council never intended its collections to take the place of a locally supported public library system, in some places like Banjul, which had no city library, the Council library did serve as a surrogate public library.

Although the nature and priority of the Council's library development work in Africa had changed over time, the purpose of individual libraries set up by the Council remained relatively unchanged. The head of the British Council's library programs, John Barnicot, wrote:

> The Council libraries are neither altruistic nor weapons for propaganda; they have a purpose which is neither a "do-goodery" nor a social service nor an effort to convert enemies into friends by the direct method.

They incidentally do good, are a contribution towards social improvement, *in the long run help people to recognize our virtues such as they are*; it is this third achievement which motivates them; the other two are by-products. (Quoted in Coombs 1988:185, emphasis mine)

In this reflective summation of the achievements and goals of the British Council libraries, Barnicot adopted a pragmatic stance, placing the Council's library work squarely in the middle, between the overtly propagandistic role of the USIA and the idealistic approach taken by the French in their efforts to spread their language and culture.

French Cultural Centers: A Humanistic Endeavor

Unlike their American and British counterparts, French leaders at the highest levels of government did not hesitate to support both public and private efforts to extend the French language and culture. Among the presidents of the Alliance Française were Victor Duruy, historian and former minister of public instruction; Raymond Poincaré, former president of the republic, who served two terms with the Alliance in the 1920s and 1930s; and Gen. Charles de Gaulle, who agreed to be honorary president of its board when the headquarters relocated in London after the fall of France. During the difficult years from 1937 to 1949, the Alliance was ably led by the author Georges Duhamel, who is credited with formulating the association's triple vocation:

1. . . . love of beautiful language. Not the language of the academy founded on an outmoded purism but a language that is clear, lively, and precise. . . . This is why education remains . . . the priority among priorities.
2. . . . respect for civilization. Not only French civilization but diverse civilizations. It is thus [that the Alliance Française] can practice dialogue between cultures.
3. . . . the cult of international friendship [and a] spirit of intellectual symbiosis. (Quoted in Bellicize 1986:111)

In leading the Alliance to adopt the ideal of pluralism and intellectual symbiosis, Duhamel's philosophy reflected important new currents of thought shared by certain liberal French intellectuals and colonial officers, some of whom were in contact with a dynamic group of black writers studying in Paris. These authors included the West Indian Aimé Césaire and Léopold Sédar Senghor, poet, reluctant political leader, and future president of Senegal. Although deeply rooted in the traditions of the Serer people, Senghor nonetheless credited some of his inspiration to studying with French ethnologists whose work in Africa contributed to his philosophy of *négritude*. For Senghor, *négritude* meant a reaffirmation of the cultural value of African civilization, which, despite its diversity, consisted of certain core values: "the quality of emotion and empathy; the quality of rhythm and form; the quality of imagery and myth, communal spirit and democracy" (Hymans 1971:68). As Senghor and his colleagues further developed this philosophy, they asserted their cultural independence from France, but they rejected neither the French language nor what they found best in French civilization.

During the late 1930s, at the time Seghor and his colleagues were first publishing their writings in Paris, a new vision of Franco-African culture was emerging among French colonial leaders in Africa. One of the chief proponents of this new doctrine was Jules Brévié, governor general of French West Africa (Afrique Occidentale Française [A.O.F.]), who wrote in 1936: "however pressing may be the need for economic change . . . our [first] mission in Africa is to bring about a cultural renaissance, a piece of creative work in human material, an association of two races" (quoted in Mumford n.d.:96). Albert Charton, who was then inspector general of education in the A.O.F., shared Brévié's ideas and attempted to redefine France's educational mission as a blending of two civilizations, African and French. Convinced that France's civilization was both superior and "universally applicable," Charton nonetheless acknowledged that "the people of Africa offered France an enormous field for research and for the enrichment of our culture" (quoted in Mumford n.d.:100, 110–11).

During these years there were numerous ethnographic and scientific missions to Africa, and gradually more African subjects were added to the school curriculum in the A.O.F., where the higher primary schools and secondary schools had previously replicated the curriculum used in France. In justifying this new approach to colonial education, Charton spoke of France's educational role in Africa as a "moral alliance" rather than a "moral conquest," and in a 1936 speech he eloquently expressed this new doctrine. After referring to the poet Paul Valéry's statement, "We other civilizations know now that we are mortal," Charton declared, "colonization will not be mortal if it ceases to be simply domination, simply exploitation . . . but extends into culture, into influence, into education . . . In this colonization is a humanistic endeavor, a profound solidarity between two peoples" (1936:383–85).

Although the French school system reached a very tiny proportion of African children prior to World War II, France did succeed in educating a small elite with a deep attachment to French culture.

When the Alliance Française expanded its work in Africa, its members included future African leaders who saw the value of reading and of improving their knowledge of French. This period also marked the first attempts by the Alliance to maintain permanent libraries in Africa. In 1948 the Dakar affiliate set up a library that, within a decade, had grown to 8,500 volumes. Even though this collection was restricted to members of the Alliance, who had to pay a fee for its use, it was nonetheless considered the best general collection available in the city, which had no municipal library. On the eve of independence there was considerable demand for books to meet the needs of study groups, youth organizations, cultural associations, and unions concerned with the education of workers. Amadou Mahtar M'bow, then a young professor and political activist, recalled that despite the high cost of books, African politicians, intellectuals, and labor leaders collected "small personal libraries whose books were passed from hand to hand" (Maack 1981:150).

Although the transition to independence in the former A.O.F. colonies occurred smoothly and with little acrimony, the French government under the leadership of Charles de Gaulle immediately took steps to promote continuing cultural, political, and economic ties between the new states and France. Much later, de Gaulle himself declared in his memoirs that he supported aid to the states of Francophone Africa "so they will speak our language and share our culture." This was also the view of Prime Minister Georges Pompidou, who stated in a 1964 debate on aid in the National Assembly: "Of all countries, France is the one that cares most about exporting its language and culture. This characteristic is genuinely specific to us. . . . This is a need of our thought, perhaps of our genius. Our co-operation is undeniably oriented, and it ought to be so, towards this expansion of our language and our culture" (quoted in Cohen 1971:204–5).

In order to encourage the diffusion of French language and thought, French embassies set up cultural centers in tropical Africa beginning in 1959, when the first center was inaugurated in Dakar by high ranking French and African officials. Within a decade there were eighteen centers, fourteen located in national capitals and four others in important cities such as Saint-Louis in Senegal and the port of Douala in the Cameroon. The overarching goal of the French cultural centers was to show "a dynamic, creative image of France through presenting diverse aspects of her culture—including cinema, theater and art as well as books" (Bilan et perspectives 1971:23). Although the first cultural centers were generally set up in rented quarters, during the 1960s most moved into buildings that either had been renovated or had been designed especially for their activities. Each facility contained a library, which usually had at least two spacious reading rooms, one for children and the other for adults; in addition, the centers also featured exhibition halls, lecture rooms, and theaters equipped for film projections. Although some centers, such as the new facility constructed in Abidjan, were impressive modern structures, one official document emphasized that "these centers were not conceived as defensive forts but as places for exchange and encounter freely open and accessible to the largest number" (Bilan et perspectives 1971:23).

Even though there had been a growing demand for books in the early years of independence, one writer remarked on a "period of distrust" before French cultural center libraries became accepted by African readers (Mandelkern 1966:11). However, their popularity was soon evident, and interviews conducted at the Centre d'Echanges Culturels de Langue Française in Dakar in 1963 revealed that the majority of readers made a special trip to the library, and some had to travel for as much as an hour. The researchers concluded that there was already a reading public in Dakar, "numerically small, but highly motivated" (Heissler, Lavy, and Candela 1965:167). At that time there were 11,000 registered library users, and of these, Africans accounted for 30 percent of the adult readers but 80 percent of the children (Heissler, Lavy, and Candela 1965:126). Ten years later, a survey of regular readers showed that Africans accounted for slightly over one quarter of the adult readers but four fifths of the adolescent users and 87 percent of the children under fifteen (Maack 1981:150). At that time an influx of students from the *lycées* meant that the proportion of Africans registered to use the adult section grew markedly. As in Dakar, other cultural center libraries had many non-African readers if they were located in cosmopolitan cities with numerous Europeans as well as other foreigners working in international organizations, multinational firms, or embassies. However, French cultural centers in cities with few foreigners have had little trouble attracting an avid readership, particularly among young people. Perhaps typical of these is the center in Brazzaville, which celebrated its twenty-fifth anniversary in 1988. At that time, 97 percent of the users were Congolese, but only 25 percent of them were adults (Gioan 1988:208). African women were not well represented among library users, and in both Brazzaville and Dakar they made up between 16 and 17 percent of the adult registrants.

The cultural center libraries in Africa were set up with the twofold mission of providing access to French books on all subjects and encouraging African authors to produce literary works in French. In addition to lending books for home use, the library staff organized study circles to encourage original writing and to discuss French and

African authors. Awards were offered to young African writers, and prize-winning works were published by the Bureau du Livre, an office set up within the French Ministry of Cooperation. Although the main work of this office was to distribute books to institutions, it also administered a book club for African readers known as Club des Lecteurs d'Expression Française, or CLEF, an acronym that means "key" in French. In 1969 the CLEF staff in Paris launched the publication of *Notre Librairie*, a periodical dedicated to African literature, with bibliographies, author interviews, and literary analysis.

Cultural center librarians in Africa and staff working in France were aware that African readers wanted and needed works that resonated with their own experience. Therefore, the promotion of African authorship has for a long time been viewed as an important element in creating a culture inspired by France but rooted in the African experience. One French cultural officer wrote in 1969: "The opportunity for France's illuminating influence, now as during the Enlightenment[,] resides in her ability to furnish other nations with the cultural instruments of their own flowering. [Our] cooperation . . . is an aid in the creation of a new culture, a culture which will certainly owe much to our influence but which will be authentically African" (Thomas 1969:5,8).

Régine Fontaine from the Bureau du Livre also emphasized the need to encourage African writing in order to "make the book a means for expressing African culture" (1974:23). Concerned with bringing readers and books together, Mme. Fontaine observed that it has not always been easy to reconcile reading with preexisting cultural values in Africa. She observed: "a silent and solitary activity, reading fits poorly into a culture dominated by oral expression and a sense of community." Furthermore, she noted that the book is considered "a culture-object . . . a sum of knowledge which belongs to the teacher, the professor and in a general way to the colonizer" (Fontaine 1974:23).

Despite certain negative connotations, books and reading, like many other foreign imports, have been enthusiastically adopted by a certain segment of young, educated Africans. Their interest in reading is consistently shown by the success of all the cultural center libraries, and as early as 1969 a report published by the French government stated that the circulation rate in the eighteen libraries in Francophone Africa was comparable to the busiest municipal libraries in Paris (Bilan et perspectives 1971:24). Although the number of center libraries increased to twenty-five by 1973, their budget has remained stagnant since the 1970s. However, in a review of the work of these centers, Fanny Lalande-Isnard remarked that the nature and extent of their services, collections, and readership remained remarkably stable during their three decades of operation (Lalande-Isnard 1992:267). At that time there were from 10,000 to 40,000 books in these libraries, which continued to be popular with African children and youth.

In virtually all cases, the French cultural center library initially served as a surrogate public library in cities that lacked any adequate municipal library structure. Although a number still continue to fill the role of de facto public libraries, this was never intended to be their function. To remedy this situation, the Ministère Français de la Coopération et du Développement began providing aid to African states to assist them in setting up public library systems adapted to their needs. The first such project was launched in 1978 in Mali, where a national public library system was created; this network included a central library and administrative unit in Bamako; forty-six rural libraries, each supervised by a local cultural heritage committee; and a railway library (*wagon-bibliothèque*) that makes bimonthly stops in six regional capitals located on the Dakar-Niger line (see Diakite and Vallet 1985:77–78). Subsequently, France funded other aid projects to launch public library systems in Benin, Togo, Senegal, Guinea, and the Cameroon. Under the terms of the contract between France and the Cameroon, the French agreed to supply books, periodicals, some furnishings, and a vehicle as well as the services of a technical assistant, while the Cameroonian government would provide appropriate quarters for libraries in five designated cities (Fontaine 1990:69).

In addition to supporting these aid projects, the Bureau du Livre has also donated and distributed hundreds of thousands of books throughout Francophone Africa, and only a quarter of these went into the French cultural center libraries. Other books were presented by French embassies to schools, youth centers, local libraries, rural community centers, and other organizations (Fontaine 1974:16). What has France gained from this effort? After posing the rhetorical question as to whether the monies consecrated to this work were well spent, one cultural officer concluded that the costs were easy to determine, but the return was immeasurable (Madelkern 1966:11).

Part 3: Comparisons and Conclusions: Justifications, Strategies, and Outcomes of Cultural Diplomacy

Britain, France, and the United States all employed similar strategies in the cultural efforts they directed toward Francophone Africa; in the most generic sense these efforts included language instruction, library collections and services, cultural programs, and book donations. The priority that each nation gave to these activities was a result of underlying ideologies that provided the foundation for its cultural diplomacy. While deeply held beliefs about culture, politics, prestige, and power shaped the nature of each country's activities in Africa, altruism was always entangled with self-interest and idealism with pragmatic reality. This idea is succinctly expressed by John Barnicot of the British Council, who noted: "[T]he Council library is not a privilege . . . bestow[ed] on people abroad; it is an instrument for enticing them to read British books and to learn about us; the benefit is mutual, but in the ultimate analysis, it is we who want readers, not the other way around" (Coombs 1988:274).

While all USIA, British Council, and French cultural center libraries aimed at attracting African readers, all were also used by expatriates who found reading a means of keeping in touch with the culture of their homeland. Undoubtedly, many other outcomes and uses were also unanticipated due to the unpredictability of readers and the independent vision of many librarians and cultural officers who chose to work in Africa. Ambiguity and paradox were inherent in the work of those who dedicated themselves to promoting the written word in countries where literacy was linked both with learning and with magic, with colonization and with liberation, with the struggle against cultural hegemony and with the desire to create a new culture that was both outward looking and deeply anchored in the African past. Despite their very real limitations, British, French, and American libraries provided at least a few African readers with alternative views of the world as well as giving them access to a selection of each country's literary heritage.

For the new African states, as for Britain and France, the independence movement and decolonization were the central issues that dominated their foreign relations during most of the Cold War years. In fact, both the British and the French focused their cultural diplomacy almost entirely on their former colonies. (By the mid-1970s only three sub-Saharan countries had both British Council and French cultural center libraries: the bilingual Cameroon, Senegal, and the Sudan [see Zidouemba 1977].) In each case, their cultural programs in Africa grew out of their respective colonial policies and represented both the continuation and evolution of beliefs and attitudes toward culture and foreign relations that were a deep-seated part of their national heritage. Cold War rivalries were peripheral to their relationships with Africa and came into play only to the degree that the presence of the USIA may have stimulated them to greater activity. For example, one French writer stressed that "the precarious state of Francophonie in Africa . . . [and] *the appearance . . . of other centers for the diffusion of competing cultures* [created a need for] *defensive action*" (Mandelkern 1966:4, emphasis mine). In a similar fashion, a cultural attaché who served in Senegal shortly after independence specifically referred to the "threat" posed to the French language "by Anglo-Saxon influence, by Islam and by the Arabic tongue" (Fralon n.d.). While both of the quotes above were written during the first decade of independence, when France felt most vulnerable to losing its influence in Africa, in 1979 Jacques Rigaud observed in a report to the minister of foreign affairs that one could scarcely read any analysis of the relative strength of English and French aside from "war communiqués where it is a question of positions to defend, bastions to conquer" (Rigaud 1980:39). However, the question of defending Francophone Africa from Communist propaganda or military incursion appears to be completely absent from any French articles or documents dealing with cultural matters.

In contrast, virtually all the cultural programs sponsored by the USIA were described in terms of their potential contribution to the Cold War struggle between Communism and the free world. For example, the goal of creating a balance of opposing viewpoints in USIA library collections was justified as a strategy for showing American commitment to the free flow of ideas, thus increasing U.S. credibility in comparison to the more strident approach used in Communist propaganda. Even Professor Charles Frankel, one of the more liberal defenders of cultural diplomacy, wrote: "The utility of an American library is compromised when . . . it is composed of books that are clearly pre-selected to deliver a message. The people who visit the library are not so naive that they do not realize the character of the institution they are visiting." He further emphasized that the library was doubly compromised when "mimeograph machines on the floor above are turning out statements defending the most recent action of the United States in foreign affairs" (Frankel 1965:34).

Other scholars have suggested that during the Cold War the USIA's strategies spanned the continuum of "information activities," from outright propaganda, to providing information of a nonpartisan nature, to the dissemination of books of lasting cultural value. However, most analysts agree that there were unfortunate consequences to making cultural diplomacy the responsibility of an agency whose primary function was informing and persuading foreign publics about U.S. foreign policy objectives. Richard Pells observes:

> From its inception, *USIA was a schizophrenic agency.* It acted as a clearinghouse for culture as well as a ministry of information and

propaganda. It was authorized both to tell the truth about the United States and to make foreigners more appreciative of America's domestic institutions and global ambitions. In setting up the agency, the Eisenhower administration reinforced and institutionalized the symbiotic relationship between American culture and American foreign policy, a relationship that was dependent on the Cold War. (Pells 1997:84, emphasis mine)

A similar critique is offered by Professor Hans Tuch, who retired to academia after a distinguished thirty-five-year career in the Foreign Service. Tuch, who accused certain USIA directors of "tunnel vision," remarked that a perennial problem confronting the Foreign Service officer was "the one-dimensional ideological approach . . . both in directing the agency's programs and in selling the agency to Congress" (Tuch 1990:15). Tuch cautioned that "if the Communist menace were to disappear or be modified as a principal issue facing the United States, the rationale for the agency's existence would be endangered" (Tuch 1990:15).

The USIA continues to exist nearly a decade after the fall of the Berlin wall signaled the beginning of the end of the Cold War. Nonetheless, Hans Tuch's warning has proved prophetic in regard to the agency's use of books as instruments of cultural diplomacy, particularly in Francophone Africa. Not only has the USIA greatly diminished its New Horizons French language translation program for Africa, it has reduced the popular, heavily used library in Dakar to a collection of six hundred circulating books supplemented by a smaller collection of reference works. The old, traditional library has now been replaced by an Information Resource Center (IRC), where books are overshadowed by an abundance of computer technology that provides the IRC with Web access as well as the ability to search a variety of CD-ROM products and online data bases. No longer "symbols of our open society and free access to information," the transformed IRCs—now restricted to an elite clientele of opinion leaders—seem to have become symbols of America's technological prowess as a nation on the leading edge of the information age (see the USIA Senegal Webpage: http://198.80.136/abtusia/posts/SGI/wwwhirc.html).

Even though the British Council's work was largely insulated from the vagaries of Cold War politics, it has now shifted greater priority to its work in Eastern Europe. At this point, there is no British Council presence in Francophone black Africa aside from its representation in Dakar. There the Council has maintained an active language instruction program, but its library has been transformed into a Resource

Centre for Teachers and Learners that now contains "2,000 of the most up-to-date British ELT [English language teaching] books and audio tapes, for children and adults. The best collection of methodology and pedagogy books for teachers." Like the USIA, the British Council in Dakar also has its own Web page and thus provides links to Britain as well as information on local activities that might be of interest to those Senegalese or expatriates who have access to sophisticated computer work stations (see the Senegal Webpage at http://www.britcoun.org/senegal/senrce.htm#aim).

Meanwhile, only the French seem committed to the immeasurable and intangible value books can provide as instruments of enlightenment, enrichment, and cultural diplomacy. In addition to supporting the libraries in centers for cultural exchange scattered throughout Francophone Africa, they have given thousands of books to other local libraries and have invested in aid programs aimed at the development of new library systems to be planned, directed, and used by Africans. Perhaps the cultural efforts of France have in the long run proved more durable because the extension and anchoring of the French language and culture are perceived as a means of facilitating the creation of a new, universal culture in which French thought and literature would play an important role. By emphasizing dialogue, mutual exchange, and a respect for African culture, the cultural diplomacy of France has evolved a philosophy that places internationalism above nationalism and views French speakers throughout the world as cocreators and co-owners of a cultural legacy not limited by political boundaries.

References

Bellescize, Gabrielle de. 1986. "Editorial." *Notre Librairie* 83:1–4.
Bruézière, Maurice. 1986. *L'Alliance Française: histoire d'une institution.* Paris: Hachette.
Bilan et perspectives. 1971. "Le Service de la co-opération culturelle, scientifique et technique avec les états francophones africains et malagaphes." *Notes et Études Documentaires,* no. 3787. La Documentation Française.
Charton, André. 1936. Untitled speech printed in *Notes et informations--Création de l'Institut Français d'Afrique noire.* Bulletin du Comité d'Études Historiques et Scientifiques de l'A.O.F.
Cohen, William. 1971. *Rulers of Empire.* Stanford, Calif.: Stanford University Press.
Coombs, Douglas. 1988. *Spreading the Word: The Library Work of the British Council.* London: Mansell.
Dadzie, E. W. 1961. "La Situation des bibliothèques publiques en Afrique." Paper presented at the Conférence Afro-Scandinave des Bibliothèques, Copenhagen, October.
Dadzie, E. W., and J. T. Strickland. 1965. *Directory of Archives, Libraries and Schools of Librarianship in Africa.* Paris: UNESCO.

Deibel, Terry L., and Walter R. Roberts. 1976. *Culture and Information: Two Foreign Policy Functions.* Beverly Hills, Calif.: Sage Publications.
Diakite, Fatogoma, and Dominique Vallet. 1985. "Au Mali l'opération lecture publique se poursuit: Bilan an VIII." *Guide du Biblithécaire, Notre Librairie,* numéro spécial.
Dizzard, Wilson. 1951. *Strategy of Truth.* Washington, D.C.: Public Affairs Press.
Donaldson, Frances. 1984. *The British Council: The First Fifty Years.* London: Jonathan Cape.
Elder, Robert E. 1968. *The Information Machine.* Syracuse, N.Y.: Syracuse University Press.
Fontaine, Régine. 1974. "Le Problème du livre face au lecteur en Afrique." *Co-opération et Développement* 47:16–23.
———. 1990. "Des bibliothèques pour les provinces." *Notre Librairie* 100:68–69.
Fralon, M., Conseilleur Culturel pour le Sénégal. N.d. "Grandes lignes de l'action culturelle." Typescript. Paris: Bureau du Livre.
Frankel, Charles. 1965. *The Neglected Aspect of Foreign Affairs: American Educational and Cultural Policy Abroad.* Washington, D.C.: Brookings Institution.
Gioan, Lydia. "Un espace vivant pour le livre: la bibliothèque du C.C.F." *Notre Librairie* 92–93 (March–May 1988):208–9.
Greffet, Philippe. 1983. "L'Alliance Française: année 100." *Le Français dans le Monde* 178:6–8.
Hansen, Allen C. 1984. *USIA: Public Diplomacy in the Computer Age.* New York: Praeger.
Heissler, Nina, P. Lavy, and A. Candela. 1965. *Diffusion du livre et développement de la lecture publique en Afrique.* Paris: Culture et Développement.
Henderson, John W. 1969. *United States Information Agency.* New York: Praeger.
Hymans, Jacques. 1971. *Léopold Sédar Senghor: An Intellectual Biography.* Edinburgh: Edinburgh University Press.
James, Henry, Jr. 1953. "Role of Information Library in the United States International Information Program." *Library Quarterly* 23:75–114.
Lalande-Isnard, Fanny. 1992. "Les Centres culturels français en Afrique." In Martine Poulain, ed., *Histoire des bibliothèques françaises: les bibliothèques au XXe siècles, 1914–1990.* Paris: Promodis–Cercle de la Librairie.
Larson, Cedric. 1951. "Books across the Sea: Libraries of OWI." *Wilson Library Bulletin* 25:433–48.
Maack, Mary Niles. 1981. *Libraries in Senegal: Continuity and Change in an Emerging Nation.* Chicago: American Library Association.
Mandelkern, Dieudonne. 1966. "Les Centres culturels français en Afrique noire et à Madagascar". *Co-opération et Développement* 13:3–12.
Mumford, W. Bryant. d. *Africans Learn to Be French.* London: Evans Brothers.
Nicolson, Harold. 1955. "The Work of the British Council." In *Report on the Work of the British Council, 1934–1955.* London: British Council.
Ninkovich, Frank A. 1981. *The Diplomacy of Ideas: U.S. Foreign Policy and Cultural Relations, 1938–1950.* New York: Cambridge University Press.
———. 1996. *U.S. Information Policy and Cultural Diplomacy.* New York: Foreign Policy Associates.
Pauchet, Marie-Pierrette. 1995. "La Bibliothèque du centre culturel français." *Notre Librairie* 120–21:263–66.
Pells, Richard. 1997. *Not Like Us: How Europeans Have Loved, Hated, and Transformed American Culture since World War II.* New York: Harper Basic Books.
Peroncel-Hugoz, J. P. 1983. "Les Cent Ans de l'Alliance Française: un irrésistible maître de l'école." *Le Monde* (Paris), 25, 26 December 1983.

Rigaud, Jacques. 1980. *Les Relations culturelles extérieures.* Paris: La Documentation Française.
Rowan, Carl. 1964. "USIA Overseas Libraries–1964." *Wilson Library Bulletin* 39:41–43, 90.
Saunders, W. L., and E. M. Broome. 1977. *The Library and Information Services of the British Council.* London: British Council.
Sussman, Jody. 1973. "United States Information Service Libraries." *University of Illinois, Graduate School of Library Science, Occasional Papers,* no. 111.
Tetu, Michel. 1988. *La Francophonie: histoire, problématique, perspectives.* Paris: Hachette.
Thomas, Robert. 1969. "A propos des centres culturels." *Co-opération et Développement* 27:5–12.
Tuch, Hans. 1990. *Communicating with the World: U.S. Public Diplomacy Overseas.* New York: St. Martin's Press.
———. 1990. "Improving Public Diplomacy: Setting More Modest Goals for USIA." *Foreign Service Journal* 67:14–18.
U.S. Senate, Committee on Foreign Relations. 1983. *Staff Report: Certain USIA Overseas Activities.* Washington, D.C.: U.S. Government Printing Office.
Zidouemba, Dominique. 1977. *Directory of Documentation, Libraries and Archives Services in Africa.* Paris: UNESCO.

Censors and Their Readers: Selling, Silencing, and Reading Czech Books

Jiřina Šmejkalová

The Nazi and Communist regimes in Czechoslovakia greatly impacted book publishing and distribution. During these periods, censorship was state controlled in an official sphere of government and was part of the processes of canon formation of literature considered officially valuable. Government constraints produced lists of *libri prohibiti*. In the 1950s the government established an explicit censorship office, the Main Board for Publishing Control (HSTD). By the 1960s HSTD was replaced by the Office for Publishing and Information, which prescribed guidelines for members of the publishing institutions. The post-1968 era in Czechoslovakia was known as a "Biafra of the Spirit" because of the government's attempts at normalization of cultural and social processes. In the 1970s and 1980s the government enforced control over the scheme of literary institutions. This was a centrally prepared publishing plan that included such institutions as paper supply and printing companies, the Ministry of Culture, publishing houses, and central warehouses. While the plan was central, each institution was relatively autonomous. By the late 1980s, many books were published outside of the official sphere. On 17 November 1989 the Cold War ended in Czechoslovakia, but previous changes in literary institutions and the economy had already contributed to the breakdown.

The history of Czech books in the second half of the twentieth century can be told as a story of silencing and closing rather than opening books. The book industry under the Nazi and Communist regimes might have differed in terms of original intentions, but what they had in common was this binding of books and their writers, editors, distributors, sellers, and readers into nets of persecutions and constraints that resulted in long lists of *libri prohibiti* (banned books). From this point of view, it might not come as a surprise when outsiders such as Louis Aragon labeled post-1968 Czechoslovakia as a "Biafra of the Spirit."

At the same time, the picture of the "oppressed" book culture becomes more complicated if we consider that, according to comparative sociological surveys, one third of the adult Czech population used to spend one to three hours a week reading books (Hepner 1975). The country developed a sophisticated translation and editorial culture, Czech book design won numerous awards at international bookfairs, and last but not least, the author of a Czech book traditionally enjoyed the position of a national hero. It would not be an exaggeration to say that a book, particularly because of the country's history of ongoing ruptures and discontinuities, has never been purely a product to be bought and sold. Rather, it has been seen as a guarantee of the continuity of national and cultural identity loaded with a "capital" of enormous symbolic and moral power. We are thus left with a question: How can we understand the actual interspaces left between the "hell" and the "paradise" scenarios of Czech cultural and intellectual history during the period of the Cold War?

A book is a specific object combining materiality with spiritual qualities, be they aesthetic, ethical, or political. This duality had produced a major dichotomy in the field of book studies. It is a dichotomy between the French tradition's concern with mentalities, that is, the intellectual background of book production and its reception, and the Anglo-American focus on the history of bibliography, or as the French book historian and theoretician Roger Chartier puts it, the distinction between the focus on the reader and the text. A number of historians and cultural critics have been trying to overcome this dualism. Chartier (1997) himself has been examining the effects of meaning produced by the transformations of the textual technologies and of reading practices. American historian Robert Darnton (1996), instead of asking which kind of canonized books contributed to the collapse of the ancien régime, was looking for books that, while being moved illegally across the French border, people actually did read prior to the French Revolution.

Within the context of the Cold War period, I am concerned with a different question. I will ask: What was the position of censorship in the process of the development of specific forms of technologies of textual production and distribution? While looking at the period of the 1970s and 1980s, I will examine how people acquired and read books the way they did in the times of the "swan song" of the socialist Czechoslovakia. Due to the limits of this rather brief account, I have to give up on the ambitious task of comparative analyses of the Czech and Slovak cultural history and will focus mostly on the Czech part of the former Czechoslovakia.

It may sound ironic that the period of the late Cold War in Czechoslovakia was called "Normalization." During this era, the newly established Communist government, supported by the presence of Soviet tanks occupying the country, was supposed to "normalize" the cultural and political residue of the 1968 "pathologies." It has often been described as the timeless period of freezing cultural and social processes into themselves. As Czech literary historian Pavel Janousek recently noted, timelessness was experienced intensively even when we were in it and "knew only its beginning without being able to imagine its end" (Janousek 1996:82). After the explosive events of 1989, the individual perception of the time "before" and "after" had changed substantially. I am even convinced that a revolution in time perception at both personal and historical levels was one of the major components of this substantial historical turnover. I would also argue, however, that this "timeless" period included an internal dynamics whose time and space analyses will perhaps be a goal for a new generation of scholars who will be less constrained by a preference for historical experience over representation. What follows is a set of starting points and opening questions rather than a completed view of culture during the Cold War.

Based on both my own experiences of studying and working in the field of Czech literature under the Czech ancien régime, I find it impossible to treat censorship as the oppressive exercise of centralized power by clearly defining "others" as the clerks of the special department of the Ministry of Culture in a Communist government or as agents of "American cultural imperialism." Who decides on the inclusion or exclusion of certain texts? It is important not to forget that the banned texts do not disappear.

My question, therefore, is how the reader's access to the text is constituted and instituted. I will look at censorship as an institutional practice of regulation taking the form of limits that can be manifested at any particular level of book production, be it chains of distribution or particular reading habits. From a more global point of view, such limits may, for example, take the form of concentration of literacy in particular parts of the world or in particular groups of society defined according to class, race, or gender. I understand censorship to be a time-related category, a far-reaching phenomenon closely related to the process of canon formation embedded within a web of social institutions. By the notion of "institution" I refer to sets of relatively strictly defined activities organized within certain structural units, such as, for example, publishing houses, and shared by their participants, including systems of regulative principles that both guarantee and reproduce their coherence. Rather than the direct prohibition of particular texts, taking a form of an "either/or" activity manipulated by the central agent, I suggest an insight into the formations of boundaries and the performances of roles that connect people and texts.

The "censorship" performed in the state-controlled "official" Czech book production in the period of the 1970s and 1980s was, however, just one part of a complex of social and cultural practices in the Normalization period. After 1968, the Czechoslovakian cultural and intellectual life was constructed as a set of at least three spheres, which, although mutually closely interrelated, were represented in both official propaganda as well as in the oppositional circles as mutually impenetrable domains. This was beyond the state-controlled sphere of books released in the so-called stone-wall publishing houses, a sphere of "self-print" texts produced within the dissident and underground circles, and a third sphere of exile books published abroad. The border between these domains was designed as uncrossable in a sense that an author once published in the *samizdat*, or exiled literary sphere, would have had very little chance of ever seeing his or her book on the shelves of a bookstore. Even the relationship between the exile and local oppositional intellectual, and consequently publishing activities, was rather complicated, since an exiled author "traveled" usually only in one direction: out of the country, with the assumption that the return gate was closed. Although their work often would have been distributed back in the country illegally, the position of exiled authors in the local alternative circles was ambiguous. The complicated relationships between these two spheres will be a matter of my further research; the limited space of this presentation allows no room for their detailed investigation.

The institutional web of the state-controlled and supported sphere to which I devote my attention here served as a tool of protecting and conserving the apparent impenetrability of all other domains and, therefore, to some extent, defied the conditions and sense of their very existence. The "official" sphere used a number of institutional and discursive mechanisms in order to build barriers to the movement of persons and texts out of and into the particular spaces. One of the most effective tools was to sentence the alternative domains into invisibility. That means, among other things, that the point would not be whether the "alternative scenes" were good or bad, they would be constructed as nonexisting in both public and even professional discussions. It was not until the late 1980s that the occasional and, of course, critical review of a book produced in an exile publishing house would have emerged in a Czech cultural journal.

Without underestimating the significance of the alternative spheres, it is important to remember that the so-called official book production targeted and involved the majority of members of the given community and actually shaped their everyday life. Moreover, it was the "official" domain that at least to a sensitive observer began to show signs of the kind of deterioration that was to become widespread throughout the whole system of the centrally operated society and economy, five years before the political turnover of 1989. After 1989, it was again this sphere that became the crucial domain of ongoing transformations, since all the others had collapsed into it and were in various ways inheriting the consequences of its past. Both émigré and dissident "men of letters" were entering remnants of this structure in order to make their texts public in the local community while struggling with rising competition and, shortly after the first immediate post-1989 boom, people's decreasing capacity as well as interest in purchasing books.

It is probably not surprising that, unlike the quite rich publicity given in the West to dissident and émigré spheres, the official system of literary production in Eastern Europe has not been particularly attractive to those participating in Western theoretical debates and has therefore been largely misunderstood. To the extent that the official sphere has received attention, it has focused on the figure "censoring" the text. By reinforcing the image of the censor as a relatively autonomous agent exercising control from above, such discussions tend to encourage the idea that getting rid of the censor exhausts the problem of censorship.

There is a dominant premise shared by many recent debates on censorship, and not only in the Czech context. These debates presuppose a world of free expression being guaranteed by the development of modern high-tech civilization and "welfare democracy," which previously just happened to be absent from the official culture. To put it differently, the powerful idea now prevails that a change of the political system and the importation of computers and copy machines will automatically open up communication through the written word. Looking at "censorship" in terms of instituted access to the text and acknowledging the limitations on the production of books in relation to particular social and historical contexts, this picture takes on another shape.

A short historical detour into the post–World War II Czech publishing and printing industry is necessary in order to challenge a number of myths operating in the post-1989 debates about "socialist" cultural processes. One of the most popular myths was that the Communist government in February 1948 exclusively created restrictive intervention into the cultural industries. It was created in order to prevent freedom of creative expression. According to this vision, state control over cultural production was supposed to be a major barrier to democratic development. It should be noted that, historically, this does not apply to many of the cultural industries. For example, the film industry was subject to state regulation even before 1948.

Moreover, the state intervention in publishing policy was not merely a Communist invention and was present already in the period of the democratic independent Czechoslovakia of 1918–38. During that period it focused on two kind of texts: the political (for example, pamphlets with anti-Semitic, Nazi, or Slovak nationalist content, some examples of left-oriented poetry) and the erotic and pornographic. It is important to note, however, that all of the censorship interventions were postpublication restrictive ones and were not intended to control the literary and publishing process as a whole by silencing particular genres or authors. By following the principles encoded in the criminal legislation, the First Republic's cultural policy had the major aim of protecting the states' interests.

Censorship during the period of the Protectorate Böhmen und Mähren had a completely different character. It was aimed at the formation and regulation of the entire cultural process and public discourse according to particularly defined anti-Czech and pro-Germanization models. The idea of a national culture as a system whose production can be unified under the umbrella of a shared/imposed common vision dominated the World War II period. At the same time, the publishing industry was experiencing a boom provoked by the intensified need of the community for readingmaterials. Nazi censorship persecuted mostly fiction and poetry written by respected Czech authors, but at the same time promoted so-called popular reading. Such a strategy was based on one of the most naive theories of "popular literature": literary trash serving as the vehicle for the "common reader" to escape from "reality"–in this case, arduous wartime living conditions–and consequently to channel a possible social rebellion.

May 1945 meant not just the desired end to the war, but it also raised the question of competing visions of continuity along two basic lines, liberal and restrictive, in other words, a conflict between the principles of the prewar and wartime cultural policy. It was long before February 1948 that the former position was lagging behind the latter. As a result, it was not the very need for regulation in book production as such that was questioned but, rather, a renegotiation among various political interest groups of the institutional mechanisms of regulation. In fact, the post-1945 central intervention in book production followed the principles of the restrictive concept of censorship of World War II with one major difference: it tried to limit the spread of the "low" literary culture in the name of promoting a vision of a national "high quality" canon (Janacek, Zach, and Tomasek 1998; Kaplan and Tomasek 1994). This basic strategy dominated book production until 1989.

Due to limited space I cannot go into a detailed analysis of all governmental and ministerial documents related to the issues of control of textual production and distribution. What is important to remember is that even without an explicit institution of censorship, post-1945 policy already promoted a notion of censorship as a planned and regulated institution aimed at the construction of a productive literary space unified under a common vision. The idea of a radical elimination of so-called literary trash was relatively new to the local cultural policy, as it had no equivalent tradition in prewar cultural policy, and it was not expressed in the cultural management principles drafted by anti-Nazi underground intellectual circles. A major dangerous aspect of the dichotomy between "low" and "high" culture is the fragile border between the two poles of this dyad and its dependency on a subjective interpretation. Once promoted as a leading principle of cultural policy, it prepared a fruitful soil for the future growth of control and repression.

Several topics dominated the post-1945 discussions about the regulation of book production: the paper, an obsessive fear from the legacy of the Nazi ideology and politics, and a declaration of war on "literary trash." The substantial achievement of this period was the introduction of permission procedures for the entire publication process. The responsible institution was the Book Council, set up by the Ministry of Education but soon replaced by the State Publication Committee (SPC), which included representatives of the writers, book producers, and readers unions named by the Ministry of Information on 4 July 1945. The SPC issued the requirement that all publishers ask for approval of lists of books released after 5 May retroactively. The basic sections of the book chains reestablished their activities in the summer of 1945: the association of distributors, the publishers and booksellers credit bank and union, and the new block of booksellers cooperatives. The ongoing conflicts among the respectable associations (such as the calls of the union for a stricter attitude of the Ministry of Information to the permission process; the increasing shortage of paper since the socialization of the Czech, not Slovak, paper industry in 1946; and the attacks on the so far private distribution companies and booksellers for not paying enough attention to books with a "progressive" content) reflected the growing tension in the literary space as well as in society in general.

Shortly after February 1948, the Communist party announced new directions in its cultural policy performed through a set of committees, which issued several lists of *libri prohibiti* for public libraries. Most importantly, a large number of publishers were eliminated in the late 1940s and replaced by over forty big state-operated publishing houses that monopolized particular fields of production such as indigenous literature, literature for children, translated literature, nonfiction, and textbooks. However, it was not until April 1953 that the first decision was made at the governmental level to establish an explicit censorship office called the Main Board for Publishing Control (HSTD) with a generous budget and an ambitious staff development plan. The board was later equipped with a regularly updated list of "forbidden issues" with which to be concerned. The difficulty of filling the vacant positions with qualified persons (the expected full staff of 271 members was never achieved) was followed by ongoing complaints about the competence of the staff members, most of whom came from a working-class background (Kaplan and Tomasek 1994).

Quotations from the unlimited number of documents issued by the HSTD in order to justify both preventive as well as postpublication interventions to both periodical and nonperiodical publications would make a tragicomic novel in themselves. In the actual publishing practice, in addition to changes in publishing legislation, the Communist government created conditions allowing the number of titles to fall from that of the prewar period while continually raising print runs. Between 1937 and 1983, the number of titles published per year in Czechoslovakia rose by 10 percent, while the total number of copies printed annually almost doubled. The most significant decline in the number of titles published occurred from 1948 to 1950, that is, within the first two years of socialized publishing, when the number of titles released annually fell from 6,640 to 3,797. Not until 1970 did that number rise above the 1948 level.

It would be a mistake, however, to interpret centralized Communist cultural politics purely as intending to create a brainwashed cultural desert, on the one hand, or as forming a "lost Reading Paradise" of oppressed but sophisticated readers who preferred buying books to refrigerators and cars, on the other—two images often disseminated by the media as well as in ambitious studies of socialized culture during the Communist era. Communist rule persisted not only because of explicitly exercised oppression but because the "social contract" between the regime and the population was quite advantageous for some of its members. After the administrative reconfiguration of the "capitalist" cultural system, the publication of low quality (so-called trash and mass) reading was almost stopped in favor of the publication of officially "valuable" literature. Regardless of the historically shifting definition of literary "value," one intention of this strategy applied during the 1950s was to canonize a selected set of texts. At the same time, the tendency to allow the number of titles to lag behind while continually increasing the size of print runs coincided with the two basic directions of Communist state cultural politics. On the one hand, there was an attempt to "democratize" the access to a text, that is, to increase the number of persons who can actually read a particular text. On the other hand, such a policy, by actually limiting the variety of texts to which a reader could gain access, limited the possibilities for individual selection.

The process of late 1960s liberation left traces in the censor's office but was too short and too weak to radically divorce the cultural sphere from the practices of central control. Although the HSTD was renamed the Central Publishing Board (UPS) in 1967, and censorship was explicitly abandoned in the amendment of article 17, law no. 81/1966 on periodical and other publications in June 1968, the fired "censors" did not even manage to clean up their desks. Shortly after August 1968, the "normalized" National Assembly passed a decision to stop the validity of amended article no. 17 and in fact reintroduced control over publications. The 1960s development was followed by a major change in the notion of censorship. It was not the newly set up Office for Publishing and Information that was supposed to make decisions over particular texts; instead, the responsibility was delegated to the members of the publishing institutions, who were risking torture and harassment for not following the prescribed guidelines (Tomasek 1996).

For further discussion, the following overview of literary institutions as they were constituted in Czechoslovakia before 1989 may be helpful. I cannot provide exhaustive analyses of all units of this structure. Here I will just briefly describe some of the institutions and their interconnections in the process of constructing editorial plans and print runs as well as in the production, storage, distribution, and sale of books in order to further explain their recent transitions.

The book production process began with publishing houses that provided the Ministry of Culture with the initial plans for books to be printed. During the late 1970s and 1980s a number of prestigious authors occupied responsible positions within this institutional system. As publishers and editors, they influenced editorial plans and print runs. As book reviewers, they regularly filled pages of two existing journals specifically devoted to literature.

The special Books Department at the Ministry of Culture not only revised publication plans in consultation with publishers but also, most importantly, divided the supply of paper assigned by the Ministry of Industry to the printing companies. The amount of available paper–strictly limited by the five-year state plan of production–dictated in a way the number of produced books. Even the authors' royalties, legislatively unified in the 1950s for all types of books, were contracted per page in the case of prose, per verse in the case of poetry. Royalties were only partially dependent on the number of printed (not sold) copies. Indeed, the main idea was to completely insulate the realm of culture against the vagaries of the marketplace and hence against those of the actual readers as consumers of the book.

Publishers informed bookstores of the title, which had passed through the corrected editorial plan by means of an internal bulletin distributed to each store. Information in the bulletin consisted of brief descriptions of the content of each book. Based on this bulletin, the bookseller was supposed to guess the expected interest of his customers one to two years before the book actually appeared on the shelf and to order a certain number of copies from the district distribution authorities (Kniha). Most of the bookstores–except those run by publishers themselves–were administratively subordinate to and even controlled by the distribution authorities.

Booksellers had very little chance to determine the character of their stores in anticipation or response to the interests of their customers. At the same time, the sellers were under certain economic pressures: their wages were partially dependent on the number of books sold, and a penalty was assessed for the inventory of unsold books stored for more than 180 days. The actual sale of books often resembled the sale of bread. Any physical contact with the book was limited. The buyer could not really open the book unless he or she asked the salesperson, whose counter was a barrier between the customers and the bookshelves. "Browsing" was unknown.

New books came out regularly once a week. Every "books Thursday," huge lines formed in front of stores early in the morning when some attractive title was supposed to appear. One may ask, What actually comprised the "attractiveness" of a book? Among the most desired texts were those that would be characterized in the United States as belonging to the "white, male-dominated canon." Not only the ambiguous relationship of Communist cultural politics to the Western modern tradition but also the connection of the works of Kafka, Sartre, Heidegger, and others to the reformists of 1968 excluded these works from publication until the mid-1980s. The stamp of "previously forbidden text" was perhaps the best advertising to attract an audience to a book. More than suggesting a "high level of cultural maturity" of the nation, the crowds surrounding bookstores every Thursday reflected the gradually increasing dysfunction of cultural production.

Used bookstores occupied a unique position in the system. Unlike in regular bookstores, where the price of the books was fixed, used booksellers could set their prices more freely. These stores became important centers for the relatively uncontrolled distribution of books that had been excluded from libraries and were no longer published after 1968. Used bookstores were also favorite gathering and reading places. The books there were situated on open shelves to be searched, seen, and touched. Nevertheless, what both new and used bookstores had in common was their involvement in the "shadow market economy," with its corruption, under-the-counter sales, and chains of "mutually supportive friendships."

The central wholesale authority (Knizní velkoobchod) collected orders from the local distribution authorities and was responsible for storing books produced by printing companies in the central warehouses (a number of mostly old buildings without basic technical equipment or air-conditioning). This authority distributed books throughout the whole state (about two thousand bookstores). Unlike publishers and booksellers, the wholesaler owned trucks for transporting books from place to place. Distribution of certain titles (approximately fifty titles per week) had to start at least four weeks before actual selling in order to keep up with the "books Thursday" system.

Even this brief account shows that the whole system had the effect of reducing the variety of accessible texts, thus unifying, conserving, and protecting canons. The aim of promoting shared values was represented in many complex practices. It must be quite shocking for an outsider to visit a number of houses of educated people in my country and to discover more or less the same collection of books in their libraries.

In spite of a centrally prepared publishing plan, each of the institutions I have described was relatively autonomous. Strict boundaries between them made the mutual coordination of their activities less and less possible. This allowed the ostensible concentration of power while encouraging a dispersal of responsibility. The resulting lack of coordination accounted for the increasing inability of particular institutions to react to changes not just inside but also outside the system of book production. For none of its participants was quite certain about the extent of his or her decision-making power, and there was no clearly defined center on which one could rely. Paradoxically, conditions within the official sphere of state-controlled literary production promoted the "attractiveness" of texts and authors who were inaccessible within that domain and provoked the regime's representatives' paranoia about the alternative textual production.

It is important to notice that, though commonly used, the Russian word *samizdat* is a rather confusing term to be applied in the Czech context, where the texts were actually manuscripts copied on typewriters by authors themselves or their mostly female friends, quite often lacking any intervention of an editor. Access to any technologically advanced means of copying, say, in the offices, was controlled by the authorities. Considering such conditions, the productivity of the *samizdat* editions may seem rather impressive. In just one instance, the Edice Expedice run by Vaclav Havel and his fellows, around three hundred texts were released, although altogether the Czech *samizdat* production consisted of nearly fifteen hundred of both original and translated titles (Horec 1997).

To construct production and distribution practices of "alternative" texts as unlawful required the implementation of a special set of laws in the Czechoslovak legal system. To simply imprison people for moving books in their cars would have contradicted one of the concerns of the regime, that is, to preserve the image of a legally controlled country. The major legal argument used by the Czech *samizdat*'s producers to defend their activities was law no. 35/1965, which "allowed" the author to retype his or her manuscript in a limited number of copies. On the front page of each copy there had to be the author's signature and a note: "Copying strictly forbidden." It was not actually writing itself but the dissemination of the text that was construed by the regime as unlawful. The only publication of a text recognized as legal in pre-1989 Czechoslovakia was defined in law no. 81/1966, "On Periodicals and Other Means of Mass Information," including the amendments of 84/1968, 127/1968, 99/1969, 131/1970, and 146/1971, and in law no. 94/1949, "On Publishing and Disseminating Books, Music, and Other Nonperiodical Publications," with amendments of 88/1950, 131/1970, and 146/1971 (Posset 1992).

In none of these laws, however, has any "unofficial" production or distribution of books even been mentioned. In legal terms, the *samizdat*, was construed as nonexisting, and consequently, the border between what was allowed and what was forbidden, between "official" and "nonofficial," remained undefined. On what grounds, then, could a traveler with a suitcase of typewritten poems by Seifert end up in court? There are only two cases when the publishers of *samizdat* were sentenced for actually producing and disseminating periodicals defined as "antistate" (Posset 1992). Most of the legal cases filed against the activists were based on criminal law, such as article 98, "Subversion of the Republic," article 118, "Illicit Entrepreneurship," and the famous article 100, "Disturbing the Peace." A person convicted of these crimes could have been sentenced to up to ten years in jail.

It is not hard to find evidence promoting Louis Aragon's "Biafra of the Spirit" images. A list of over 150 writers and translators was issued by the Czechoslovak authorities in the early 1970s expelling them from the writers union, which in practical terms meant losing the license for having their work published. Their work was erased from the editorial plans of publishing houses, bookstores, and libraries. All twenty-five literary journals active in the country were eliminated, and in the twelve publishing houses over 80 percent of the editors and executives, including 2,000 journalists (that is, half the members of the journalists union), lost their positions. Together with thousands of academics and other professionals, they ended up in manual jobs or in exile (Renner 1989:101). From August 1968 to 1970, nearly 140,000 people emigrated from Czechoslovakia. The total number of direct victims of the dismissals is estimated to be as high as 300,000. A full picture of the number of persons, titles, and volumes banned or removed from the official institutions cannot be reconstructed today, since precise data are lacking, especially from the provinces (Renner 1989:100, 101). It can be said, however, that the hysteria of the ruling Czechoslovak post-1968 regime over books and their "movements" across various borders would have hardly found a comparison in post–World War II Europe.

Despite the unlimited number of actions actually enforcing the borders among particular spaces, the performative stability of the official sphere became more and more problematic in the face of its gradually increasing institutional weakness in the 1980s. The deterioration of the performed consistency in the practices within the "book chain" became apparent in the growing inefficiency of the central distribution, rising prices of paper, decreased quality of the book binding, and increasing conflicts between the demand and supply of books. Queuing crowds in front of bookstores and a corrupted "under the counter" sale system were the most obvious consequences of the inefficient state cultural politics.

By acting as though existing institutions were fully legitimate entities that functioned to achieve commonly desired goals, individual members of the literary institutions performed the roles of "authors," "editors," and "sellers." Not only did people perform what they considered to be their own roles, but they also acted in anticipation of the possible reaction of an imagined audience. By assuming a role within this network of performances, individual actors stabilized the institutional system. Daily experiences were made to appear natural and integrated into a larger unity through the performance of consistency. The appearance of consistency was desired and, under certain historical conditions, necessary for the effective maintenance of the identities of both the ruling regime and its opposition.

Nevertheless, both individuals and texts have constantly challenged the performed consistency of the system in many ways. To understand how such gestures met the institutional system, it is important to recognize that concepts of "authorship," "public sphere," and "market" acquired meanings and significances quite different from those prevalent in Western cultural and social contexts. The connections between an author's name, historical actions, and written work were unstable. For example, many excluded writers were publishing under someone else's name (often not just a pseudonym but a name belonging to another actual person who was willing to take that risk). More than financial exchange, interpersonal bonds and mutual trust were at stake here. Some authors who were forbidden to publish their own work were allowed to support themselves with translations. The works of writers who had been denied access to the biggest publishers in Prague could have been released in small district publishing houses. An author may have been restricted from publishing works for adults but tolerated writing for children. "Authorship" was defined in terms of "where" and "how" rather than "whom." The reformulation of the line between the person, the name, and the text that resulted from the policies instituted within the official sphere of literature actually eroded the boundaries between the official, émigré, and dissident spheres and challenged the controlling intentions of the official state system.

In spite of the dramatic character of the end of the Cold War in Czechoslovakia, the transition of the whole institutional system did not start suddenly on 17 November 1989. Disproportion within the web of literary institutions as well as mild economic reforms introduced by the Communist government gradually contributed to the breakdown of the performed consistency of the system. Already in 1988, the director of the central wholesale authority publicly discussed the problem of warehouses overfilled with unsold books, on the one hand, and, on the other hand, the profound lack of books demanded by the market. Due to difficulties in filling the state production plan, the printing companies used to move into the central warehouse over 40 percent of the whole year's production during the last quarter of the year. At the same time, booksellers began refusing to order books that they were unable to sell (e.g., explicitly proregime poetry or fiction) because they had to pay a penalty for unsold books remaining in the store for more than 180 days. The number of unsold books stored in the warehouse increased by 25 percent between 1980 and 1988.

Not only the time needed to produce a book (minimally, two to three years) but also the strictly fixed assignment of paper, printing colors, book-binding glue, and other products made it almost impossible to coordinate print runs with readers' actual demands. As early as January 1989, the printing and paper production authorities, which controlled one of the crucial elements that determined access to the printed text, opened themselves to both local and international market pressures and raised the price of paper by 30 percent. This move confused financial obligations among state publishing, production, and distribution companies. To paraphrase Cold War propaganda discourse, the times were pregnant with change.

One may ask at the end of all this explanation, Where is the angry censor who completes lists of *libri prohibiti*? By leaving out the censor I do not want to hide the fact that after 1968 in Czechoslovakia a list was issued of hundreds of writers whose books were excluded from the libraries and editorial plans, a list that also included a number of translators. Consequently, for many years the works of Hemingway, Brecht, Morgenstern, and Lorca were not available because the people who translated them were persona non grata. The role of the censor certainly was quite an effective and active part of the cultural scene. At the same time, as I have tried to show, reference to this role cannot exhaust the complex question of censorship in cultural and social practices.

I hope I have challenged the simplistic model of "censorship," which is derived from its own internal utopian idea that the administrative exclusion of certain texts can generate expected effects on the reception of these texts and can produce desired changes in the "reeducation" of a particular community. I have tried to express my suspicion about models of an autonomous Censor, a victimized Author, and a deprived Reader rooted in the seductive "oppression/ domination" explanatory dichotomy. Rather, I am interested in institutions and their structures and in the performances that form systems of censorship—not simply as the disapproval of certain texts but as the institutionally limited access of the reader to the text. Although the censors did have a particular role to play in this system, when they and the political and social forces related to them disappeared in 1989, the other actors still continued to hold on to some of their familiar discourses and performative habits. It took a few days to clean up the censors' offices, but the vestiges of the former institutions, though in their post-1989 transitional forms, continued to frame cultural practices. Instead of a conclusion, I would just add that the concept of "censorship" is one of the most seductive methodological frames for drawing a black-and-white picture of burning books, suicidal authors, and brainwashed readers. I would argue that paradoxically enough, particularly because of its apparent seductive methodological power, if we manage to go beyond the notion of censorship, defined as a genocide of bodies and texts, it can became a challenging tool of understanding complex daily experiences and "structures of feeling"– to use R. Williams's expression–that shaped and constructed the totalitarian social and cultural experiment in the period of the Cold War.

Note

This essay is part of a larger research project supported by a British Academy Small Research Grant. Some of the results of this project have been published in my essay "Marketing Silence: On the Transformation of the Czech Book," *Cultural Policy* 5:2 (1999): 199–218.

References

Altieri, Charles. 1990. *Canons and Consequences: Reflections on the Ethical Force of Imaginative Ideals.* Evanston, Ill.: Northwestern University Press.
Chartier, Roger. 1997. Interview conducted 25 April in *SHARP News* 6:2 (Spring): 4–5.
"The Czechoslovak 'Black List.'" 1983. In George Schöpflin, ed., *Censorship and Political Communication in Eastern Europe.* London: Francis Pinter. 29–31.
Darnton, Robert. 1996. *The Forbidden Best-Sellers of Pre-Revolutionary France.* London: Fontana Press.
Hepner, Vladimir. 1975. *Pruzkum ceske verejnosti ke knize a k jejimu sireni* (Survey of the Czech public's attitude to the book and to its distribution). Prague: Ustav pro vyzkum kultury.
Horec, Jaromir. 1997. "Vztah nakladatele a spisovatele v ceskych kulturnich dejinach" (The relation between the publisher and the writer in Czech cultural history). *Tvar* 8:13:13.
Janacek, Pavel, Ales Zach, and Dusan Tomasek. 1998. Internal materials on censorship and publishing in Czechoslovakia from 1945 to 1948 prepared at the Institute of Czech Literature of the Czech Academy of Science in Prague.
Janousek, Pavel. 1996. "Spor o Lukese. Kapitola z ceske literarni kritiky pocatku osmdesatych let" (A controversy over Lukes. A chapter from Czech literary criticism of the early eighties). In *Normy normalizace* (Norms of normalization). Utav pro ceskou literaturu AV CR, Slezska univerzita. Prague: Opava. 82-90.
Kaplan, Karel, and Dusan Tomasek. 1994. *O cenzure v Ceskoslovensku v letech 1945–1956* (On censorship in Czechoslovakia in the period 1945–1956). Sesity pro Soudobe dejiny AV CR, Svazek 22. Prague: Ustav pro soudobe dejiny AV CR.

Posset, Johanna. 1992. *Ceska samizdatova periodika 1968-1989* (Czech *samizdat* periodicals, 1968-1989). Brno: Tovarna na sitotisk ve spolupraci se Spolecnosti pro reklamu a tisk R & T.

Renner, Hans. 1989. *A History of Czechoslovakia since 1945*. London and New York: Routledge.

Tomasek, Dusan. 1996. *Pozor, cenzurovano! aneb ze zivota soudruzky cenzury* (Attention, censored! or, from the life of the comrade censor). Prague: Vydavatelstvi a nakladatelstvi MV CR.

Control of Literary Communication in the 1945–1956 Period in Poland

Oskar Stanislaw Czarnik

Following the Soviet invasion of Poland in 1944, Polish Communists created censorship authorities to control literary communication in the country. Beginning with a censor's office within the temporary government, several offices were established to control literary communication through preliminary and secondary control or censorship. This essay describes these authorities and the control they exercised over the Polish publishing industry. It lists examples of preliminary and secondary censorship. Preliminary censorship used trusted editors and senior officials in publishing and press offices to assure that books, publications, and entertainment complied with Communist ideology. Authorities limited the publication of books through censorship or control of printing houses, paper supplies, copyright, and importation of books. Secondary censorship limited the distribution of books and artistic works and sometimes removed undesirable texts from circulation. Published works that did not represent "Socialist realism" were removed from circulation. However, the one area of literary communication the censors could not control was reading. Readers sought out private libraries and previously published works to escape the control of the censors.

The control of literary communication in countries ruled by Communists was a multifaceted activity. Censorship proper served to control texts for publication. It controlled literary and scientific works, informational texts and columns, as well as any products of intellectual effort and artistic creativity. The results of that control could not be undermined; the Communist system excluded any possibility of appeal against the censor's decision.

Apart from that, there was preliminary control that evaluated texts before they were sent to the censor's office. This type of activity was the task of specified trusted persons, such as some editors in publishing houses and the press head offices, senior officials in scientific institutions, and some activists in literary and artistic organizations. Preliminary control served to verify ideas and to eliminate controversial artistic concepts. Its second objective was to form the text according to the binding ideological requirements. This type of control played an immense role in the Stalinist period, but its role diminished in some countries (e.g., in Poland) after the political changes of 1956.

Secondary control gained quite a stable position in the Communist system. The authorities watched and evaluated the process of reception of printed or disseminated texts using different methods. There was a need to know whether reception was correct or not, whether it instigated any ideological doubts or any other unexpected developments or not. If necessary, new decisions were made: to limit the reception of the work or withdraw it from cultural circulation. This variety of control was the responsibility of some experts of the Communist party, political police, and some artistic and literary critics privileged by the authorities. As a result, sometimes a work that passed censorship and was eventually published fell out of literary circulation after some time.

Preliminary, proper, and secondary censorship was enhanced by other control measures. An immense role was played by the publishing policy of the state, strict limitation of foreign cultural relations, and nonstop checking of the contents of library holdings. The above activities together created a certain system of control that was comprehensive, consistent, and seemingly effective. This system, which had been developed in the Soviet Union in the 1920s, was introduced into the countries of Central Europe.

The Genesis and Powers of Communist Censorship in Poland

From July 1944 to April 1945 the Soviet army drove German troops out of Poland. In that period Soviet State security people destroyed a significant part of the Home Army (AK, or Armia Krajowa) that had previously fought against Hitler's occupation. Similarly, some underground institutions (public, cultural, educational) active during the German occupation in the structures of the underground state maintained by the Polish government in London were eliminated. Those who had escaped fascist terror now became victims of violence.

Protected by the Soviets, in July 1944 Polish Communists began to create new state authorities and at the same time a new system of control of public life. A temporary government (PKWN, or Polish Committee of National Liberation) officially established censorship, already active at that time in Lublin, a city liberated in July 1944 from Hitler's occupation. The censor's office was a unit within the Security Department.

The bureaucratic career of the new office developed rapidly. At the beginning of 1945 the Ministry of Security of the new temporary government created a Central Bureau of the Press, Publications, and Performances Control. This institution, reporting to political police, was entitled to control a major part of public communication in Poland. However, the legal situation of the bureau was not clear yet. Three political centers competed with each other in the area of control. General administration, called to life by the Communist party, demanded that censorship be added to its structures. Some senior officials situated outside the Communist party, collaborating with the new authorities, suggested this solution. At that time another rival appeared on the political scene. The Ministry of Information and Propaganda established at the beginning of 1945 controlled the production of paper, the work of printing houses, the size of book impressions, and periodicals circulation; moreover, it produced evaluations of the Polish press from a political angle. Heads of the ministry wanted to take over censorship and form a separate censor's division within the ministry. Thanks to this, the system of control would become uniform, meaning one ministry would exercise it. This solution gained the support of some political dignitaries.

Hidden competition inside the power apparatus lasted almost a year. The general administration was the weakest rival and was eliminated within a few months, whereas the Ministry of Information and Propaganda started a fierce fight, its senior officials showing their intention to extend the exercised control over the entire literary communication. There was one element that played an important role. Public opinion in Poland and in the Western countries evaluated visible links between censorship and state security service as something very negative. There was an apparent need to find a proper way out of this problem and to camouflage this shameful relationship. That is why on 15 November 1945 the government made a new decision. The main office of the Press, Publications, and Performances Control was created. From that moment on, the censor's office seemed an independent body.

The main office was a ministry-level agency, and it had branches in all major administrative centers throughout the country.[1] Nevertheless, its independence was fictitious, and the winner still remained a vassal. Censorship operated strictly according to general and specific recommendations issued by the Political Bureau of the Polish Workers Party and later the Polish United Workers Party Central Committee (the

Communist party). Orders were passed confidentially at least once a week. They named forbidden authors and texts, specified subjects that were to be passed over in silence, and indicated also some official, ideological, and literary publications that were beyond criticism. Censorship continued to cooperate secretly with the Ministry of Security. Political police played an important role in controlling the cultural life. The relationship lasted a long time—until the eventual collapse of the Communist system in Poland in 1989–90.

The censorship institutionalized in 1944–45 was of a preventive nature. It was authorized to control texts before their dissemination. Its decisions were arbitrary; the controlled body had no right of appeal. In this respect that system of control differed quite distinctly from the censorship that had existed in Poland in the interwar period. Texts were controlled after publication; the author or publisher of the confiscated work had the right of appeal.

The resolution adopted by the government on 15 November 1945, followed by legal regulations approved in 1946 and 1947, granted extensive powers to the main office of the Press, Publications, and Performances Control. Briefly put, they were as follows: (1) preventive control of texts meant for publication in the press and in book form; (2) censorship of texts disseminated through other channels of literary communication (e.g., theater, cabaret, cinema, and radio); (3) issuance of permission to establish periodicals; (4) approval of the size of book printings and periodical circulation, a major influence on the appropriation of paper quotas; (5) a decisive voice in the area of imports of foreign publications to Poland; and (6) the control of private and state-owned printing houses. In this fashion, censorship controlled texts of any kind: literary works and cookbooks, religious dissertations and obituaries, theater posters and music scores, religious books and advertising prospectuses. A ban on publishing a certain work was a professional and political secret, and partial interference did not leave any visible, official traces in the printed text.

After gaining a decisive influence over contemporary communication, the main office started to control the past. The Division of Book Collections, operating within the structure of censorship, compiled from 1945 to 1947 seven lists of forbidden printed works being withdrawn from bookshops and libraries. After 1950, under the influence of the censor's office, the Ministry of Education and the Ministry of Culture introduced other similar lists. All in all, a ban on access covered over three thousand books, including historical works as well as old and contemporary literary works, both Polish and foreign. Among the withdrawn publications there were also some novels by Charles Dickens, Honoré de Balzac, and Jack London.[2]

Ever more extensive powers of the censor's office speeded up the fall of the Ministry of Information and Propaganda. It was closed down in 1947, and the main office of the Press, Publications, and Performances Control inherited its powers. Political and bureaucratic competition in the area of control came to an end.

Selected Examples of Preliminary and Secondary Control

Preliminary control exercised by many institutions also affected the literary and scientific texts themselves. The publication of the Polish Literary Bibliography, which was prepared by a special team of the Institute of Literary Studies of the Polish Academy of Sciences, provides an instructive example.

A number of editors and officials of the institute, entitled to carry out internal control, filed their fundamental objections in 1950. They demanded that twenty-eight Polish periodicals (primarily religious and émigré publications) and seven Western scientific and literary periodicals be removed from the bibliography. The *American Slavic and East European Review*, *British Book News*, the *Kenyon Review*, the *New York Times Book Review*, the *Partisan Review*, the *Saturday Review of Literature*, and the *Times Literary Supplement* were among those removed. Diligent controllers suspended the publishing of several volumes of this bibliography for several years. Finally, the book appeared after the fall of Stalinism in Poland in 1956 and was published with numerous separate supplements.

Preliminary censorship also distorted other scientific studies. In an article on a Polish literary journal, *Sygnaly*, published in Lvov from 1933 to 1939, the names of Polish writers who had emigrated after World War II were removed. Also any mention was removed of some foreign literati such as Louis Ferdinand Céline, André Gide, Aldous Huxley, André Malraux, and Heinrich Mann. In another publication on the Polish periodicals *Poprostu* and *Karta*, which were published in Vilna in the interwar period, a reproduction of the title page of one of the periodicals was falsified in order to remove the name of Czeslaw Milosz, who emigrated from Poland after the war. The above events quite frequently, in fact, resulted from both external pressure as well as individual conformism and servility–to accurately tell one from another remains a difficult task. Preliminary control ended at the Institute of Literary Studies in 1956.[3]

The system of internal control also affected the activity of the artistic community. At the beginning of 1949 a new phase began in the cultural policy of the state. During the general congress of the Polish Writers Trade Union in Szczecin, socialist realism was recognized as the ideal artistic method. Political authorities adopted the assumption that the Polish Writers Union (already without the adjective "trade") was an ideological training organization preparing its members in a proper implementation of the official method. Participation in this program became obligatory for all writers of the union. Worthy of note is a certain quite characteristic sign. In 1950 heads of the union set up within their organization the so-called creative sections serving the purpose of ideological formation and the artistic improvement of writers. Separate sections were established for prose, poetry, drama, translation, and children's and young people's literature. The initiative was put in effect mainly through group evaluation of ideas and artistic concepts. During the meetings the writers presented their literary concepts and read fragments of texts, whereas the task of the discussion participants was to criticize those elements that were found to be "inadequate" or "ambiguous." In this fashion, the activity of the section fulfilled the function of collective preliminary censorship. Forced "work" in the sections began to be phased out during the decline of Stalinism and eventually became extinct in the spring of 1956. As mentioned above, cultural policy makers watched the reception of texts that entered cultural circulation very carefully. When it was indispensable, they intervened.

It was secondary censorship that stopped the dissemination of literary works by Jean-Paul Sartre and Albert Camus. In October 1947 the Maly Theater in Warsaw staged a play by Sartre called *Huis-clos* (*No Exit*), while in February 1948 the Polish Army Theater in Lodz staged another play by the same author, *La Putain respecteuse* (Polish title: *Ladaczica z zasadami*). At the same time, a fragment of *L'Etranger* (*The Stranger*) by Camus appeared in a Marxist periodical, *Kuznica*. Several months later, Communist critics launched a campaign against existentialist philosophy and literature, defining them as "destructive" and "reactive." Certain works were immediately removed from literary circulation. The reception of existentialism became possible only after 1956 in the already totally different political and cultural atmosphere.

The alertness of secondary censorship also affected literature defined as "progressive." In December 1952 Bertolt Brecht's Berliner Ensemble toured Poland, performing in Warsaw, Krakow, and Lodz. The staging of *Mother Courage* by Bertolt Brecht, the Gorki-based *The Mother*, and a play by Heinrich von Kleist, *The Broken Pitcher*, received an enthusiastic reception. The journals *Przeylad Kulturelny* and *Nowa Kultura* published articles by Konstanty Puzyna, Andrzej Wirth, and Jerzy Pomianowski. These authors came forward with a thorough assessment of the artistic concepts of the famous theater artist.

Additionally, they expressed the idea that after Brecht's visit in Poland the concept of socialist realism ought to be modified. The artistic values and the achievements of the Berliner Ensemble should enrich literature committed to the cause of creating a new social order. At that time the editors of the *Pamietnik Teatralny* (Theatrical Diary) began to prepare a special issue devoted to the tour.

Political authorities found that the above proposals became an ideological provocation. "We did not find this theater a model of socialist realism," "Brecht, especially in theater, does not represent socialist realism" sounded the accusations of senior officials of the Communist party. The Ministry of Culture warned the editorial board of the *Pamietnik Teatralny* not to publish articles emphasizing the artistic merits of Brecht's work. The result was a foregone conclusion. The publication about the Berliner Ensemble was reduced to a small note. For three years silence was kept about the whole matter, and the special issue on Brecht came out only in August 1955, when political and cultural changes in Poland were already at an advanced stage.[4]

Political Requirements and Changes in Book Production

At the onset of the 1945–56 period the book market in Poland was partly capitalistic. Private enterprises and some cooperatives played an immense role in the publishing sector, particularly from 1945 to 1947. Private publishers produced 55 percent (in 1945) and 48 percent (in 1947) of all book titles. Playing a prominent role in the cultural life of the country, in 1947 they published about 70 percent of adult fiction, 80 percent of children's books, and 80 percent of printed music. In this category of publishers, one can identify institutions set up in the nineteenth century, at the beginning of the twentieth century, in the interwar period (e.g., Gebethner i Wolff, S. i M. Arct, Trzaska, Evert i Michalski, and Ksiaznica Atlas), as well as after World War II (e.g., E. Kuthan, Krakow Publishing Society, and T. Nalepa i Spolka).[5]

Communist authorities were forced to temporarily tolerate the above trend. During the war, with Nazi and Soviet occupation, Polish culture lost about 70–80 percent of its bookshops' stock and library holdings. The printing industry was more than half destroyed. Now, after the cataclysm, only private owners could immediately restart their businesses, provided they had the necessary funds and technical facilities. The textbooks they produced were the foundation for the reconstruction of national education. Though books produced by private publishers were controlled by the censor's office, Communist leaders treated them as a necessary evil. The gradually introduced limitations were meant to ensure the predominance of the state in this area of literary communication.

The first step was forced nationalization of the printing industry. In 1946 almost all of the printing houses became the property of the state; the few exceptions to this rule were practically negligible. At the same time, stringent regulations affected the distribution of paper, which was in the hands of the Ministry of Information and Propaganda. Already in 1945 two different prices were introduced for printing paper: a lower price for publishers associated with the authorities (e.g., publishing houses that belonged to the state and the Communist party) and a higher price for the remaining publishers and printers. After the Ministry of Information and Propaganda was scrapped in 1947, the distribution of paper became the responsibility of a special commission, in which the decisive voice belonged to a representative of the censor's office. Additionally, private publishers were obliged to submit general annual and detailed quarterly plans. The purchase of paper was possible only provided that publishing plans were approved by the censor's office. Had they not met this requirement, the purchase of paper would be prosecuted as a political and economic crime.

The authorities also used another effective measure: limiting the copyright. Some private publishers and cultural associations acquired copyright, enabling them to publish all the books by some old Polish writers. On 4 April 1946 the State National Council, a temporary legislative body established by the Communists, issued a decree suspending those rights. At the beginning of 1947 the Ministry of Culture transferred exactly the same rights to publishing houses set up by the new authorities. The described donation was at the same time an act of force—private publishers did not receive any compensation.

The political and administrative decisions also limited the implementation of contracts signed during the war by some booksellers and publishers with contemporary Polish writers. Printing of the works was planned after the war, whereas the money paid to many writers as an advance payment helped them in their difficult material situations during the Nazi occupation. Communist propaganda attacked these contracts violently as contracts "forced by situation" and demanded that they be annulled.

In 1948, under political and administrative pressure, a new regulation was introduced. The validity of the above contracts was to expire on 1 April 1949. Publishers who had not published the purchased works by that time lost any right of compensation for any copyright acquired during the war.[6] The effects of these activities were visible. The participation of private publishers in the production of

112 *Control of Literary Communication in Poland*

books dropped immensely, and in 1950 their share in all published titles was only 8 percent. After 1950 only a few religious organizations continued publishing as a side activity. Publishing now became the monopoly of the state.

A development that followed was the visible concentration and centralization of publishing. In 1949 the Central Publishing Commission was set up and in 1961 the Central Office of Publishing Houses, Printing Industry, and Bookselling. This institution was now in charge of distributing paper among publishing houses as well as controlling their publishing and financial plans. The Central Office approved the specialization and activity programs of the publishing houses now reporting to it. The individual publishers became contractors in a general plan. Nevertheless, some state-owned publishing houses achieved outstanding results in the dissemination of literature (e.g., the Panstwowy Instytut Wydawniczy [PIW], Czytelnik, and Wydawnictwo Literackie). After 1956 they often held talks with the censor's office in order to save the publication of some works that had been rejected by cultural policy decision-makers. Some publishing institutions set up at that time operate today, thanks to internal changes introduced after the fall of the Communist system in Poland in 1989–90.

In the 1950–56 period the number of books published and the general size of their print runs went up. This growth was due to significant dissemination of old literature, both Polish and foreign. A visible effort was made to introduce into cultural circulation works by such authors as Homer, Molière, William Shakespeare, Jonathan Swift, Daniel Defoe, Stendhal, Emile Zola, Jules Verne, and Romain Rolland as well as Jan Kochanowski, Adam Mickiewicz, Juliusz Slowacki, Henryk Sienkiewicz, and Stefan Zeromski. Generally speaking, hundreds of Polish and foreign writers were being published. However, the literary repertoire was the object of permanent scrutiny and censor's limitations, particularly in the case of contemporary literature. Millions of copies of texts representing the official trend, namely, socialist realism, were printed at that time. They filled libraries, bookshops, and huge bookstores. Millions of copies of propaganda prints kept in wholesale warehouses were later taken directly to paper mills as scrap paper. The book market became to a major extent a system of arbitrarily governed distribution.

The Book Reader and Book Reading in a Totalitarian System

The above-presented system of control covered practically all stages of literary communication, starting from the writing of the text to the production of the book. Only one element still remained a secret: book reading.

Cultural policy decision-makers assumed that they could exert a prominent influence on the activities, interests, and opinions of readers. It is true that part of the reading public, such as schoolchildren, was affected by these arbitrary decisions. The reading of some texts, political and literary, was obligatory or at least recommended in some institutions. The reading of these texts thus resulted from necessity, sometimes conformism, or real interest. All in all, the influence of politics over book readers and reading seemed obvious and stable.

From time to time some cautious warnings would shake this confidence. In 1951 one librarian wrote in a professional journal that Poznan workers showed her open disregard for the entire official propaganda in books. They openly expressed their independent tastes and tried to find contemporary works that were free of primitive political bias. In 1954 some journalists wrote about the preferences of young people who remained faithful to old, popular literature (adventure, historical, and fantastical novels). Another author confirmed that young people totally rejected contemporary Polish and Soviet works written in line with the binding ideological requirements. Another librarian stressed in his report written in 1955 that workers from a major Warsaw factory borrowed mostly popular books, whereas the works of socialist realism aroused interest exclusively in old Communist activists. At the same time, a bookseller in Lodz wrote in his letter to one of the journals that Communist party activists did not pay attention to Marxist literature, and only a certain Catholic priest would come to buy books by Marx and Lenin in his bookshop.[7]

Communist dignitaries tended to neglect such information for a long time. The situation in their opinion was obvious: some readers have "false" awareness, formed by the previous "bourgeois" ideology. Thus one ought to gradually change the mentality of the reading public and form reading preferences accordingly. Only in 1954, during the declining phase of Stalinism, did the political authorities allow scholars to conduct research on book reading as an object of studies that exists irrespective of current political tendencies. In fact, one ought to ask a question: How did it happen that some readers crossed the limits of controlled literary communication? It seems that a critical reader had three strategies to choose from that ensured internal freedom in a strictly controlled system of communication.

1. *Reading independently of the system.* Private book collections were used; literary communication was also based on books published before World War II. Individual borrowings from colleagues at work

or friends were quite frequent. Sometimes the already heavily damaged books were being recopied by hand; copying them on a typewriter at that time was still connected with too many problems. In some cases, interesting publications could be found in public libraries where the "cleansing" of the collections had been conducted but not too thoroughly. The above reading strategy was quite stable and continued to prevail during the entire period of Stalinism.

2. *Reading as an escape*. In the discussed period, old literature enjoyed particular popularity. Readers used both earlier editions of books as well as contemporary publications. In spite of ideological limitations, the artistic repertoire was diversified. What was read were masterpieces of Western and Eastern European literature, as well as Russian and American works, particularly novels. Part of the reading public linked this reception of the achievements of the past with total rejection of contemporary literature written according to ideological requirements. Reading became a refuge; great cultural traditions protected the reader in spiritual terms against everyday violence in public life.

3. *Reading in search of heresy*. Readers reading propaganda texts and works in the spirit of socialist realism could perform a certain experiment. Sometimes in the course of reading a basic question was asked: How does the book read depart from the party line and at the same time signalize changes in the cultural policy, in the censor's activity? This pattern of reception was quite frequent from 1954 to 1956, toward the end of Stalinism. Rivalry within the Communist party between "liberals" and "hard-liners" strengthened the political and cultural ambiguities. It was at the time of the above crisis that readers' attention was attracted by *The Thaw*, a 1956 novel by well-known Soviet writer Ilea Erenburg. The work, average as it was in artistic terms, was regarded as a testimony of ideological and cultural changes in the Soviet Union. Also at that time the *Poemat dla doroslych* (Poem for Adults) by Adam Wasyk, a well-known writer and party activist, expressed radical rejection of official propaganda and social changes introduced by Communist authorities. The work appeared in the journal *Nowa Kultura* (New Culture) in August 1955. Pawel Hoffman, the editor-in-chief of this journal, was dismissed immediately after the text was published, but the text, recopied by hand many times, continued to function in the cultural life, causing many ideological and literary disputes toward the end of 1955 and at the beginning of 1956.

Events speeded up. The armed rising of Poznan workers in June 1956 and the autumn 1956 political turn brought important changes into public life as well as into literary communication. After 1956 it still remained subject to control, but from that point onward the evolution toward freedom and the process of coming out of isolation were ever more visible.

Notes

1. Mieczyslaw Ciecwierz, "Ograniczenie tresci prasy w okresie PKWN i Rzadu Tymczasowego," *Kwartalnik Historii Prasy Polskiej* 4 (1983): 63–83; Mieczyslaw Ciecwierz, "Ksztaltowanie sie panstwowego aparatu nadzoru i kontroli prasy w latach," *Kwartalnik Historii Prasy Polskiej* 2 (1944–48): 27–63.
2. Stanislaw Adam Kondek, *Wladza i wydawcy* (Warsaw, 1993), 29–46.
3. Jadwiga Czachowska, "Zmagania z cenzura slownikow i bibliografii literackich w PRL," in *Pismiennictwo–systemy kontroli–obiegi alternatywne,* ed. Janusz Kostecki and Alina Bruulzka (Warsaw, 1992), 2:214–36; Krystyna Tokarzownna, *Cenzura w Polskiej Bibliografii Literrackkiej*, 237–50.
4. Marta Fik, *Kultura polska po Jalcie* (London, 1989), 87, 95, 172–73.
5. Adam Bromberg, *Ksiazki i wydawcy* (Warsaw, 1966), 20.
6. Stanislaw Adam Kondek, *Wladza i wydawcy* (Warsaw, 1993), 47–71.
7. Stanislaw Adam Kondek, "Stracone zludzenia. Klopoty dysponentow obiegu ksiyiki z rzeczywistoicia czytelnicza w latach, 1952–1955," in *Instytucje V-publicznosc–sytuacje lektury. Studia z historii czytelnictwa*, ed. Janusz Kostecki (Warsaw, 1997), 6:222–53.

International Harmony: Threat or Menace? U.S. Youth Services Librarians and Cold War Censorship, 1946–1955

Christine Jenkins

> We think of the Resistance as being a part of war and invasion, but actually it is the core of everyday life. . . . It means a new sense of world brotherhood–and the will to express it.
> Bertha Mahoney Miller, "Peacetime Resistance"

The traditional stance of youth services librarians has been strong advocacy on behalf of children's books that promote intergroup cooperation and international understanding. With the onset of the McCarthy era, however, books with an intergroup and international focus became politically suspect, and librarians found themselves confronting both unspoken and overt "blacklists" of so-called subversive titles and authors. During the Cold War, librarians in the United States who served children and young adults were subject to demands from political pressure groups to remove or restrict books and other library materials viewed by those groups as pro-Communist propaganda. Many librarians succeeded in actively resisting these pressures. They did so, however, in ways that were largely invisible to their contemporaries outside the field. Thus far, their strategies of resistance have gone unnoticed by historians as well. ALA youth services leaders' rhetoric and strategies of resistance–quiet, positive, and active–effectively countered pressure groups' censorship efforts and, in doing so, maintained librarians' professional jurisdiction over the selection and evaluation of books for young readers.

Children's libraries and librarianship originated in the Eastern urban centers of the United States during the final decades of the nineteenth century.[1] Along with social work, teaching, and nursing, children's librarianship was a female-intensive "social housekeeping" profession that was part of Progressive era efforts to assimilate and

Americanize the burgeoning immigrant populations of that time.[2] Early children's librarians supported and extended this "melting pot" ideal to promote a mutual understanding between immigrant and native-born children. This professional conviction was reflected in the children's literature of the time, which took an international approach to folklore, fiction, and nonfiction for children. In the decades that followed, the social and political tensions inherent in a multicultural society, plus the international upheavals of the Great Depression and two world wars, only deepened librarians' commitment to literature and programming on behalf of intergroup (interracial) harmony and international understanding, and American children's librarians met the founding of the United Nations and of UNESCO with understandable enthusiasm.[3]

After three years of no conferences due to wartime travel restrictions, the American Library Association (ALA) held its first postwar annual conference in late June 1946. The conference theme was "Gearing Libraries to a New Epoch," and the theme of intergroup and international cooperation, plus the importance of the United Nations and UNESCO, was stressed throughout the conference.[4] The ALA youth services divisions' conference programming included a presentation on evaluating materials about foreign countries (specifically those that would promote understanding of the U.S.S.R. among young American library users), and the division's Booklist Committee reported that it had compiled two annotated lists of young adult books with "about one third of the books listed tend[ing] to further racial or international understanding."[5]

The importance of understanding between diverse groups and nations was reflected in other books singled out that year for special recognition. The winner of the 1946 Newbery Medal–the highest award for children's literature–was Lois Lenski's *Strawberry Girl*, a realistic story of the hardscrabble lives of agricultural workers in rural Florida.[6] Among the runners-up for the medal was Florence Crannell Means's *The Moved-Outers*, another realistic story about the Japanese American experience in World War II relocation camps (and one of the first novels about this experience for readers of any age).[7] Two picture books with positive portrayals of Russia, Becky Reyher's *My Mother Is the Most Beautiful Woman in the World* and Lee Kingman's *Ilenka*, were also among those honored by the ALA children's librarians in 1946.[8]

At the same time, however, a number of Americans were beginning to view the U.S.S.R. with growing uneasiness. One of the earliest postwar anti-Communist campaigns was inaugurated in December 1945 by the U.S. Chamber of Commerce when its board approved the preparation of a report on "the menace of Socialism in Europe, and its effect upon this country."[9] This report, a forty-page pamphlet titled *Communist Infiltration in the United States: Its Nature and How to Combat It*, was published in 1946 with an initial print run of 400,000 copies and distributed through the Chamber, the American Legion, and other business and patriotic organizations.[10] In March 1947 President Truman gave his speech outlining the Truman Doctrine of Communist "containment" in Eastern Europe, and less than two weeks later Truman signed Executive Order 9835, an antisubversive program of mandated loyalty oaths for all federal employees.[11] Much of the outlook described in the Chamber's 1946 pamphlet was now national policy. The Cold War had begun.

In 1948 the Chamber of Commerce published another widely distributed pamphlet, *A Program for Community Anti-Communist Action*, which would became a basic textbook for groups and individuals interested in "rooting out the Reds" in schools, libraries, organizations, and the media. This fifty-six-page text was an outline for the establishment of local anti-Communist organizations to act as watchdogs for possible Communist infection. The Communist virus, the pamphlet declared, might enter the community through any number of avenues, including mass media, voluntary organizations, public education, and the public library. Among the most dangerous vectors were the ostensibly benign Communist front organizations that "masquerade[d] as promoting peace, justice to minorities, and civil rights" in order to prey upon the gullible.[12] Teachers and public education were appropriate targets for investigation, as were librarians: "Librarians are likewise not beyond public scrutiny. . . . Pro-Communist studies are promoted in library literature as objective or recommended studies. The real danger in this field is not usually the attitudes of the librarians themselves. It is in the fact that *many of their important book review sources are infiltrated by Communists or sympathizers*" (emphasis in original).[13] This critical differentiation between naive librarians and subversive reviewers was not a view shared by librarians or reviewers themselves. Many of the editors and most of the reviewers writing for their "important book review sources" (such as *Booklist*, the *Horn Book*, and the *Library Journal*) were in fact current and former librarians.

Censorship attempts became more prevalent as the American Legion, the Daughters and Sons of the American Revolution (the DAR and SAR), and other "superpatriot" groups grew increasingly active in their campaigns against domestic subversion.[14] The proceedings of postwar ALA conferences reflect librarians' growing awareness of the impact of anti-Communist "cultural vigilantism" on American libraries. The first mention of Cold War censorship problems in ALA conference proceedings was in 1947, at two programs sponsored by the Young People's Reading Round Table (YPRRT) and the American Association of School Librarians (AASL). On 1 July Los Angeles school librarian Marion Horton spoke. Her school district had recently been involved in a bruising fight over *Building America*, a series of supplemental social studies texts, and *Land of the Soviets*, a pamphlet by Marguerite Stewart which had been challenged by a local SAR chapter.[15] Her talk ranged over the same areas of intergroup and international understanding that librarians had always championed, but Horton warned her audience:

> The House Subcommittee on Un-American Activities is trying to prove that Communism is being fostered by current moving pictures and books. Alarming signs of hysteria are found on every side. . . . Complacently we say, "Oh, it couldn't happen here." . . . But it can happen in any part of the country. Witness the recent uproar over Howard Fast's *Citizen Tom Paine* in New York and over *Building America* and the Stewart pamphlet on Soviet Russia in California. These are symptoms of the rising tide of intolerance and the suppression of freedom of thought and inquiry throughout the country.[16]

Two days later, young adult librarian Eleanor Kidder gave a talk on reading guidance for teens that succinctly summed up librarians' "best practice" in maintaining young people's right to read: "Have a good reason for every title in the collection and then accept them without further apology."[17]

Successful Strategies of Resistance

As ALA youth services leadership sought ways to protect children's library collections, they contended not only with groups and individuals from outside the library but sometimes with colleagues from inside the library as well. Whatever the source, however, effective responses had to be found that would keep the books they valued on the library's shelves and available to young readers. The strategies they developed were strategies of resistance that took forms that could be described as quiet resistance, positive resistance, and active resistance.

Although well aware of the activities of censors, librarians might choose to deliberately ignore campaigns against the authors or books in their collections, a strategy that might defuse and neutralize the conflict. To the quiet but often effective resistance of deliberate disregard, librarians might add the tactic of positive resistance by featuring and promoting books that were under attack. Finally, in cases where the attack was too threatening to ignore, librarians could directly counter and challenge attackers through active resistance. No matter how forceful and vigorous their opposition to censors, however, librarians' responses would be expressed in the civil words and polite, businesslike tones that reinforced their position as middle-class professional women.

Quiet Resistance: Maintaining Strategic Silence

Some Red-hunters believed that librarians were simply "hear no evil, see no evil" naïfs whose ignorance of the potential for Communist subversion in libraries could be remedied via the publications of the Chamber of Commerce or the American Legion. Once librarians were aware of the danger, their critics reasoned, they too would become active and vigilant in the battle against Communist propaganda in the library. In many cases, however, librarians' silence was not due to any lack of political awareness but was, rather, a strategic silence to shield their collections from procensorship vigilantes.

Strategies for effective resistance to the efforts of would-be censors took several forms, the first being the apparent nonresponse that is actually passive but purposeful resistance. The presentations of Horton and Kidder at the ALA's 1947 conference were delivered to an audience of several hundred youth services librarians. In addition, the texts of both presentations were published in the November 1947 issue of the *ALA Bulletin*, which would have been sent to that year's more than 17,000 ALA members.[18] These were the first ALA presentations and the first published coverage of Cold War censorship in the library press, and both focused on attacks targeting children's and young adult library materials. It is highly unlikely that youth services librarians were not cognizant of the potential threat to their own libraries. Even so, the ALA youth divisions' official publication, *Top of the News*, contained no coverage of this concern in 1947 or 1948. Some might interpret this absence to youth librarians' general lack of awareness of the world outside their libraries. A more likely explanation is that ALA youth services librarians had made a deliberate decision not to give official recognition to those who visited the library to "root out the Reds."

The selection and evaluation of reading materials for children and young adults were key professional responsibilities of school and public youth services librarians. Librarians took their role as gatekeeper seriously, and a book was scrutinized with great care before being added to the collection. However, once it was part of the collection, principled librarians could not simply reverse their considered positive evaluation of a book. Quiet resistance was librarians' first line of defense.

One children's department head who described an incident in her library during the 1950s exemplifies this. Representatives of a veterans group came to her brandishing the above-mentioned children's picture book, *Ilenka,* and demanding that it be taken off the shelves because the title character was "a happy little Russian girl, and no little Russian girls could possibly be happy." The librarian said she would reexamine the book in light of this complaint, and the group left, apparently assuming that she would acquiesce to their demand, and the book would be permanently removed. Instead, she took the book home, read it, and thought about it. The book went back on the shelf.[19]

Positive Resistance: Promoting Controversial Books

Throughout the early years of the Cold War, the activities of promoting international and intergroup understanding and of resisting censorship went hand in hand. Librarians and teachers represented by ALA and the National Education Association (NEA) had many common interests, and the ALA-NEA Joint Committee was formed in 1931 as a liaison committee "to facilitate and promote joint studies and other cooperative activities by the two associations."[20] As members of both the library and the education communities, school librarians were particularly visible in this work and provided most of the committee's activist energy. The Joint ALA-NEA Committee's most visible activity in the 1940s and 1950s was in compiling annotated lists of recommended books for classroom use that were published annually in the *NEA Journal.*[21]

At the February 1953 meeting of the Joint ALA-NEA Committee, members generated a list of eighteen future projects for the committee. Included on this list were "the identification of intellectual freedom as an issue of crucial concern to both associations" and an exploration of "the common interest of ALA and NEA in the effects of attacks on the public discussion of such issues as UNESCO."[22] As a result of this meeting, the committee began producing a monthly column for the *NEA Journal.*[23]

"The Bookshelf," a series of annotated bibliographies, debuted in the September 1953 issue with a list titled "Citizenship" that included several books on the UN and democracy: *A Fair World for All* by Dorothy Canfield Fisher; *Partners: The UN and Youth* by Eleanor

Roosevelt; and *Democracy*, coauthored by Willard Goslin.[24] At that time, all three authors and books had been placed on the "REaD READING" lists of proscribed books targeted by several superpatriot pressure groups.[25] The October 1953 list celebrated United Nations Month; the December 1953 list was in honor of International Brotherhood and Human Rights; the February 1954 list highlighted books on juvenile delinquency and included books on the causes of prejudice.[26] The September 1954 list on citizenship included books on the UN plus *American Government* by Frank Magruder, a text that was facing an energetic censorship campaign at that time.[27] The October 1954 list focused on international relations and included more books on the UN and its role in creating "citizens of the world."[28] The January 1955 list was titled "Human Freedom" and again featured Fisher's *A Fair World for All*, which had recently been removed as recommended reading from the *Girl Scout Manual*, and Henry Steele Commager's *Freedom, Loyalty, Dissent*, a critical look at the erosion of First Amendment rights.[29] The February 1955 issue's list, "Brotherhood," included books on the history of school segregation and racial prejudice "appropriate for use in coordination with Brotherhood Week."[30] The April 1955 issue reprinted ALA's 1954 list of Notable Books, which included books by Lillian Smith, Norman Thomas, and Elmer Davis, all authors then included on lists of subversives.[31] Thus, in 1953, 1954, and 1955–peak years of the McCarthy era–the Joint Committee's members were both promoting intergroup cooperation and international understanding and defying censorship through their repeated recommendations of precisely the authors and titles then under attack by Red-hunting pressure groups. This work exemplifies the strategy of positive resistance to censorship favored by ALA youth services divisions.

Active Resistance: A Direct Response to a Direct Challenge

There were, however, times when a direct challenge rated a direct–and firm–response from ALA youth services librarians. An illustrative example of active resistance as a mode of dealing with challenges to books in children's library collections may be seen in the handling of a complaint against the 1952 Caldecott Medal winner, *Finders Keepers*, by William Lipkind and Nicolas Mordvinoff.[32] This picture book is a humorous story of two dogs that quarrel over the ownership of a bone but who, when threatened by a larger dog, join forces to keep and share the bone between them. The book's illustrations have an abstract, modern look, the figures are exaggerated and representative rather than realistic, and the palette is comprised entirely of red, yellow, black, and white.

Figure 1. Spotted dog from Finders Keepers *by William Lipkind, illustrated by Nicolas Mordvinoff (Harcourt Brace, 1951). Complainants charged that the large dog represented the United Nations, in part because they believed its spots resembled the outlines of "the U.S., Great Britain, Germany, Formosa, and Japan." Illustrations adapted from* Finders Keepers, *copyright 1951 by William Lipkind and Nicolas Mordvinoff and renewed 1979 by Maria Lipkind and Barbara Mordvinoff, reprinted by permission of Harcourt, Inc.*

On 7 March 1952 Elizabeth Gross, Newbery-Caldecott Committee chair, announced the names of that year's Newbery and Caldecott Medalists and Honor Books (runners-up). The Caldecott Medal was awarded to a team of comparative newcomers to the children's picture book world, author William Lipkind and illustrator Nicolas Mordvinoff, for their artistically innovative picture book, *Finders Keepers*.[33] Two weeks later, Mildred Cotton and Jean Arnold, public librarians in the small town of Goshen, Indiana, wrote a letter to Gross expressing their "deep disappointment that such an inferior book" had been chosen for the

Caldecott Medal. Their criticisms were leveled at what they perceived to be the book's potentially subversive content. According to Cotton and Arnold, the entire story was an allegorical account of the Korean War, with the two smaller dogs representing North and South Korea and the larger dog representing the UN. As evidence for this interpretation, they cited the book's red and yellow colors ("the exact shades used in the Russian flag"), several pages containing a hammer and sickle motif ("a curved line bisected by a second line"), maplike shapes in the depictions of the bone (Korea) and the large dog's spots ("the U.S., Great Britain, Germany, Formosa, and Japan"), and a cartoon face on the back cover that they believed bore a strong resemblance to the face of President Harry Truman. Thus, the book was clearly a subversive text aimed at urging North and South Koreans to "unite and drive the United Nations out of Korea." They ended the letter by stating that they thought the pictures "wildly grotesque," the story not "uplifting," and the whole book "entirely amoral."[34]

Elizabeth Gross sent a prompt reply to their letter. She began by thanking them for letting her know their opinion of *Finders Keepers*. "It [their opinion] is a minority one, but we are fortunate indeed in that we live in a country where such opinions and accusations as you have stated may be freely expressed." She acknowledged that the illustrator, Nicolas Mordvinoff, was Russian by birth, but his family had fled Russia during the Revolution, and she thought it unlikely that he would create a book for the purpose of promoting the current Russian government. Her harshest words were reserved for the practice of perceiving subversive messages where none existed:

> It is possible, of course, to read any meaning that we wish into a story or drawing. Your remarks, however, concern me[,] for nothing will help to advance the cause of Russian propaganda more than to insert implications of Communism, even unto its symbols and insidiousness in Korea, into a story and illustrations where none were intended by the author and the artist. To imply that the face on the back of the cover could be even a cartoon of President Truman is, I think, an insult to the President of the United States.

Gross ended her letter by assuring Cotton and Arnold that hundreds of people ("librarians, educators and artists, for whose intelligence, integrity and patriotism I have the highest respect") had examined the book, and none had found it subversive. The book was, finally, a picture book illustrated in a modern style whose moral, if anything, was one of "cooperation and respect for the rights of others."[35]

125

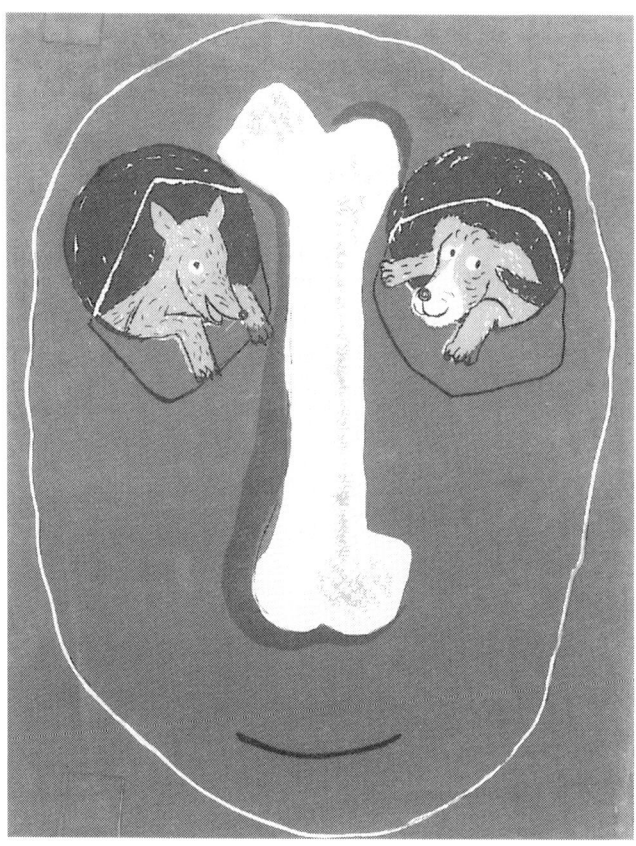

Figure 2. Cartoon face, back cover of Finders Keepers *by William Lipkind, illustrated by Nicolas Mordvinoff (Harcourt Brace, 1951). Newbery-Caldecott committee chair Elizabeth Gross wrote, "To imply that the face on the back of the cover could be even a cartoon of President Truman is, I think, an insult to the President of the United States."*

Although the author/illustrator team of William Lipkind and Nicolas Mordvinoff were relative newcomers to children's book publishing, they had received notice (and gained notoriety) the previous year with their first collaboration, *The Two Reds*, a picture book about a friendship between a red-headed boy and a red-furred cat that was named a 1951 Caldecott Honor Book.[36] *The Two Reds* was published in the fall of 1950, a time when McCarthy's Red-hunting campaign was becoming increasingly active and publicized. The book was considered daring both for its modern artwork and for its teasingly "subversive" title. In fact, the New York City toy store F. A. O. Schwartz canceled a planned window display of the book precisely because the potentially provocative title (plus the illustrator's Russian name) might lead some to view the display as a pro-Communist statement.[37] As Fritz Eichenberg, a popular children's book artist of the time, said of the book, "It takes great courage, for reasons too numerous and obvious to mention, to name a children's book *The Two Reds*."[38]

There are several interesting points in the correspondence between the Goshen librarians and Elizabeth Gross regarding *Finders Keepers*. First, there is the language and tone of their letter of complaint, which was similar to the insistent, hair-splitting argumentation and indignant tone of many other complaints lodged by pressure groups such as the American Legion against a wide variety of individuals and groups suspected of subversion during the McCarthy era. Mildred Cotton and Jean Arnold wrote from a community not far from Indianapolis, home of the American Legion's national headquarters. It is possible they were members of an American Legion Auxiliary themselves and/or were inspired by patriotic organizations' publications, such as the American Legion's Firing Line, which produced a continual stream of accusations of subversion targeting a wide range of people, organizations, and publications expressed in a rhetorical style similar to that of Cotton and Arnold's letter. It is equally likely that their interpretation of *Finders Keepers* was independent of any specific outside source but simply reflected the assumptions and literary/artistic interpretations of ordinary McCarthy era citizens who believed that covert Red propaganda in children's books was a real danger to the country.

Elizabeth Gross countered their complaints in the thoughtful, firm, and ladylike manner typical of the women of ALA's youth services divisions, a manner that could combine intelligence, graciousness, and reproof in a single sentence. She answered their letter promptly and began by thanking them for sharing their thoughts with her. She followed this by reminding them that they were privileged to live in a country where such minority viewpoints could be expressed—a not-so-subtle rebuke to would-be censors. In a manner that contrived to be both direct and indirect, she granted that any meaning might be gleaned from any text or picture, depending upon the individual reader, but followed this with words that resisted and defused their attack by stating that the act of finding hidden subversive messages where none exist was in itself subversive. It was also a social error, for in the positive etiquette of ladies and ALA youth services librarians, one made the public assumption that one's friends had honorable intentions, and children's authors and illustrators, especially those receiving the Newbery and Caldecott Medals, were most assuredly the friends and equals of the children's librarians who bestowed these honors. Gross maintained her semihostess stance in the following paragraph as she introduced and explained Mordvinoff's pre-Revolution Russian parentage to Cotton and Arnold, a point the letter-writers had not raised but upon which she was eager to educate them. Gross called next upon their common professional ties by evoking the judgment of the many librarians, educators, and artists who endorsed the book and closed her letter and lesson by reinterpreting the book and suggesting an alternate "moral" of cooperation and respect. It is impossible to know what the effect of Gross's letter was, though it appears that Cotton and Arthur may have been disturbed by it—both were ALA members when they wrote in 1952, and both dropped their memberships the following year. It must be noted, however, that both appear to have returned to the professional fold by rejoining ALA in 1954 and maintaining their ALA membership in the years that followed.[39]

Gross wrote as a representative of the Newbery-Caldecott committee, whose choices represented the criteria and judgment set by the ALA youth services division. Potential for controversy did not deter her committee from choosing the next book from a previously controversial author/illustrator team. As the chief arbiters of quality in children's books, ALA youth services librarians were a very critical audience, but once a book had been approved by them (as demonstrated by the Newbery or Caldecott Medal, placement on a list of ALA notable books, or favorable reviews in professional journals), that book would be defended, usually in a manner that defused debate through reasonable but firm resistance. More often, however, no active defense would be needed, because an ALA award or honor was generally sufficient testimonial to a book's worthiness to immunize it against any criticism, however serious. Once a text made it past the gatekeepers of children's collections, its future availability in American libraries was assured.

The traditional stance of children's librarians was strong advocacy on behalf of children's books that promoted intergroup cooperation and international understanding. With the onset of the McCarthy era, however, books with an intergroup and international focus became politically suspect, and librarians found themselves confronting both unspoken and overt "blacklists" of so-called subversive titles and authors.[40] The ALA youth services leaders' rhetoric and strategies of resistance—passive, positive, and active—effectively countered pressure group censorship and maintained their professional jurisdiction over the selection and evaluation of books for young readers. Youth services librarians' work in promoting international and intergroup understanding and in resisting censorship were in fact complementary professional responsibilities. As Bertha Mahoney Miller, founder and first editor of the *Horn Book*, noted in her January 1946 article, "Peacetime Resistance":

We think of the Resistance as being a part of war and invasion, but actually it is the core of everyday life. Every life is effective or ineffectual according to the strength of its Resistance to evil, its will to goodness. "For each one of us to have in his heart an impregnable fortress—that is the way to salvation." So Paul Hazard wrote with the enemy in control of his country. In its most personal sense, Resistance means refusal to surrender to our own weaknesses. In a wider sense, it means thinking things through and then expressing ourselves vigorously and responsibly.

In times like these, Resistance means remembering every day the widespread suffering of innocent men, women, and children, near and far, and helping now. It means bearing in daily remembrance all those who have recently laid down their lives in hope. It means a new sense of world brotherhood—and the will to express it.[41]

Notes

1. For a fuller history, see Harriet G. Long, *Public Library Service to Children: Foundation and Development* (Metuchen, N.J.: Scarecrow Press, 1969); Fannette Thomas, "The Genesis of Children's Services in the American Public Library, 1875–1906" (Ph.D. diss., University of Wisconsin-Madison, 1982); Sybille Anna Jagusch, "First among Equals: Caroline M. Hewins and Anne C. Moore: Foundations of Library Work with Children" (Ph.D. diss., University of Maryland, 1990).

2. For coverage of other female-intensive "social housekeeping" professions with Progressive era origins, see Walter I. Trattner, *Crusade for the Children: A History of the National Child Labor Committee and Child Labor Reform in America* (Chicago: Quadrangle Books, 1970); Laurily Keir Epstein, ed., *Women in the Professions* (Lexington, Mass.: Lexington Books, 1975); Dominick Cavallo, *Muscles and Morals: Organized Playgrounds and Urban Reform, 1880–1920* (Philadelphia: University of Pennsylvania Press, 1981); Joyce Antler, *The Educated Woman and Professionalization: Struggle for a New Feminine Identity, 1890–1920* (New York: Garland, 1987); Robyn Muncy, *Creating a Female Dominion in American Reform, 1890–1935* (New York: Oxford University Press, 1991); Murray Levine and Adeline Levine, *Helping Children: A Social History* (New York: Oxford University Press, 1992); Molly Ladd-Taylor, *Mother-Work: Women, Child Welfare, and the State, 1890–1930* (Urbana: University of Illinois Press, 1994).

3. Jean Thomson, "UNESCO Month," *Top of the News* 3 (October 1946): 4.

4. "United Nations Week, September 3–9, 1946," *ALA Bulletin* 40 (July 1946): 247; Luther Evans, "Keynote Address," *ALA Bulletin* 40 (July 1946): 248.

5. "ALA Proceedings, Annual Conference, Buffalo, NY, June 16–22, 1946," *ALA Bulletin* 40 (September 1946): 48.

6. Lois Lenski, *Strawberry Girl* (New York: Lippincott, 1945).

7. Florence Crannell Means, *The Moved-Outers* (Boston: Houghton Mifflin, 1945).

8. Lee Kingman, *Ilenka* (Boston: Houghton Mifflin, 1945); Becky Reyher, *My Mother Is the Most Beautiful Woman in the World*, illustrated by Ruth Gannett (New York: Lothrop, 1945); "*Horn Book* Honor List," *Horn Book* 22 (July–August 1946): 256–59.

9. Peter Irons, "American Business and the Origins of McCarthyism: The Cold War Crusade of the United States Chamber of Commerce," in Robert Griffith and Athan Theoharis, eds., *The Specter: Original Essays on the Cold War and the Origins of McCarthyism* (New York: New Viewpoints, 1974), 78.

10. U.S. Chamber of Commerce, *Communist Infiltration in the United States: Its Nature and How to Combat It* (Washington, D.C.: U.S. Chamber of Commerce, 1946); Donald F. Crosby, S.J., "The Politics of Religion: American Catholics and the Anti-Communist Impulse," in Griffith and Theoharis, eds., *The Specter*, 18–39.

11. Louise Bilebof Ketz and Joseph G. E. Hopkins, eds., *Dictionary of American History*, rev. ed. (New York: Charles Scribner's Sons, 1976), 7:121; David Caute, *The Great Fear: The Anti-Communist Purge under Truman and Eisenhower* (New York: Simon and Schuster, 1978), 268–72.

12. U.S. Chamber of Commerce, *A Program for Community Anti-Communist Action* (Washington, D.C.: U.S. Chamber of Commerce, 1948), 25.

13. Ibid., 26–27.

14. Robert Iverson, *The Communists and the Schools* (New York: Harcourt Brace, 1959), 175.

15. Kimball Wiles, "Building America: A Case in Point," *Educational Leadership* 19 (November 1948): 108–14.

16. Marion Horton, "Invitation to Reading," *ALA Bulletin* 41 (November 1947): 436–37.

17. Eleanor Kidder, "Reading Guidance for Young People," *ALA Bulletin* 41 (November 1947): 443.

18. *ALA Handbook of Organization 1999–2000* (Chicago: ALA, 1999), 149.

19. Kay Meadows (pseud.), telephone interview, 2 April 1992.

20. Patricia Pond, "A.A.S.L.: Origins and Development of a National Professional Association for School Librarians, 1896–1951" (Ph.D. diss., University of Chicago, 1982), 375–85; Joint ALA-NEA Committee, "Report: 1931–32," *ALA Bulletin* 26 (April 1932): 278.

21. Joint ALA-NEA Committee, "Report: 1941–42," *ALA Bulletin* 36 (October 1942): 680–83.

22. Joint ALA-NEA Committee, "Summary of Report," in *NEA Proceedings* (Washington, D.C.: NEA, 1953), 305–6.

23. Ibid.

24. "The Bookshelf," *NEA Journal* 42 (September 1953): 361.

25. For example, Mrs. Myrtle G. Hance, "REaD-READING: A Report on Our San Antonio Public Libraries, Communist Front Authors and Their Books Therein" (San Antonio, Tex., 1952).

26. "The Bookshelf," *NEA Journal* 42 (October 1953): 456; "The Bookshelf," *NEA Journal* 42 (December 1953): 582; "The Bookshelf," *NEA Journal* 43 (February 1954): 120–23.

27. "The Bookshelf," *NEA Journal* 43 (September 1954): 382.

28. "The Bookshelf," *NEA Journal* 43 (October 1954): 462.

29. "The Bookshelf," *NEA Journal* 44 (January 1955): 57.

30. "The Bookshelf," *NEA Journal* 44 (February 1955): 108.

31. "The Bookshelf," *NEA Journal* 44 (April 1955): 242.

32. William Lipkind, *Finders Keepers*, illustrated by Nicolas Mordvinoff (New York: Harcourt Brace, 1951); *NEA Journal* 44 (April 1955): 242.
33. "Caldecott Award, 1951," *Top of the News* 8 (March 1952): 17.
34. Mildred Cotton and Jean E. Arnold, letter to Elizabeth Gross, 22 March 1952, Series 10, box 1, Bixler Papers, Antioch College Archives.
35. Elizabeth Gross, letter to Mildred Cotton and Jean E. Arnold, 31 March 1952, Series 10, box 1, Bixler Papers, Antioch College Archives.
36. William Lipkind, *The Two Reds*, illustrated by Nicolas Mordvinoff (New York: Harcourt Brace, 1950).
37. Betsy Hearne, "Margaret K. McElderry and the Professional Matriarchy of Children's Books," *Library Trends* 44 (Spring 1996): 757.
38. Fritz Eichenberg, "Artist's Choice: *The Two Reds*," *Horn Book* 27 (July–August 1951): 239–40.
39. *ALA Directory, 1951–1955* (New York: R. R. Bowker, 1951–55).
40. For further information on censorship campaigns targeting political "subversion" in library materials, see Caute, *The Great Fear*, 454–55; Anne Lyon Haight and Chandler B. Grannis, *Banned Books: 387 B.C. to 1978 A.D.*, 4th ed. (New York: R. R. Bowker, 1978), 109–18; Marjorie Fiske, *Book Selection and Censorship: A Study of School and Public Libraries in California* (Berkeley: University of California Press, 1959), 45–63; for an actual "blacklist," see Hance, *REaD-READING*.
41. Bertha Mahoney Miller, "Peacetime Resistance," *Horn Book* 22 (January–February 1946): 9.

Le Comité de Défense de la Littérature et de la Presse pour la Jeunesse: The Communists and the Press for Children during the Cold War

Thierry Crépin

French children's periodicals underwent some significant changes between the years 1933 and 1954. French publishing houses and press agencies came under attack for being unduly influenced by and saturated with subversive American cartoons and comics. Numerous French comic strips created and endorsed by different morality leagues and Communist political groups appeared. The new French comic strips during this period were modeled after their more popular American counterparts; however, they were drawn by French authors and displayed Communist ideals. The strips utilized the brightly colored techniques of the American strips, trying to capture the imagination and attention of the children that read them. These French-born strips were designed to combat the widespread appeal of the American strips. The French comic strips and comic books were used as tools for the supposed intellectual and political education of the youths they targeted. American comic strips during this period were campaigned against, being painted as highly corruptive, perverse publications that assaulted the morality of the youth of France. Repeated attempts to get legislation passed that would enforce the newly created offense of "youth demoralization via the press" were made but were never entirely successful. The result was that the influence of American comic strips was never completely replaced and still had a devoted following among French youth during this time period.

Most historians of the comics held the Communist party responsible for the adoption of the law passed on 16 July 1949 on publications for youth. This law established some control over the press for children, which published most of the comic strips at the time, and established a new offense: the demoralization of youth via the press. The Communists had started producing and criticizing this media at the beginning of the 1930s. This interest grew sharply after the Liberation due to the educational movements of the Communist activists, who were at the forefront of the movement against foreign comic strips, the origin of the Act of July 1949. Yet the Communist representatives did not approve of its final version and voted against it.

In the context of the beginning of the Cold War, the Communists lost control of the process of regulation of the press for children. As a result, they set up an organization aimed at purifying (effectively, from their viewpoint) the press for children: le Comité de Défense de la Littérature et de la Presse pour la Jeunesse (Committee of Defense of Youth Literature and Press).

From 1933 to 1949, the Communists tried to launch a progressive press for children at a time when this press was being influenced by American comic strips. In spite of an early denunciation of the hegemony of these new pictures, they failed to get measures that would have banned them when the July 1949 law was voted. And though le Comité de Défense de la Littérature et de la Presse pour la Jeunesse launched a vigorous campaign at the beginning, its action petered out in 1952 after three years of battle only, and the assessment of the committee's action was quite mixed.

On the eve of the Second World War, the French press for children underwent a profound mutation brought about by the launch of *Le Journal de Mickey* on 19 October 1934 by the director of the press agency Opera Mundi, Paul Winkler, with the backing of Hachette. So far, publishing firms whose success had stemmed from the methods dating back to the turn of the century had dominated the market. They published small, poorly colored comics with stories illustrated by pictures. *Le Journal de Mickey* revolutionized all this with its large size and the bright colors of comic strips coming from the United States: *Mickey, The Katzenjammer Kids, Jungle Jim, Little Annie Rooney,* and others. Very popular with young people, the magazine quickly reached a circulation of 350,000 issues a week, something that had never been achieved before by a comic strip. This success encouraged other publishing firm managers to copy Paul Winkler: Italians such as Ettore Carozzo's Librairie Moderne and Cino Del Duca's Editions Mondiales; French people keen on American culture such as the Dupuy family and their group, Excelsior Publications; and even the very moderate Catholic Editions du Petit Echo de la Mode. The Société Parisienne d'Editions (SPE), which had dominated the press for children until 1934, had understood the lesson and replaced its old comics with new, trendy publications. In 1938 eleven newspapers, which made up almost half the press for children, published American as well as Italian, English, and Yugoslavian comic strips that engrossed the young readers' attention. *Mandrake, Flash Gordon,* and *King of the Royal Mounted* appealed to them more than *Les Pieds nickelés* and *Bibi Fricotin.* However, dynamic publishers managed to resist this momentum and assert their originality, in particular, militant editors such as the priests of the Union des Oeuvres with *Cœurs vaillants,* which had been capitalizing on the publication of *Les Aventures de Tintin et Milou* since 1930. But the Communist comic strips, as well as almost all the others, were hit by the groundswell coming from America. The magazine *Mon camarade* was created in July 1933 by the French Communist party and was edited by Georges Sadoul. He inaugurated a style of great austerity and extreme graphic poverty and set himself the task of raising children's political awareness. But in December 1936 the magazine became like all the others, with bright colors. Apart from its small size, it became as attractive as *Journal de Mickey.* Georges Sadoul thus tried to defeat the commercial press on its own ground. Nevertheless, there remained a major difference: all the pictures were drawn by French authors and promoted the Communist ideal, even if they imitated the American model.

This groundswell was stopped by the war. The last American comic strips were published at the beginning of the summer of 1942 in the comic magazines published in the unoccupied part of France. As early as the autumn of 1940, the editors had started replacing them with serials drawn by young French cartoonists. Most of them took up the style of American comic strips, as described by Raymond Poivet:

> Confrontés à la fois à un problème imprévu et urgent, la seule solution possible qui s'offrit à nous fut de nous inspirer, voire de copier, hélas!, les excellentes séries américaines dont nous pouvions encore disposer.
>
> Moi-même et ceux de mes confrères qui ont fait leurs débuts sous cette contrainte admirative en avons gardé, et en garderons les stigmates jusqu'à la fin de notre carrière.[1]
>
> [As we were faced by a problem both urgent and unforeseen, our only solution was to draw our inspiration from, even unfortunately plagiarize, the excellent American strips that were still available.
>
> I and some colleagues of mine who started out under the constraint of this admiration for American models have kept and will always keep stigmata of this passion until the end of our careers.]

The collaborationists, who launched *Le Téméraire* in January 1943, a comic strip relaying Nazi propaganda, were well aware of this influence. The format of the new magazine was inspired by that of *Robinson,* a weekly created by Paul Winkler in 1936, and its main comic strips, *Vers des mondes inconnus* and *Marc le Téméraire,* were copies of the adventures of *Flash Gordon* and *Secret Agent X-9.*

At the Liberation, new authorities coming from the ranks of the Resistance banned all the comic strips published during the German occupation. The minister of information, facing a shortage of paper, did not allow the publication of the press for children before the spring of 1946. As early as November 1945, he set up a committee that examined the applications for the right to publish comic strips for children. Bent on renewing the press for children, the committee ruled out systematically the editors willing to publish American comic magazines, which were thought to be not educational enough.[2] Due to this censorship, it was only later that Paul Winkler, Cino Del Duca, and Ettore Carozzo came back on the market of the press for children and with far less success than before the war, except for *Tarzan*, which dominated the market with a circulation of over 200,000 copies. Their collections of complete stories glorifying American heroes came up against fierce competition from the comic strips launched by small French editors whose cartoonists plagiarized American comic strips shamelessly. *Tarzan* remained one of the few American heroes that fascinated youth as much as before the war. Children preferred truly French characters from the Resistance, such as those created by Marijac in *Coq Hardi* or by the authors of *Vaillant*, another new comic strip created at the Liberation by Communist militants from a Resistance organization: the Front Patriotique de la Jeunesse. In June 1945 this comic appeared after an underground one: *Le Jeune Patriote*. In this way, its publishers managed to bypass the law of the minister of information, who had suspended the publication of comics.

In April 1945 those militants joined an organization ruled by the Communist party: the Union de la Jeunesse Républicaine de France (UJRF). In July this organization founded the Union des Vaillants et Vaillantes, a nonreligious children's movement. One of its leaders, Madeleine Bellet, soon took over the editorship of the comic. She was assisted by a small young team headed by René Moreu, the editor. Roger Lécureux, the editor's secretary, who used to read Paul Winkler's comics as a child, largely helped to create a format inspired by *Robinson*. Comic strips gradually structured comics. Some series were undoubtedly influenced by American models. *Les Pionniers de l'espérance* reminded one of *Flash Gordon, Lynx Blanc, Jungle Jim,* or *Yves le loup, Prince Vaillant* while delivering the special message of comics. The reconstruction and renewal of the country, the resistance to tyrants, science and progress or friendship, and an admiration for the U.S.S.R. and popular democracies are the main preoccupations of *Vaillant*'s cartoonists and writers. However, after taking advantage of *Vaillant*'s privileged position to become largely successful until the spring of 1947, the cartoon strips that were then published by the Vaillant editions saw their readership decrease. This situation caused great concern among the leading team, all the more so as a feminine version of the comic book, *Vaillante,* had been a failure. The Communists attributed their failure in part to the disloyal competition of newspapers that published American comic strips.[3]

American comics had been the target of educators and censors of all kinds: Catholics, nonreligious activists, and Communists. As early as 1938, Georges Sadoul, the editor of *Mon Camarade,* had written a synthesis of his ideas on this matter in a brochure entitled *What Your Children Read.*[4] In this text he denounced the capitalist methods of press agencies that published foreign comic strips. He also denounced the ideological indoctrination of young readers by a fascist propaganda and the incitement to crime and debauchery by indecent and ugly pictures. Only on this particular point did he agree with the other educators. However, his discourse never lapsed into an anti-American one, unlike that of Father Bethléem, who was a renowned leader of Catholic publications before the war. Moreover, Sadoul wanted the public authorities to take steps to protect French cartoonists from foreign competition. These themes continued to inspire the Communist rhetoric on the children's press after the war despite a marked decrease in the number of comic books publishing foreign comic strips. However, the start of the Cold War caused a notable change: from then on American comic strips were accused only of perverting French youth and of ruining French cartoonists and editors. Danger came from America and America only! In *l'Humanité* in October 1947 the caption of a photograph showing a boy reading a comic book dramatized this situation while calling for vigorous reaction: "Ce petit garçon sera-t-il la proie du journalisme yankee, assassin des esprits juvéniles?" [Will this youth be the prey of Yankee journalism, the murderer of young minds?][5] Paul Winkler, the American director of *Opera Mundi* who represented William Randolph Hearst's syndicate in Europe, was violently taken to task and slandered as he was accused of being in France as an American agent. Cino Del Duca, who was Italian, was attacked by the Communist press, which reproached him with being a fascist in the past, an assertion that had been totally made up by Sadoul before the war. In spite of their systematic denials in the columns of the Editions Mondiales' editor, Communist journalists regularly echoed these libels.[6]

In spite of repeated, early calls from cartoonists and morality leagues, the governments of the Popular Front and of Vichy never legislated on the press for children. At the Liberation, the minister for national education worked on a draft paper inspired from a bill that had been put forward in October 1940 by the moral action trust (Cartel d'Action Morale). But no sooner was it written than it was forgotten. Two years later, Pierre Bourdan, the minister for youth and arts, revived the project. The ministers who dealt with the press for children, the Fédération Nationale de la Presse Française, the Union Nationales des Associations Familiales, and the Union Patriotique des Organisations de Jeunesse (UPOJ), were invited to take part in a committee in charge of drafting a bill. Communist Madeleine Bellet sat on this committee as a representative of the UPOJ.[7] Exasperated by the slow work of this committee, the Communist group at the National Assembly broke the fragile common front of educators that had prevailed since the Liberation. On 20 May 1947 they tabled two bills about the press for children. Bill no. 1374 was largely inspired by Pierre Bourdan's work, which advocated a moral reconstruction of the country. This was dear to the men and women from the Resistance; it also intensified the repression of unsound comic books, which were supposed to glorify debauchery and crime. Bill no. 1375 aimed at protecting French editors and cartoonists from the spread of foreign comic strips by radical means: the limitation of foreign comic strips to 25 percent of the total space per comic, taxation of comic plates, setting of a minimum price per comic plate, and the creation of a special stamp for all French comics.[8] Moralism, patriotism, and protectionism dominated these bills, but they were not discussed, and Pierre Bourdan's bill did not even reach the National Assembly.

Perhaps the press for children would have been forgotten but for a press campaign fostered by youth movements, family associations, and morality leagues that kept the matter in the news. A decisive step was taken in January 1948 when Vincent Auriol, the president of the Republic, asked the Conseil Supérieur de la Magistrature to tackle the problem of juvenile delinquency, whose increase was thought to be partly due to the evil influence of bad comics. André Marie, the minister of justice, announced to the Conseil de la République on 26 February 1948 the setting up of a new commission whose work was to be completed this time. No doubt the Communists first rejoiced when hearing this statement before becoming quickly disillusioned. If the various bills that had been drafted since the Liberation had all been influenced by the three-party system, it was no longer the case of the text, which was adopted on 2 July 1949 by representatives and enforced on 16 July.[9] The parliamentarian talks on the different articles were "un bel exemple de l'entrée en guerre froide des sociétés occidentales" [a superb example of how Western societies joined in the Cold War].[10] Powerless, the Communist representatives witnessed the making of a moralizing and repressive law that ruled out their educational and protectionist ideas. They even discovered that this law could backfire on their own comics due to the addition of the sin of lying, which, according to article 2, couldn't be shown in a favorable light. The Communists realized that the interpretation of the offense of youth demoralization could be turned against them. Having failed to ban the representation of public schools and family associations on the control committee that was established by the bill in order to supervise the press for children, the Communists became even more opposed to this bill. When article 12 on the setting up of quotas on foreign comic strips was dropped, the Communist representatives decided to vote against the law.

Even before the law was voted on, there was a counterattack from the Union des Femmes Françaises (UFF), an organization of former Résistance women formed in 1943 that was in the Communist sphere of influence. During the third national congress of the UFF in Marseilles in June 1949, Elsa Triolet urged the delegates to examine what their children read. It resulted in this new claim:

> Nous demandons que nos écrans soient épurés des films pernicieux de gangsters d'outre-Atlantique, et que nos librairies soient débarassées des publications immondes dont nous abreuve l'Amérique, et qui risquent de ternir la fraîcheur et la pureté de notre jeunesse.[11]
> [We demand that our screens be purified from pernicious American gangster films and our bookshops be rid of the infamous publications that America feeds us, because they are likely to blemish the freshness and purity of our youth.]

A few days later, on 8 July 1949, taking advantage of a conference about children's literature, the UFF founded a defense committee of youth literature and press. It also created two book prizes with quite big awards in order to reward books for young people and books of poems for children.[12] No sooner was the committee created than it appealed to people to improve youth literature and fight the corruption of the press for children. They immediately obtained seventy-four signatures from people who belonged to the Communist party or backed it, from Elsa Triolet to Louis Aragon as well as Pierre Seghers. But the signatures of people such as Jean-Marie Domenach, editor of the left-wing Catholic journal *Esprit*; Pierre Ménard, head of the information department at the Ligue Française de l'Enseignement and chief editor of his comic, *Francs-Jeux*; and Germaine Peyroles, leader of the Mouvement Républicain Populaire (MRP) showed that the UFF sought the largest support possible even outside the Communist circle.[13]

From the beginning the committee followed a strategy defined by Communist leaders and launched a vigorous information campaign before its action petered out. The first Congrès Mondial des Partisans de la Paix had taken place at the same time in Prague and in Paris in April 1949, less than one year after the creation of the peace movement at the initiative of the Kominform at the end of summer 1948. The Communist party had rapidly linked the objectives of its propaganda to those of the Kominform and of the peace movement.[14] As early as 1949, the rhetoric of the committee was marked by this influence. From then on, not only did it denounce the immorality and criminality of foreign comic strips but it also accused them of war-mongering. A representative for the Aisne Department, Paulette Charbonnel, who had spoken passionately at the House of Commons in order to condemn the law of July 1949 on behalf of the Communist group, explained the motivations that were supposed to guide the militants of the UFF in their new fight:

> Nos amies en ont assez de donner des héros pour la guerre et veulent donner des héros du travail, des héros pour la vie. C'est pour cela qu'elles vont de bon coeur créer nos Comités de défense de la littérature enfantine, car donner de bonnes et belles lectures à nos enfants, c'est aussi lutter pour la paix et pour la vie.
> Avant de lancer leurs bombes atomiques, les fauteurs de guerre sentent la nécessité de préparer les esprits pour un nouveau conflit. Avilir, corrompre notre jeunesse, la détourner du travail et de la bataille revendicative, c'est aussi une façon de recruter des mercenaires pour une guerre impérialiste.[15]
> [Our friends are fed up with giving birth to war heroes and want to give birth to heroes of labor, heroes of life. That is the reason why they will readily create our Defense Committee for Children's Literature, because giving good, wholesome reading material to our children also means fighting for peace and life.
> Before dropping nuclear bombs, warmongers feel the necessity of preparing minds for a new conflict. Debasing, corrupting our youth, diverting them from work and the struggle of collective protest are also the means to recruit mercenaries for an imperialist war.]

Due to this propaganda, the committee had difficulties in recruiting new members. A lot of parents and educators who shared the committee's aim for the children were probably put off by watchwords that were too clearly identified with the action of the Communist party. Communist papers such as *Les Lettres Françaises*, *Femmes Françaises*, *Bâtisseurs d'Avenir*, and *La Revue de la Presse Enfantine* backed the actions of the committee. Although some prominent people such as Laurent de Brunhoff joined the committee, it was quickly isolated. The second father of the famous elephant Babar even agreed to represent the committee at the Peoples' Congress for Peace in Vienna in December 1952.

At the beginning of the autumn of 1949, the committee started an itinerant exhibition in the Communist towns outside Paris in order to make people aware of the problems of the press for children. Starting in Montreuil in October, the exhibition then went to Aubervilliers, Saint-Denis, and Argenteuil. This kind of action was not original at all, and it had already been used the year before by the Direction de l'Education Populaire of the Ministry of National Education.[16] It was taken up by the Ligue Française de l'Enseignement and the Catholic youth movements. But unlike their predecessors, the militants of the committee not only praised the good comics, that is, the Communist ones, but they also promoted literature for young people with a view to promoting books. According to them, "dans le meilleur des cas, et alors même qu'elle n'est pas à proprement parler nocive, la presse enfantine n'est pas un aliment intellectuel suffisant. Tout au plus peut-elle apporter une distraction, mais elle ne saurait en aucun cas aucun cas remplacer le livre" [in the best case, whereas children's publications are not harmful, strictly speaking, they are not satisfactory intellectual fare. They may at best provide entertainment, but in no way can they possibly replace books].[17] The committee called for the creation of libraries for young people. In order to help librarians choose their books, they invented the Bibliothèques des Enfants et des Jeunes (BEJ, Libraries for Children and Young People). The BEJ were made up of four standard parcels containing seven, nineteen, thirty, and ninety books. A bigger parcel included the smaller one, so parcel B included the seven books of parcel A plus another twelve books. There was a great variety of books: "albums, contes, romans, nouvelles et documentaires destinés à instruire et à distraire les jeunes de quatre à dix-sept ans" [albums, tales, novels, and documentaries designed to educate and entertain youngsters from four to seventeen], as well as classics by Jules Verne, Mark Twain, Théophile Gautier, and renowned contemporary writers such as Georges Nigremont and Charles Vildrac.[18] The BEJ's main originality lay in the fact that it included Soviet books, but not too many, hardly 10 percent of the total.

At the same time, the committee endeavored to organize new types of exhibitions capable of appealing to a wide audience. Its greatest popular success was probably the organization of a yearly exhibition of books for sale, which took place four times from 1950 to 1953 just before Christmas in the sixth *arrondissement* of Paris. Organized by

Charles Vildrac, it went beyond a mere means for authors to advertise their books thanks to the active involvement of cabaret artists and cartoonists. But it also revealed the limits of the committee. This exhibition was marred by a hasty preparation conducted by volunteers. The members of the UFF and the Francs et Franches Camarades took an active part in its organization, but their isolation laid bare the reluctance of Communist activists to defend the children's press as well as children's literature. As to the most committed activists who would have agreed to sell the books, they were often unable to help people choose for want of knowledge about the books for sale.[19] But this event remained exceptional. Most of the time the committee activists delivered tracts and a leaflet entitled *Ne laissons pas corrompre notre jeunesse*. From 1952 the activity of the committee decreased because it was no longer supported by the Batailles du Livre, which had been stopped in the spring by the Communist party.[20] Moreover, the committee failed to become a mass organization. In March 1952 there were only a few hundred members.[21] Its leaders then tried to relaunch it by turning it into an independent association of the UFF named le Comité National de Défense de la Presse et de la Littérature pour la Jeunesse, with an honorary committee and a secretariat. It was chaired by Gustave Monod, an eminent person who was an honorary director of secondary education. It was still run by a Communist activist, Paulette Charbonnel. Its main activity was to organize seminars that were followed by the publication of a special issue of the journal *Enfance*, which dealt with the press for children, in November 1953. The movement then ceased to exist.[22]

The assessment of the committee is mixed. Its main purpose, the setting of quotas for foreign comic strips, was a failure. It was only later that the socialist representatives were convinced of the interest of the protectionist argument of the Communist representatives. Two days after the passing of the bill on 4 July they tabled a bill taking up the clauses imposing a minimum 75 percent of French drawings and texts in a comic. Although it was accepted by the Assembly on 22 December 1950, it was once again rejected by the Conseil de la République. This proposal was then forgotten and never discussed, and similar texts were tabled by the Communist party in the following years.[23] Paradoxically, it is within the control and supervising commission of the youth publications that had been set up by the law of July 1949 that the committee exerted its greatest influence. Yet it unrelentingly denounced its lack of efficiency. Two of its members sat on this commission: Madeleine Bellet, who was a delegate of the Communist youth movement, L'Union des Vaillants et des Vaillantes, and Raoul Dubois, the delegate of the nonreligious youth movement, the Francs et Franches Camarades. Within the commission they managed to create a common front of educators with the Catholic representatives. Communist publications were never censored, contrary to the fears the Communist representatives expressed in 1949. The commission issued barely two recommendations between 1950 and 1954.[24] And on the contrary, thanks to the alliance of educators, article 13 of the law was strictly enforced; the import of foreign comics for the young was submitted to the authorization of the information ministry after the commission had given its green light. Thus, three albums that were hostile to the Communist fighters in Asia could not be imported in France. The first one, *Bernard Chamblet en mission au pays jaune,* which described the war in Indochina, was drawn by Etienne le Rallic, who was a French patriot.[25] The other two books were about the adventures of Buck Danny by the Belgian authors Jean-Michel Charlier and Victor Hubinon: *Ciel de Corée* and *Avion sans pilote.* They related the fight of American pilots against the Communist Korean army.[26]

Conclusion

At the beginning of the thirties the Communists discovered the role played by the press for children in children's intellectual and political education. Their action in that field remained discreet until 1945. At that time they successfully launched *Vaillant,* an attractive comic. They also fought vigorously against the comics that published American comic strips, which were accused of corrupting and soiling the young by their immorality. Although the Communists played a major part in the preparation of the law on publications for the young, they lost hold of the project with the beginning of the Cold War. They then created le Comité de Défense de la Littérature et de la Presse pour la Jeunesse, whose action and rhetoric were strongly marked by the political and ideological struggle of the Communist party.

The committee's action should be assessed in a very qualified way. It failed to make people aware of the problem of the press for children. On the other hand, its leaders were more successful within the control and supervising committee thanks to their attitude, which was more practical than ideological. However, they did not manage to stop the American influence on the French children's press. In June 1952 they were powerless when Paul Winkler relaunched the *Journal de Mickey,* which was the symbol of the American youth culture. The comic outnumbered all its competitors as early as 1954 with a weekly circulation of 628,000, that is, four times as many as *Vaillant.*

Notes

1. Letter of 25 October 1987 by R. Poïvet to the author.
2. Archives Nationales (AN) F41 2047. Note of 1947: "La Presse enfantine depuis la Libération."
3. The creation of *Vaillant* has been studied at length, especially by Bruno Rossignol, "Du Jeune Patriote au journal le plus captivant: Vaillant (1945-1950)" (D.E.A. de l'Institut d'Etudes Politiques de Paris) supervised by Pascal Ory, 1982; and by Gil Plas, "Vaillant (1946-1950)," *Le Collectionneur de Bandes Dessinées* 52 (Winter 1986-87): 14-24.
4. G. Sadoul, *Ce que lisent vos enfants* (Paris: Bureau d'Edition Paris, 1938).
5. Armand Monjo, "L'Offensive du dollar contre les cerveaux d'enfants," *L'Humanité*, 25 October 1947: 4.
6. Archives de la Préfecture de Police (APP) 169.854/0.
7. Centre des Archives Contemporaines (CAC) 880437/7. Report of the committee's meeting of the UPOJ of March 1947.
8. Journal Officiel de la République Française (JO), documents parlementaires, 20 May 1947: 983-84.
9. JO, Lois et décrets, 19 July 1949: 7006-8.
10. Pascal Ory, "Mickey Go Home! La Désaméricanisation de la bande dessinée (1945-1950)," *Vingtième Siècle, Revue d'Histoire* 4 (October-December 1984): 80.
11. "Notre programme: Ensemble, sauvons la vie," *Femmes Françaises*, 25 June 1949: 11. Elsa Triolet was the wife of the famous Communist poet Louis Aragon.
12. Marianne Milhaud, "Pour une littérature saine, qui fasse de nos enfants des héros du travail et de la vie," *Femmes Françaises* 243, 16 July 1949: 3.
13. "Ne laissons pas corrompre notre jeunesse," Comité de Défense de la Presse et de la Littérature pour la Jeunesse, 1950, 2.
14. Lilly Marcou, *Le Kominform* (Paris: Presses de la Fondation Nationale des Sciences Politiques, 1977), 293.
15. P. Charbonnel, "Donner de bonnes et belles lectures à vos enfants, c'est aussi lutter pour la vie, pour la paix," *Femmes Françaises* 252, 17 September 1949: 6.
16. Marie-Claire Hermann, "L'Exposition des livres d'enfants voyage," *Les Lettres Françaises* 286, 17 November 1949: 3; Pierre Delatre, "L'Exposition de la presse enfantines est ouverte à Argenteuil," *Libération*, 30 November 1949: 3.
17. Louise Mamiac, "Ils demandent des livres," *Femmes Françaises* 246, 6 August 1949: 15.
18. Tract of the committee of 1951 kept in the Centre National de la Bande Dessinée et de l'Image in Angoulême.
19. Raoul Dubois, "Littérature buissonnière," unpublished manuscript, 251.
20. On this topic, see Marc Lazar, "Les Batailles du livre du P.C.F. (1950-1952)," *Vingtième Siècle, Revue d'Histoire* 10 (April-June 1986): 37-50.
21. Tract of the committee of March 1952 kept in the Centre National de la Bande Dessinée et de l'Image.
22. Ibid.
23. Ory, "Mickey Go Home!" 83.
24. CAC 900208, art. 2. Minutes of the fifth meeting of 29 June 1950 and minutes of the fifteenth meeting of 18 December 1952.
25. CAC 900208, art. 2. Minutes of the second meeting of 31 March 1950.
26. CAC 900208, art. 2. Minutes of the nineteenth meeting of 15 October 1953, of the twenty-third meeting of 24 June 1954, and of the twenty-fourth meeting of 28 October 1954.

Reading in the Context of Censorship in the Soviet Union

Valeria D. Stelmakh

This essay discusses the reading of literature in the environment of censorship preceding the disbandment of the U.S.S.R. The Soviet authority's mission was to forestall the collapse of the Communist regime by attempting to strengthen censorship and other repressive measures. The author considers censorship as a social system with powerful control over information and reading, restricting the public's access to the world's various cultures. Some specific features of the cultural situation under censorship are emphasized: the high prestige of literature, which was almost the only source of spiritual freedom; the creation of the black market for books as an alternative to the official book publishing and distribution system; the reproduction and dissemination of illegal literature and texts (*samizdat*). The author explains the role of the *spetskhran*—a closed special library collection of forbidden literature. The author states that because of censorship during this period and the constant struggle against it, there is a huge impediment to many areas of development caused by the energy spent by readers to overcome the prohibitions rather than create cultural treasures.

The period preceding the disintegration of the U.S.S.R. and the collapse of the Soviet regime (from the 1960s to the beginning of the 1980s) had a number of distinctive features that are important for the analysis of reading. Clear signs of decline characterized it. On the one hand, modernizing tendencies were gathering speed, accompanied by a change in the social structure—a sharp increase in the percentage of the population living in towns and a growth in the number of well-educated people—the cultural pressure from below that undermined the foundation of power and its ideology. The process of eroding the regime and discrediting Soviet norms and values was a distinctive feature of these years.

On the other hand, the regime's attempts to forestall the impending collapse and to stabilize the situation included strengthening censorship and other repressive measures. At this time, the society had been living under an almost complete blockade on information, combined with a sophisticated system of misinformation and total censorship. The censorship of the Soviet period as distinguished from, for example, that of czarist Russia had a number of specific features. First, it was not restrained by any provisions of law and hence was arbitrary and not accountable to anyone; second, it was carried out, for the most part, before publication; and lastly, it was performed in secret and anonymously.

By the beginning of Gorbachev's *Perestroika,* or economic restructuring, the range of the forbidden literature gradually grew wider and was eventually virtually all-embracing. The special restricted access collection, known as the *spetskhran,* had become an independent system within libraries to which were consigned not only publications openly hostile to the regime but also completely innocent works. Thus, by 1985 the *spetskhran* of the Lenin State Library of the U.S.S.R.–one of the largest in the country–contained more than 1 million items. About 30,000 to 35,000 items were added to its stock each year.

The problem of reading in such conditions is often understood as open or secret resistance–on the one hand, a controlling and punitive regime, on the other, a suppressed and downtrodden people. However, there was no uniformity in the attitudes of different social groups to life under censorship–open struggle, secret dissidence, open support and approval, trusting acceptance, and many other attitudes. Censorship was able to become an all-pervasive, total system, rather like a cancerous cell infecting the whole body, only because of the interaction between state bodies and the various social groups due to self-censorship within the society. People working with the written word–directors of publishing houses, editors, authors, librarians, and booksellers–narrowed still further the areas of openness. They interpreted any wish of the regime, official or unofficial, as an absolute prohibition. Regardless of the instructions from the chief organ of state censorship (Glavlit), the publishing houses published a number of books with their own marking: "Not for sale," "For in-house use," "On the right of manuscript," and so on, thus narrowing the sphere of their distribution.

The librarians who carried out checks and purges of library stocks often demonstrated even greater vigilance than required by the Glavlit orders. In the 1970s among the staff members of the service department of the Lenin State Library of the U.S.S.R. there were specially appointed persons–"politcontrollers"–who, apart from their regular professional functions, had to perform additional control over the literature lent from the general stocks (not from the restricted access collections), thus exercising censorship over percolation of the avant-garde aesthetics to the reader, the aesthetics that introduced new ways of thinking and a new outlook on life and social behavior.

The writers union and other creative unions such as the cultural groups acted as bearers of the recognized aspect of the socialist culture. To the outside world this appeared to be a conflict between literary groups and tendencies. Finally, the readers themselves would quite often suggest to the library's authorities that this or that publication should be transferred from the general stock to the *spetskhran* collection. One of such letters concerned, for example, the three-volume edition of *The History of the Communist Party of France*, published in Paris in 1964.

Thus, when analyzing the problem of reading in the context of censorship, one should not discuss the activity of a specific state body but rather the complex social mechanism that controls the very possibility of texts going into circulation. Control over readers is possible only where the state has a complete monopoly of book publishing and distribution. In the 1970s and 1980s such a system, typical of a totalitarian state, was finally in position, and state publishing comprised over 80 percent of all printed output. The essence of the state's book strategy consisted of forcing the public to read what was prescribed for it, not allowing people any space outside state control. The obligatory literary selection should be the only one accessible to the whole of the country's population. Here are several aspects of this policy:

1. A consistent reduction of the range of the published titles. In the mid-1980s, in spite of broadening readers' demands and new cultural contingents coming along, the number of the published titles was almost the same as in the 1960s: in 1985 it was only 100.6 percent of the 1970 figure and 104 percent of that for 1980.

2. An unrestrained growth in the print runs of the literature that was permitted and approved of by the state authorities. This was mostly mass ideological literature intended for the lesser educated and middle-brow groups. The total print run of the books and brochures in 1985 was 164.2 percent of the 1970 figure.

3. A consistent reduction in the production of journals and other serials, which are the most innovative sort of publication. In 1970 there were 5,968 titles, in 1985, 5,180.

4. A particularly harsh prepublication censorship of foreign literature, primarily in the humanities and socioeconomic disciplines. Books on politics, international relations, sociology, philosophy, cybernetics,

semiotics, linguistics, and so on were hardly ever published, and those that did enter the country were immediately sent to *spetskhran*. In the mid-1980s foreign publications made up 80 percent of the stocks of the *spetskhran* of the Lenin State Library of the U.S.S.R.

5. Extraction from the library collections and the book trade network of the published titles in accordance with Glavlit lists and directives.

There was discrimination against all groups of readers, but it was directed primarily at the best-educated part of the society: the literary, social, and scientific elite. It was this particular group that, despite its constant growth, was deprived of the possibility of publishing its work and having free access to information. The natural reaction of the reading public was the urge to escape the boundaries of what was permitted. A characteristic feature of this period was the development of "shadow," parallel forms of cultural life. One of these was the black market in books. In the 1970s and 1980s the black market was an active part of society. Buying books directly from other people was how 35 percent of Soviet adults acquired books for their own homes, and 68 percent of families living in major cities bought books only on the black market.

A special study of the range of books on the black market carried out by the Sector for the Sociology of Reading and Librarianship of the Russian State Library in 1988 showed that the titles on sale on the black market constituted 21 percent of the published lot. On the black market, the most expensive categories of books were: 1. Russian literature from the nineteenth and early twentieth centuries and Russian Soviet literature by authors such as Anna Akhmatova, Osip Mandel'shtam, Boris Pasternak, Mikhail Bulgakov, Igor' Severianin, Aleksei Remisov, Fedor Sologub, and others; 2. the best examples of twentieth-century foreign literature that had rarely been published in the U.S.S.R. such as Marcel Proust, Jorge Luis Borges, John Dos Passos, F. Scott Fitzgerald, and others; 3. *tamizdat*, or works by prohibited Russian and Soviet authors in editions published abroad such as Alexandr Solzhenitsyn, Boris Pasternak, Vyacheslav Ivanov, and others (those who traded in such books dealt with a very limited group of trusted people); 4. religious books such as the Bible, the Koran, and the Talmud as well as the works of Russian religious philosophers; 5. books on foreign philosophy, psychology, and ethics published within the U.S.S.R. in very small editions and books in limited editions marked "For academic libraries"; 6. books by Russian and foreign literary scholars, especially in structuralism and semiotics, such as Yuri Lotman, Mikhail Bakhtin, and Boris Eikhenbaum. Thus, the black market was directed toward readers' actual requirements, and it restored to society, albeit only partially, that which the system had taken away.

A unique phenomenon in scale and in its role in the society was *samizdat*. *Samizdat*, in this case, would be everything that was reproduced and distributed without the official permission of the authorities. This term appears regularly in works describing the social and cultural situation in the U.S.S.R. from the 1960s through the 1980s.

Samizdat appeared right after the October coup, when the revolutionary censorship had been introduced. Still, during the Stalin period *samizdat* as a serious segment of the unofficial culture did not exist. Those separate cases of reading the illegal texts were just a marginal phenomenon. This can be accounted for with a number of reasons. The process of stratification of the society and erosion of the regime from the 1930s to the 1950s had not yet acquired the evident and widespread character as in the subsequent decades. Moreover, as a result of the Second World War the society became more consolidated, and the authority of the state power was strengthened. Also, the repressive measures that were used for eradication of the slightest manifestation of dissidence maintained the atmosphere of fear in the country.

Samizdat of the 1960s through the 1980s was no longer just separate "subversive" books or literary schools in opposition but already a system of the creation and distribution of unofficial "information" uncontrolled by the state. The people involved in the distribution and reading of *samizdat* were no longer separate heroes or tiny separate groups but whole social strata in whose orientation the illegal literature became the antipode to the official ideology and culture. *Samizdat* was a form of opposition to the regime and an assertion of the right of the individual for "one's own" reading. Its distribution could not be stopped by any punitive sanctions of the authorities.

There are no statistical and sociological data on the reading of *samizdat*. Not only its collection but the mere stating of separate cases was impermissible from the point of researchers' ethics. That is why we can use only the experts' opinions, the recollections of contemporaries, and our own personal experience. When defining the boundaries of distribution and reading of *samizdat* its present researchers use, as a rule, such metaphors as "the entire country," "the whole people," and "the entire society." Nevertheless, *samizdat* was a characteristic of a special segment of the society, specifically, of the intelligentsia, by whom we mean not simply the well-educated part of the society but its comparatively small group—the social and cultural avant-garde who could find their own way to culture.

A. Suetnov, the researcher and bibliographer of *samizdat*, notes that the starting number of copies of an illegal book was about fifteen to twenty. The final number would not exceed two hundred; the monthly spontaneous run could be about 50,000. From this A. Suetnov considers that the one-time *samizdat* audience was about 200,000 readers. Still, in spite of its small number, this was the group of cultural leaders who opposed state power and its repressive machinery, thus preserving the cultural and moral potential of the society.

There was a marked change in the nature and composition of the documents distributed through *samizdat*. In the sixties and early seventies, *samizdat* was primarily literature, such as brilliant unpublished books (e.g., Pasternak's *Doctor Zhivago*, the novels of Solzhenitsyn, and Bunin's diary), the poetry of poets who had been prohibited, repressed, or never published (such as Osip Mandel'shtam, Anna Akhmatova, Nikolai Gumilev, Marina Tsvetaeva, and Iosif Brodskii). There were copies of Russian translations of Hemingway's *For Whom the Bell Tolls*, Orwell's *1984*, and Djilas's *New Class*. Expert assessment suggests that over three hundred works were in circulation in *samizdat* then. This was the initial phase of rethinking our past and appropriating the cultural heritage that had been hidden from society.

In the subsequent decade, it was primarily political *samizdat* that was produced and read. There were philosophical works, bulletins, and chronicles of the human rights movement, foreign émigré journals (e.g., *Kontinent*), and also literary works from the new wave of émigré writers such as Maksimov, Kopelev, Aksenov, and others. These changes in the repertory were evidence of a new phase in the development of society. The growth of independent public opinion and the formation of groups that began to oppose the regime actively brought it about. It was these groups that took on the production and distribution of *samizdat*. The emergence of these groups facilitated the self-realization of unofficial culture and its institutionalization. Its significant features included the creation of original texts, which had been rare in the *samizdat* of the 1960s; the appearance of homemade, uncensored political journalism, which testified to consolidation and simultaneously to clearer differentiation of *samizdat* readership; the widening range of documents and greater opportunities for their reproduction, especially setting up channels through which manuscripts could be sent to the West to be published and sent back to the U.S.S.R. (*tamizdat*); the setting up of stable avenues of distribution within the U.S.S.R.; improvements in technology for the reproduction of texts within the U.S.S.R., including the acquisition of printing capability and the beginning of the practice of reprinting texts for a fee.

As a result, *samizdat* was distributed far more widely. The pressure of the censor grew correspondingly, and repressive measures from the authorities and the KGB became tougher. But they were unable to terminate *samizdat*. This, by the mid-1980s the readership of *samizdat* was clearly differentiated. Its creators and the top layer of distributors merged with human rights activists and were engaged in open opposition to the regime. For the other groups, reading *samizdat* was a form of symbolic identification with the opposition. Such reading did not help well-educated readers to lift up their heads and start to take action. The intelligentsia took part in official Soviet life and publicly approved the actions of the authorities while making up for it by reading forbidden texts at home.

Nevertheless, in reading and thinking through "their own" literature the intelligentsia worked out alternative models of social behavior and culture. Reading illegal texts was a demarcation line dividing the intellectual avant-garde from the general reader. Beyond these islands of freedom was a different reality where another sort of literature ruled and where—as Orwell predicted—ignorance was strength.

In the mid-1980s, the general reading public comprised about 161.2 million people, about 40–50 million of whom could be called active readers, in the opinion of experts. This enormous audience of readers lacked the cultural depth required to find their own way in literature and had no access to the channels through which unofficial texts were distributed. The mass reader had to be content with the selection offered by the state publishers. As was shown above, this comprised only a limited range of books and a restricted choice of authors, the so-called books for the general public. For these readers, the censorship and the whole ideological apparatus constructed an artificial cultural universe, regulated, well-ordered, and confined.

Surveys of readers and the analysis of demands from mass library users that we carried out in the 1970s and 1980s show that fiction was the most popular. The most popular authors were modern Soviet writers. In the 1960s and 1970s, the range of authors read was reasonably broad. In the last decade of Soviet power, a small group of officially approved authors emerged, the so-called literary generals. These authors, who were published in massive editions every year, blocked readers' access to other literature.

However, because of the narrow range of the published titles, the general public was not satisfied. Only 40 percent of reader demand was satisfied. This group particularly felt keenly the book shortage in mass literature. This is not to say that mass culture did not exist in the U.S.S.R. It did, but in a specific variation with its own ideological features. Its goal was not entertainment and relaxation but brainwashing intended to inculcate Soviet ideology into the public's mind. It was heavily politicized, using ideological symbols—"us and them," "friends and enemies," "socialism and capitalism," and so on. It lauded the cult of work in the name of the state and derided rest and relaxation. In this sense Soviet literature did not fit the formula of mass culture and was simply bad literature, but it was issued in huge print-runs. A whole range of standard genres was absent from Soviet mass literature—women's fiction, melodrama, comics, and so on. There were severe limitations on detective stories, science fiction, and adventure stories. One could buy these books only on the black market, where they cost the equivalent of the average monthly wage.

It was not only "high" literature that was subject to censorship. Mass literature was dismissed as "false propaganda for a hostile ideology and the bourgeois way of life." Some elements of the unofficial culture created by the educated elite did filter down to the wider public, such as political jokes or tapes of the songs of Vysotskii and Okudzhava. But basically the behavior of the general reading public under censorship and ideological restriction was different from that of the avant-garde. These readers did not know and could not know what they were missing. The general reading public accepted and believed the official line on their superiority over the other countries and times, expressed in slogans such as "The Soviet people are the best-read people on earth" and "The U.S.S.R. is a great book power." In this sense, the Soviet reader constructed by the slogans was not merely a slogan but did exist—it came to coincide with readers' own assessment of themselves.

Conclusion

Right after the fall of the Soviet empire public opinion was manipulated, if not with the aim of justifying Soviet censorship, then at the very least in order to downplay its fatal role in society for more than seven decades. Thus numerous researchers suggest that the regulatory function of censorship had a positive result in encouraging the illegal distribution of texts on a large scale.

As soon as library special collections were opened, two ideas began to circulate in the library profession. One stressed the positive role of the closed collections in saving the nation's cultural heritage from destruction. The other argued that their existence did not entail any infringement of readers' rights, as anyone who really needed access could get it. Also, the claims are made that it was the constant struggle against the censor that helped our culture develop its unique traits (implication, our ability to read between the lines, etc.).

All these and similar arguments are myths created and circulated by those groups that were involved in the activities of the censorship and ideological authorities. In Soviet totalitarian society, censorship could not be anything but a mighty hindrance to social, cultural, and economic development. The battle against censorship was a great tragedy for our literature and its readers. The intellectual potential of the nation was diverted from its proper purpose into overcoming prohibitions rather than creating spiritual treasures. In this struggle talent degenerated, gifts were wasted, and projects turned to dust.

Symbolic Censorship and Control of Appropriations: The French Communist Party Facing "Heretical" Texts during the Cold War

Bernard Pudal

The author examines the methods used by the French Communist party (FCP) during the Cold War to control and neutralize the effects of anti-Communist or heretical texts as challenges to its ideology. The FCP was faced with a free publishing market and therefore followed a symbolic censorship action plan. This involved denouncing critical texts as enemy propaganda, either as forgeries or as part of an anti-Communist project, and discrediting their authors to avoid discussion of the arguments put forward. The climate of the Cold War with its bipolarization of ideology, perceived threat of a Third World War, idealization of the U.S.S.R. by Communists, and their world vision of history as a conspiracy against Communism contributed to successful implementation of the plan. The blurring of truth into opinion, the encouragement of Zhdanovjan campaigns denouncing other intellectuals, and the FCP's prohibition of critical confrontation encouraged intellectuals within the party to suspend their professional and scholarly critical mindset and accept plausibility over truth. Internal censorship was practiced through controlled reading programs that limited the exposure of other party members to heretical writings.

The situation in France was different from that of those countries where Communist parties controlled the state, where publishing and distribution were completely under their control, and censorship, therefore, was totally efficient. During the Cold War, the French Communist party (FCP) had to deal with a "free" publishing market and a circulation of "heretical" texts (from its point of view). A lot of these texts, which were considered at the time by the FCP as forgeries made by specialized "agencies" or as stories inspired by anti-Communism, are nowadays recognized by the scientific community as either studies or valid testimonies.[1] But it is important to note how long it took for these "heretical" texts to be recognized as interesting, and so we may wonder how the FCP managed to "neutralize" these texts or restrict their critical power, thus protecting itself against their dangerous effect. As the FCP could not forbid the publication of critical texts, it had to elaborate a complex political symbolic action plan that varied according to the texts and the audiences that were concerned in order to control the way these texts were appropriated. I would like to outline this partially effective action plan.

Undoubtedly, there were intellectuals, journalists, and politicians with reviews, associations, and financial supports at their disposal who tried to limit the influence of the FCP. They remained rather marginalized, even though they held relatively important positions and applied themselves to distributing and making available the texts that we called "heretical."[2] Exploiting the theme of "the rehabilitation of the thinker misunderstood by his contemporaries," the history of the intellectuals nowadays aims to consider the most well known among those people as visionaries.[3] Among those are Raymond Aron and Boris Souvarine, whose articles and analyses have been reprinted.[4] Moreover, Jean-Louis Panné recently devoted a biography to Souvarine, in which the latter is "a sentry of the free world," resisting all alone the illusions around him during the Cold War.[5] However, despite these individuals and unlike the tendencies in other Western countries, the French intellectual field has been attracted by the FCP, and the world of Communism itself (from the simple electors to the party's intellectuals) resisted any calling to question during the hardest period of the Cold War with a remarkable consistency (a practice still sometimes present today). It was the idealization of the U.S.R.R. that made such behavior possible (which, retrospectively, appears to be mystifying).

Analytical Framework

How did the FCP succeed in exerting this power of attraction? How did French non-Communist intellectuals fail to maintain a "critical mind"? How did other intellectuals, party followers, or Communists take part in the Zhdanovjan ideological campaigns? Jeanine Verdès-Leroux (I oversimplify her thought) asserts that, on the one hand, most of the self-sufficient intellectuals were not Communists and that, on the other hand, the Communist intellectuals, allied with the self-taught, working-class intelligentsia of the FCP, made up an outcast intelligentsia lacking in titles and works and therefore dependent on the Communist institution and its "cultural markets."[6] Within the FCP, analyzed as a "total institution" (Goffman), the latter engendered party spirit principally characterized by a resentment of the self-sufficient intellectuals. This analysis of a frustrated intelligentsia, of intellectuals "against intellect" (Kolakowski), was inspired by Max Weber and Pierre Bourdieu. It also revived the conservative tradition of the exposure of uprooted intellectuals, and that is perhaps the reason for its success. This analysis was based on the reading of Communist texts of the time (the theory of the two sciences, social realism, an exposure of psychoanalysis) and also on discussions with intellectuals unable to understand their own past. The emphasis was put on the irrational nature of the stand taken by the Communist intellectuals and executives. Even if Verdès-Leroux's sociopsychological analysis does explain some aspects of the Communist intellectuals' identity, it is still oversimplistic, and it has been rightly criticized.[7] On the one hand, the theory was unable to explain the favorable reception of the FCP either from the "self-sufficient" intellectuals, Communist or not (e.g., Aragon, Jean-Paul Sartre, Maurice Merleau-Ponty until *Les Aventures de la dialectique*, Marcel Prenant, etc.), or from those who became "self-sufficient" (J.T. Desanti, François Furet, Annie Kriegel, etc.). In summary, it oversimplified the multiple modes of joining Communism. On the other hand, having limited her explanation to the internal logic of the institution without using a sociohistorical analysis, Verdès-Leroux failed to demonstrate the factors that could make something unbelievable believable (under certain circumstances). Without disputing the contributions of Verdès-Leroux, I think it would be more heuristic to consider that an analysis of the internal logic is inadequate to give an account of the symbolic censorship phenomenon. As Eric J. Hobsbawm wrote, "In the wars of (secular) religion of the twentieth century, the historian could not separate the myth from the countermyth, illusion from counterillusion, any more than a specialist of the sixteenth century could separate the Protestant Reformation from the Catholic reactions."[8] Consequently, we have to analyze these mechanisms of symbolic censorship by trying to understand how the internal logic (obviously not confined to resentment, lack of education, the interests of alienated intellectuals, or self-taught intelligentsia) was combined with the external logic. I assert that only the combination of these two types of logic is able to clarify the effectiveness of the action plan of symbolic censorship used by the FCP.

Forgery, False Forgery, Truth, and Propaganda

The Cold War is still a war. This truism must be underlined if we want to understand the social logic guiding appropriations of the texts. From the end of 1947 to 1956, the possibility of a Third World War, moreover, a nuclear war, was not inconceivable. The Chinese Revolution (1949), the fights for national liberation, the Korean War (1950), the anti-Communism of the Western world (from the Marshall Plan to McCarthyism), on the one hand, and the extension of the

Soviet system to the popular democracies (Prague, the partition of Germany), on the other hand—these elements give substance to the war menace. The great strikes of November–December 1947, marked by violence, occurred in a climate of civil war and strengthened the menace. This menace has been politically and symbolically exploited by each camp. In the Communist world, Zhdanov's report of 30 September 1947 defines the vision of a world rushing toward a Third World War. This report is also a criticism against the "opportunism" of the French and Italian Communist parties (which was a necessary prelude to the future proceedings, purges, and other actions based on ideological vigilance and respect of orthodoxy) and a fight for peace.

As for the period 1940–44, this situation of crisis reinforced the heteronomous logic of the intellectual fields, intensified the preexisting divisions, politicized all the attitudes, whether literary, philosophical, scientific, pedagogical, and so on, bringing them down to one characteristic only: for or against the U.S.S.R.[9] This climate of ideological civil war had a lot of consequences: every critical text was suspect, and it couldn't be the project of a contradictory evaluation; every dissidence became a drama, and therefore the psychological and social costs of the "exit" and "voice" considerably increased. To make symbolic censorship efficient, which meant to forbid access to the texts or to neutralize their reading, it was necessary to substantiate the idea that the heretical texts were due to enemy propaganda either because they were forgeries or because they were included in an anti-Communist intellectual project, a technique that allowed them to be dismissed.

In this logic of war, the vision of history as a conspiracy had been used more or less successfully in different circumstances. According to Gérard Belloin, who was a young executive and a local leader of the FCP at the beginning of his career and later an official and an assistant director of the central school of the FCP, then a journalist, one of the most distributed books to the Communists militants was *La Grande Conspiration contre la Russie* of Michel Sayers and Albert E. Kahn, published by Editions d'Hier et Aujourd'hui in 1947. *Les Cahiers du Communisme* of October 1947 praised it, advising each militant to read it and think about it. Although the vision of history as a conspiracy was not Marxist, it was very popular and widespread. These Cold War years, following the Second World War, were indeed especially favorable on each side to the popularization of cryptic hermeneutics, both in spy novels and films.[10] Every critical text was consequently included in the category of false, considered as a forgery or as a result of anti-Communist propaganda. This category of false emerges neither from the logic of a debate nor from the "learned discussion." To avoid the critical discussion of a text, it was necessary to discredit the authors themselves, whose nosography was developed: policeman (Nizan), renegade, apostate, spy, ex-Nazi or fascist, and so on. These labels were put on the "persons," and that is the reason why a trial became a tool of disqualification. There were a lot of trials, besides the famous ones (Kravchenko, Rousset). Etienne Fajon, in his report on the degradation of the Communist press during the meeting of the Central Comittee of 26 March 1952, mentions 139 trials against *L'Humanité*.[11] The form of a trial, actualized or not, makes an author a suspect, whether he is guilty or not. The same type of disqualification was systematically exploited, while the charges against the "defendants" differed according to the case. *I Choose Freedom* of Kravchenko (1947), for example, was presented (in *Les Lettres Françaises*) as a forgery made by a renegade, hostage of the CIA. If this characterization was then possible, it is because forgeries were common practices. Some authors (Bessedovsky, Yves Delbars) proposed their "literature" to the press eager for scoops: *France Soir, Combat, L'Aurore, Ici-Paris*, and unscrupulous editors. Thus were published the memories of a ghost Soviet officer and ectoplasmic marshals, false memories of General Vlassov, a false letter of Jan Masaryk, an invented correspondence between Stalin and Tito, Budu Svanidze, false memories of Maxime Litvinov (with a preface by the English historian E. H. Carr!), or the memories of a "confidant of Malenkov." These forgeries justified to a certain extent the vision of a general conspiracy given by the FCP. Boris Souvarine never stopped to denounce this type of literature for its effect of interference with real testimonies.[12]

The case of "Tasca" presents an example of a complex mixture of the false and real truth. A former executive of the Italian Communist party who had become an anti-Communist, he collaborated in 1940 with the Information Services of Vichy and accumulated information and files on the FCP. In the books he published after the Second World War about the policy of the FCP during "la drôle de guerre" and after the Soviet-German Treaty (1939), he radically questioned the official version (in which the FCP had been totally patriotic and antifascist from the beginning to the end of the war) given by the FCP after the Liberation. Even if the sources are firsthand, the political past of the author (who published under the pseudonym of Amilcare Rossi) brought discredit on the author in the eyes of the Communists and of all intellectual circles (the distrust of the news paper *Le Monde,* among others). Because of his past, Tasca owned firsthand sources, and, for the same reason, his books have been discredited. Boris Souvarine is in the same situation because of his collaboration with Albertini. At the time of the Rajk trial (1949), François Fetjö wanted to publish an article in *Esprit* to denounce the fabrication of the trial. Emmanuel Mounier received a visit from Pierre Courtade, who informed him that Fetjö "was a fascist, policeman and collaborator."[13] These disqualifications were the most spectacular symptoms of the heteronomy of the intellectual fields. They muddled up the "thresholds" (*seuils* for Genette) of the texts to such an extent that readers had to be suspicious, even if they had read the texts. This means, up to an extreme point, that testimony could be considered as "plausible" and, at the same time, condemned for its inclusion into a political project; thus "the effect of reading" is neutralized by the cognitive distance between the "known" and the "recognized." This misfortune befell Claude Lefort when he stood up for *I Choose Freedom* in *Les Temps Modernes*. Sartre published his article in the column "Opinion" and wrote his "disapproval of the tone more than of the analysis, the tone of an indictment in a world that is nowhere innocent and not governed by imminent reason" (*Les Temps Modernes*, February 1948). In this context, the truth (always relative) deteriorates first into "plausible," then into "opinion," which is associated in the reader's mind with falsity or even forgery. Consequently, taking this state of the intellectual fields into consideration, the authorities of mediation could no longer be governed by specific intellectual logic, restricting at least partially the protagonists and their ability to discuss and evaluate the texts. The FCP could impose this functioning onto the field of criticism because of its importance due to its role in the Resistance ("the party of the shot ones") and to the role of the U.S.S.R. against Nazism, and also due to the different places occupied by the FCP in the intellectual world (at the National Committee of Writers, for instance) and in the working world. The FCP was also in harmony with other ideological tendencies that had their own logic (such as anti-Americanism).

The *Remise de soi* and the Plausible

In this binary symbolic climate (true/false, for/against, betrayal/loyalty, war/peace, bourgeois science/proletarian science), the protagonists had to classify themselves, not without difficulties at times. The lack of autonomy of the intellectual fields increased the tendency for *remise de soi*, which wags called "the party spirit."[14]

Certain types of the social logic studied by Verdès-Leroux then produced their effects. Two large groups can be distinguished: militants and self-taught executives, on the one hand, and intellectuals, on the other hand.

The *remise de soi* of the working executives of the FCP diverted them from reading the heretical texts: at best, they heard about them in critical articles of the Communist press. Their entire reading space was occupied by directed readings, which varied according to the militant levels. In each "section" of the FCP, there was a person in charge of education who advised the militants in their personal reading selections, compiled the library of the cell, and tried, with a variable success, to substitute fundamental readings (the Soviet novels or books of Communist writers: André Stil, Pierre Courtade, Louis Aragon, Elsa Triolet, Pierre Lafitte, Paul Eluard) for decadent readings. For specific readings, the militant had to make a personal study in a notebook: on the left page, he had to write the "important facts," "principal ideas," and required readings. On the right page, he had to write his "personal thoughts." An advisor in charge controlled this notebook. Among such fundamental reading, one can find *Fils du peuple* of Maurice Thorez (general secretary), reprinted in 1949. The FCP launched the "book battles" in order to diffuse the readings he recommended.[15] The readings that were supposed to offer salvation did not always live up to readers' expectations and therefore were a source of disappointment. The doctor Hervé Lucia, analyzing the book battle in Aubagne, asserts that "it has been a splendid flash in the pan during one afternoon, completely put out in less than a week."[16] This functioning of the FCP, which justifies our talking about "total institution" in reference to the FCP, suited only a minority of militants whose private and public lives were incorporated in the Communist world. However, even these militants could have doubts. Gérard Belloin became a reader of *Le Monde* in the early fifties but justified his guilt (he was giving money to the bourgeois press, wasn't he?) by the necessity of having knowledge of the "enemy's arguments." However, the status of the truth changed: "When *L'Humanité* wrote something, I thought it was true, but when *Le Monde* wrote the same thing, I thought it was truer."[17] When truth needs something truer, it is no longer real truth . . .

As for intellectuals (those who were Communists, party followers, or momentary associates like Jean-Paul Sartre), they finally had to submit to the rules imposed by both sides: the FCP and anti-Communist authors. These rules were based on the heteronomy of intellectual fields, and the intellectuals were caught in the trap of a committed intellectual. They were more or less predisposed to this functioning according to their different capacities for autonomy

(autonomy is an ideal seldom reached due to the necessity of numerous institutional mechanisms), and consequently they chose different tactics: from a silent stand back to a marginal resistance, from a limited agreement to the fight for peace, or "Zhdanovjan," campaigns, including the denouncement of other intellectuals.

Annie Kriegel, thinking retrospectively about the time when she was an activist involved in the Communist ideological fights, poses the problem correctly when she says, "Truth, in each field, is partly delegated, and this delegation is convincing only if it is scattered among specialists and experts who are submitted to contesting and confrontation."[18] However, the FCP's strategy tended to symbolically forbid all critical confrontation. It forced the social agents to make a bet based on their social stand and fundamental values, which are the basis of the delegated confidence, and forced them to believe in something "plausible." These bets were different according to situations and people. Annie Kriegel, for example, remembered that she tried to justify the Rajk trial using the concept of "plausible" and answering the following question: "Was it thinkable that Rajk had been a traitor?" The mere appeal to "plausible" can be analyzed as an implicit and subconscious distancing.

One should elaborate a precise sociology of different kinds of adhesions to the Communist universe. Some intellectuals considerd the *remise de soi* wanted by the FCP too far from their intellectual conceptions. The leadership of the FCP understood that and tried to arouse a guilty feeling within these individuals. The FCP advised them to give up the old conceptions, and it constructed a sociological theory to explain their ability to be influenced by "bourgeois propaganda." The FCP finally asserted that under every doubt lay a potential betrayal. That is why the intellectuals "in doubt" were obliged to choose the "most plausible," which required the renunciation of their professionalism. We must take into account their populism, the legitimacy of their fundamental values, and the old links of conflict, especially in the Resistance and in concentration camps. Because of their intellectual role, they were not able to agree with the truth of heretical texts, although they might also have been plausible.

Conclusion

We understand now why the publication in 1956 in *Le Monde* of the secret report of Nikita Khrushchev at the Twentieth Congress of the Communist Party of the Soviet Union (CPSU) was so important. Indeed, it forbade comparison of different types of *remise de soi*, comparison allowed during the Cold War. The reaction of the FCP

160   Symbolic Censorship

to the report was varied. Some people considered that their fundamental choices were not questioned and that the intellectual Communists would play a new role in the necessary coming *aggiornamento*.[19] On the contrary, those who were the most implicated in the "Zhdanovjan logic" considered the report as a mistake of the CPSU. Therefore, they became allied with the working-class party's executives to conquer its preeminence in the internal conflicts. Finally, those who joined the FCP by the conformity of the anticonformity, those who joined it for a short while, considered the report as a revelation that liberated them from their old commitments. "It is not simple: neither Stalinism, nor Man."

Notes

1. For an example of such studies, see, among others, the work of Angelo Tasca about the history of the FCP from 1939 to 1945 and the work of Boris Souvarine about the U.S.S.R. See also the famous book of Kravchenko, *I Choose Freedom* (translated into French in January 1947), *La Condition inhumaine* of Jules Margoline (1949), *Echappé de Russie* of Antoni Ekart (Paris, 1949), *Déportée en Sibérie* of Margarete Buber-Neumann (1949), and *Onze ans dans les bagnes soviétiques* of Elinor Lipper (Paris, 1950).
2. Pierre Gremion, *Intelligence de l'anticommunisme (Le Congrès pour la Liberté de la culture à Paris, 1950-1975)* (Fayard, 1995).
3. Nicolas Baverez, "Raymond Aron, le visionnaire mal-aimé," *L'Histoire* 209 (April 1997).
4. Bris Souvarine, *Chroniques du mensonge Communiste*, textes choisis par Branko Lazitch et Pierre Rigoulot, Commentaire/Plon (1998).
5. Jean-Louis Panné, *Boris Souvarine* (Laffont, 1993), 358.
6. Jeanine Verdès-Leroux, *Au service du Parti. Le Parti Communiste, les intellectuels et la culture (1944-1956)* (Paris: Fayard/Minuit, 1983).
7. Marie-Claire Lavabre, Marc Lazar, note critique sur *Au service du parti*, *Communisme* 5 (1984): 138-41. The authors wrote: "reading [the book of Verdès-Leroux] we understand what the Communist culture during the Cold War was, but we do not catch its meaning" (141).
8. Eric J. Hobsbawm, "Histoire et illusion," *Le Débat* 89 (March-April 1997): 137.
9. Gisèle Sapiro, "La Raison littéraire. Le Champ littéraire français sous l'occupation (1940-1944)," *Actes de la Recherche en Sciences Sociales* (March 1996): 111-12.
10. For an example of hermeneutics, see Alain Dewerpe, *Espion* (Paris: Gallimard, 1996). For discussions of the spy novel, see Erik Neveu, *L'Idéologie dans le roman d'espionnage* (PFNSP, 1985) and "Les Miroirs troublants de la soviétologie spontanée," *Politix* 18 (1992).
11. Etienne Fajon, rapport au CC du PCF du 26 mars 1952, Archives du CC du PCF, 1 AV 45/2069.
12. Panné, *Boris Souvarine*, 358.
13. Annie Kriegel, *Ce que j'ai cru comprendre* (Laffont, 1991), 454.
14. *Remise de soi* means giving complete confidence to the party, largely giving up one's own views and judgments and replacing them almost entirely with those of the Party (*fides implicita* in Latin).

15. Marc Lazar, "Les Batailles du livre du PCF (1950–1952)," *XX Siècle*, 37–49.
16. *La Nouvelle Critique* 25 (April 1951): 66.
17. Gérard Belloin, manuscrit autobiographique, inédit, 1997–98.
18. Kriegel, *Ce que j'ai cru comprendre*, 457.
19. Bernard Pudal, *Prendre Parti. Pour une sociologie historique du PCF, 1920–1980* (PFNSP, 1989), 336.

American Literature in Cold War Germany

Martin Meyer

During the Cold War period following World War II, the United States made a decision to reestablish culture in Germany rather than risk Soviet expansion into Western Europe. Due to the atrocities committed by Germany during the war, it was hard to understand why the United States switched political partners in the immediate postwar period, but publishing American views in Germany was regarded as essential to propagating democratic principles in Europe. The intention was to reach German intellectuals through literature so they would become mouthpieces for democratic principles and a market economy. Germans were reeducated through books and magazines containing scholarly works, fiction, plays, and poetry. Armed Services Editions (ASE), paperback books shipped to American soldiers during the war, and Overseas Editions (OSE), books printed in English and translated into other languages after the war, were the backbone of American published materials. In addition, American money was channeled to European political magazines, such as *Der Monat* and *Encounter*, thought of as having influence on the intellectual elite of Western European countries. Several international literary conferences held during the late 1940s and early 1950s became battlegrounds for words. The conflicts centered on cultural freedom and the spreading of capitalist and Communist ideas by the United States and the Soviet Union, respectively.

American Literature in Defeated Germany

When Germany was finally defeated in the spring of 1945, the United States was ready to offer new food for thought to all Germans who wanted to catch up with international intellectual developments. Cooperating closely with the U.S. government since the spring of 1942, the American book industry had already been shipping millions of paperback books called Armed Services Editions (ASE) to U.S. soldiers around the globe. Many of these ended up in German hands in 1945, and particularly the young readers were grateful for any material that did not have the taint of Nazi propaganda. Although the ASE were never meant to serve reeducation purposes, they no doubt fulfilled that function. Their successors, the Overseas Editions (OSE), were meant to "give the people of Europe a picture of what Americans are like and what we had been doing since communications were closed," as Robert Ballou and Irene Rakosky wrote in 1946.[1]

The OSE looked much like the ASE, but, unlike their senior partners, the OSE were not only published in English but also in other languages such as French, Italian, and German. They were distributed in more than twenty countries, no doubt boosting interest in American literature in Europe.[2] In Germany, American literature was certainly popularized by Alfred Kazin's *On Native Grounds*, which was first published in 1942. Kazin's *Interpretation of Modern American Prose*, as the subtitle reads, was translated by the German emigrant Hans Sahl in the Office of War Information (OWI) and then distributed in Germany in the OSE series in both English and German. Even today, copies of both editions can be found in many German university libraries. The fact that an American publisher's edition of *On Native Grounds* is still in print today shows that the people in charge of selecting material for the ASE and OSE programs were literary experts with a good sense of pragmatism.

Many other important books by first-rate American intellectuals were made available in postwar Germany. Looking back on this period, the German scholar Hans-Joachim Lang concluded in 1972: "There was not a publication voluminous enough not to get translated. And the selection made was excellent."[3] For example, F. O. Matthiessen's *American Renaissance*, first published in 1941, was available in German as early as 1948, as was the two-volume edition *The Growth of the American Republic* by Samuel Eliot Morrison and Henry Steele Commager (1930). These books could be read in German in 1949–50. By this time, over three hundred American books had been translated, not counting the OSE.[4] Clearly, this would have been impossible without active support by American offices. The Office of the Military Government of the United States (OMGUS) in Germany had installed a so-called Information Control Division (ICD) within which the Publications Branch (PB) was in charge of supervising publishing in Germany.[5] Officers of the PB were responsible for controlling what was published in the recently defeated country, and it was also their job to offer new reading material suitable for reeducation purposes in the U.S. occupation zone. The PB selected titles for translation at a flat rate of $250 to U.S. publishers for each title chosen, managed copyright questions, and ran a translation unit in Bad Homburg.[6]

Publishing in Germany after World War II

A brief look at the book-publishing situation in Germany during the immediate postwar years will help explain why new books were hard to find. Many of the printing facilities had been destroyed during the war, and those that were still working were requisitioned by the occupation forces. Paper, of course, was rationed, and publishers in the American occupation zone were often assigned their contingent only after a license for a particular book project had been granted by the Publications Branch, provided, that is, the publisher had received a license to run his publishing business in the first place. As a result, only 2,400 titles were published in Germany in the years 1945-46. This number reached 8,900 in 1947 and increased to 13,400 in 1948.[7]

Even books printed like newspapers were welcome. Between December 1946 and October 1949, some 3 million copies of *Rowohlts Rotations Romane* were sold and read, even more with each copy passing through many hands. If I may use the term "romance" instead of "novel," the alliteration Rowohlts Rotations Romane even translates into English as "Rowohlt's rotary [press] romances." Ernest Hemingway's prewar publisher in Germany, Ernst Rowohlt, is sometimes credited with having started this series, but it was actually his son, Heinrich Maria Ledig-Rowohlt, who published these books. In 1946 Ledig-Rowohlt was contacted by the Information Control Division in Stuttgart, which suggested that he should start publishing quality literature, especially for the younger generation. ICD officers are also likely to have shown him how this could be done. The ASE and OSE had been printed on "rotary presses," and this method would also work in Germany.[8] The main difference between them and Rowohlt's novels was that *Rowohlts Rotations Romane* looked like newspapers whereas the American titles resembled paperback books. Later, in 1949, Ledig-Rowohlt traveled to New York to study "pocketbook" production and started his first paperback series in Germany in 1950.[9]

Morality and Politics

It is not easy to understand why America would have helped Germany in any way after discovering the atrocities committed, mainly by Germans, during World War II. In his autobiography, Arthur Miller called it "an ignoble thing" that America switched political partners in the immediate postwar period. During the war Russia had been the ally and Germany the enemy. Yet within a year after the end of World War II, America started to accept Germany as a new partner and looked upon the Soviet Union as the new opponent: "[T]his ripping off of Good and Evil labels from one nation and pasting them onto another," Arthur Miller wrote in *Timebends* in 1987, "had done something to wither the very notion of a world even theoretically moral. If last month's friend could so quickly become this month's enemy, what depth of reality could good and evil have?"[10]

Who, except maybe politicians, would dispute that politics and morality make strange bedfellows? More often than not, *Realpolitik* prevails. While it is the writer's job to bring up painful subjects, it is the politician's job to decide pressing political issues, sometimes even "by making choices among soiling possibilities," as the American novelist Thomas Berger phrased it in 1954.[11] In order to gain a fuller perspective, we will look at what the Soviets were doing in terms of *Kulturpolitik* in their occupation zone.

Soviet *Kulturpolitik* and the Battle of the Congresses

As early as August 1945, the Berlin-based Aufbau-Verlag received its requested publishing license from the Soviet Military Administration (SMAD). Only a month later the first issue of its magazine *Aufbau: kulturpolitische Monatsschrift* appeared as the official organ of the Kulturbund zur demokratischen Erneuerung Deutschlands (Cultural Alliance for the Democratic Renewal of Germany). The president of the Kulturbund, Johannes R. Becher, had fled the Nazis in 1933, finding refuge in Moscow. It had been Becher who had co-organized the First International Writers' Congress for the Defense of Culture in Paris in June 1935.[12] A number of famous writers had participated, including André Gide, André Malraux, E. M. Forster, Aldous Huxley, Bertolt Brecht, Heinrich Mann, Boris Pasternak, and Theodore Dreiser, to name but a few. Ten years later, Becher was in charge of cultural affairs in Berlin in his new capacity as president of the Kulturbund, which became the center for all cultural activities in postwar Berlin.[13] The writer and politician Ernst Niekisch (1889–1967), who had been sentenced to life in prison for opposing the Nazis in 1939, had left East Germany in 1954 because he was disillusioned with its socialism. He put it in a nutshell when he stated in his memoirs: "The Soviets were trying hard to win over the bourgeois intellectuals for their cause."[14] While the Soviets tried to convince the "bourgeois intellectuals," the Americans addressed the "non-Communist left" in Europe. Either group could be reached through books and a proven commitment to culture. Once convinced of either the capitalist route or the Communist way, these intellectuals would become mouthpieces, some people apparently thought, and help to pave the way toward Communism or capitalism.

When mainly Western intellectuals met in West Berlin in the summer of 1950, the battle of the congresses, begun in Paris in 1935, had long been resumed. Since 1945, writers had been meeting at international conferences in Wroclaw (August 1948), New York (March 1949), and Paris (April 1949).[15] In the last days of June 1950, from 26–30 June, authors, scholars, and philosophers gathered in West Berlin for an international conference bearing the programmatic title Congress for Cultural Freedom. Only a week later, the Second Congress of German Writers was scheduled to take place in East Berlin (4–7 July 1950). Thus the stage was set for the battle of words. No director of a Cold War drama could have come up with a more appropriate timing, for on 25 June, the day before the Congress for Cultural Freedom started, North Korea began its assault on South Korea. By the end of the meeting, the Congress for Cultural Freedom concluded with a manifesto read by Arthur Koestler calling for, among other things, the right to free speech, including the right to disagree with political authorities. "Human beings become slaves when they are deprived of the right to say 'No!'" the second of twelve propositions read.[16] All in all, the manifesto claimed that the West promised freedom, democracy, and tolerance, whereas the East had nothing to offer but mind control, dictatorship, and totalitarianism.

The Second Congress of German Writers in East Berlin, meeting only a few days later, was the forum that offered a chance to respond to the Congress for Cultural Freedom's manifesto. Perceived as a provocation, it prompted reactions that revealed its meaning through the very language chosen. In the words of the president of the Kulturbund, Johannes R. Becher, the participants in the Congress for Cultural Freedom were no longer writers but "henchmen of the war-mongers" and "gangsters in literary disguise."[17] A dialogue with these people, Becher claimed, was impossible, and he therefore refused any discussion. According to the magazine *Aufbau*, which published Becher's speech, he also said: "We not only hate these people who have humbled themselves into becoming writers of the warmongers, we also feel repugnance and disgust for this anti-Bolshevist riff-raff.... No, we will not permit offensive material of this kind to be distributed in the German Democratic Republic."[18] No doubt, Becher's use of the first-person plural sent a signal to his audience that said a discussion of the issue was not on the agenda.

American Weapons in the War of Ideas

In the mid-1960s it became known that the Congress for Cultural Freedom had been funded at least in part by money made available through American intelligence offices. As was disclosed in a 1976 U.S. Senate report, the Church Committee Report, the United States had taken up the challenge of Soviet cultural diplomacy at least as early as 1947. As far as publishing books was concerned, it stated: "Well over a thousand books were produced, subsidized or sponsored by the CIA before the end of 1967. Approximately 25 percent of them were written in English. Many of them were published by cultural organizations which the CIA backed."[19] Some of these were written under the supervision of intelligence officers, while others were published without the writer having any clue about his or her manuscript finding the approval of a third party. Why the books were sponsored was addressed by a comment made by the chief of the CIA's Covert Action Staff. In 1961 he stated: "'Books differ from all other propaganda media, primarily because one single book can significantly change the reader's attitude and action to an extent unmatched by the impact of any other single medium.'"[20] Clearly, books were regarded as weapons in the war of ideas.

Money was also channeled to magazines thought of as having influence on the intellectual elite of the respective countries. Among the best-known journals receiving support through the American taxpayer were *Der Monat*, founded in Berlin in October 1948, and *Encounter*, started in London in October 1953. Their focus was on politics and culture. *Der Monat*, for example, published the proceedings of the Congress for Cultural Freedom. As far as American literature in Germany is concerned, the highly regarded international journal *Perspektiven* was extremely influential.[21] It was published simultaneously in various countries between 1952 and 1956, called *Perspectives* in the United States and Britain, *Profils* in France, and *Prospettive* and *Prospetti* in Italy. Funded through the Ford Foundation and published by the New York–based organization Intercultural Publications,[22] the German edition, *Perspektiven*, absorbed the literary periodical *Das Lot*, including its highly motivated international staff. Between 1947 and 1952 the editors of *Das Lot* had been publishing avant-garde poetry from many countries, including the United States. Once absorbed by *Perspektiven*, editorial control was gone. Addressing the transatlantic modes of transport for poetry in the postwar decade, the German scholar and translator Klaus Martens came to the conclusion that *Perspektiven*'s main purpose was to exercise control over what was published and to offer German readers more American poetry than had been published by *Das Lot*.[23]

Scholars in literature prefer discussing aesthetic dimensions of texts rather than dealing with material issues such as why books get published or translated. Therefore, not many studies are available on the role American institutions played in reestablishing postwar culture in Germany. It seems, however, that the literary experts working for *Perspektiven* had less qualified colleagues in public relations offices who wrote fiction intended to mold public opinion. In 1951, for example, the Frankfurt-based Rudl publisher came out with what was called a "documentary novel" entitled *The Big Rape* by James Wakefield Burke. The setting of the novel is Berlin in the spring of 1945 during the Russian invasion. Predictably, the victims are German women, the victimizers are Russian soldiers, and sharp Americans entering Berlin in July 1945 are the saviors. Burke, who claimed he had been public relations advisor for General Clay in Berlin in 1947–48, published his book in Germany in English a year before it came out in New York, where it was published by Farrar, Straus and Young in 1952.[24] Here, I believe, we have a pretty good candidate for the list of books sponsored by American authorities as described in the Church Committee Report. Laudable as the publication of that report was in the midseventies, would it not be wise now to envisage a date for disclosing the information therein so far reserved for the eyes of U.S. senators?[25] Who were the authors, what were the titles, and what were the names of the publishers in the United States and abroad that received money to propagate messages and material deemed useful in the days of the Cold War? If Washington and ideally also Moscow opened their archives, we might learn from the mistakes made in the past.

Conclusion

After 1945, in a unique historical situation, Washington's choice was perceived as being one between helping Germany or risking Soviet expansion into Western Europe. Publishing American views was regarded as essential to propagate democratic principles. The publishing machinery that had worked so well during the war was now used to reeducate Germans. Many scholarly works, plays, and fiction by Americans were made available in English as well as in translation. This clearly boosted American literature and had an effect on postwar writers in Germany on the lookout for new literary examples. The questionable role is that played by agencies not under political control. What democratic legitimacy did they have to publish books whose purpose seems to have been to incite hatred? We have no reason to be self-righteous as today we are spared the decisions that had to be taken then. We have a right, however, and an obligation, I believe, to study what was instrumental in shaping literary taste and Cold War sentiments in postwar Germany and Europe, respectively. What has also been demonstrated is that the role of American literature in Cold War Germany cannot be comprehended without a basic understanding of Soviet policies and of German commissars on a cultural mission defined in Clausewitz's language. "Peace," Johannes R. Becher wrote in September 1944, "is the continuation of war against fascism by other means, mainly ideological means."[26] The cultural Cold War was in full swing.

Notes

This article was written in memory of Martin Schulze (1928-2000).
 1. Robert O. Ballou and Irene Rakosky, *A History of the Council on Books in Wartime, 1942-1946* (New York: Country Life Press, 1946), 85.
 2. Whereas more than 120 million paperback books were published as ASE between 1943 and 1947, OSE amounted to about 3.6 million.
 3. Originally: "Kein Werk war zu dick, um nicht doch übersetzt zu werden. Dabei muß man die Auswahl als hervorragend bezeichnen." Hans-Joachim Lang, "Vorbemerkung," in *Nordamerikanische Literatur im deutschen Sprachraum seit 1945: Beiträge zu ihrer Rezeption*, ed. Horst Frenz and Hans-Joachim Lang (Munich: Winkler, 1973), 106. For the history of American literature in Germany, see also Harold Jantz, "Amerika im deutschen Dichten und Denken," *Deutsche Philologie im Aufriß*, ed. Wolfgang Stammler, vol. 3, 2nd ed. (Berlin: Erich Schmidt, 1962), especially "Die amerikanische Literatur in Deutschland," 361–69. See also Lawrence Marsden Price, *The Reception of United States Literature in Germany*, University of North Carolina Studies in Comparative Literature, vol. 39 (Chapel Hill: University of North Carolina Press, 1966), which includes a detailed bibliography. Political implications are discussed in Hansjörg Gehring, *Amerikanische Literaturpolitik in Deutschland 1945-1953: ein Aspekt des Re-Education Programms*, Schriftenreihe der Vierteljahrshefte für Zeitgeschichte, vol. 32 (Stuttgart: DVA, 1976).
 4. See Birgit Bödeker, *Amerikanische Zeitschriften in deutscher Sprache, 1945-1952: ein Beitrag zur Literatur und Publizistik im Nachkriegsdeutschland*, Neue Studien zur Anglistik und Amerikanistik, 60 (Frankfurt am Main: Lang, 1993), 194.
 5. OMGUS was the successor of SHAEF (Supreme Headquarters of the Allied Expeditionary Forces). ICD was the successor of PWD (Psychological Warfare Division).
 6. Bödeker, *Amerikanische Zeitschriften*, 194.
 7. See Karl August Kutzbach, *Autorenlexikon der Gegenwart: schöne Literatur verfaßt in deutscher Sprache mit einer Chronik seit 1945* (Bonn: Bouvier, 1950), 474, 479, 483. For comparison, 77,900 titles were published in 1997.
 8. Ballou and Rakosky, *A History*, 75.
 9. See Kurt Pinthus, "Ernst Rowohlt und sein Verlag," in *Rowohlt Almanach 1908-1962*, ed. Mara Hintermeier and Fritz J. Raddatz (Reinbek: Rowohlt, 1962), 36.
 10. Arthur Miller, *Timebends: A Life* (New York: Grove Press, 1987), 160.
 11. Thomas Berger, review of *A Woman in Berlin* (New York: Harcourt, Brace and Co., 1954), *Socialist Call* (November 1954): 24.

12. Erster internationaler Schriftstellerkongreß zur Verteidigung der Kultur. See Peter Coleman, *The Liberal Conspiracy: The Congress for Cultural Freedom and the Struggle for the Mind of Postwar Europe* (New York: Free Press, 1989), 3f. According to his biographer, Horst Haase, Johannes R. Becher played an important role in preparing, organizing, and staging the Paris congress in 1935. See Horst Haase, *Johannes R. Becher: Leben und Werk*, Schriftsteller der Gegenwart, 1, 2nd ed. (Berlin: Volk und Wissen, 1987), 116f. Roger Shattuck even sees links between the Paris congress in 1935 and the First All-Union Congress of Soviet Writers held in Moscow in August 1934. See Roger Shattuck, "Writers for the Defense of Culture," *Partisan Review* 51:3 (1984): 401.

13. See Horst Engelbach and Konrad Krauss, "Der Kulturbund und seine Zeitschrift *Aufbau* in der SBZ," in *Zur literarischen Situation 1945l-1949*, ed. Gerhard Hay (Kronberg/Ts.: Athenäum, 1977), 177. Horst Haase identifies Becher as the man who formed cultural policies in Soviet-occupied Germany after Becher's return to Berlin in June 1945. See Haase, *Johannes R. Becher*, 187.

14. Originally: "Die Sowjets gaben sich Mühe, die bürgerlichen Intellektuellen für sich zu gewinnen." Ernst Niekisch, *Erinnerungen eines deutschen Revolutionärs*, vol. 2: *Gegen den Strom 1945-1967* (Cologne: Verlag Wissenschaft und Politik, 1974), 53.

15. Congress of World Partisans of Peace vs. Sidney Hook's International Day against Dictatorship and War.

16. Originally: "Der Mensch wird zum Sklaven, wenn er des Rechtes beraubt wird, 'nein' zu sagen." Quoted in *"Als der Krieg zu Ende war": literarisch-politische Publizistik 1945-1950*, ed. Bernhard Zeller, 4th ed., Sonderausstellungen des Schiller-Nationalmuseums, Katalog 23 (Munich: Kösel, 1995), 548. Among the men attending the Congress in 1950 were Ernst Reuter, Ignazio Silone, Sidney Hook, Arthur Koestler, Melvin J. Lasky, Hugh R. Trevor-Roper, Raymon Aron, Karl Jaspers, Alfred Weber, Dolf Sternberger, Peter de Mendelssohn, Nicolas Nabokov, Eugen Kogon, Richard Löwenthal, and Theodor Plievier.

17. Originally: "Handlanger der Kriegshetzer" and "literarisch getarnte Gangster." In ibid., 550.

18. Originally: "Wir hassen diese Leute nicht nur, die sich zu den Schreibern der Kriegshetzer erniedrigt haben, wir empfinden auch Abscheu und Ekel vor diesem antibolschewistischen Gesindel. . . . Nein, wir werden es nicht zulassen, daß solch ein Schund und Schmutz in der Deutschen Demokratischen Republik verbreitet wird." In ibid., 550f., originally published in *Aufbau: kulturpolitische Monatsschrift* 6:8 (1950).

19. *Final Report of the [U.S. Congress, Senate] Select Committee to Study Governmental Operations with Respect to Intelligence Activities*, 94th Cong., 2nd sess., SR 94-755, Book 1 (Washington, D.C.: GPO, 1976), 193.

20. Ibid.

21. "Nach *Lot* und *fragmente* ist die längerlebige Zeitschrift *Perspektiven* (1952-1956) von kaum zu überschätzendem Einfluß." Klaus Martens, "Wege und Auswirkungen der übersetzerischen Vermittlung amerikanischer Lyrik in der Bundesrepublik Deutschland (1945-1956)," *Mitteilungen des Verbandes deutscher Anglisten* 3:2 (September 1992): 15.

22. "Die *Perspektiven* wurden, so ist bereits dem Impressum der ersten Ausgabe zu entnehmen, von der New Yorker Gesellschaft *Intercultural Publications* herausgegeben, von der *Ford Foundation* finanziert und in Deutschland bei S. Fischer (Frankfurt a.M.) verlegt." Ibid., 21.

23. "Vielmehr wird offenkundig, daß es nunmehr ganz deutlich in den *Perspektiven* um amerikaseitige zentralisierte Steuerung der vermittelten Literatur ging. Eine zielseitige Auswahl durch deutsche–oder einer deutschen Zeitschrift verbundene–Herausgeber, die auch ihre eigenen Texte lancierten, war nicht erwünscht." Ibid., 23.

24. Frankfurt am Main: F. Rudl Verleger-Union, 1951. Also published as *Die grosse Vergewaltigung*, trans. Werner Asendorf (Frankfurt am Main: F. Rudl Verleger-Union, 1952) and as *Frau komm: Berlin 1945*, trans. Ursula Lyn, Amsel-Kriro, 9 (Berlin: Amsel Verlag, 1953, 1956). It was slightly rewritten and published once more as *Arli* (Ottawa, Ill.: Caroline House, 1978).

25. "The material italicized in this report has been substantially abridged at the request of the executive agencies. The classified version of this material is available to members of the Senate under the provisions of Senate Resolution 21 and the Standing Rules of the Senate." *Final Report*, 179. Frank Church wrote in his "Letter of Transmittal": "Despite security considerations which have limited what can responsibly be printed for public release the information which is presented in this report is a reasonably complete picture of the intelligence activities undertaken by the United States, and the problems that such activities pose for constitutional government." Ibid., iii.

26. "'Der Friede . . . ist, was unsere Aufgaben betrifft, die Fortsetzung des Krieges gegen den Faschismus mit anderen Mitteln, vor allem mit ideologischen Mitteln.'" Quoted from a paper by Johannes R. Becher entitled "Zu unseren Kulturaufgaben" dated 25 September 1944 in Haase, *Johannes R. Becher*, 187. Becher became minister for cultural affairs in the German Democratic Republic in 1954.

A Cold War Best-Seller: The Reaction to Arthur Koestler's *Darkness at Noon* in France from 1945 to 1950

Martine Poulain

Arthur Koestler's *Darkness at Noon* served as the pioneer publication denouncing Stalinist strategies. First released in 1940 in London, Jewish publishers reissued subsequent French editions of *Darkness at Noon* in the mid-1940s amidst a climate of Communism, facing major obstacles that included a paper shortage. The Communists regarded paper as a rare commodity in war-torn Europe, and it would not easily be turned over to anti-Communist movements. Publicly heralded in France, *Darkness at Noon* survived Cold War Communist censorship and underground book sales. While French Communist party members abhorred Koestler's message and his successful publications, Western critics and democratic-minded European readers clung to the revolutionary statements envisioned in the book. This essay describes the difficulties, from lack of funds to political warnings, the author and publishers experienced when attempting to release the work. It also follows the various reactions to *Darkness at Noon*, both exceedingly positive and sharply negative.

Jonathan Cape published *Darkness at Noon* in London in 1940. Arthur Koestler, the author, was a Hungarian Jew who had lived in Berlin and Paris and had belonged to the German Communist party, been a reporter for an English newspaper during the Spanish Civil War, been imprisoned in Málaga and released through the intervention of his newspaper, and chose to recount the Moscow trials of 1938 in a work of fiction. Arthur Koestler's novel, the first important book denouncing the Stalinist reign of terror, had worldwide success and prompted unusually far-reaching discussions. These debates became particularly virulent, and more so in France than elsewhere.

Publication of the English Edition

In *Hieroglyphs*, Arthur Koestler related the genesis of the idea and the writing style of *Darkness at Noon*.[1] The novel, written in German and translated into English by his companion of that time, Daphne Hardy, was begun during the summer of 1936 and completed in April 1939. The first edition was published in 1940 in London, where Koestler was a refugee.

In France, Pierre and Robert Calmann-Levy, descendants of an important dynasty of publishers of Jewish origin, only published the book after the war, in December 1945.[2] The Nazis had closed down the publishing house during the war, a measure consistent with their policy of keeping French publishing Aryan.

Robert Calmann-Levy got in touch with Allen Lane, the publisher of the pocket edition during the war, perhaps in 1943 or 1944. The French edition, entitled *Le Zéro et l'infini*, was an immediate success. In this essay I hope to analyze the tormented triumph of the book. The reading of Koestler's novel was greatly affected by the international political context of the moment, when the Cold War commenced in 1947. French national politics were directly influenced by its presence in terms that became increasingly conflictual, even to the point that discussions turned into harmful denunciations.

Let me remind my foreign colleagues that the French Communist party (FCP) had an important following at the end of the war. It was part of the government in 1947, and until 1956 it represented more than a fourth of the electorate. The deterioration of relations among political currents that had been allied during the Resistance was aggravated in 1947. This uncompromising political context in France had a direct impact on the reception of Koestler's novel.

The French Edition

The Calmann-Levy archives include a wealth of documents concerning the French editions of Arthur Koestler's work, but they do not solve all the mysteries. The French translation, under the direction of Penguin Books, was late in coming.[3] Throughout 1945, Robert Calmann-Levy, who had acquired the rights to another of Koestler's books (*Arrival and Departure*, or *Croisade sans croix*), planning to publish it after *Darkness at Noon*, worried and complained that he had not received the long-awaited translation. His major problem, apart from the delay in receiving the translation, was the paucity of available paper. In France, where the war had just ended, the paper supply was strictly controlled,[4] and there was very little of it. At last, on 28 December 1945, Arthur Koestler received a telegram from Robert Calmann-Levy announcing the publication of his book in an edition of 20,000 copies, according to Koestler's wishes. From the moment of publication, the editor intuited the success that the book was to have.

It is interesting to observe the precision and the regularity (about a letter a week) of Robert Calmann-Levy's correspondence with Koestler, keeping him informed of his book's success. Throughout 1946 and 1947, Robert Calmann-Levy sent Arthur Koestler an abundance of clippings discussing the book, gave him details about sales, and informed him of further editions, which often delayed the publication of other books by Koestler because paper was so scarce. Arthur Koestler faithfully answered all these communications on his blue paper. An initial good feeling developed into a real friendship between the two men.

The publisher prepared a new edition of 10,000 copies in February 1946.[5] It was immediately sold out. On 28 March he let Koestler know that a third edition of 20,000 copies is planned.[6] That edition turned out to be 44,000 copies–immediately out of print.[7] On 3 May 1946 Robert Calmann-Levy told Arthur Koestler that a fourth edition of 20,000 copies is planned (30,000 will actually be printed), while 15,000 copies of *Arrival and Departure* have already been reserved by bookstores.[8] On 11 July 1946 Calmann-Levy wrote Koestler that 115,000 copies of *Darkness at Noon* had been sold, and a fifth edition of 20,000 copies was under way.[9] Seventy thousand copies were immediately reserved by bookstores in Paris and throughout France. Robert Calmann-Levy undertook an edition of 100,000 copies early in 1947. More than 300,000 copies of *Darkness at Noon* were sold in France between 1945 and 1948.[10]

Public Acclaim

Clearly, there was an impassioned public acclaim for *Darkness at Noon*. The press did not lag behind this general acclamation. From the time of its publication and throughout the entire year, numerous reviews were dedicated to the book.

Le Figaro published an article full of praise for the book on 9 February 1946, appreciating that it had "violently stirred public awareness" and that "hallucinating scenes leave the reader with vivid impressions." The author of the review, who briefly recounted the accusations of the Moscow trials and evoked "the rise of the Stalinist dictatorship," which is the context of the book, emphasized that Arthur Koestler's novel is a perfect illustration of "the conflict between revolutionary action and moral ideas."[11]

In *La Minerve* of 22 February 1946, Yves Gandon praised the novel as well. In his summary of Koestler's theme ("is the individual only a pawn on a chess board, or has he an independent existence?"), he considered that the novel illustrates the conflict between "two moralities which cause dissension in the world," one Christian and humane, the other materialist with its point of departure being that "the end justifies the means." Observing that Arthur Koestler was able to write as analyst as well as novelist, the critic judged *Darkness at Noon* to be "without question, a work of exceptional merit."

There are endless examples of critical acclaim for Koestler's book, praising his qualities as an analyst and a writer. All accounts of the work assess it as a lucid exemplification of the tendencies of the Communist regime in the U.S.S.R. (the term *totalitarian* is often used) as well as an examination of the effects of power on human psychology. The book was to play an important part in the reflections of many liberal Democrats and to inspire certain evaluations of the Soviet regime. This was the case with Raymond Aron, for example, when he published *Le Grand Schisme* in 1948.[12]

Communist Hostility: A Growing Campaign of Denunciation

The Communists' attitude toward *Darkness at Noon* can only be understood in the context of the Cold War, which exacerbated their outlook and their behavior. Hardly favorable, and that is a euphemism, toward a book that denounces the Stalinist trials or an author who is an ex-Communist, during the early months of 1946 the Communists maintained a contentious posture while they established a strategy of suspicion.[13]

In *Action* of 5 April 1946 Claude Roy dissipated illusions and instilled doubts.[14] Is Roubachof's indecision not that of "a counterfeit man, completely cut off from the universe and other men?" "In this book written in 1939 and published in 1940, it could be said that there is no national-socialist menace, no *Wehrmacht*, that Munich had never been, that Mussolini was never born, that Hitler is inconceivable, that Soviet Russia reigns without peril, alone in the world, its existence concerning only itself."

If all the ingredients of the future campaign of denunciation are there, they are present in a euphemistic form. Arthur Koestler's theses are discussed, not denounced. The tone will become harsher, since Communist strategy will change in the autumn of 1947. A new strategy dictated by Moscow replaced that of the sacred union adopted during the Resistance and then at the Liberation: confrontation was the new tactic. The FCP's attitude had already evolved since it left the government in May 1947. During a meeting of nine European Communist parties in the autumn of 1947, Andre Jdanov presented this new direction and introduced the creation of the Kominform. The French and Italian Communist parties were roundly reproached for their attitudes of collaboration with their governments.

The enemy was designated: American imperialism. This radicalism had immediate effects on the attitudes of the FCP concerning cultural and intellectual matters: *Les Lettres Françaises* was taken in hand, all "class enemies" were denounced, and so on. Arthur Koestler, like Victor Kravchenko, whose French translation of *I Chose Freedom* appeared in the fall of 1947, took on symbolic values.[15] They both became active renegades who falsified the image of the Soviet Union and of Communism as it was evolving. They had to be denounced.

Censorship and Censure

The Communist press alternately applied silence (boycotting the book, no longer discussing it), censorship, and invective. According to several Koestler specialists, the Communist party went to see Robert Calmann-Levy to ask him to renounce further editions of the novel.[16] Koestler echoed this pressure in his autobiographical essays: "The communists tried to intimidate the publishers of the book. When they did not succeed, they bought up entire stocks of it in bookstores in the suburbs and throughout the country, and destroyed them. As a result, the book was sold on the black market, for four or five times its real price, between editions."[17] He queried his publisher in a letter of 8 June 1946 and was reassured that there had been no pressure put upon him.[18] Did Calmann-Levy try to dissimulate the intensity of pressure and censure under which he had to work? No further archival information is available to help us clarify that question today.

The Communists found the success of Koestler's book intolerable and, even more so, the discussion of the Soviet regime that it incited. In 1947 Roger Garaudy, member of the party's National Committee, published a pamphlet entitled *Literature for Gravediggers* in which he harshly denounced *petit-bourgeois* writers one by one: Jean-Paul Sartre, François Mauriac, André Malraux, and Arthur Koestler.[19] The FCP clarified its doctrine during the late 1940s before engaging in "the battle of the book" during the fifties.[20] Laurent Casanova, member of the National Committee, presented this doctrine in June 1947: "There is a reactionary art just as there are reactionary politics. . . . There is an avant-garde art just as there are avant-garde politics."[21] What should be encouraged are "the exalting virtues of an optimistic literature," based upon the values of the masses: "using the people's life experiences as a point of departure, a certain number of moral values belonging to our time and our nation may be defined. . . . As long as there is action among the masses, the essential cultural values may really be found in the struggles of the masses." Intellectuals and artists should serve those values, and their enemies are denounced:

Mr. Koestler and Mr. Dos Passos formulate their ideological arguments in a foreign country, and many defeatists in countries weakened by the war draw strength from those arguments, which find resounding echoes in France. American films bearing a foreign ideology invade our cinemas, American books inundate our bookstore shelves, foreign film companies and publishing houses, through economic and cultural exchanges, even settle in France, contributing to the degradation of our own national character.

This thesis, presented as a defense of a popular, anti-imperialist tenet, displays an overt nationalism that merits further discussion.

In 1950 Jean Kanapa published an even more virulent attack in the form of a pamphlet entitled *The Traitor and the Proletariat, or Koestler and Company, Ltd.*, dedicated to *Darkness at Noon*.[22] Kanapa condemned the support and solidarity that consistently helped Koestler in his role as head of an organized campaign. The disparagement not only targeted *Darkness at Noon* but Arthur Koestler himself: "Koestler's activity, beginning with the *Testament of Spain*, is entirely devoted to a literary justification of the unjustifiable: first, desertion and then, still worse, treason."[23] His heroes are merely "traitors to their people, to the revolution, turncoats among the proletariat." Arthur Koestler represents nothing more than the derisive efforts of a bourgeoisie literature "to disclaim an already existing socialism, the workers' movement, the enormity of its aims, the courage of its militants, the nobility of its leaders."[24]

Neither Darkness nor Noon: *Esprit, Les Temps Modernes*

Faithful to what was to become its tradition, *Esprit* sought a "middle way." Martin Brionne dedicated an article to Koestler's book in May 1946 with a significant title: "Neither Darkness nor Noon."[25] Reproaching the conspiracy of silence as well as the imprecations of the Communist press, Martin Brionne did not really confront Koestler's book; he digressed endlessly in his arguments and did not conclude anything. Considering that Koestler's novel posed the question of modern Machiavellianism (does the end justify the means?), Brionne proposed a parallel between the early stages of Communism and early Christianity. Shouldn't Communism, as a young religion, be pardoned for its errors?[26]

A year later, *Esprit* discussed the book once again, this time in an article by Bertrand d'Astorg.[27] Admitting the book's success, he criticized the Communist party's diatribes against it but at the same time indicated his reservations.[28] Even the American ambassador in

Moscow understood that the Russians were waging a battle against a fifth column, d'Astorg argued.

Doesn't every revolution pass through phases when one must consider that the end justifies the means? Spelling out the real reasons for his reticence, his need to believe in a brighter future, Bertrand d'Astorg pointed out, "For if the U.S.S.R. is not the country of socialism—even a faltering, marred socialism—where can the socialist look for it: in the United States, because there is an antitrust law there dating from 1904?"[29] He concluded his article with an appeal to a new European intelligentsia, a third force, ready to reconstruct a church, be it without God or clergy, a third force from which Koestler would be excluded because of his skepticism toward the European Left.

We know that Arthur Koestler's relations with Jean-Paul Sartre, who founded *Les Temps Modernes* in 1945 in collaboration with Raymond Aron, Maurice Merleau-Ponty, Simone de Beauvoir, Jean Paulhan, and others, were stormy.[30] When Koestler returned to Paris in 1946, he met with Sartre and his group. In February 1949 their relationship was severed on the grounds of political incompatibility. But between 1949 and 1950, *Les Temps Modernes*, Sartre, and Beauvoir were not yet fellow travelers of the FCP, as they became in 1952. Even though it was impossible for them to condemn the Communist regime, they did publish critical articles in their magazine.[31] Between October 1946 and January 1947, Maurice Merleau-Ponty published three articles in *Les Temps Modernes* directly inspired by his reading of Koestler's works, *Darkness at Noon* and *The Yogi and the Commissar*. These articles form the core of his book, *Humanism and Terror*, which was published by Gallimard in 1947.[32] As Claude Lefort recalled in the preface to a later edition of the book, "The planning of *Humanism and Terror* took shape when Merleau-Ponty was reading Arthur Koestler's *Darkness at Noon*."

Far more ample than his earlier analytical works, this book by Maurice Merleau-Ponty was several hundred pages long and quite close in spirit to the assessments in *Esprit*. After 1950, when he radically refused Stalinism, he left *Les Temps Modernes*.[33] Within the limited framework of this essay, it is impossible for me to give a detailed account of Merleau-Ponty's position. As Claude Lefort so rightly emphasized, throughout his book Merleau-Ponty and his double are present, confronting each other and disagreeing without ever seeing each other. Maurice Merleau-Ponty summed up his incapacity to take a firm stand, considering himself to be "in an inextricable situation": "One cannot be an anti-Communist and one and not be a Communist." He constantly weighed the blemishes of capitalism against the abuses of Communism.[34] Declaring himself a

Marxist, Merleau-Ponty reproached Koestler for not being the least bit of an historian, for being pre-Marxist.[35] The accused in the Moscow trials may therefore be subjectively innocent and objectively guilty. The Yogis are not at grips with the Commissars; the same man is perhaps now Yogi, now Commissar, according to the point of view he adopts toward a given historical act.[36]

Maurice Merleau-Ponty, haunted by the fear of a third world war, which he deemed imminent, was equally put off by the inadequacies of both liberal and Communist worldviews (one must "remind the Marxists of their humanist inspiration" and "remind democracies of their fundamental hypocrisy"). However, in expressing an argument that will be used for a long time thereafter, he considered that "any criticism of Communism . . . really aims at the very existence of the U.S.S.R. and must be considered as an act of war," a war that must be avoided at all cost.[37]

Conclusion

The study of reactions to Arthur Koestler's novel sheds a good deal of light on postwar and Cold War French society. Hundreds of thousands of readers evidently tried to formulate an opinion with the help of a book. Can that not be considered an outstanding example of the role of reading as a public exercise in reasoning? Readers' horizons and expectations influence their way of reading. One can estimate that there were three types of readers: those who modified their worldview and acquired a fuller understanding of the Communist system through reading Koestler's book; those, on the contrary, who reinforced their own outlook, either because they shared Koestler's views and found grounds to confirm their points of view in the book or because they disagreed entirely with Koestler's opinions and considered that the book shamelessly presented events in a distorted, invented, or falsified manner (such was the reaction of the Communists);[38] and those who might include readers such as Merleau-Ponty or d'Astorg, whom the book would leave at an intermediary stage—their previous points of view were neither confirmed nor weakened. Successive reading will lead the reader to an eventual modification of his or her world outlook.

This incident shows how deeply France was divided between two radically opposed currents of influence. The intelligentsia was most often sympathetic toward the pro-Communists. Today, such a lack of awareness of Soviet totalitarianism seems not only incomprehensible but also reprehensible. However, it is also useful to understand what led to this blindness. There is no doubt that the nearness to the war explains the gratitude felt toward the Soviet Union. But the reluctance to acknowledge the Stalinist oppression for what it was must have to do with a rapport with oneself and with the world, as Claude Lafort remarks so rightly in his preface. The mourning for a lost ideology, mourning for a lost belief in a better world was—at the end of the war— the most terrible bereavement in history; for many people, it was intolerable. It was the need to believe that constituted the group of readers who were willingly impervious to some of their reading.

Notes

1. All references to Arthur Koestler's various autobiographical writings are taken from the remarkable edition of his collected *Oeuvres autobiographiques*, re-edited by Phil Casoar in the Robert Laffont edition (Coll. Bouquins, 1994). In his preface, Phil Casoar evokes the facts we are concerned with within this text.
2. For the history of the Calmann-Levy editions, see Jean-Yves Mollier, *Michel et Calmann-Levy ou la naissance de l'édition moderne: 1836-1891* (Paris: Calmann-Levy, 1984).
3. The agreement between Penguin and Calmann-Levy that relegated Calmann-Levy to the role of a subcontractor with Penguin for the French rights was an example of the singular conditions in publishing after the war. This situation soon became unacceptable for Robert Calmann-Levy, who corresponded with Allen Lane about procuring full rights as French publisher of *Le Zéro*. Arthur Koestler seconded him in this effort. A good sport, Allen Lane quickly agreed to withdraw and allow Calmann-Levy and Koestler to establish a direct contract, which was signed in 1946.
4. *Action*, founded in September 1944, was increasingly directed by the FCP: "*Action* was a refuge for the intellectual Communists in discord with Jdanovism. But it was a short-lived refuge and, through an elaborate process that escaped its participants, it became a strictly Communist publication." Jeanine Verdes-Leroux, *Au service du parti. Le Parti communiste, les intellectuels et la culture, 1944-1956 et 1956-1958* (Paris: Fayard-Minuit, 1983, 1987).
5. Letter to Arthur Koestler, 18 February 1946: "You will see from the enclosed clippings that almost all the critics have been immensely enthusiastic!" Letter of 27 February 1946: "Only a thousand copies left of first edition of *Zero*. Second edition at twenty thousand in course of print. Congratulations." Letter of 14 March 1946: "Almost 10,000 copies of the new editions, which should be out within the week, is already reserved." Calmann-Levy Archives.
6. "I'm doing my utmost to find the paper for a third edition of 20,000 copies." Letter from R. Calmann-Levy to A. Koestler, 28 March 1946, Calmann-Levy Archives.
7. "The new edition, of which 30,000 copies are already ordered, will be on sale within ten days." Letter from R. Calmann-Levy to A. Koestler, 25 April 1946, Calmann-Levy Archives.
8. Letter of 3 May 1946, Calmann-Levy Archives.
9. "We are thinking of a fifth edition of 22,000 copies, but if we manage to get hold of more paper, we'll print more." Letter of 11 July 1946, Calmann-Levy Archives.

10. After this success, Calmann-Levy became A. Koestler's official French publisher, while prior to this, Koestler had accepted the proposals of various publishing houses. Charlot had published *Le Yogi et le commissaire* in 1945. In its articles, the press often associates the two books, very much related in content but different in form (one a novel, the other an essay). In 1946 Charlot published *La Lie de la terre*, an autobiographical book recounting Koestler's war years and particularly his internment in the Vernet prison camp. Before the war, Albin Michel had published *Un Testament espagnol* in Denise Van Moppes's French translation.

11. "Le Zéro et l'infini," signed Les Alguazils (*sic*), *Le Figaro*, 9 February 1946.

12. Gallimard, 1948. Raymond Aron is also responsible for another collection (*Liberté de l'esprit*), with the collaboration of Manes Sperber. Both men are Arthur Koestler's friends. Koestler, in his letters, often suggests that his editor consult them for their advice on matters concerning the publication of his work.

13. In January 1946, *Les Lettres Françaises* published an article on *Le Zéro* with a tone that astonishes R. Calmann-Levy, who writes to Koestler: "Enclosed you will find three reviews of *Le Zéro*: a magnificent one in *Lettres Françaises*, considering its definite tendency toward Communism; still, it could not refrain from writing about your book." Letter from R. Calmann-Levy to Koestler, 4 February 1946, Calmann-Levy Archives. We must remember that Jacques Decour and Jean Paulhan founded *Les Lettres Françaises* in September 1942. Though a Communist sensibility was present from the outset, it was "taken in hand" by the Communist party in the autumn of 1947.

14. *Action*, founded in September 1944, was increasingly directed by the FCP: "*Action* was a refuge for the intellectual Communists in discord with Jdanovism. But it was a short-lived refuge, and, through an elaborate process that escaped its participants, it became a strictly Communist publication." Verdes-Leroux, *Au service du parti.*

15. *J'ai choisi la liberté*, published by Albin-Michel in October 1947. On 13 November 1947, *Les Lettres Françaises* published an article entitled "What Made Kravchenko," supposedly written by a certain Sim Thomas and received from the United States. Extremely troubled by several similar articles published in the weekly, Victor Kravchenko accused both *Les Lettres Françaises* and *l'Humanité* of defamation. The trial took place early in 1949. The repercussions of the Kravchenko affair were even more pronounced in French society than those caused by *Le Zéro*. But one reaction cannot be understood without the other.

16. Phil Casoar mentions this interdependency in his preface to Koestler's *Oeuvres autobiographiques.* Pierre Debray-Ritzen assumes that "the publisher R. Calmann-Levy received a FCP delegation headed by Jacques Duclos in 1945. They ordered him to relinquish publication of *Le Zéro et l'infini* in France. The publisher went ahead with his plans." Arthur Koestler, *La Herne* (1975).

17. Koestler, *Hiéroglyphes.*

18. "I gather from an article by Randolph Churchill that Communist circles in France have tried to put pressure on you to prevent the publication and reprinting of *Le Zéro*. I would be grateful if you could give me full information about this affair. If you want me to treat the information or part of it confidentially, please tell me." A. Koestler to R. Calmann-Levy, 8 June 1946, Calmann-Levy Archives. R. Calmann-Levy's answer in June 1946: "About the issue concerning *Le Zéro*, we have never been pressured to cease publishing or re-editing, and all the stories in the French press are nothing but journalistic rumors." Calmann-Levy Archives.

19. Roger Garaudy, *Une littérature de fossoyeurs* (Editions Sociales, 1947).
20. Marc Lazar, "Les 'Batailles du livre' du Parti communiste français (1950–1952)." *XXe Siècle* 10 (1986).
21. Laurent Casanova, "Le Communisme et l'art," lecture given by L. Casanova at the 11th Congress of the FCP, 25–28 June 1947.
22. Jean Kanapa, *Le Traître et le prolétaire*. The title is an unmistakable allusion to Koestler's *The Yogi and the Commissar*, published during the same period.
23. He pretended to have fought in the Spanish Civil War, but he has never been anything but a "petit bourgeois adventurer," "complacently released by Franco . . . at the intervention of Lady Astor" and the Vatican. Arthur Koestler, in fact, "deserted." A simple adventurer, Koestler "surrendered to the Phalangists, simply looking for a thrill and for the mark this gesture would make on his future undertakings." Kanapa, *Le Traître et le prolétaire*.
24. Further on, Kanapa continues: "[To publish Koestler is to favor] the return of the Nazis . . . because if Koestler attacks Communism and the Communists the way he does, it is because the Communists are the best defenders of our national independence." Ibid.
25. Martin Brionne, "Ni zéro ni infini," *Esprit*, 1 May 1946: 692–702. This catch phrase will be used as a gesture of defiance against the book. José Corti, for example, the well-known postwar Paris bookseller who was to become a publisher of famous books as well, fervently opposed Koestler's book because of his solidarity with the Soviet Communists and refused to sell the book in his shop, replying to customers who asked for it, "Je n'ai ni *Zéro* ni infini." The anecdote says a lot about the passionate reactions caused by the book, as well as the agreement with these reactions by a broad social segment, including a very prestigious bookseller who exercised censorship in this case, refusing to sell a book of which he disapproved. That such behavior was not always found shocking is an indication of the state of mind of that period, when people were quick to join some group and to accept the many signs that signified belonging.
26. "What I am trying to break down, with these all too brief lines, is the opposition Koestler has forced us into; I should like to say that for the Christian, humanity is not zero, and man alone must not be everything; that for the Communist all hope is not lost when a man is still someone, and that a singing humanity cannot be a mass of larvae. And while underscoring these points, I am trying to keep from misusing–as various extremists have done–Koestler's admirable book." Brionne, "Ni zéro ni infini."
27. "My bookseller told me a month ago that people were standing in line at Calmann-Levy's shop to buy *Le Zéro et l'infini*." Bertrand Astorg, "Arthur Koestler, prix Nobel 1960," *Esprit* 10 (October 1947): 378–98.
28. Concerning the way the book was received, it is worth quoting from the beginning of d'Astorg's article: "The book has caused a stir. It has had excellent reviews in the literary columns of the big dailies where the usual trend is to review only the dullest love stories. Its impact was immediately weighed in on a political scale: The RLP must recommend it to its members and *l'Aube*, to its followers. As for the Communist party, it sent out the signal to boycott and exclude it totally. Claude Morgan, in *Les Lettres Françaises* did not hesitate (just when we are celebrating the anniversary and the glorious celebrations of the Red Army) to sow discord (a scandalous book comes out . . .) and to affront the publisher by reminding him, with a certain amount of bad taste, that the Jews owed a lot to the glorious Red Army and

therefore . . . the Calmann brothers would have been most astonished three years ago, in the London gardens of our delegation where they happily waited to obtain the rights for such an excellent novel, if they had been told at the time that the book would also result in them having their origins tossed in their faces." Ibid.

29. Ibid.

30. In *Hiéroglyphes*, Arthur Koestler refers to this. There is a delightful little book by Pierre Pachet on the same subject, a commentary on a sculpture by Jean-Louis Faure entitled *Jean-Paul Sartre and Simone de Beauvoir Refusing to Shake Arthur Koestler's Hand,* in Jean-Louis Faure and Pierre Pachet, *Bêtise de l'intelligence* (Nantes: Joca Seria Eds., 1995).

31. Michel Winock retraces the major political developments in Sartre's trajectory, together with his team on *Les Temps Modernes*, in *Le Siècle des intellectuels* (Seuil, 1997).

32. Maurice Merleau-Ponty, *Humanisme et terreur: essai sur le problème communiste* (Paris: Gallimard, 1947). Reprinted in 1980 with an introduction by Claude Lefort (Idées Gallimard).

33. This rupture is formalized in the publication of the *Aventures de la dialectique* by Maurice Merleau-Ponty in 1955 by Gallimard. In it is a chapter on "Sartre and Ultra-Bolshevism."

34. "The Marxist criticism of capitalism remains valid, and it is clear that today, anti-Sovietism includes the same components of brutality, pride, instability, and anxiety that were present in fascism. On the other hand, the revolution is now at a standstill: it is sustaining and worsening the dictatorial apparatus while renouncing revolutionary freedom for the proletariat in its Soviets and its party as well as the humane functioning of the state." Merleau-Ponty, *Humanisme et terreur,* 49.

35. "Political action must be judged not only from a moral point of view but equally according to the historical context and the dialectic situation when it is taken." Ibid., 121.

36. "However good-willed we may be, we act without a precise understanding of the objective sense of our actions, we build an idea of a future based only on probabilities, asking something of the future. We may be condemned for this, for events are unequivocal. A man cannot eliminate his own presence in terms of freedom and judgment . . . nor can he contest the competence of the tribunal of history, because when he acts he involves others and, eventually, all mankind." Ibid., 158.

37. An example of the constant activity of the author-reader Maurice Merleau-Ponty is his discussion, in the preface to *Humanisme et terreur*, of the way his own ideas are received. He feels he's been misunderstood in his efforts toward a middle way. He evokes the "violent reproaches" he had to deal with because of his remarks about "this famous and little known book . . . which has not been read," readers being carried away by their emotions. Merleau-Ponty points out: "When only a third of our study had appeared . . . people who usually did not get involved in polemics . . . sat down at their desks and threw themselves into writing and, in a tone of moral reprobation, composed refutations lacking the merest trace of lucidity: sometimes making us say the opposite of what we were saying, sometimes ignoring the problem we are trying to state." Ibid., 60. The Communists had, in fact, accused him of justifying "a victorious Hitler," while the liberals claimed that he was justifying the Moscow trials.

38. In *Les Staliniens, une expérience politique, 1944–1956* (Fayard, 1975), Dominique Desanti describes the role of *Zéro et l'infini* in Communist circles as "an agent of contrast and consequently federation."

Library Secret Fonds and the Competition of Societies

István Király

The competition between the socialist/Communist social system and the capitalist social system elicited a need for secrecy. This ideological battle took place during the Cold War, which is conceptually defined as "the *unarmed* development of a competition between antagonistic social systems" where the goal is to "suppress" or "liquidate" the competition. This organized secrecy played a part in structuring life within each of these systems. The secret collections in Romanian libraries consisting of banned books contributed directly to this secrecy. Library secret fonds were used to control the circulation of information within a system or throughout other systems. These prohibited materials were withdrawn from circulation and kept confidential. Libraries kept lists of these fonds separate from the regular collection, and these lists were kept and updated throughout the years. During the Communist regime in Romania, the lists of forbidden books were considered "an efficient instrument for the political struggles from the inside of the Communist party." Library secret fonds are a symbol of the antagonism between the two political systems of the Cold War.

In this essay I intend to analyze, using Romania an as example, the secret fonds as specific products of the societies of real socialism founded–by project and from the beginning–in competition with capitalism and with Western democracies.

When they use the term "Cold War," historians mean quite different periods, processes, and events. I will not debate their theories. I am interested in the *conceptual essence* of this term. I will try to define it in view of finding the extent to which it is able to present the internal and external structuring generated by competitive relationships between two antagonistic social systems.

As an expression, "Cold War" defines in its conceptual meaning the unarmed development of a competition between antagonistic social systems, that is, a competition where the permanent and essential stake has been and has remained an expectation of suppressing and liquidating the competitive partner. Though this competition was structured and restructured in various manners and intensity in space and time, the stake, that is, the prospective objective of one system's liquidation by the other one, has still remained unaltered in its essence.

When speaking of social systems, I do not refer to a certain number of countries and states but instead make reference to projects of social organization that are put into practice in such a way that, in their structuring, the tendentious articulation of their relationship with a competitive partner defined by ideology and perception is fixed. From the first country, and simultaneously with the victory of the Bolshevik revolution in Russia, socialism was set up with the view of liquidating capitalist society's injustice throughout the globe. Additionally, the last countries that have remained bastions of the socialist regime cannot renounce their global judgment on the nature of the capitalist system. For this reason, the relation is, on the one hand, interiorized and, on the other, exteriorized by actions, ideologies, and perceptions arranged in a definite way by the relation's nature itself as well as by the conjuncture politics of "administering" conflictual matters. The main elements of this structuring are perception of the self, perception of the competitive partner (enemy), and perception of the competition's determined situations. The same structure yields "glissando" but in a different direction, both toward the inside and toward the outside. And the competition's results, as we can see it nowadays, when the Soviet block has disintegrated, are not decided, in fact, as depending on given situations but on the ability of the two systems to have integration, during historical and situational oscillations, the essential stake itself of the competition. That is, depending on the extent to which they could or could not integrate on all levels (economic, political, ideological, and so on each time), they could be subjected to this essential stake. Although, for example, the politics of "peaceful coexistence" between systems seemed to succeed in its ideological integration (by "delay")[1] and, to a certain extent, on the plan of external politics (by "realism"), the countries of real socialism failed in the economic integration of the stake. And renouncing partially the stake under the form of Gorbachev, *glasnost* and *perestroika* have rapidly resulted in the block's integration and, in fact, in its disappearance.

Toward the inside, the same structure of perceptions is directed to avoidance and disconnection of system crises. For the West, this matter became evident during the crisis of 1929, which, together with problems inherited as a result of the First World War and together with competition from the U.S.S.R., resulted in unleashing the Second World War. For the U.S.S.R., the problem of its own system's crises is raised concomitantly with the NEP (Novaia Economiceskaia Politika) politics, being afterward strongly ideologized and occulted.

Library secret fonds, as the characteristic library fonds of a socialist system, are connected to all elements and all directions of the structure of competition between systems. They carry out and determine the perception of the self, that of the enemy and the conjunctural perception of the competition's "state," both for the internal construction and for the external relationships and oppositions of the system. They are tools and means of controlling the circulation of information, on the one hand, in the inside of the system and, on the other hand, between the systems. So they are, under the conditions of the Cold War, instruments of ideological struggle, of propaganda, and of ideas, that is, the very essential means of achieving a competition between systems.

But beyond their purely competitive nature, library secret fonds are connected, ontologically speaking, to another principle that, in its turn, occupies a specific place and role in building the global reach of the socialist system. In question is the principle of the secret's category, which has acquired such a central and essential role in the internal structuring and relationship of real socialist society, that it cannot be found anywhere but in history?

Secret and Socialism

The specific place occupied by the category of secret in structuring the global reach of real socialism has deep roots in the history of the Communist movement itself. Almost all Communist parties that have emerged as being the dominant political force in a socialist country have had a period of illegality in their history. Illegality, for a political movement, means a secret organization and a proper contact, organizational and practical, with the category of secret.

Emerging as victorious, arriving with or without external aid, at power, and legal as well, the Communist parties resuscitate the accumulated experience of their contacts with the category of secret. All this is done under the form of a competition and under that of an inclination toward its utilization. They have characterized and accompanied all Communist parties, along all the road covered by their domination and in all countries in which they have been or are in power.

Communist parties pass through the experience of their contact with the category of the secret, having at their basis a certain particular ideology as well. This ideology, the Marxist-Leninist one, is totalitarian in essence, aiming, on the one hand, at the liquidation of social relationships of the capitalist system and, on the other hand, at assuring an "aware" control of all spheres of social life. This is supposed to build a state party that disposes of all means for controlling the society conceived as an indivisible integer, found in a historical competition.

Binding themselves in a total restructuring of political, economic, administrative, and cultural entities of the societies they dominated, Communist parties were able to utilize the category of secret, and the proceedings of concealment, in an extremely extended and varied way. From secret policies and political processes conceived and conducted in secret, to the system of generalized denouncement of the hypertrophied system of state secrets, to the complicated mechanisms needed to maintain the function of these secrets, Communist parties proved competent in and an uncommon inclination for the utilization of the secret.

The engagement of the category of secret in structuring a social globalism induces, however, at the same time, a typical fixation in the categorial organization of the secret itself. So in spite of the utilitarian, surprising variety of secrets, in the countries of real socialism a systemic tendency of these societies exists in order that, within them, the typically characteristic and dominant form should become state secret. This tendency is explained not only by the preponderance of state properties but, rather, by the preponderance of the part played by the socialist state as a source of absolute subjective right in organizing and controlling social life.

The tendency of state secret to become a dominant and, later on, the uniquely recognized form of secret in socialist society may be very clearly demonstrated by following the progress of Romanian legislation. It shows very clearly, both in special legislation and in the more applicative zones of the *Criminal Code,* that the direction of all forms of the secret, legally recognized in society (for example, also the professional secrets, those of service), should become something other than parts of state secret. The latter term came to cover the entire sphere of all nondestined data from the beginning of publicity. All that is not destined for publicity from the beginning becomes the secret that directly interests the Romanian socialist state.

This Communist legislation—in this particular case, the Romanian one—has opened the category of the secret toward the horizon of a proliferation, inconceivable under other conditions, and, at the same time, the sense itself of the legislation that, instead of settling secrets with regard to their content's spheres, becomes a means of assuring their defense. In other words, this legislation is not, in its essence, something other than the public interdiction form of state secret itself.

I do not have sufficient space to analyze the evolution of this legislation. I have done so on another occasion.[2] It is very important, however, for the theme of my discussion to emphasize that the tendency is to proliferate, clearly totalizing the state secret as a typical form of secret in socialism, perfectly covering the period 1953–68, during which the legislation had an important role in avoiding a de-Stalinization in Romania. Then, passing through the cardinal points 1969, 1971, 1973, and 1976–77, this legislation accompanies—as a dark alter ego—the so-called politics of peaceful coexistence between systems as well as Romania's approach to the movement of nonaligned countries presented as an apparent alternative to the "politics of blocs." It is the same legislation that, on the one hand, paves the way for emphasizing the non-Stalinist tendencies that dominated Romanian politics and life at the end of the 1970s and throughout the 1980s.

The more the system seems to appear "toward outside," so much the more in reality it shrinks in the secret, that is, in the secret that is proper to it and congenital. It regulates both the external and the internal relationships of the system.

Romanian Libraries' Secret Fonds

By library secret fonds, I mean the library fonds constituted as a result of the secret interdictions of publications. Functioning and administration of such fonds also supposes the building of a multi-level secret structure by which such interdictions are applied and preserved.

In Romania they appeared through a discrete and gradual process together with the Sovietization of the country. This fact justifies the hypothesis that the "practice" of the library secret fond was actually born long before in the crucibles of cultural politics and libraries in the U.S.S.R., being then instrumentalized in all countries under Soviet influence. Having, however, insufficient information on the birth of library secret fonds, I will concentrate on their analysis in Romania.

The above-given definition of secret fonds has to be maintained as a rule for both interpretation and utilization of the term. They are a product formed and articulated not only during time but also in a more discreet, maybe even ingenious way and, therefore, possibly a misleading one.

In Romania and, perhaps, in the other former Communist countries of Europe, library secret fonds appeared in the foundations of some fonds of interdicted publications. These fonds had been constituted on the basis of Article 16 of the Armistice Convention signed between the Romanian government and the governments of the United Nations on 12 September 1944. As a result, by a decree signed by King Michael I on 4 May 1945, the publications printed in Romania between January 1917 and August 1944, containing Iron Guardist, fascist, Hitlerist, chauvinistic, and racist ideas, were interdicted. The libraries had to withdraw these publications from circulation, store them, and make their separate inventory. To consult them it was necessary to obtain a special approval from the head librarian, and they could be viewed only in the library.

Until 1949 several lists appear consecutively, the most sizable that of 1948, having about five hundred pages. But what is characteristic, however, of these prohibitive lists is the fact that they are entirely documents of public settlement, specifying the criteria of their being made up but also the sanctions brought about by their being encroached upon. But in 1949, a new volume of lists appeared, entitled "Undiffusible Publications," which, unlike the public character of the previous lists, became "of internal circulation," advising in its foreword that the withdrawal of publications from circulation should be made "tactfully and with discretion."

In 1949 the interdiction became of "internal use," and the operation of withdrawing publications became a discreet and confidential act. Obviously, the application of such interdictions supposes setting up a confidential administrative network as well, that is, creation within the framework of the librarians' professional community of a group based on criteria of confidence and devotion.

The creation of this ideological and administrative apparatus, as well as the withdrawal operation, lasted years. The list no longer referred to publications of the extreme right, but it included, on the basis of the Stalinist theory of internal and external intensification of the struggles between antagonistic social classes and systems, any "reactionary," "directly or indirectly hostile" publication.

In parallel with and as a result of the 1953 modification of the legislation regarding state secret, in 1955 a new list appeared by which professional secrets in the working place were assimilated, at a lower degree, to state secret. It no longer contained either justifications or instructions, since the confidential mechanism of application was already well known. The content of this list aimed mainly at printed literature from capitalist countries as well as anti-Marxist and anti-Communist publications. At the same time, all lists mirrored the internal situation and conjuncture of Communism, being–in Romania–an efficient instrument for the political struggles from the inside of the Communist party. In 1957 the last list appeared in which the year of its start-up is mentioned. It was followed by six notebooks, the last one being perhaps "edited" in 1963.

In conclusion, from a historical point of view, the fact itself of printed works' interdiction gradually loses its public character and becomes a completely secret operation. In this process one can trace the deepening and gradually sinking depths of secret. By this, however, the secret not only deepens but actually extends. The lack of "instructions" annexed to the lists does not mean their disappearance but their transfiguration. By detaching themselves from the determined lists, the instructions cease being mere orientations of application for certain lists, but they become secret documents of organization and separation of the whole structure of libraries, sketching both their public physiognomy and their secret one.

The tendency by which some secret instructions come to structure some public institutions is extremely significant for understanding the direction toward which the role of secret evolves in real socialist societies. In fact, all fundamental documents regulating the structure and functioning of libraries in Romania bear the stamp of secret by instructions and categories of all library fonds (usual, documentary, special). In other words, the whole public sphere of libraries is drawn in secret and is delimited by secret. There will be no relaxation of this tendency; on the contrary, it becomes more emphasized, going toward aberration, up to the last moment of the existence of socialism.

In the same way, the publications coming from abroad, together with those contravening the external or internal politics of the Communist party, as well as those attacking the socialist system, were, and have remained until the end, permanent targets of the process of secretization. From the beginning to the end, library secret fonds have remained means and tools of the struggle and competition between systems, both on an ideological level and on the level of information circulation.

Notes

1. Victor Sapeykov, *La Coexistence pacifique à qui elle est profitable* (Moscow: Editions de l'Agence de Presse Novost, 1979): "They [the reactionary politicians] state that socialist countries consider pacific coexistence as a means of cheating the Occident's vigilance, of gaining time for increasing their military potential, with the aim of, let's say, extending their sphere of influence in the world" (11), and then, "The ideology of the working class presents as unavoidable the passing to Communism throughout the world, it points out personal means and methods for performing this passing" (50).

2. Together with Ionut Costea and Doru Radosav, in 1995 I edited a volume entitled *Fond Secret. Fond "S" Special. Contributii la istoria fondurilor secrete de biblioteca din Romania. Studiu de caz. Biblioteca Centrala Universitara "Lucian Blaga", Cluj-Napoca, 1995* [Secret fond. Special "S" fond. Contributions to the history of library secret fonds in Romania. A case study. "Lucian Blaga" Central University Library, Cluj-Napoca] (Cluj-Napoca: Editura Dacia, 1995). The volume contains 160 pages of documents from the secret archives of the "Lucian Blaga" Central University Library in Cluj, on the basis of which the library secret fond was constituted and functioned.

Cold War Librarianship: Soviet and American Library Activities in Support of National Foreign Policy, 1946-1991

Pamela Spence Richards

The author examines the international rivalry between the United States and the Soviet Union during the Cold War and how ideological premises were used to bring libraries into the conflict. In the aftermath of World War II, the two superpowers were left with international hostilities that carried over into cultural institutions. Libraries served as important tools in the implementation of their respective governments' foreign policy. Instruments used in the Soviet Union were the Ministry of Culture's journal, *Bibliotekar'*, and the Communist party's Comecon (Council for Mutual Economic Assistance). *Bibliotekar'* targeted public librarians and influenced them against the perceived capitalist agenda of imperialism abroad. As a result, many libraries became involved in a campaign to raise domestic consciousness toward international foreign policy. Comecon concentrated on subsidizing higher education in librarianship to foreign students, and many foreign countries, financed by the Soviet Union, joined in the campaign. The United States was limited in ways to influence library collections. However, the Foreign Agents Registration Act enforced by the U.S. Congress was one way, through U.S. Customs, to stop the flow of Soviet materials into the United States. Another way was through the United States Department of State Libraries (USIS), controlled by the United States Information Agency (USIA). Overseas USIS libraries were forced to support American foreign policy. McCarthyism in America and socialism in Communist countries had a large impact on political agendas. Consequently, political philosophies developed during the Cold War curtailed national library activities and by the same token affected international foreign policy.

Libraries in the United States and the Soviet Union, like most cultural institutions in those two countries, were drawn into the ideological battle between the two superpowers that prevailed for almost half a century following World War II. During this Cold War, as the world's nations divided into two hostile camps, the superpowers used their libraries to tout their own economic and cultural superiority at home and to win the allegiance of the populations of other countries. Soviet and American libraries' involvement in the rivalry followed widely differing patterns, reflecting the two nations' contrasting governance of cultural institutions. In the U.S.S.R., the direction of all aspects of intellectual and cultural life derived from decisions made centrally by the Communist party in Moscow. The activities of all publicly accessible libraries in the Soviet Union were subordinated to the implementation of party goals, including those goals having to do with foreign policy. But in the United States, where the individual states' jurisdiction in cultural matters is jealously guarded and where some of the greatest library collections are privately owned, the degree of involvement of different types of publicly accessible libraries in the Cold War varied greatly. Only in the arena of federally run overseas libraries is it possible to speak of their total subordination to government policy aims. This essay attempts to describe the ideological premises upon which, on both sides, libraries were perceived as important in the international rivalry; to demonstrate how librarians on both sides were drawn into the rivalry; and to show how their participation affected professional life in American and Soviet libraries.

Ideological Premises

The Communist party saw libraries in the Soviet Union as important agencies in the creation and maintenance of a socialist society. According to Lenin, all of the people's needs could be met by socialism, and socialism could only be built by "improving" the political education of the people. Increasing literacy was thus only a means toward the specific end of building socialism. Implicit here is that not all reading was seen as good and that library workers had to be vigilant lest bourgeois or religious books crop up in their collections.[1] In the United States, by contrast, public libraries were conceived of as forums of intellectual diversity. Both the general public and most government leaders tended to perceive all reading as a good thing. The underlying assumption of America's library founders was that if citizens would just read widely enough, the republic would be safe from misrule.[2]

As the Soviet Union began to take an active role in international affairs after 1945, its libraries, as state-run organs of propaganda, automatically involved themselves in the state's international campaigns. But in postwar America, when the U.S. government began to articulate a distinctly anti-Soviet position, the harnessing of its diverse public, private, and academic libraries into the service of national foreign policy goals was a much more complicated task.

Soviet Libraries and Librarians in the Service of Soviet Foreign Policy

Following the turbulent years 1946–48, when the American-Soviet confrontation over the future governance of Eastern Europe ended the last vestiges of wartime collaboration, Soviet libraries and librarians were actively drawn into the campaign of raising domestic consciousness about the importance of the international struggle for socialism. In 1948, articles in the Ministry of Culture's monthly journal, *Bibliotekar'*, aimed at public librarians, began aggressively to denigrate America's right to international leadership and to warn against the dangers of the hegemony of American-style capitalism.

The single most popular accusation hurled at America was that of racism, which in Soviet eyes made the United States peculiarly unsuitable for the leadership of a world that even Harry Truman described as "90% colored."[3] A 1948 *Bibliotekar'* article on "Bourgeois Libraries in the Service of Reaction" pointed out that only 99 of the existing 734 public libraries in the southern states of the United States had services for black readers, adding that "in fact the Negro population of the U.S. in general lacks the most elementary library services."[4] One month later *Bibliotekar'* returned to the theme of racism, remarking in a report on the openings of Department of State–sponsored USIS libraries in Latin America that "the funds spent on these libraries would be more than adequate to open scores of public libraries for American blacks, but for them the love of Uncle Sam does not extend."[5]

Another favorite theme of *Bibliotekar'* (which was circulated free of charge to the U.S.S.R.'s thousands of public libraries) was the danger inherent in the United States' extension to foreign countries of its reactionary brand of librarianship, serving only the interests of the middle class. In November 1948 *Bibliotekar'* focused on U.S. stewardship of Japanese public libraries under the U.S. occupation, saying that the American advisors simply played into the hands of the Japanese reaction and that Japanese libraries were actually worse off than they had been before the war, since now "their budgets are subsumed by the police force."[6] But the threat of American ideological infiltration through libraries was not just limited to places under American occupation, it was dangerous for a country even to accept aid from the United States. *Bibliotekar'* claimed that, under the pretext of lending aid to suffering European libraries, USIS libraries were actually infiltrating them with their "microfilming installations."[7] *Bibliotekar'* further claimed that the United States was using UNESCO "as a means of spreading its influence safely under the flag of international cooperation."[8]

One way of arming Soviet librarians against the threat of American influence was to convince them of Soviet cultural superiority over all other countries, especially the United States. In July 1948 the Soviet Writers' Union urged a campaign for stressing the priority of Soviet science, which is "rightly proud of Russian primacy in the invention of the steam engine, electric light, radio and in creating the first airplane."[9] One month later *Bibliotekar'* called on librarians to carry this campaign into the libraries and to watch out for Soviet bibliographies that "parrot critical Western under-valuation of Soviet science." The journal included a list of reference books in which searches on the history of Soviet science could safely be done, as well as a list of suggestions for book exhibits on the science of the fatherland.[10]

Exporting Soviet Librarianship

In the course of the 1950s, following the foundation of the Council for Mutual Economic Assistance (Comecon) in 1949, the Communist party began aggressively to export the principles and practices of Soviet librarianship. While there would eventually be a worldwide network of Soviet cultural centers with modest libraries, the Soviets emphasized the less expensive method of organizing professional conferences and seminars at Soviet libraries for librarians from socialist or nonaligned countries and of subsidizing continuing and higher professional library education for overseas students at Soviet institutions.[11] Certainly these measures raised the professional standards in many of the targeted countries. They also served the purpose of politicizing librarianship by training librarians to act as "active agents in the class struggle." The importance of this ideological training of foreign librarians for countering the threat of American influence was stressed in a 1981 Soviet report on international socialist collaboration on bibliographic control. The author noted that the underlying purpose of all the collaborative activities of the past two decades was "the development of a common socialist culture" that would strengthen the various "brother socialist countries in three ways: (1) by helping to build a stronger scientific and technical base; (2) by assisting in the development of a 'proper orientation' to encroaching Western social ideas; and (3) by arming the brother socialist countries in their struggle with bourgeois, reformist, and revisionist ideologies."[12] The author explained this as meaning that librarians in socialist countries needed to evaluate the information streaming in from Western sources "with class consciousness and a partisan approach."

Socialist librarians also needed to be warned of the ideological dangers lurking in Western information technology. A recurring theme of the Comecon library professional conferences of the 1970s and 1980s was the need to counter the overseas influence of MARC, which was expanding its original function of making the Library of Congress cataloging machine readable by other American libraries and becoming an international system for the exchange of bibliographic information in machine-readable form. The Soviets claimed that this enabled the United States to exercise an ideological influence on the information activities of participating countries.[13]

The majority of the continuing education conferences supported by Moscow were organized specifically for librarians in the Comecon countries, which by the late 1970s included Mongolia, Vietnam, and Cuba. But in 1975 an expensive conference specifically for librarians of nonsocialist, nonaligned countries in Africa, Latin America, and Asia was staged consecutively in Moscow and Alma-Ata, Kazakhstan. Delegates from sixteen countries listened to speeches by ethnic Kazakhs and Uzbekis on the benefits derived by their cultures from Soviet rule and on the importance of librarians being active in the ideological struggle against capitalist imperialism.[14]

By far the most effective method used by the Soviets for exporting their worldview (including their foreign policy) through libraries was their massive program in subsidizing higher education in librarianship to foreign students. The single most important site for this was the Krupskaia Institute for Culture in Leningrad (now the St. Petersburg Academy of Culture), which between 1978 and 1985 annually hosted an average of one hundred such students in its five-year diploma program.[15] In addition, between 1974 and 1991 the Krupskaia Institute awarded the doctorate (*kandidat*) in librarianship to twelve Vietnamese, two Sudanese, two Cubans, two Syrians, two Afghanis, and individual librarians from Cambodia, Laos, Guinea, Kenya, and Iraq.[16] Thus nearly two thousand librarians were returned to their home countries fluent in Russian and convinced of the advantages of a centrally controlled library service active in the battle against Western ideas. A number of these graduates became influential in the cultural development of their home countries. A Vietnamese graduate of the Krupskaia Institute, for example, is currently the director of the National Library in Hanoi.[17]

American Libraries and Librarians in the Service of U.S. Foreign Policy

Like their Soviet counterparts, American leaders saw libraries as important in the ideological battle at home and abroad, but the U.S.

Congress had limited means at its disposal to influence the contents of public, private, and academic library collections. One such means was the U.S. Customs Service. As early as 1944, Congress moved to cut off the flow of Soviet materials into the United States by enforcing the exclusionary Foreign Agents Registration Act, which required booksellers of Soviet materials to register as agents of a foreign power; to place on file in Washington one copy of all books and periodicals they offered for sale; and to send to Washington, within forty-eight hours, the name and address of every person to whom they sent publications.[18] Despite the objections of such eminent librarians as Ralph Shaw of the National Library of Agriculture that these restrictions inhibited scientific research, libraries, together with educational institutions, did not secure a specific exemption from the elaborate screening of Soviet literature until 1962.[19]

The tailoring of public library collections to reflect the federal government's anti-Soviet foreign policy was most often a result of popular pressure at the local level. Senator Joseph McCarthy's anti-Communist campaign in the late 1940s and early 1950s derived much of its influence from the country's general cultural aversion to Communism and from its underdeveloped appreciation of the importance of civil liberties for oppressed minorities.[20] Especially in the South and in regions influenced by the South, library collections and activities promoting racial integration were branded as Soviet-inspired and as subversive to "the American way of life," and they were suppressed by popular demand.[21] Identification of Communist internationalism with forced "race mingling" resulted in many local public libraries, especially those in segregated areas, adopting an aggressively anti-Soviet stance. But even in industrialized nonsouthern states like New Jersey and California, campaigns of patriotic organizations for the labeling of "dangerous" books led to self-censorship by cautious librarians. One indication of how intimidated some librarians were by self-styled "patriots" was the refusal in 1955 of three school librarians who opposed book banning to permit their faces to be photographed for an Edward R. Murrow television program on the right wing's book-banning campaigns: only the librarians' silhouettes and hands appeared on the nation's television screens. The organizer of one of the California book-banning campaigns, however, had no such fears of public retribution: Mrs. Anne Smart of San Francisco, a self-appointed book censor, appeared full-face on the Murrow show to defend her list of subversive books and to tell the American public that "books are dangerous. They have caused revolutions."[22]

The hardening of the U.S. government's policy toward the U.S.S.R. in the late 1940s, coupled with the outbreak of the Korean War in June 1950, brought with it more aggressive government attempts to influence academic library collections, over which it had no legal authority. The U.S. National Security Council's declaration on 25 November 1948 that "there can be no advancement of the interests of the communist and non-communist world by mutual collaboration" threatened many long-standing international scholarly arrangements;[23] and indeed in 1951 the Federal Bureau of Investigation (FBI) actually seized a box of library exchanges bound for Prague, Czechoslovakia.[24] In 1951 the House Committee on Un-American Activities, searching for pro-Communist textbooks, demanded the submission of course reading lists from over seventy American colleges and universities.[25] Inevitably, this led to self-censorship on the part of professors and a decrease in the assignment (and library purchase) of books that might be seen as sympathetic to the Soviet Union. By the mid-1950s cooperation with the FBI as a defense against accusations of subversion by congressional committees had become the policy of Harvard University, where the Russian Research Center regularly cleared all its purchases with the FBI.[26]

Exporting American Librarianship

The libraries that the U.S. Congress most successfully forced to support American foreign policy were, of course, those that it paid for directly, namely, the overseas USIS libraries of the United States Information Agency (USIA). Founded by President Eisenhower in 1953 at the height of the Korean War and McCarthyism, the USIA suffered from the beginning, both at home and abroad, from popular perceptions that it was simply a propaganda machine for the U.S. government.[27] The USIA inherited close to a hundred overseas libraries and cultural centers originally set up by the Office of War Information during World War II. President Truman's January 1950 speech calling for a "Campaign of Truth" against Communism gave new urgency to the work of "selling America" abroad, but in the months leading up to the USIA's founding in August 1953, Senator Joseph McCarthy denounced the overseas libraries as riddled with pro-Communist books and administered by Communist sympathizers.[28] The USIA was thrown on the defensive by McCarthy's aides' widely publicized identification of "subversive" books in USIS collections, including those by best-selling authors Dashiel Hammett and Howard Fast.[29] Consequently, the USIA instituted an elaborate, politically safe method of book acquisition by its Bibliographic Division, which was required to prepare annual reviews of some six to eight thousand books for possible acquisition by the USIS libraries. Books were approved on the basis of four criteria: (1) how well the book supported U.S. policy; (2) congressional or domestic reaction to the book; (3) the book's acceptability to other cultures; and (4) whether the book was comprehensible to a foreign audience. Among the books that the USIA refused to shelve in the 1950s were Norman Mailer's *The Naked and the Dead* (1948), James Jones's *From Here to Eternity* (1951), and William Lederer's *The Ugly American* (1958). Commented one USIA officer at the time: "We have drifted into a system where anything the least controversial is pushed aside."[30]

After 1961 and the Cuban missile crisis, there was an even greater emphasis on subordinating the activities and collections of the USIA libraries and cultural centers to U.S. government policy.[31] In early 1970 *Publishers Weekly* ran a story describing the refusal of the USIA to stock a European USIS library with a number of books it had requested because their authors were not consistently laudatory of either the United States or its policies. The ban included such bulwarks of the American intellectual establishment as Henry Steele Commager, Louis Henkin, and former ambassador to Japan Edwin Reischauer.[32] In their stead, the USIA's Washington headquarters sent to the field lists of recommended conservative authors like Frederich August von Hayek, William Buckley, Allen Tate, and Max Eastman.[33] The USIS libraries' connection with American policies was so clear in foreign eyes that by the late 1950s the libraries were more often attacked than any other U.S. installations abroad (although in fairness it must be said that it was a lot easier to attack a library building than the Voice of America).[34] Mobs besieged USIS libraries in Algiers, Athens, Baghdad, Beirut, Calcutta, and Taipei in the 1950s and Rome, Cairo, Surabaya (Indonesia), Brussels, and Saigon in the 1960s.

During the administration of President Jimmy Carter (1976–80) the libraries' collections were politically diversified, but security constraints increasingly limited the foreign public's access to them.[35] (By 1980 more than seventy USIS libraries had been either bombed or burned down.)[36] Despite the hopes of some idealistic American professionals that the USIS libraries would serve as demonstration libraries, and despite the success of the publicly accessible Amerika Häuser libraries founded in the American zone of Germany in the late 1940s, USIS libraries have had only limited impact on librarianship in their host countries, and that influence was most often the result of demonstrations of modern library technology. For security, financial, and policy reasons, the USIS libraries increasingly concentrated their focus on a limited elite target audience of local opinion leaders (journalists, academics, graduate students), with all patrons by 1991 having to pass through a security check by an armed guard.

At the height of the Cold War, two American library leaders, perhaps rankling under the federal government's apparent indifference to librarianship's strategic potential, insisted that the profession involve itself in the ideological struggle. Library educator Lawrence Thompson saw librarianship as a tool for cementing strategic military alliances, commenting in 1952 that "it is essential that our allies know not only something of our skills in warmaking but also something of our skills in things of the spirit. Specifically, we can export the Anglo-American variety of librarianship."[37] Librarianship could also be a key to maintaining America's technical lead over the Soviets. In a keynote address delivered before the Special Libraries Association in 1956, Jesse Shera, dean of the library school at Case Western Reserve University, warned of the pioneering information processing being done in Moscow by the All-Union Institute of Science and Technology and asked his audience: "What new bibliographic achievements have we to show since the UNESCO Conference on Improving Bibliographic Services met in Paris in 1950? On our own ability to put knowledge to work may rest the very future of our civilization and the perpetuation of our cherished way of life. We are engaged in a grim game; we may not long hold all the high cards, if indeed we do now, and—make no mistake about it—this time we are playing for keeps."[38]

Conclusion

For half a century, the United States and the Soviet Union were not only each other's principal military adversaries but also each other's ideological and moral rivals. In that sense the Cold War profoundly shaped the public philosophy and cultural life of each country, including its libraries. We have seen how the Soviets prioritized the education of foreign librarians, while the Americans built a large chain of USIS libraries to exhibit selected American publications and American library technology. Ultimately, Soviet fears about American influence infiltrating into socialist cultures through American information technology were borne out: American electronic utilities, online databases, and bibliographic formats ultimately prevailed over the information organization and processing techniques of both UNESCO and the former Soviet Union. However, many emerging nations retain the centralized information infrastructures they adopted under Soviet tutelage, and these are still run by Soviet-trained professionals. The next decades will show how the tensions produced by this mixed legacy of the Cold War rivalry in librarianship will resolve themselves.

202 Soviet and American Library Activities

Notes

1. K. I. Abramov, *Istoriia bibliotechnogo dela v SSSR* (Moscow: Kniga, 1980), chap. 7.
2. Jesse Shera, *Foundations of the Public Library* (Chicago: American Library Association, 1949), 217.
3. Quoted in Michael S. Sherry, *In the Shadow of War: The United States since the 1930s* (New Haven, Conn.: Yale University Press, 1995), 146.
4. B. Kozlovskii, "Burzhuaznye biblioteki na sluzhbe reaktsii," *Bibliotekar'* (May 1948): 28.
5. B. Kozlovskii, "Burzhuaznye biblioteki na sluzhbe reaktsii," *Bibliotekar'* (June 1948): 40.
6. B. Kozlovskii, "O iaponskikh bibliotekakh i ikh amerikanskikh nonechiteliakh," *Bibliotekar'* (November 1948): 32.
7. Kozlovskii, "Burzhuaznye" (June 1948): 41.
8. Ibid.
9. *Literaturnaia Gazeta*, 17 July 1948, quoted in Werner Hahn, *Postwar Soviet Politics: The Fall of Zhdanov and the Defeat of Moderation 1946-1953* (Ithaca, N.Y.: Cornell University Press, 1982), 83.
10. N. Vil'chur, "Propaganda literatury vydaiushchikhsia deiateliakh otechestvennoi nauki i, tekhniki," *Bibliotekar'* (August 1948): 6.
11. For a more detailed account of Soviet overseas information assistance, see Pamela Spence Richards, "The Reconfiguration of International Information Infrastructure Assistance since 1991," *Bulletin of the American Society for Information Science* (June-July 1998).
12. I. G. Gorbacheva, *Sotrudnichestvo evropeiskikh sotsialisticheskikh stran v realizatsii programmy universalnogo bibliograficheskogo ucheta* (Moscow: Moscow State Institute of Culture, 1981), 6.
13. Ibid., 7.
14. Egypt, Bangladesh, Venezuela, Guinea, Zaire, India, Congo-Brazzaville, Mexico, Yemen, Peru, Senegal, Syria, Somalia, Tunisia, Sri Lanka, and Ethiopia. See R. Ia. Varaksina, "Seminar bibliotechnikh rabotnikov stran Azii, Afrika i Latinskoi Ameriki 'Planirovanie natsional'nykh bibliotechnykh sistem' Moskva/Alma-Ata 4-11 sentiabria 1975g," *Bibliotekovedenie i Bibliografiia za Rubezhom* 57 (1976): 72-94.
15. Interview with Larisa P. Moskalenko, since the 1960s Dean of Foreign Students at the St. Petersburg Academy of Culture (formerly the Krupskaia Institute), St. Petersburg, 24 October 1997.
16. Dissertations in library science, typed list in the archives of the St. Petersburg Academy of Culture, St. Petersburg.
17. Interview with Galina Verganova, Associate Dean for International Relations, St. Petersburg Institute of Culture, New York, 24 April 1998.
18. American Russian Institute, "Special Libraries Conference on Russian Materials, November 17, 1945, New York City," mimeographed report, Slavic and Baltic Division, New York Public Library, 33.
19. Ibid., 18; "Libraries Exempt from Ban on Communist Literature," *Library Journal* 87 (15 November 1962): 41-56.
20. Richard M. Fried, *Nightmare in Red: The McCarthy Era in Perspective* (New York: Oxford University Press, 1990), 9.
21. See especially Louise S. Robbins, "Racism and Censorship in Cold War Oklahoma: The Case of Ruth W. Brown and the Bartlesville Public

Library," *Southwestern Historical Quarterly* (July 1996): 18-46.

22. "Murrow's TV Program Exposes Book Banning," *Library Journal* 80, (15 September 1955): 1245.

23. Sigmund Diamond, *Compromised Campus: The Collaboration of Universities with the Intelligence Community 1945-1955* (New York: Oxford University Press), 54.

24. Ibid., 208.

25. Fried, *Nightmare in Red*, 100.

26. Diamond, *Compromised Campus*, 47.

27. Robert E. Elder, *The Information Machine: The United States Information Agency and American Foreign Policy* (Syracuse, N.Y.: Syracuse University Press, 1968), 33.

28. Walter L. Hixson, *Parting the Curtain: Propaganda, Culture and the Cold War 1945-1961* (New York: St. Martin's Press, 1997), 52.

29. Fried, *Nightmare in Red*, 34.

30. Hixson, *Parting the Curtain*, 123.

31. Elder, *The Information Machine*, 255.

32. "New USIA Ban on Certain Books Overseas," *Publishers Weekly* 196, (15 December 1970): 19-20.

33. "USIA Moves to Right in Book Selection," *Library Journal* 95, (1 February 1970): 435.

34. Hixson, *Parting the Curtain*, 124.

35. "New Views on Overseas Libraries," *Publishers Weekly*, 29 March 1978: 22.

36. Donald Hausrath, "International Communication Agency," in *Encyclopedia of Library and Information Science* (New York: Marcel Dekker, 1981), 32:95.

37. Lawrence S. Thompson, "Books Are Basic beyond the Bosphorus," *ALA Journal* 46 (1952): 195.

38. Jesse Shera, "Keynote Address Delivered before the Special Libraries Association," *Special Libraries* 47 (September 1956): 322-26.

Foreign Libraries in the Mirror of Soviet Library Science during the Cold War

Boris Volodin

This essay focuses on how the political climate of the Cold War-era U.S.S.R. affected Soviet librarians' ability to study and write about libraries in capitalist countries. The author refers extensively to papers published in major Soviet library science journals from the 1920s to the early 1990s to support his views. Examples are given of the influence of Cold War politics on the work of Russian library science researchers. The author uses contemporary material to trace the effects of the political on Soviet librarians' view of the international library community. Volodin also makes a clear differentiation between publicly expressed "politically correct" views and unpublished, unbiased research by significant Soviet librarians. The article discusses the profound impact made in bibliographic research by humanities scholars who chose library careers to avoid the intellectual constraints enforced elsewhere in Soviet academics. The author concludes by pointing out that librarians in the former Soviet Union are still unable to consider the effects of the Cold War on their profession as past history due to the stagnant climate of research and education. He describes the continued intellectual isolation perpetuated by the domestic focus of the popular Russian library science journals.

Before the Cold War

The end of World War II brought new hope for an integration of domestic library service in the world community. Advanced ideas were thriving in the mid-1940s, as fundamentally differentiated from the period immediately before the war, when the focus on international experience promoted in the first days of Soviet power had been totally rejected.

The earlier strategies, generally influenced by Vladimir I. Lenin and Nadezhda K. Krupskaia, were to stimulate Soviet professional librarians to active studies and use of foreign achievements. The interest, however, was mainly in matters of organization and technology like interlibrary loan, international book exchange, or the union catalog. Subsequently, Soviet library science came to embrace Lenin's idea of a "Swiss-American" system involving a range of exciting modern practices for a nationwide library service functioning in the best possible way, likewise to be achieved through organizational and technological solutions. Another library-related instruction, formulated in Lenin's major work "Materialism and Empiriocriticism," may be thought of as almost programming: "to be able to reject their reactionary trend, to be able to follow an independent policy, combating any policies of enemy forces of classes."[1]

Within such political frames, as the most significant Russian library scientist in the first half of the twentieth century, Lubov B. Khavkina, maintained in 1918, libraries were turned into an instrument in the party struggle, gradually inclining toward trend chasing and biased opinions.[2] Studies of library services abroad have been subject to specific constraints, but even thus constrained, the scope of international studies in the 1920s can be defined as extremely broad. Articles on the subject appeared in professional journals at regular intervals. Domestic monographs on foreign library services were both prepared and published, and major works of foreign colleagues were translated into Russian. International contacts were established and maintained.

In the 1930s, however, foreign experience had no use whatever in the U.S.S.R., socialism being established in "an isolated country" where every attainment was to be regarded as the perfect implementation of decisions prompted by superior wisdom. By the late 1930s foreign subjects were actually nonexistent in the professional press. Thus, while publications on foreign library services totaled twenty-two in 1935, only one such paper was published in 1939.

Yet in the early 1940s, when World War II was on, the Russian library community appeared to show great interest in foreign experience. With the constraints relaxed under the new political conditions, issues of foreign library experience were again addressed in publications and conference papers. And by the end of the war in 1944, Lubov Khavkina in one of her papers proposed changing the very nature of investigations in foreign library experience. She believed that "rather than being reviews or compilations, they ought to be intended as efforts in scholarly research complying with every appropriate requirement."[3] With the advent of the Cold War the hope of Russian librarians for a way out of professional isolation fell apart.

The First Years of the Cold War

As did the spheres of science, education, and culture in general, library service first experienced the Cold War in the form of the anticosmopolitanism campaign unleashed in 1949. Naturally, the campaign was to affect studies of international experience. The effect was tangible not only with regard to library services in capitalist countries. In the popular democracies, the new pattern of library research promoted "window dressing" for socialist library development presumably based on in-depth study, adaptation, and use of the Soviet experience. Thus S. Gruia, library administrator at the Romania Culture Ministry, wrote: "Lenin's doctrine of cultural revolution and his instructions on library services have been our permanent guidelines in establishing and developing the library network and in enhancing Communist propaganda."[4]

Since the scheme would fail in Eastern European countries with more developed library systems and certainly in Czechoslovakia and East Germany (GDR) with their long library traditions, the professional press preferred to ignore them. By contrast, library services in the capitalist world were occasionally discussed in Soviet professional periodicals, though only to denounce one or another government's "reactionary policy."

For the most part, the content of such publications could be illustrated by the title of an important paper on foreign libraries: "Bourgeois Libraries in the Service of Reaction." The intention, actually forced on the author, was presented as follows: "Militant, offensive criticism of the bourgeois library system, its theoreticians and propagandists, eradication of every trace of servility to *inostranshchina* [foreign ways] will be the contribution of Soviet librarians to the common struggle of advanced forces against reaction."[5] As a rule, the essays started with an individual story to convince readers of the antipopular, reactionary policies pursued by library services in the country in question. Thus descriptions of American corporate libraries in the highest-circulation professional journal, *Bibliotekar'*, were designed to denounce their exclusive attention to corporate services.[6] None of the papers contained profound theorizations or in-depth analyses. The common subjects were individual cases of "reactionaries" reported from France, Germany, Great Britain, Italy, or the United States. Typical publications about the United States can be judged by their titles, with problems formulated to imply the solutions, such as "U.S. Public Libraries in a Blind Alley," "Circulation Decreasing in U.S. Libraries," "What Is behind 'Free Reading' in U.S. Public Libraries?"[7]

Papers on these subjects were undoubtedly commissioned. Moreover, the commissions were forced on such superior professionals as Anna G. Kravchenko, who had intimate knowledge of particular features of many types of library services across the world. Findings from her resident studies in Germany, Denmark, and the United States in the 1920s were presented in a series of her publications.[8] During the Cold War, Kravchenko had to promote official views of events in a given country. A typical example is her essay on library service in France. The discussion ran as follows: "Library service in France has been severely handicapped to date . . . The reactionary French Government is spending the people's money for the army, police and gendarmes to 'put the working people down.' . . . [It] cannot and would not provide the required resources for the country's library system."[9] The only positive values were assigned to libraries operated by the Communist bodies. The negative values were due to the country's library authority, Direction des Bibliothèques de France et de Lecture Publique, as the author puts it, dominated by the "American party." The author finds the principal "mouthpiece" of the worship of American masters in Wall Street and of their "culture" in the person of Julien Caen, director of the National Library and head of the Direction des Bibliothèques. His work was to be appreciated in the U.S.S.R. at a later date.[10] Likewise at a later date, special emphasis was to be attached to his concentration camp and active antifascist fighting experiences in World War II. The essence of reforms in France after World War II can be illustrated in particular by the union catalogs of major libraries in several countries, compiled with the assistance of the UNESCO library section and using an American methodology. In addition to France, Kravchenko listed Denmark, Switzerland, and some other countries. The underlying idea was described as "the way for U.S. librarians to know for certain what books are lacking in U.S. libraries."[11]

An acquaintance with Kravchenko's publications on library services in the United States, France, and other capitalist countries readily suggests general political frames with no attempt at adequate professional analysis. Nevertheless, it would be wrong to follow the authors of the above-mentioned publications in "denouncing" her effort, if only in another chronological context. At the same time, it was Kravchenko who prepared the unique multivolume research of the past and current (at the time) conditions of library services in France, Germany, Switzerland, and the United States, certainly not to be published then. A typewritten copy held by the National Library of Russia gives evidence of the author's superior professional qualities and erudition.[12]

The anticosmopolitanism campaign had a profound impact on library service, with some of the consequences over a range of manifestations still evident to date. One such manifestation was library employment of major humanities scholars and key professors and lecturers trying to escape the repressions. In addition to often being useful in libraries with their unique professional knowledge, they were offered a certain extent of freedom from ideological pressure in doing important bibliographic research. As a result, the period proved a hotbed for a series of unprecedented bibliographic achievements in Russian libraries. The library-librarian dialogue with the outside world could not be interrupted, proceeding in the form of intellectual contacts. Rather than direct contacts in actual time and space, that is, with contemporary colleagues in other countries, there were dialogues with past generations. With respect to contemporary humanities and international librarianship, the government policy pronounced a total ban on objective studies or multi-aspect analyses of international library theory and practices.

The Cold War after the Thaw

The situation changed radically in the mid-1950s, the years of Khrushchev's "Thaw." The typical library research of the period addressed practical aspects, provided in-depth analysis, and sought professional contacts. There was a strong interest in the world library community. The most important publications were prepared by Irina Ju. Bagrova, Rudjero S. Giljarevski, Juri V. Grigorjev, Boris P. Kanevski, Maya B. Nabatova, Valentina M. Os'kina, Tatjana I. Skripkina, Tatjana Stupnikova, and Natalya I. Tjulina. The revue *Bibliotekovedenie i Bibliografija za Rubezom* (International Library Science and Bibliography) by the Lenin State Library in Moscow became the main source for research and analytical information as well in the field of foreign library experience in the U.S.S.R.

Of course, severe criticism and exposure of bourgeois ideology were required as the background of any research dealing with foreign library theory or practice. However, in the first years of the Thaw the "exposures" were in the nature of rather genteel, often quite formal "rules of the genre." The character of denouncing sections in professional papers and publications on issues of foreign library theory and practice changed rapidly in the mid-1960s. Yet there was a certain balance of the "practical," that is, professional analysis with a positive motivation, and the "antibourgeois," that is, purely ideological analysis. In many cases the latter was merely a formal though inevitable element of the publication.

The situation of a conditional equilibrium changed drastically when Iu. V. Andropov came to power in 1982 and remained almost the same until M. S. Gorbachev's *Perestroika*. For some time any more-or-less fundamental rationalizations about library theory and practices in capitalist countries without proper ideological colorings were actually vetoed. With regard to socialist countries there was a new surge in advertising for the triumph of Soviet library ideas and their benefits for the rest of the socialist community. The new focuses were represented in the formalization of the socialist library science as the "true" library science. Ideologists of the science appreciated its achievements to the extent of considering foreign experience unnecessary in formulating their fundamental ideas, propositions, concepts, and so on. The results are evident in the actually ambiguous position of the Russian library service to date. Some of the most important contradictions ought to be mentioned. In the absence of new textbooks and manuals, students are still using standard Soviet texts focusing on Soviet library science values and library services in an integral centrally governed state.

On the level of professional awareness, common sense suggests independence of domestic and international experiences. The leading Russian professional journal, *Bibliotekovedenie* (Library Science), generally addresses domestic issues, with essays on foreign library theory and practices only published by way of a special exception. The latter are confined to a separate periodical, the *Bibliotekovedenie i Bibliografia za Rubezhom*. An undoubted exception is made for informatics, permitting no juxtaposition of domestic and international experience. However, many approaches to potential applications are based on the traditional, in the Soviet library science notions of foreign library experiences as advanced technology. Thus no account is taken either of the historical context of library services in individual countries or of the philosophy of the information society itself. The majority of Russian librarians are still unable to consider the effects of the Cold War as past history.

Notes

1. V. I. Lenin, *Complete Works*, 18:364.
2. L. B. Khavkina, *The Book and the Library* (Moscow, 1918), 104.
3. L. B. Khavkina, "Topical Problems of Studies in the Foreign Library Experience and Conditions for the Studies," paper presented at the Moscow State Library Institute (1944), NLR, Manuscripts, F.321.K.2.It.4, Sh.6.
4. S. Gruia, "Development of Library Service in the Romanian People's Republic," *Bibliotekar'* 9 (1954): 46.
5. B. Kozlovski, "Bourgeois Libraries in the Service of Reaction," *Bibliotekar'* 5 (1948): 35.

6. G. B. Koltypina, "Reference Service in the Service of a Businessman: (U.S. 'Business Libraries')," *Bibliotekar'* 5 (1950): 40–43.
7. The articles by A. G. Kravchenko were published in the journal *Bibliotekar'* from 1948 to 1953.
8. See A. G. Kravchenko, *Towards an Integrated and Large Library Economy* (Moscow, 1929) and *A Review of Libraries and Schools for Adults in Germany and Denmark* (Moscow, 1929).
9. See A. G. Kravchenko, "Marshallization of French Libraries," *Bibliotekar'* 10 (1950): 42.
10. See M. I. Rudomino, "Julien Caen (1887–1974)," *Bibliotekovedenie i Bibliografia za Rubezhom* 57 (1976): 39–56.
11. Kravchenko, "Marshallization," 39.
12. Manuscript, National Library of Russia, St. Petersburg, F. 1119.

Finland Pays Its Debts and Gets Books in Return: ASLA Grants to the Finnish Academic Libraries, 1950-1967

Ilkka Mäkinen

This essay examines the political and historical context, implementation, and effects of the ASLA program and especially how it was used to fund the purchase of American books for Finnish academic libraries during the years 1950-67. In 1949 the U.S. Congress passed a law (P.L. 81-265) that transformed Finnish payments on the loans acquired from the United States after World War I into a fund. Out of the fund, grants for travel in the United States were given to Finnish researchers and specialists. Finnish institutions of higher education were given grants in order to acquire American scientific and scholarly books as well as technical equipment. In Finland the program is known according to its Finnish acronym: ASLA (Amerikan Suomen lainan apurahat, or Grants from Finland's American Loan). Today it is called the ASLA-Fulbright program. The essay describes the relation of the ASLA program to the United States, cultural diplomacy in general, and how the program influenced Finnish academic libraries. Sources include published congressional documents and Finnish archival sources, especially papers of the Helsinki University Library, its chief librarian, Lauri O. Th. Tudeer, and the Council (later Board) of Scientific Libraries.

When browsing the shelves of Finnish academic libraries you often find books printed in the 1940s and 1950s that bear a label with the following dedication:

This book has been presented to Finland
through ASLA funds
by
The Government of the United States of America
as
an expression of the Friendship and Goodwill
which
the People of the United States
hold for
the People of Finland.

During the years 1950–67, Finnish academic libraries received books, periodicals, and other materials, such as microfilm readers, as gifts in excess of $650,000 from the United States. The activity was based on a law passed by the U.S. Congress that had turned Finnish payments on the interest and principal of loans acquired from the United States after World War I into a fund. Out of the fund, grants for travel in the United States were given to Finnish researchers and specialists so that they could acquire American scientific and scholarly books as well as technical equipment for Finnish higher education institutions.

The Americans knew the program by the number of the law stipulating it (Public Law 265, 81st Congress); for the Finnish, the program is best known according to its acronym, ASLA (Amerikan Suomen lainan apurahat, or Grants from Finland's American Loan). Presently, the program is still functioning, even though the acquisition of books ceased in the 1960s; the travel grants remain. The program is known today as the ASLA-Fulbright program, which indicates that the specific Finnish program is combined with the more general Fulbright program.[1]

Besides describing how the ASLA program came into existence, my interest in this essay is to evaluate the structural effects of the program on the Finnish academic library system. The effects were much more than just a growing number of American books on the shelves, even if that was a meaningful thing in itself. As a side effect of the program, the cooperation between the libraries assumed institutionalized forms. The American influence on the academic libraries also reflected the wider picture of the academic world in Finland. After World War II, the traditional connections of the Finnish academic institutions to Germany were broken. Before the war, there were very few English-language books among the textbooks in the university curricula, but there were German books in abundance. A large share of the scientific works for international distribution was written in German. The German language was used by the disciplines of science and the humanities and, hence, was widely taught in secondary schools. This was, of course, not confined to Finland; the German language dominance in science was an international phenomenon. After World War II, it was American culture and the English language that gained the dominant position. For historical reasons the Russian language has never been a genuine option for Finns. In searching for the structural effects of the program, I am compelled to concentrate on the prehistory or genesis of the first years of the program. I will attempt to shed light on the historical and political context of the ASLA program.

As far as Finland is concerned, my perspective is based on that of a leading figure among Finnish academic librarians, Dr. Lauri O. Th. Tudeer, the chief librarian of the Helsinki University Library, which is also the National Library of Finland. His correspondence and documents, as chief librarian and leader of the academic library world in Finland, are my principal source of information. I have also studied the documentation of the legislative process in the U.S. Congress concerning this matter.

Relief after the War

There were already plans within the United States during World War II that pertained to ensuring the distribution of American books to war-devastated libraries.[2] The war had severed the lines of transportation, and for many years Continental Europe was cut off from the United States. The need for American scientific and technical books and periodicals was strongly felt. On the other hand, because it had not been possible to deliver them to buyers or exchange partners, there were great stockpiles of publications in American libraries and other institutions that had been accumulating during the war. Consequently, exchange relations also broke down and had to be reestablished. The American Book Center (ABC) for War Devastated Libraries, Inc. was established in 1945 in order to coordinate and implement a worldwide relief effort for libraries. In 1948 it was reorganized into a new organization called the United States Book Exchange, Inc. (USBE). USBE's main function was thought to be the exchange of publications, but at least in the beginning, it continued coordinating book donations.

Private American foundations had vast relief processes and had funded the operations of other organizations. The Rockefeller Foundation was active in the library field. Even Finnish librarians were able to benefit from ALA-operated visits or study periods in the United States, funded by the Rockefeller Foundation after the war. It also funded subscriptions to American social science periodicals, a project coordinated by the American Social Science Research Council.

After the war, Finnish librarians started to reestablish the broken exchange relationships with institutions abroad. The need for relief was also great because of the damage of the war and the lack of hard currency after many years of isolation. The lack of technical literature was extreme, as the largest library in that field, the Library of the Institute of Technology (today the Helsinki University of Technology), had been completely destroyed in an air raid. The need for technical literature was of a strategic nature, because Finland had to create a new metal industry to manufacture the products that would be given to the Soviet Union as part of the war reparations.

Dr. Tudeer was very involved in taking care of the international relations of Finnish academic libraries. He had had contacts with American librarians even before the war, especially with the ALA and the Library of Congress. Soon after the war, he tried to restore these contacts. He worked with the Library of Congress to reestablish the exchange agreement and with the ALA International Relations Office, which delivered book donations to Finland. Tudeer also arranged study tours for Finnish librarians organized by the ALA. The ALA also channeled donations financed by the Rockefeller Foundation. For example, in 1947 Helsinki University Library was one of the recipients of a complete set of the Library of Congress catalog of printed cards (167 volumes).[3]

Immediately after the war, help from the Finnish Ministry for Foreign Affairs was needed to get the acquisition of foreign books going again. In the beginning of 1946 there began to arrive signals from the United States about the possibilities of acquiring literature from that country. Soon the lack of a Finnish coordinating organ was felt. Out of necessity, the Finnish delegation in Washington acquired a central role in the dispatching of books. The head of the Legation, Minister K. T. Jutila, at least once personally took care of choosing duplicates from the stock shelves of the Library of Congress. He was well qualified to understand the meaning of books for libraries and research, because before his diplomatic career he had been a professor at the University of Helsinki and responsible for the Library of Agricultural Sciences at the Faculty of Agriculture and Forestry.

In February 1946 the Legation sent to the Foreign Ministry a memorandum describing the situation of the available book donations. The memorandum took quite a strong attitude in favor of coordinating the book acquisition operations on the Finnish side. Many libraries such as the Helsinki University Library, the Library of the Institute of Technology, and the Library of the Central Laboratory, which was a private research center owned by the pulp and paper industry, had all requested from the Legation or directly from the American institutions (especially the Library of Congress and the ALA) information about the possibilities of acquiring books. Minister Jutila stressed that the rational acquisition of literature presupposed detailed negotiations with the American organizations and an acquisition program based on these negotiations. A difficult problem was financing the cost of book transportation, because the libraries and the Legation had so little hard currency.

The Legation asked for advice from the Ministry and proposed that a small committee be established in Helsinki to collect book requests from libraries and other institutions and to transmit through the Ministry a coordinated list of requested donations from the United States. The American Book Center for War Devastated Libraries had notified the Legation that Finland would receive part of the literature collected for European countries. The organization had asked the Legation to name a couple of representatives to participate in the negotiations, during which the distribution of available books would be agreed upon. A precondition was that there existed in Finland a Center for Finnish Libraries to take care of the distribution of books in Finland and to coordinate information about the needs of libraries. The committee proposed by the Legation could function in that capacity. During that period, Finland seems to have been the only country benefiting from the ABC program that had fought on the wrong side in the war. Generally, the aim of the Center was characterized as follows:

> The Center proposes to conduct soon after January 1, 1946, a national campaign to stockpile printed materials useful for scholarly investigation and for the physical, economic, industrial, and social rehabilitation of Allied nations in war areas. Such materials will be solicited as gifts from publishers, learned societies, educational institutions, scholars, scientists and other individuals throughout the United States, and will be collected at a national receiving point where they can be sorted and distributed to the recipient countries.

In an early phase, the ABC was given the job of distributing literature stockpiled by government agencies.[4]

It is apparent that it was on Chief Librarian Tudeer's initiative that a coordinating organ, the Section for Literature of the Committee of University Rectors, was established in 1946. It seems to have been an ad hoc organ solely for the purpose of coordinating book requests and distributing books to libraries. Tudeer had considerable correspondence on these matters with the American Book Center and the CARE organization, which took care of transporting the bookcases.

It is possible that the time-consuming and troublesome work for the Section for Literature gave Tudeer the idea of proposing to the Ministry of Education that a regular committee make plans for cooperation among the Finnish academic libraries be nominated. He made the proposition at the beginning of 1947, and soon the committee was at work. It worked actively during the years 1947–50. The postwar years were a kind of New Deal period in Finnish public administration. Many things were reorganized, and reforms were made despite a lack of money. This period was also active for the planning of academic libraries. There were a number of committees working in this field. The most important among them was the Committee for Scientific Libraries, as its name was, perhaps a little inaccurately, translated. It convened for discussion almost ninety times, giving, besides its own written report, its expert opinion on many matters pertaining to academic libraries. It functioned as if it were a permanent board. It also organized a collection of information about Finnish academic and special libraries based on which a "Guide to Finnish Academic and Special Libraries" (in Finnish) was compiled and published. The report of the committee was an extensive document that laid the foundation for the development of Finnish academic libraries for a long period. When the committee ended its work in 1950, there was a general feeling that it should, somehow, continue to operate. The creation of a Council of Chief Librarians was proposed in the report. The Ministry of Education was reluctant to establish an organ of that kind, apparently for economic reasons. Nevertheless, very soon an unofficial cooperative organ was needed for the specific needs of the ASLA program.

ASLA Grants in the Congress

The history of the ASLA program starts in the aftermath of World War I. The newly independent Republic of Finland obtained loans from the United States, as did many other European countries, to manage through the first difficult years. The total sum of the loans was $8.3 million. Finland paid back its loans yearly. During the Great Depression other countries that had received loans from the United States ceased to pay back what they owed, but Finland continued to pay. Prior to World War II, the American press had given credence to Finland for this exceptional behavior. The fact that Finland persisted in paying its debt, even during the years of the war, aroused admiration. Finland and the United States fought, in practice, on different sides during the years 1941–44, even if the United States did not declare war on Finland (diplomatic relations were severed by the United States in 1944). Despite this state of affairs, Finland tried stubbornly to submit its payments. These efforts earned the small country a lot of international goodwill, which, of course, was one of the main reasons it had continued to pay.[5]

In addition to the constant debt paying, the Winter War, which began when Russia attacked its tiny neighbor in November 1939, also raised Finland into international awareness. Being a cobelligerent with Germany in 1941-44 only temporarily disturbed the goodwill earned by Finland. Soon after the war the comradeship between the United States and the Soviet Union turned into a Cold War. Finland's position seemed threatened in the same way as during the Winter War, although there was no overt aggression. In the peace treaty signed in 1947, Finland had to give a large piece of its land area to the Soviet Union and pay huge war reparations. Some 400,000 people had to be resettled. The Soviet Union was again putting pressure on Finland, and it seemed uncertain if the country could retain its democratic system. Finland seemed to be doomed to fall into the hands of the Soviet Union and Communism.

Finland again paid its semiannual payments in 1947. In December 1947, resolutions to help Finland were introduced both in the Senate and the House of Representatives. According to these resolutions, the rest of the Finnish debt was to be transformed into a fund from which grants would be given to Finns who travel to the United States in order to study and do research. Books were not yet mentioned in these resolutions.[6]

Now that the ASLA program has been integrated with the more general Fulbright program, it is easy to forget whose idea it originally was to transform the Finnish debt into an educational fund. The real father of the ASLA program was David Hinshaw (1882-1953), a former aide to Theodore Roosevelt and an advisor to Herbert Hoover. Hinshaw had worked as the public relations manager of a large oil company but was also known as a writer. His Quaker convictions led him into international philanthropy. After the Second World War he came to Finland to inspect the Quaker relief work and, based on what he saw, wrote a book entitled *An Experiment in Friendship* (1947), in which he proposed that the sums paid by Finland be used to the benefit of the country itself. Later he published a larger book about the country, *Heroic Finland* (1952). In the foreword of the latter book the director of a Finnish relief organization, Arvo Puukari, describes how in 1947, while visiting Hinshaw's New York office, he overheard him discussing the details of the Senate resolution on the phone with Senator H. Alexander Smith. Smith wrote the text of the resolution, gained supporters for it, and in every way worked for its smooth passage through Congress. Both Hinshaw and Smith were Republicans; however, Democrats also supported the resolution. A similar resolution was made in the House of Representatives. The resolutions had been sent to the congressional committees, where they stayed. The Department of State considered the Finnish situation so uncertain that it advised those who had made the proposals to wait.

The Soviet Union had prevented Finland from taking part in the Marshall Plan in 1947. In the spring of 1948, the Soviet Union proposed to Finland the same kind of defense agreement that it had made with its Eastern European satellites. Finns were able to negotiate a much more moderate agreement than was done with Romania or Hungary. After the signing of the agreement, there began a time of stabilization in Finland's position. From the point of view of the United States, Finland's situation had stabilized to the extent that it was felt that resources sent to Finland would not go to waste. This made it possible to arrange the rest of the Finnish payments in the proposed way. In January 1949 the same members of the Senate renewed their proposal. Besides Senator Smith, who introduced the resolution, there were numerous other supporters such as Senator William Fulbright. Concurring initiatives were also made in the House of Representatives. In every way, interest in Finland was at its peak in Congress.

When he introduced his proposal on 6 January 1949, Senator Smith (N.J.) said that he now was "advised by the State Department that the way ahead is clear, and that the Department has no objection to the proposal. In collaboration with the State Department, and in response to suggestions that came to me from the Acting Secretary of State, Hon. Robert Lovett, the new joint resolution has been slightly revised and given a somewhat wider application than was afforded by the draft I introduced last year. The purpose, however, is the same." From the point of view of the present essay, the most important new feature in the proposal was contained in the b-clause, where it was stated that the funds could be used for the "selection, purchase, and shipment of (1) American scientific, technical, and scholarly books and books of American literature for higher educational and research institutions of Finland, and (2) American laboratory and technical equipment for higher education and research in Finland."[7]

The Senate proposal also got support from the organization that supervised the implementation of the Smith-Mundt Act, or the United States Information and Educational Exchange Act, namely, the United States Advisory Commission on Educational Exchange. The Commission's action, which was taken on the recommendation of George V. Allen, assistant secretary for public affairs at the State Department, specifically endorsed the proposal for use of the Finnish debt payments.[8]

Why Were Books Included?

There were clear signs in the American legislation concerning cultural relations and information activities that the distribution of

American books and publications abroad had gained interest. It was felt that the printed material could convey the right picture of the principles directing American policy, life in the United States, and so on. The message in books and publications was considered to be more enduring and more influential than the information transmitted by the more immediate media such as radio that affected larger populations. In January 1948 Congress passed the Smith-Mundt Act, the purpose of which was to authorize and finance U.S. information activities such as Voice of America transmissions abroad. American information libraries established abroad were also referred to in the law. In the Smith-Mundt Act cultural exchange was specified on a wider basis than in the Fulbright Act. The Smith-Mundt Act considered "the interchange of persons, knowledge and skills," and in paragraph 202 it was clearly stated that the Department of State was authorized to arrange for the exchange of books and periodicals between the United States and other countries.

The proposal concerning Finland was introduced at the same time that the American information policy was in a period of change. Kraske has described a tension in the policy concerning information and American libraries abroad. On the one hand, there was the cultural view (supported by the ALA) that honored the best American public library traditions even in American libraries abroad. On the other hand, there was the view that information activities could be a direct tool of U.S. foreign policy.[9] Relief programs originating from private initiatives (such as ABC, CARE, ALA-sponsored programs financed by the Rockefeller Foundation) had been characteristic both during and after the war. Libraries that the Americans had established abroad during and after the war were seen first of all as specimens of the free American library ideals and American culture in general, even if they were established by the Office of War Information (OWI).[10]

The Cold War and the hardening of attitudes in the United States resulted in a growing tension between the information and culture points of view. When the Smith-Mundt legislation was under preparation, there was discussion as to whether cultural relations should be seen as an inseparable part of the foreign policy and whether they should be modeled to support the goals of U.S. foreign policy. In the ALA, the situation was noted with growing concern. At a conference in January 1948 at the State Department, the ALA representative tried to defend a view that "the information library and cultural activities will be handicapped in making their natural long-time contribution if they are misused by the information boys for propaganda." It was apparent that American libraries abroad more and more were understood primarily as outposts of the State Department and only secondarily as libraries.

The same George V. Allen who asked the Advisory Commission to support the Finnish program said bluntly in July 1948: "Our information program is nothing more, nor less, than an instrument—one of the instruments—in achieving the foreign policy of the United States."[11]

In both the Senate and the House of Representatives the resolutions concerning the Finnish program were scrutinized in the appropriate committees.[12] Senator Fulbright presented the report of the Senate committee. In the committees, reciprocity was added in the legislation by widening the financing of American citizens to travel and stay in Finland. The Senate report states the following about books: "It is entirely proper that cultural interchange should include scientific, technical, and scholarly books and books of literature, as well as laboratory and technical equipment and materials for higher education and research. This is a vital operation also in harmony with the spirit of the resolution." The report specifically refers to the experiences that the State Department had gained during the year it had administered the Smith-Mundt Act. The machinery created for that purpose could be used for the implementation of this program also. Thus, the Finnish program became closely tied to the Smith-Mundt Act and a move in the policy of containment. Both the Senate and the House reports mention that the State Department had made proposals concerning the contents of the act.

The Finnish program was considered in the House committee report as experimental and flexible, even conditional. If it did not produce the desired results, it could be terminated, and the money could be used for other purposes. The Finnish program differed from the Fulbright program in that it was dollar-based, whereas the Fulbright program was based on local currencies. It was also pointed out that the Finnish program was exceptional and, seen in relation to the size of population, even more generous than the average benefits offered by the other programs. The State Department had unofficially let it be known that it thought the resources between personal exchange and exchange of educational material should be split more or less evenly. Clearly, it seems that the thought of using the resources to deliver books and equipment originated from the State Department. The arrangement was meant to strengthen Finland as a democratic Western country. Here it was not a question of mass propaganda but strengthening the identification with the West of those who were (or would be) in leading positions.[13]

Kraske confronts two opposite lines in the conduct of U.S. cultural relations. First, "the shift from short-term information and propaganda objectives, which characterized the early 1950s toward more sophisticated long-range attempts in the early 1960s, to build international understanding through education, brought greater recognition to general cultural activities and an expanded role in the information program."[14] When the Finnish program was shaped in Congress, the report of the House committee stressed the importance of careful long-range planning: "This is not an emergency undertaking in which the premium is to be on quick results. It is a long-range program in which the premium is to be placed on sound planning at the start" (p. 6). In this respect the Finnish program was ahead of its time. The conditions for creating the program were also exceptionally favorable.

The exceptionality of the Finnish program lay in the fact that no American taxpayers' money was directly needed. Another important feature was that the initiative came from the Americans. The legislative process was completely in the hands of Congress and the Department of State, and there was no need for an official agreement with Finland. The only thing the Finns could do was to make certain attempts at individual lobbying and deliver necessary background information to Hinshaw.[15] Making the Fulbright agreement with Finland was much more difficult.

The Fulbright agreement with Finland was not made until 1952, even if Finland was among the first countries to be offered this option in 1947. The Department of State tried persistently for many years to make the Finns accept the agreement, which was clearly economically advantageous for Finland. But the Finnish government wanted to be absolutely sure that an agreement of this kind did not disturb the relations between Finland and the Soviet Union. The agreement was almost final in 1948, but the Finnish government let it drop. One must bear in mind that the Soviet Union had prevented Finland from taking part in the Marshall Plan in 1947. Officially, the Soviet government did not comment on the matter when the Fulbright agreement was finally made in 1952, but soon after the signing there were nasty articles in the Soviet press that also found their way into the Finnish left-wing newspapers. At that time, the situation of Finland was already so steady that the policy of needling had no effect. The initiative concerning the Finnish debt was probably seen in the Department of State as a convenient way to attain the same goals as with a Fulbright agreement. The Americans maintained a low profile policy toward Finland in order to avoid arousing Soviet suspicions.[16]

The Implementation and Its Effects

During the fall of 1949 Dr. Tudeer had a busy time trying to get to know how Public Law 81-265 would be implemented. The Finnish minister in Washington, K. T. Jutila, was the first one to whom he directed his inquiries. As the matter was in the hands of the Department of State, it was natural to try to find out about it through the Finnish diplomatic representative, who, even before, had proved to be valuable in library matters. Tudeer's first priority was to secure the interests of libraries in the organizations that were to be established to handle the distribution of funds. It was not clear how the Americans were going to proceed, and Tudeer wanted to make sure that they were aware of the interests of libraries.[17]

Another natural addressee of inquiries was the Library of Congress. Tudeer asked the deputy librarian, James B. Childs, about the grants, their distribution, and the organizations that would do the actual work: "I think some sort of board in the United States will make the decisions, but will there also be an advisory committee in Finland for the purpose?"[18] The Library of Congress was not directly involved in the implementation, but, as it became clear later, it had influence over the process.

The next person to whom Tudeer turned was the public relations officer at the American legation in Helsinki, Henry F. Arnold, who was to be a central person when the practical arrangements of the ASLA program were determined. He informed Tudeer personally that he already had sent a proposal to Washington for the procedures in implementing the program. He had, however, no knowledge about the time schedule. In any case, the final decision of how the funds would be distributed was in the hands of the Department of State. Arnold had proposed that a Finnish committee be nominated to take care of the applications for funds. The nongovernmental committee would consist of seven prominent cultural personalities. Then there would be subcommittees consisting of representatives of special fields to aid the main council. The idea of subcommittees was a direct response to Tudeer's remark that the representation of libraries' interests would be essential. Arnold agreed but thought that there would not be a representative of the libraries' interests in the main committee. Arnold also supposed that a share of 40 percent of the annual funds would be reserved for books.[19]

In January 1950 Tudeer discussed the matter with the chairman of the Finnish American Grants Committee, Professor Eino Saari. Already in this early discussion, many of the topics that were to be later eagerly debated were considered. Their conversation proves that there were no specific plans on how to handle the funds for book distribution. Tudeer wrote in his promemoria concerning the discussion with Saari, "It would perhaps be possible that an unofficial library council could get the matter at its responsibility until an official board is established." Another matter that was dealt with in the negotiation between Tudeer and Saari was what kind of institutions would be the recipients of books. The phrase in the law referred to "higher educational and research institutions of Finland." Universities and colleges would clearly be included. Certain departmental libraries would also be among the recipients as well as the Library of Parliament and libraries at independent research institutes of the state. Private research institutes were not self-evident beneficiaries, because the books should, also without difficulties, be at the disposal of researchers and the general public. Further, Professor Saari agreed with Tudeer that the "debt-money" should not be used to pay for serials, multivolume works, and periodicals that libraries had started to pay for out of their own funds. An interesting point in Tudeer's notes is a passage that was struck over: "Saari supposed that there is no need to reserve these funds for a special American Institute. He was sure that the Finnish Committee had no interest in this, but he was afraid that the American Legation would back up that kind of institute." This proved later to be true. Tudeer and Saari discussed further personal travel grants and the microfilming of newspapers, which was also meant to receive ASLA funds (this project will not be touched upon in this essay).[20]

Some light on how the distribution of the ASLA funds was handled in the United States is to be found in a letter to Tudeer from the Librarian of Congress, Luther H. Evans. Evans was well aware of the matter, although he stressed that the Library of Congress had no responsibility for the administration of Public Law 81-265. Representatives of the Library had recently discussed the matter in some detail with the officials of the State Department. The central position of the American Legation in Helsinki was emphasized in Evans's letter. The most important individual decision-maker in the process was the public affairs officer of the Legation in Helsinki. "In making its recommendation to the State Department the Legation, of course, consults with an advisory committee established in Finland for the purpose and with interested Finnish groups," Evans had written. When Evans wrote his letter, the first distribution of funds had already taken place in the spring of 1950. Evans had gotten the impression that the proposal was made by a provisional Finnish committee, "which I am told was established specifically for the purpose in January 1950." In reality it seems that it was Tudeer himself who in great haste had made the first proposal to the Finnish main committee. Evans expressed the hopes of the American side of the issue. He stated that a permanent Finnish organization would be established to take care of making proposals at the time of the next round. "If by that time the Scientific Library Council has been established by the Finnish government, the council would certainly appear to be a logical source from which the Legation might seek advice.

If a convenient opportunity presents itself we shall suggest to the Department in December that it consider the Scientific Library Council in any review it may make of the allocations of books."[21]

The first allotment of funds for books was $58,000. Tudeer's proposal was not accepted as such, but only one recipient was added; otherwise, only the sums were changed. The sums proposed for Helsinki University Library and the Library of the Institute of Technology were changed so that they were to receive the same sum, $12,700 (in Tudeer's paper, $14,000 and $8,000). This procedure stressed the great need for technical literature. During the following years the priority of the Helsinki University Library was restored. The only institution added to Tudeer's list was the American Institute at the University of Helsinki, and it received $2,300.

USIS director Henry Arnold sent a letter to each of the recipients notifying them of the allocated sum as well as background information and practical advice. He stressed that allocations would be flexible from year to year, and "the fact that a certain amount has at present been allocated to any particular institution, does not imply that future amounts will remain identical nor, that all institutions receiving allotments now will continue to do so. Changing needs of eligible institutions, and alterations in program emphasis may result in wide variations over a period of time in allotments made." The procedures described in the letter remained approximately the same until the end of the 1950s.[22]

There were no conditions regarding the contents of the books in Arnold's procedures, other than that the books should be American scientific, technical, and scholarly books or works of American literature. There were no political limitations, and it was always a matter of normal, neutral library operation. The first ASLA books began to arrive in Finland in September 1950. The Department of State had made a contract with CARE for the handling and transportation of the books. As far as it is to be seen in the documents, the only case where the required books could not be delivered were the books that were not American or that were out of print.

Finns Proposing, State Department Disposing

In the next selection process during the fall of 1950, the forms that were going to be fairly permanent for many years were found for the distribution of ASLA funds. The most important task for the Finnish side was to establish a permanent body to make the distribution proposals. In a letter to Tudeer, Henry Arnold, public affairs officer, raised a number of important issues that summarized the pertinent discussion. The discussion included Arnold and Ms. Thelma Passo, the librarian of the USIS library in Helsinki, together with the Finns Tudeer, Helle Kannila, lecturer in library science at the College of Social Sciences, and Marjatta Havu, librarian at the Institute of Technology. According to Arnold, it was

> the intention of the United States Government in administering Public Law 265, to permit the Finnish people to make the basic recommendations for the allocation of funds and the selection of persons to visit the United States under the program. It was a pleasure therefore to learn that the Council of Scientific Libraries, even though that Council does not yet have an official existence, might assist this office in allocating funds available during the 1951 fiscal year for the purchase of books and other items for libraries in Finland.

Public libraries and libraries connected with primary and secondary schools were not included among the recipients of funds, but special libraries that were part of research institutions and all college and university libraries were eligible to receive items from P.L. 81-265 funds. Further, Arnold remarked that "in making its recommendations, the Council of Scientific Libraries is first of all requested to set up certain criteria or standards which should govern the recommending of allocations." Such factors were, according to Arnold, "the urgency for certain materials, the shelf space in existence for making books and other materials immediately available, the importance of any particular library in the immediate and future development of Finland." Arnold had requested that Thelma Passo be permitted to attend meetings of the Council of Scientific Libraries at which P.L. 81-265 allocations were discussed. He said he believed this would be "helpful to the Legation in becoming acquainted, first-hand, with the progress of the Council and, reciprocally, should prove helpful to the Council in providing answers to such questions pertaining to the making of allocations that Miss Passo might be able to supply."[23]

The unofficial Council of Scientific Libraries held its first meeting on 10 October 1950 with a single issue on the agenda, namely, to make a proposal for the distribution of ASLA funds for books. Those present included the chief librarians of the biggest academic libraries, a representative of the Finnish Library Association, and representatives from the two leading Finnish scholarly academies. The Americans distributed the money exactly as the council proposed. In his letter informing the recipients, Arnold wrote: "This allotment is based on recommendations made by the Finnish Council of Scientific Libraries."[24] Arnold also sent a special letter to Tudeer to thank him for the council's activity.[25]

Evans's letter, cited earlier, and Arnold's sighs of relief in the fall of 1950 show how much importance the Americans put on the fact that there would be a permanent body taking care of the distribution of the ASLA funds. This was in line with a principle in American cultural relations policy, that is, that American authorities should not meddle in the business of local actors. It was true, on the other hand, that American officials, usually librarians of the USIS library in Helsinki, participated in the meetings of the Council of Scientific Libraries during the first years of its existence. Usually they did not say much on the decisions whether a certain institution should receive money or not, but there were exceptions. In most cases, they made only general remarks.

On some occasions, the American representatives wanted to widen the circle of institutions receiving more funds than what the Finnish librarians were willing to allocate. Thelma Passo, who took part in the first meeting of the council, remarked that the funds referred to in the law were not solely meant for university people but also for wider circles. She stated that the council intended to draw the borders too narrowly. The Finnish librarians wanted to keep the number of recipients at a lower level, although representatives of the academic associations defended smaller institutions.[26]

American Preference

The question whether the American Institute at the University of Helsinki should receive funds had already come up in the discussion between Tudeer and Professor Saari in January 1950. Later, Arnold energetically supported allocating funds to the institute, which was to be a constant and privileged recipient during the whole ASLA books period. This is one of the rare overt efforts of the Americans to influence the way Finns proposed the distribution of the funds. Of course, the institute was a useful part of the university, and receiving funds for it was not a terrible imposition. In a letter written to Tudeer in September 1950, Arnold wrote about the American Institute. "In view of the very limited supply of books in the fields of American literature, language and culture available to Helsinki University students in their Institute reading room, the Legation is interested in the growth of that collection. For this reason, it is proposed that a minimum of $3,000 from the 1951 fiscal year funds be made available to the American Institute of Helsinki University."[27] At its first meeting, the Council of Scientific Libraries diligently proposed $3,000 for the American Institute. As he spoke about the issue, Tudeer expressly informed the other members that this was Arnold's wish.[28]

At the same meeting, funds were not proposed for the Workers College at Kiljava, which was the other institution that Arnold wished to receive funds. Apparently, the college had not made an application. Before the meeting, Arnold had written Tudeer about his visit to the college:

> Last week, I had the pleasure of visiting the new workers' college that is located at Kiljava in Nurmijärvi. I believe this school is to be operated by SAK [Union of Labor Associations] for the benefit of workers throughout Finland. One of the obvious needs of the institution is books, and I believe that American books and periodicals in the field of economics and related subjects would prove of tremendous value in connection with work of this institution. May I suggest, therefore, that the Council give consideration to allocating a portion of the funds under P.L. 265 to the library of this institution. My guess would be that a sum from $500.00 to $1000.00 would be adequate to meet the initial needs.[29]

At the end of 1950, Arnold moved back to the United States. There he began to supervise the Voice of America transmissions in Finnish from the beginning of 1951. Maybe it tells something about Arnold's interest in the Finnish labor unions that the second program in these broadcasts included an interview with a Finnish Workers Union delegation.[30] Americans, and also most of the Finns, regarded it as important that the Finnish labor unions should remain in the hands of Social Democrats instead of slipping under the control of Finnish or Soviet Communists.

In the next distribution of funds, the Council of Scientific Libraries proposed something for the Workers College. A letter by Arnold's successor, David G. Wilson, to Tudeer may have had some influence. He emphasized that "in this connection, the Legation is of the opinion that the library of the Ammattiyhdistysopisto [Workers College] at Kiljava is clearly eligible for an allocation, and hopes that the Committee will give favorable consideration to the very modest request which that institution has made for books."[31] The principles of distribution stated earlier were here rather liberally interpreted. In the allocation for 1951, the Workers College got a modest sum ($125), the first and last it received. It is probable that the Americans found other ways of supporting the moderate Finnish labor movement.

The question of how wide the available funds should be spread was under discussion again in the fall of 1951. Tudeer and Public Relations Officer Wilson had had a talk about whether the Tampere Public Library was eligible for funding. In his letter written in November 1951,

Wilson returned to the issue. He had come to the conclusion "upon further consideration that for the present it is advisable to continue application of last year's ruling that public libraries and libraries connected with primary and secondary schools are not included."[32] In any case, Tampere was allocated $350 for the acquisition of a microfilm reader. During the fall of 1952, the American representative strongly supported Tampere at the meeting of the Council of Scientific Libraries: "'Tampere is unique in Finland,' 'higher institutions' should have a wider interpretation, public libraries are such." Tampere was at the time the most important industrial city in Finland, which may explain the interest of the Americans. On the other hand, there were also Finnish members who supported Tampere. Again in 1953, Tampere got $500. In the distribution proposal, an explanatory note was added, stating, "The Tampere Public Library—for literature in industrial and engineering sciences." The public library in Oulu also received funds "for literature in the fields of psychology, pedagogy and sociology."

The Effects of the ASLA Books

During the early years of the 1950s, the quantitative significance of the ASLA funds for the Finnish academic libraries was at its greatest. This was due to the weakness of the local currency, the Finnish mark, and the low level of the acquisition funds of the libraries. The ASLA funds were added on top of the budgeted funds. If we convert the dollars into Finnish marks, in the Helsinki University Library the ratio between the normal budgeted acquisition funds and ASLA funds during the first two years of the system was rather even, 60 to 40, and still 65 to 35 in the third year. After that, the share of the ASLA funds began to decline in comparison to the regular budget. Approaching the 1960s, the share of the ASLA funds diminished to less than 10 percent and even lower until during the last years of the system, when it became insignificant. In the other, bigger libraries, the trend was similar; in smaller institutions it was even more dramatic due to the low original level of funding. The ASLA funds diminished in absolute terms, but the most important reason was the significant rise in the budgeted acquisition funds.[33] Finland was getting onto its feet economically, and more funds were allocated to the rapidly growing higher education system. In any case, the economic and symbolic importance of the ASLA funds was apparent at a time when the situation was at its worst.[34]

The literature acquired with the ASLA funds was mostly fresh and had been selected to meet the goals of the libraries, universities, and other institutions. In that respect, these books were better than direct donations, which were unpredictable and often outdated. Many libraries used the funds to subscribe to journals, both those that were lacking because of the wartime isolation and the new ones. For example, Helsinki University Library used ASLA funds to order 115 journals with their back volumes, altogether around 2,000 volumes. The original idea of the Americans was to use the funds to purchase books, and they sometimes tried to get the libraries to order fewer journals.

The greatest effect of the ASLA funds was, of course, the sharp growth in the acquisition of American literature. Concerning the Helsinki University Library, one of the signs of this was the fact that before the war, the library had to borrow American literature from other Scandinavian countries, whereas during the 1950s the direction of interlibrary loans was reversed. There are no separate statistics about the use of ASLA books, and in general it is difficult to evaluate the factual effects of the American books after the war, but in some fields source analysis has been conducted concerning the period beginning with the 1950s. In the Finnish sociological dissertations the enormous share of the American sources is evident during the 1950s; there was a clear change of paradigm.[35]

The lasting effects of the ASLA program are to be found in the network of Finnish academic libraries. The first cooperative organ in the field, the Council (later the Board) of Scientific Libraries, was established originally to make proposals for the distribution of the ASLA funds. Americans required that there should not be unnecessary duplication in acquisitions, which enhanced cooperation in acquisitions, growth in interlibrary loans, and better union catalogs, among other things. There are many features that indicate that taking part in the distribution process had structural and operational effects on Finnish academic libraries, even pointing toward an academic library system or network. Coming together for discussion, even if, in the beginning, it was only for distributing the funds, created opportunities for new kinds of cooperation. The results are difficult to determine objectively, but at least Finnish librarians have always been eager to adopt modern methods and equipment that presuppose interlibrary cooperation.

The ASLA program for books acquired a permanent form during the 1950s. The operation was run more and more by the Finns themselves. The last ASLA funds allotted for the acquisition of books was received in 1967. Since then, all available funds have been reserved for personal travel grants. The ASLA-Fulbright program is still flourishing. My own institution, the Department of Information Studies at the University of Tampere, has, during the last few years, had the great pleasure of having two distinguished American scholars visiting as Fulbright professors.

Appendices

TABLE 1
ASLA GRANTS TO FINNISH ACADEMIC LIBRARIES

Year	Amount
1950	$ 57,000
1951	77,000
1952	75,000
1953	55,000
1954	50,000
1955	50,000
1956	45,000
1957	50,000
1958	50,000
1959	40,000
1960	15,000
1961	27,000
1962	20,000
1963	20,000
1964	10,000
1965	5,000
1966	6,500
1967	9,000
Total	$661,500

TABLE 2
THE MOST FAVORED LIBRARIES

Helsinki University Library	$104,400
Helsinki Institute (University) of Technology	80,278
Library of the Swedish University of Turku (Åbo Akademi)	67,776
Library of the University of Turku	69,757
Library of Parliament	32,547
American Institute, University of Helsinki	28,110
Library of the University of Jyväskylä	24,135
University of Helsinki, Institutional Libraries of the Section of Mathematics and Natural Sciences	22,450
University of Helsinki, Institutional Libraries of the Faculty of Medicine	20,400
Library of the Student Union, University of Helsinki	20,344
Library of the College of Social Sciences (now University of Tampere)	20,116
Helsinki School of Economics	14,275
Swedish School of Economics (Helsinki)	14,251
Library of the College of Veterinary Medicine	13,350
Library of Agriculture, University of Helsinki	11,250
Forestry Library, University of Helsinki	11,200

Notes

I am indebted to many persons in connection with the preparation of this essay. I would especially like to thank Professors Osmo Apunen, Maxine Rochester, Paul Solomon, and Elin Törnudd, Dr. Jyrki Iivonen, Chief Librarian Esko Häkli, the personnel of the Fulbright Center in Helsinki, and those who arranged the Paris conference, where the first version of this paper was read.

1. About the ASLA-Fulbright program in general, see *Finnish-American Academic and Professional Exchanges: Analyses and Reminiscences*, ed. William Copeland et al. (Espoo: Foundation for Research in Higher Education and Science Policy and United States Educational Foundation in Finland, 1983), and *Shaping Nations: Fifty Years of Finnish-American Academic Exchanges* (Helsinki: Fulbright Center, 1999).

2. For general information on American international activities for libraries before, during, and after World War II, see Beverly J. Brewster, *American Overseas Library Technical Assistance, 1940-1970* (Metuchen, N.J.: Scarecrow Press, 1976), and Gary E. Kraske, *Missionaries of the Book: The American Library Profession and the Origins of United States Cultural Diplomacy* (Westport, Conn.: Greenwood Press, 1985).

3. About the distribution of the catalog, see Brewster, *American Overseas Library*, 235. The official correspondence of the chief librarian in the archives of the Helsinki University Library contains information on the aid Finland's academic libraries received after the war.

4. Ministry for Foreign Affairs memorandum no. 13010, 16 March 1946, copy in the Papers of the Board of Scientific Libraries, National Archives (Helsinki), attached to a memorandum from Minister K. T. Jutila, no. 1045/130, 6 February 1946 (copy) and a copy of letters from the ABC, 31 October 1945 and 31 January 1946.

5. For relations between the United States and Finland before and during World War II, see Michael R. Berry, *American Foreign Policy and the Finnish Exception: Ideological Preferences and Wartime Realities, 1941-1945* (Helsinki, 1987).

6. *Congressional Record*, 15 December 1947, 11358-11360.

7. *Congressional Record*, 6 January 1949, 86-87.

8. *Department of State Bulletin*, 6 February 1949, 171. See also *Department of State Bulletin*, 13 February 1950, 251.

9. Kraske, *Missionaries*, 232. See also Henry J. Kellermann, *Cultural Relations as an Instrument of U.S. Foreign Policy: The Educational Exchange Program between the United States and Germany 1945-1954* (Washington, D.C.: Department of State, 1978), 6-9.

10. About the nonpropaganda character of the OWI libraries, see Pamela S. Richards, "Information for the Allies: Office of War Information Libraries in Australia, New Zealand, and South Africa," *Library Quarterly* 52:4 (1982): 325-47.

11. Kraske, *Missionaries*, 232-35.

12. U.S. Senate, *Committee on Foreign Relations, Rept. 740*, 81st Cong., 1st sess.; U.S. House, *Committee on Foreign Affairs, Rept. 1195*, 81st Cong., 1st sess.

13. See Kraske, *Missionaries*, 247.

14. Ibid., 252.

15. See, e.g., Jussi M. Hanhimäki, *Rinnakkaiseloa patoamassa. Yhdysvallat ja Paasikiven linja 1948-1956* (Containing Coexistence: the United States and the Paasikivi Line, 1948-1956) (Helsinki: Suomen Historiallinen Seura, 1996), 71.

16. *Shaping Nations*, 8; "Department of State Policy Statement, December 1, 1949. Finland," in *Foreign Relations of the United States 1949*, vol. 5 (Washington, D.C.: U.S. Government Printing Office, 1976), 443.

232   *Finland Pays Its Debts*

17. Tudeer to Jutila, 28 October 1949, official correspondence of the Helsinki University Library (HUL), Db1.12. Another important contact for Tudeer in the United States was his friend and former colleague Karl-Emerik Olsoni, who often visited the United States and in the end stayed there. He kept Tudeer well-informed about the American library and other news, created contacts (e.g., with the Library of Congress and the Department of State), and offered in general his services. Letters from Olsoni to Tudeer are in Tudeer's private papers in the HUL Archives.

18. Tudeer to Childs, 12 November 1949, official correspondence, HUL, Db1.12.

19. Tudeer's memorandum, 18 November 1949, HUL, MA 3.3. ASLA-muistioita.

20. Promemoria, 18 January 1950, Papers of the Board of Scientific Libraries, National Archives (Helsinki).

21. Evans to Tudeer, 11 August 1950, Papers of the Board of Scientific Libraries, National Archives.

22. Arnold to Tudeer, 16 February 1950, Papers of the Board of Scientific Libraries, National Archives.

23. Arnold to Tudeer, 12 September 1950, Papers of the Board of Scientific Libraries, National Archives.

24. Arnold to Tudeer, 24 October 1950, Papers of the Board of Scientific Libraries, National Archives.

25. Arnold to Tudeer, 25 October 1950, Papers of the Board of Scientific Libraries, National Archives.

26. Minutes of the meeting of the Board of Scientific Libraries, 18 October 1950, Papers of the Board of Scientific Libraries, National Archives.

27. Arnold to Tudeer, 12 September 1950, Papers of the Board of Scientific Libraries, National Archives.

28. Minutes of the meeting of the Council of Scientific Libraries, 18 October 1950, Papers of the Board of Scientific Libraries, National Archives.

29. Arnold to Tudeer, 2 October 1950, Papers of the Board of Scientific Libraries, National Archives.

30. *Department of State Bulletin*, 22 January 1951, 151.

31. Wilson to Tudeer, 9 November 1951, Papers of the Board of Scientific Libraries, National Archives.

32. Wilson to Tudeer, 11 November 1951, Papers of the Board of Scientific Libraries, National Archives.

33. Based on the data in the annual reports of Helsinki University and other educational institutions and libraries, 1947–67.

34. For appraisals of the program, see Eino Nivanka, "ASLA Grants to the Finnish Research Libraries," *ASLA* 4 (1965): 6–8, and "Finnish Research Libraries Thankful for Asla Books," *ASLA* 2 (1967): 10.

35. Erik Allardt and Krister Ståhlberg, "Social Sciences," in *Finnish-American Academic and Professional Exchanges: Analyses and Reminiscences* (Helsinki, 1983), 49–53.

Romanian Libraries Recover after the Cold War: The Communist Legacy and the Road Ahead

Hermina G.B. Anghelescu

There is an urgent need for current leaders to stem the neglect suffered by Romanian libraries during the Communist years by acknowledging the importance of the library as an institution and by providing financial support to move the libraries into the realm of the developed countries. Historically, Romanian libraries developed in much the same way as libraries did in countries in Western Europe: monastic and ecclesiastical libraries, court libraries, and private collections, some becoming college libraries, and public libraries created to support education for all citizens. Independence in 1877 led to the creation of universities and the establishment of an academic library system. There was, however, a derailment in this continued development of libraries in Romania under the forty-five years of Communist rule. Its effects are still being felt today as the country struggles with a high inflation rate; an abandonment by authorities as they focus on more immediate problems; a lack of specialized faculty to teach new skills and technology to library school graduates, along with an outdated curriculum; an "anybody can do it" attitude toward librarianship; an outdated infrastructure; a critical "knowledge lag"; damaging attitudes adopted under Communism; and a lack of management expertise. The library, under Communism and the legacy of Communism, is presented interchangeably, through an exploration of the library system, the librarians' status, professional associations, the library's image in society, cultural policies, collections, censorship, infrastructure, and mentalities.

Historical Context

The early history of Romanian libraries followed a pattern similar to that of libraries in Western Europe. The first libraries in the three Romanian principalities, which constitute the territory of today's Romania (Wallachia, Moldavia, and Transylvania), were monastic libraries dating from the fourteenth century. The invasions of migratory peoples took their toll and delayed the cultural development of these lands. It was during the sixteenth, seventeenth, and eighteenth

Figure 1. National Library of Romania (current locale, former Stock Exchange), Bucharest. Photo by author.

centuries that the reigning princes started the court libraries by acquiring illuminated manuscripts and incunabula from Europe and Asia Minor.

Court libraries coexisted with private libraries that belonged to the scholars and the dignitaries of the time.[1] School libraries, which in the beginning were part of the ecclesiastical libraries, became independent during the sixteenth century and started their activities in conjunction with colleges. Prince Constantin Brâncoveanu founded the St. Sava College Library in Bucharest in 1679. The princes who succeeded him on Wallachia's throne contributed to the enrichment of the collections of this library, which in 1838 acquired the status of National Library, harboring 10,000 volumes.[2]

During the eighteenth century, the national emancipation movement led to the development of an educational system for all citizens and, consequently, to the emergence of public libraries during the following century. The end of the Russo-Turkish war (1828–29) marked the end of the Ottoman domination over the Romanian principalities. At this time the czarist empire imposed the Organic Regulations, which represented restrictive constitutions, upon Wallachia in 1831 and Moldavia in 1832. The establishment of the first public libraries in the Romanian principalities dates back to the age of these regulations.

The commission that drafted the Organic Regulations for Wallachia took into account the fact that the two lands needed public instruction and libraries. Article 63, point 13 mandates the allocation of an annual budget for "the maintenance of public schools in the capital city [Bucharest] and in two other towns of the Principality, of the Printing shop, and of the Library."[3] In 1833 four new articles were added to the Organic Regulations with specific stipulations for libraries. These four items comprise the first public library legislation in Romania.[4]

In 1859 the Romanian state was founded when Wallachia and Moldavia elected the same ruler, Alexandru Ioan Cuza, a prince educated in Paris.[5] Cuza's reforms prepared the way for Romania's independence from the Ottoman Porte, the government of the Ottoman empire, which was achieved in the year of 1877. The foundation of the Romanian state, along with the accelerated economic, educational, and social development of the nineteenth century, coincided with an increase in the need for knowledge. This led to the creation of universities and the establishment of the academic library system: the Central University Library in Iași (1870), the Central University Library in Cluj (1872), and the Central University Library in Bucharest (1891). In 1866 the Library of the Romanian Academy was founded. Beginning in 1901, it functioned as a national library until 1955, when the Central State Library was established. At present the former supports academic and scholarly research with a retrospective focus, while the latter institution focuses on current materials. After 1989 the Central State Library changed its name and became the National Library of Romania.

The Library System in Romania

In 1990 the public library network in Romania consisted of the Bucharest Municipal Library, 40 county libraries, and 2,823 libraries at municipal, city, commune, and village level.[6] In 1997 the Ministry of Culture, which funds and supervises the public libraries, decided to place them under the jurisdiction of the local authorities. Due to high inflation, the ministry was no longer able to subsidize public library activity. This was indicative of decentralization, a natural consequence of the demise of Communism, but in reality this was nothing else but abandonment, since the local authorities, confronted with many other issues, simply ignored the library, which at the time was not viewed as a high priority from a financial standpoint. "When the Municipal Council has to decide where to invest first—in acquiring new books for the municipal library or in a new topping for the main road—it goes without saying that the money will go into the road, as everybody uses it, compared to the library, which is used only by a fraction of the population." Gheorghe

Macsim, who was the director of the Prahova County Library in Ploiesti for forty years, revealed this information during a personal interview.[7]

The academic library system includes the main academic library and the libraries of different departments located within each university—a total of forty-three.[8] This network, together with that of 10,956 school libraries in middle and high schools, is under the jurisdiction of the Ministry of Education.[9] The Central University Library in Bucharest, which saw its collections turned into ashes during the popular revolt of 1989, is the first Romanian automated library accessible via the Internet.[10] The automation of some other libraries is still only in an incipient phase.

There is also a system of special libraries (a total of 2,908 in 1990),[11] concentrated mainly in Bucharest. These libraries are overseen and funded by the ministries they serve. For instance, the Central Pedagogical Library depends on the Ministry of Education, the Central Medical Library serves the needs of the Health Ministry and its subordinate institutions, and the Central Military Library depends on the Ministry of Defense, while the Library of the National Institute of Information and Documentation assists this national body.

The Status of Librarians

Prior to 1990, the government subsidized all library activities in Romania—book and periodical acquisition, buildings and their maintenance, and staff salaries. I have to point out that the budget the government used for allotments to libraries was far from enough for collection development money or salaries. The low salaries and the low prestige of the library profession were some of the major reasons why not many people felt attracted toward this particular career. In 1989 the Central State Library—the premier library of the country—had only 250 employees, 175 of them possessing a graduate degree focusing primarily on foreign languages or history.

Library education was discontinued in the 1970s, when the Ministry of Education decided to close the only library school, part of the University of Bucharest. The assumption was that anyone holding a graduate degree could fulfill a librarian's tasks, which had been viewed as a simple method of bringing books to readers and then reshelving them. At present, this is the image of the profession of librarian that persists in today's Romania. Practicing librarians are also concerned with the public image of their profession to the extent that they even avoid mentioning their real profession on their business cards.[12]

Figure 2. National Library of Romania (new locale), Bucharest. Photo by author.

In 1990 the Department of Library and Information Science started as part of the Faculty of Letters at the University of Bucharest. The curriculum is still far from meeting the objectives of preparing librarians for the twenty-first century.[13] The graduates are more book historians than experts in library and information science. The curriculum concentrates on classes in Latin, Church Slavonic, book and library history, cataloging, and classification. The main reason for this trend is that specialized faculty required to teach courses on new technologies, collection development, information retrieval, data conversion, use and users of library services, reference services, and the preservation of library materials are nonexistent.

Professional Associations

During the 1980s, all professional associations were outlawed in Romania. Angela Popescu-Brădiceni, the director of the Central State Library, explained this annihilation: "It was because of the government's paranoia. They saw a potential anti-Communist plot in any meeting which brought together in the same place a group of several people."[14] Therefore, the Romanian Library Association ceased to exist. The Council of Socialist Culture and Education (the Ministry of Culture at that time) cut all the funding for IFLA membership fees. Popescu-Brădiceni's efforts to reintegrate Romanian libraries into the international library community had remained

Figure 3. Central University Library, Bucharest. Photo by author.

unsuccessful in spite of all the memos she sent to the Council of Socialist Culture and Education.[15] During this decade, Romania adopted an isolationist stance in politics that drastically diminished the country's participation in international scientific meetings of any kind. Romania's presence at IFLA conferences was only sporadic.

In 1990 two library associations came into existence: the Romanian Association of Education Librarians (Asociația Bibliotecarilor din Învățământ din România–ABIR), which brings together school and academic librarians, and the Romanian Association of Public Librarians (Asociația Bibliotecarilor din Bibliotecile Publice din România–ABBPR) for public librarians. Unfortunately, even today these two associations continue to act as separate entities, and they show no sign of cooperation. However, the positive side is that, in 1990, they both joined IFLA.

Image of the Library in Society

The low prestige of the library as an institution stemmed from the fact that Romania's party and government leaders had not made use of the libraries themselves, their education being limited to a thorough knowledge of the texts of Marxism-Leninism. In addition to other cultural institutions such as theaters, cinema theaters, opera houses, philharmonic societies, and museums, libraries were part of the generic domain of culture. The supreme goal of a socialist economy was the production of material goods. The cultural domain produced spiritual goods that were impossible to measure in quantifiable parameters. As a consequence, this domain was completely marginalized. If the other cultural institutions were considered as a sort of a "Cinderella" because they at least produced limited profits from the tickets they sold, libraries were even worse–they were Cinderella's Cinderella, synonymous with the maid's maid–they generated absolutely no annual revenue.

The visionary public addresses delivered by president Ceașescu on different festive occasions, such as the congresses of the Romanian Communist party, which were targeted to showcase the accomplishments of the nation during the five-year plans, had never mentioned libraries or their roles in society. Ceaușescu used to talk about the crucial importance of research and development and about putting into practice the latest conquests of science and technology "for the general progress of society and for raising the material and spiritual well being of the people."[16] The cultural-educational chapter of his speeches alluded to the "molding [of] the new man, conscious builder of socialism and Communism."[17] The institutions that were targeted as vehicles to achieve this task included the press, radio, television, and cinematography, together with literature and the arts.[18]

The Romanian Communist party's programmatic documents,[19] which were the product of a council consisting of members of the Central Committee of the party, had not mentioned the libraries. They targeted the role of literature and the arts for the aesthetic development of the masses.[20] The mission of the mass media was "to work for the generalization of the advanced experience gathered in all the sectors of socialist construction, . . . to secure the large exposition of the views and proposals of the working people, of all citizens in connection with the activities carried out in various fields of economic and social life."[21] Scientific research in all fields (industry, agriculture, biology, physics, chemistry, and mathematics) was to take place in the labs of the research institutes.[22] It appears that neither Ceaușescu nor his counselors were aware of the mission of libraries! It is as if these institutions did not exist at all.

Ceaușescu wanted to commemorate his glorious reign with the famous Victory of Socialism Boulevard crossing from East to West Bucharest's historical downtown. At the Western extremity, the largest building in Europe was erected–the People's House, a monumental North Korean-style construction that remains unfinished even today. The Eastern extremity was reserved for the edifice of a national library. In spite of the fact that libraries had been ignored and had received insignificant subventions on behalf of his government, Ceaușescu wanted to leave the stamp of his "golden age" with a library of national scale. Despite the fact that the building was not yet finished, in June 1989, a few months before his dramatic end, Ceaușescu inaugurated the book exhibition, consisting mostly of his own works and the party documents, organized in the entrance hall (the only finished room of the eight-story building). He cut the inaugural ribbon, and the fatal year of 1989 was carved on the frontispiece of the edifice.

The governments that followed Ceaușescu's fall paid as little attention to the libraries as their predecessors. This trend is, in large part, due to skyrocketing inflation and other priority issues that the Romanian economy has faced for the last decade. The construction of the National Library was put on hold, and it continued to be one of the many abandoned structures that was characteristic of the Romanian capital city of the 1990s. Since its very first design stage, the construction of this building was not conceived to be architecturally accommodating to meet the needs and requirements of a modern library. It would have been the first library construction in Communist Romania. All public libraries in Romania are located in buildings erected before World War II for various purposes. For instance, the National Library in Bucharest is situated in the former Stock Exchange, an architectural art déco jewel; unfortunately, it is far from being able to accommodate the needs and operations of a library, especially a national library.[23]

Cultural Policies

During the forty-five years of Communist domination, one of the major objectives of the government's policy was to disseminate culture among citizens belonging to all social strata throughout the urban and rural areas of the country. In real terms this translated into a phenomenon of mass indoctrination with the dogmas of Communist ideology. For the purposes of this study, the government's objectives had two major strategies: the creation of a special publishing house whose mission was to publish propagandistic texts that would illustrate the socialist doctrine, and the creation of a national network of public libraries whose intended use was to house and disseminate these texts. The mission of the Political Publishing House (Editura Politica) was to translate into Romanian and to publish the works of the three fathers of socialism: Karl Marx, Friedrich Engels, and Vladimir Ilich Lenin. It is obvious that their works, documented in multiple volumes and copies, were to occupy the many shelves of any Romanian library.

Figure 4. Mihai Eminescu Central University Library, Iași. Photo courtesy of the library.

After the 1965 election of Nicolae Ceaușescu, general secretary of the Romanian Communist party and president of the Socialist Republic of Romania, his personal manifests were placed next to the works of Marx, Engels, and Lenin. The monumental thirty-two-volume opus of the sociopolitical thinking of Romania's president was published in mass editions and grouped under different series, for example, *Romania: Achievements and Prospects; Romania on the Way of Completing Socialist Construction: Reports, Speeches, Articles; Romania on the Way of Building up the Multilaterally Developed Socialist Society: Reports, Speeches, Interviews, Articles; Romania: Past, Present, Prospects.* These series were then regrouped by theme, for example, Science, Progress, Peace, Socialist Humanism, and then translated into the five official UN languages (French, English, German, Russian, and Spanish). The Meridian Publishing House (Editura Meridiane), which had reserved an entire department for this purpose, published the editions in foreign languages.

The main hall of the various libraries—public, academic, special, and school—had at least one large portrait of the president surrounded by his most recent works. Once in the reading room, other displays and mottos portraying the "deep thought of the country's supreme commander" met readers. The destruction of these works—the entire world viewed them flying through the air, catapulted out of the windows of the headquarters of the Romanian Communist party during the live

Figure 5. Braşov County Library, Braşov. Photo courtesy of the library.

broadcast of the December 1989 revolt—symbolized the end of a gloomy period for the Romanian people, a time characterized by acerbic demagoguery and obfuscation.[24] These works were the first items to be weeded from any library collection after the fall of Communism. Fortunately, a certain number of copies were preserved in order to facilitate research into this bleak era in Romania's history.

Collections

Collection development policies required only the acquisition of books and periodicals published in Romania. Given that everything was government controlled and centralized at the ministry level, it was not difficult to record the current national publishing output in the national bibliography (*Bibliografia Republicii Socialiste România*).[25] In 1971 Romania published 5,000 titles. In 1989 a significant decline occurred, and the twenty-four publishing houses published only 1,000 titles. The main reasons were drastic censorship and a sharp rise in the cost of paper. A spectacular increase in the number of private publishers after 1990 (in 1994 there were 2,300 publishing houses compared to only 24 in the pre-1990 period) led to bibliographic chaos. The new publishers were not aware of the legal deposit regulations, so the National Library had no longer received the legal deposit copies. The situation returned to normal only after a new legal deposit law was passed in 1996 due to the increased efforts of the National Library to familiarize publishers with ISBN and CIP standards.

Because of the lack of hard currency, Romanian libraries became isolated from the international circuit of knowledge. It was only through international exchanges that Romanian libraries were able to obtain foreign publications; however, they still could not get the latest *Encyclopaedia Britannica* via exchange. In 1990 the most recent encyclopedias in the reference section of the National Library were dated from the 1970s. "The [National] Library's last edition of the major international chemistry journal *Chemical Abstracts* is dated 1972. At Romania's national library 'the knowledge lag is 10 to 15 years' behind what is available outside the country," wrote Blaine Harden in an article published in the *Washington Post* on 28 December 1989.[26]

The precarious situation of the Romanian library collections was assessed by numerous teams of Western librarians who had come to Romania, particularly after they had seen the collections of the Central University Library in Bucharest engulfed by flames. In 1990 massive shipments of books and periodicals were sent to Romania as a result of several international programs aimed at restoring and updating Romanian library collections.[27]

The exchanges with the sister countries, that is, the socialist countries, were extensive, even though it is hard to believe that readers were anxious to come to the library to find out what was going on in neighboring Bulgaria or Albania or other Communist countries that had shared the same fate as theirs.[28] Library statistics compiled during the Communist regime cannot be verified for accuracy and, hence, require cautious interpretation. The figures do not reflect the reality–from the number of volumes held by a library to the number of library users.[29] In a study on Romanian libraries, Steve Amery ironically states: "The official source for library statistics in Romania is *Anuarul statistic al României*. It is at best unreliable, at worst not to be trusted.... For libraries to have an estimated population served of 26,700,000, in a country with a population of 22,755,260 is quite an achievement."[30]

Censorship

Prior to 1989 there were twenty-four publishing houses in Romania. All of them were government owned, and all of them were subject to severe ideological control. The publication of any book was completely government subsidized except for one–Editura Litera–a vanity press

Figure 6. Lucian Blaga Central University Library, Cluj-Napoca. Photo by author.

where an author had to finance the publication of his or her own work. However, the publication was not guaranteed. Usually Editura Litera published the manuscripts rejected by the other publishing houses for various reasons, the main one being the content, which did not agree with the party line.

The *sine qua non* condition in order to be employed by a publishing house was to be a member of the Romanian Communist party. This implied that the worker was faithful to the Communist ideology and, at the same time, capable of being a censor and an editor in order to ensure that the ideas that could undermine the government would not reach the press and, implicitly, the readers. Paradoxically, one of the few works dedicated to the history of libraries in Romania did not pass the censor, and its author was forced to self-finance the publication of his book.[31]

For example, works written by authors of Romanian origin and who lived abroad, such as Eugène Ionesco, Emil Cioran, Tristan Tzara, Princess Marthe Bibesco, and many others, were not published in Communist Romania. It was not the content of their writings but merely their status of émigrés that prevented publication.[32] At present, the publishing houses, which had mushroomed after 1990, have made their fortunes by publishing the works of the banned authors of the Communist era. These particular authors belonged to a "black list" of expatriates and were considered to be in the category of people who wrote in negative terms about the government in Bucharest or about Communism in general. If their original works were mailed to Romania from anywhere in the world, a vigilant commission of censors that operated under the Ministry of Post and Telecommunications would index them. Most of the books were sent to the Central State Library to be placed in the famous "Fond S." In reality, the calembour "S" special/secret meant "forbidden." This collection of "noxious" materials consisted of books and periodicals on religion (Marxism taught atheism), monarchy (King Michael was forced into exile in 1947), Nazism (Romania had its own fascist movement, the Iron Guard, during the pre–World War II period), or even history (works that analyzed sensitive aspects of Romania's history such as the controversial provinces of Transylvania or Bessarabia).

The first list of forbidden works was published as early as 1945,[33] immediately after the advent of Communism. It was followed by a more complete one in 1948, unequivocally titled *Lista publicațiilor interzise* (List of forbidden publications).[34] Similar lists followed, but they ceased to be officially distributed. They had restricted and "confidential" circulation and bore the seal of the ideological bureau of the Central Committee of the Romanian Communist Party, which had distributed them through the Council of Socialist Culture and Education (turned into the Ministry of Culture in 1990).

Every county library had a Fond S that was more or less substantial. "The Fond S was distinct from the current circulation fond; it was separately classified and stocked, and it was preserved under special security conditions."[35] There were ordinances that regulated the consultation of the Fond S publications. They explicitly required librarians to keep a discerning eye on the people who had asked for permission to consult these fonds and to keep track of the themes that these users were interested in, which led to the creation of a list of researchers interested in taboo subjects.[36] Policy stated that researchers had to submit a written request to the library director in order to be allowed access to these materials. In spite of all the oppressive restrictions that they were required to enforce, there were several library directors who assumed the risk of approving access to documents officially considered "hostile, Horthyst, anti-Communist, and chauvinistic."[37] "On the contrary, I used to encourage those asking for access to this genre of literature. However, I could not admit it publicly," the director of an academic library confessed to me.[38]

During Ceaușescu's reign, the secret fonds abounded in materials that included only one sentence alluding to his dictatorial regime. Multivolume encyclopedias such as the eight volumes of the *Encyclopedia of Philosophy* were banned since they contained articles with negative comments on the state of Romania or on Communism.[39] The famous sixteen-volume *Encyclopedia of Religion* was withdrawn for two explicit reasons: the subject—religion—and the editor—Mircea Eliade, a Romanian who had left the country in 1944 to settle and teach in the United States.[40]

The political situation got worse, and the complete obliteration of anti-Communist literature was desired. Ordinances were issued to this effect requesting physical destruction of the materials in the Fond S.[41] "I haven't destroyed anything. No copy. No book. We hid everything from the politicians' sight and from all those who could have accused us of not having done it. I preferred to close my eyes pretending I saw nothing, and to let the librarians take these materials home. In this way not only did we save the book as a physical object, but also the ideas these books contained," Traian Brad, director of the Octavian Goga County Library in Cluj-Napoca, expressed to me during an interview.[42]

In 1990, throughout Romania the "S" fonds were incorporated into the general collections of the library. The cards with the bibliographic description were integrated into the general card catalog. They continue to bear the "S" symbol so that future generations of researchers would know that their predecessors had once been denied access to these documents.

The Infrastructure

Basic equipment vital to facilitating the research process, namely, copiers (taken for granted in the West), were considered luxury items in Romania. "To photocopy a document in a library, one had to obtain special authorizations, signatures, and stamps before a single copy was made," stated Mary Nell Bryant.[43] Any method of duplication was severely limited and kept under strict surveillance. The unauthorized ownership of a typewriter constituted a felony and, therefore, was penalized by law. Individuals who had been granted authorization for the ownership of a typewriter had to register it with the police annually.[44]

The printed card and the card catalog continue to represent the only method of access to the collections in many Romanian libraries, except for the Central University Library in Bucharest, already mentioned. The efforts to automate Romanian libraries have been isolated for two main reasons: the lack of money and the cooperation among libraries. The inflationist economy has priorities other than to introduce new technologies to these types of institutions. In addition, policy-makers do not recognize the integral connection between the advancement of the nation toward democracy and the support that is necessary for the creation of a modern library network.

Figure 7. Library of the Polytechnic University, Timişoara. Photo by author.

Presently, a significant number of libraries still do not own computers. There are libraries that have only one computer available (computers with CD-ROM drive are rare), placed in an office, with no concept of a local area network. With the absence of a modern telephone and communications system, the Internet remains just a pipe dream for many libraries in Romania. Due to the support of international organizations, such as the Soros Foundation for an Open Society, progress is being made toward the universal employment of online access.

Mentalities

During the Communist regime libraries served as vehicles to disseminate propagandist material for mass indoctrination. Even today, their mission continues to be the preservation of the national cultural heritage and collection development. Their focus has been mostly on quantity rather than quality. The desire to facilitate access to documents or to improve service, keeping the end-user in mind, remains only a desideratum. The way out of this passivity, which characterizes Romanian libraries, implies a paradigm shift that, in its turn, involves mutations in librarians' attitudes.

The societies of the Communist block have never been concerned with consumer satisfaction, nor have libraries. The librarians' mission was, rather, to be the guardians of the books that were part of the national cultural heritage more than to do their best to obtain a certain book or article that a certain researcher particularly needed.[45] The exception was when a "comrade" of the nomenclatura requested that material. In this case, no effort would have been spared.

Interlibrary loan was not the solution for all requests and was used only in special instances. In that case, the request had to be approved by the director of the Central State Library (this operation was centralized at the national level), and the entire process could take almost two years. By the time the requested book had reached Romania, the researcher had already published his book! It was the same cycle for the requests of Romanian books that were needed abroad. *Festina lente* seemed to have been the motto. It is this mentality that needs to change. Unfortunately, it went hand in hand with another dictum of the Communist era: "We pretend to be working and the government pretends to be paying us," which led to very low productivity, specifically in Eastern European countries. It is high time to change attitudes in this area. However, changing mentalities, attitudes, and behaviors is a slow phenomenon requiring long periods of time.

One of the most advanced Romanian public libraries in terms of the automation of its operations is the Octavian Goga County Library in Cluj-Napoca. At present, its online catalog provides access to almost 45,000 titles in the library's holdings.[46] But more important than the retrospective conversion of its collections is the Community Information Center established within this library, with the mission of providing online access to various local information sources, from bus and train schedules to job postings, from health providers to entertainment in the Cluj area. This is a novelty in the panoply of services that a public library has undertaken to offer in Romania, and it is a proactive example worth following by other public libraries. Changing attitudes is not impossible.

Romanian libraries mirror the lack of managerial experience at the national level. The euphoria of the "December revolution" has caused a few libraries to change their top management directors and department heads—who had been political appointees.[47] However, the new management, although politically immaculate, lacked leadership and managerial skills. After 1990 several Romanian libraries, confronted with this managerial vacuum, found themselves adrift in choosing to implement radical change. Eliminating certain people who stood for symbols of the ended era was imperative within Romanian society in general. As for libraries today, they need young leaders with modern visions to take them into the twenty-first century. However, training leaders is not an overnight process.

Conclusion

Romanian libraries continue to be confronted with the vestiges of the Communist regime, which translate into the nonexistence of adequate library buildings, the lack of specially trained staff, and outdated collections. It is almost a miracle that Romanian libraries survived as institutions during the forty-five years of Communist neglect. At present, they are affected by the precarious financial situation caused by the skyrocketing inflation, which has characterized the Romanian economy since 1989. With very few exceptions, the modernization of Romanian libraries and the integration of their collections into the international information circuit, along with the diversification of the services they ought to offer to their users, will be the task of tomorrow's librarians.

The Communist government's neglect of libraries portrays a lamentable heritage, the roots of which will remain visible if the new politicians continue to ignore these institutions. The time has come for national leaders to perceive libraries as information centers that serve and empower the community and as institutions meant to provide access to information for all members of the society. They ought to recognize the importance of the library as an institution that supports the country's advancement toward democracy and to provide the financial support needed to help Romanian libraries acquire the status that libraries enjoy in the developed countries of the world.

Notes

1. A remarkable number of libraries and archival collections were established in Transylvania. The Teleky-Bolyai Library was founded in Târgu Mureş in 1653 by a former chancellor of Transylvania. The Batthyaneum Library in Alba Iulia was established in 1784, and the Brukenthal Library was founded in 1784 in Sibiu. In Wallachia, some of the best-known private collections of the seventeenth century were those of the Cantacuzino and Mavrocordat families. In Moldavia, Prince Dimitrie Cantemir was renowned for his eighteenth-century library.

2. Corneliu Dima-Dragăn, *Biblioteci umaniste româneşti: Istoric, semnificaţii, organizare* (Romanian humanistic libraries: history, significance, organization) (Bucharest: Editura Litera, 1974).

3. *Regulamentul Organic* (Organic Regulations) (Bucharest: P. Z. Karkaleki, 1832), 25.

4. Paul Oprescu, "Infiintarea si dezvoltarea bibliotecilor publice româneşti în epoca Regulamentului Organic" (Establishment and Development of Romanian Public Libraries at the Time of the Organic Regulations). *Studii si cercetari de bibliologie* 1 (1955): 47.

5. Kurt Treptow and Marcel Popa, *Historical Dictionary of Romania* (Lanham, Md.: Scarecrow Press, 1996), 83.

6. *Anuarul statistic al României* (Romania's Statistical Yearbook) (Bucharest: Comisia Centrala pentru Statistica, 1990).

7. Interview, 7 August 1997, Ploieşti.

8. *Anuarul statistic al României.*

9. Ibid.

10. The URL for the Central University Library in Bucharest is http://www.bcub.ro.

11. *Anuarul statistic al României.*

12. The Romanian librarian introduces him- or herself as "professor," "philologist," or "licentiate in history." Large libraries have an "editor" position for the person in charge of issuing the local bibliography. Other librarians use the name "documentalist," a neologism few laypeople beyond the library science sphere are familiar with.

13. They offer three-year college-level courses and four-year faculty-level courses.

14. Interview with Angela Popescu-Brădiceni, 13 August 1997, Bucharest.

15. Letters from the Central State Library to the Council of Socialist Culture and Education. Correspondence at the archives of the National Library of Romania.

16. Nicolae Ceauşescu, *Report of the Central Committee on the Activity of the Romanian Communist Party between the Twelfth Congress and the Thirteenth Congress and on the Future Activity of the Party with a View to Attaining Romania's Economic and Social Development Targets under the 1986-1990 Five-Year Plan and, in the Long Run, until the Year 2000* (Bucharest: Editura Politica, 1984), 29.

17. Ibid., 57.

18. Ibid., 63-64.

19. *Programme of the Romanian Communist Party for the Building of the Multilaterally Developed Socialist Society and Romania's Advance toward Communism* (Bucharest: Romanian News Agency–AGERPRES, 1975).

20. Ibid., 163-65.

21. Ibid., 166-67.

22. Ibid., 100-102.

23. The Bucharest Municipal Library is situated in the city's downtown area in a house built by an oil man for his mistress during the interwar period.

24. I was in the building of the Central State Library in Bucharest (the future National Library) during the popular uprising against Ceauşescu on 21 December 1989. We were not allowed to join the popular revolt; on the contrary, the heavy cast-iron door of the building was bolted, following the instructions received from the party committee of the district in which the library is located. We can say that "the revolution" passed by the library without the librarians being allowed to join it. At the same time, the director, Angela Popescu-Brădiceni, foreseeing the possibility of government overthrow, ordered a silent removal of the permanent exhibit "Homage to the President," displayed along the corridor leading to the director's office. Her instructions were "to carefully box the books" so that they could be taken to a safe place, far from the possible collective fury that could have led to the destruction of other books if the door of the library had been forced by the revolutionaries. When the library staff was allowed to leave the institution, there were only empty cases on the second floor of the library.

25. *Bibliografia Republicii Socialiste România* (Bibliography of the Socialist Republic of Romania), changed into *Bibliografia Nationala* (National Bibliography) in 1990, published by the National Library, with ten series.

26. Blaine Harden, "Romanian Library Topples Ceauşescu's Literary Monuments," *Washington Post*, 28 December 1989: A26.

27. Opritsa D. Popa and Sanda J. Lamprecht, "Romania and United States Library Connections," *Advances in Librarianship* 18 (1994): 196–99.

28. The National Library continues to have an Oriental collection with Chinese, Mongolian, and Vietnamese books received on an exchange basis; they are not cataloged, as there is no Romanian librarian who knows these languages.

29. "When we had to fill in the forms for the *World of Learning*, we had to report an ascending curve for the bibliographic units in the library holdings. We've tried to remain modest when reporting increasing figures," confessed Gheorghe-Iosif Bercan in 1997. Bercan was the librarian elected in January 1990 by open vote of the staff of the National Library to become the national librarian. In order to justify its efficiency to the Council of Socialist Culture and Education, the National Library had to report a number of 1,000 users per month. Needless to say, it was not able to attract that many readers, primarily during winter months, when due to energy savings programs there were numerous power and heat shortages that brought the temperature in reading rooms down to 40°F (5°C). It would have been too adventurous to do research under these circumstances. At this point the staff was asked to tour the reading rooms to sign the readers' book with their name, the name of their family members, of their friends, and of their neighbors–people who had never set foot in that library. This was the way the planned figure was met.

30. Steve Amery, "Romanian Libraries: Past, Present and Future," in Kathleen de la Peña McCook, Barbara J. Ford, and Kate Lippincott, eds. *Libraries: Global Reach, Local Touch* (Chicago: American Library Association, 1998).

31. Corneliu Dima-Drăgan, *Biblioteci umaniste româneşti: Istoric, semnificatii, organizare* (Romanian Humanistic Libraries: History, Significance, Organization) (Bucharest: Editura Litera, 1974). In this case, it was not the subversive content of the book but the author's political attitude: Dima-Dragan was an anti-Communist. He defected in the 1980s to go to Canada. A few years later he was assassinated. The moment Dima-Dragan left Romania he was considered a "traitor," and, consequently, his works were no longer thought to be worth consulting in libraries. The works were transferred to the Fond S.

32. If, however, their writings were published, they were very much altered, and all of the passages that were not in agreement with the official view were removed. The volumes were "abridged editions" or "selected writings," the selection being made to meet the propagandistic purposes of the government.

33. *Lista publicatiilor scoase din circulatie* (List of publications withdrawn from circulation), published in the *Monitorul Oficial* and in booklet format.

34. Ionut Costea, István Király, and Doru Radosav, *Fond Secret. Fond "S" Special. Contributii la istoria fondurilor secrete de biblioteca din Romania. Studiu de caz. Biblioteca Centrala Universitara "Lucian Blaga", Cluj-Napoca, 1995* (Secret fond. Special "S" fond. Contributions to the History of Library Secret Fonds in Romania. A case study. "Lucian Blaga" Central University Library, Cluj-Napoca) (Cluj-Napoca: Editura Dacia, 1995), 39.

35. István Király, "Fonds secrets ou fonds interdits?: Une esquisse d'histoire des fonds secrets des bibliothèques de Roumanie," *Bulletin des Bibliothèques de France* 39:6 (1994): 79.

36. Ibid.

37. Dimitrie Poptamas, director of the Mureş County Library, interview, 26 August 1997, Târgu Mureş.
38. Corneliu Stefanache, director of the Mihai Eminescu Central University Library, Iaşi, interview, 11 July 1997, Iaşi.
39. Paul Edwards, ed., *The Encyclopedia of Philosophy*, 8 vols. (New York: Macmillan, 1967); Opritsa D. Popa and Sanda J. Lamprecht, "Romania and United States Library Connections," *Advances in Librarianship* 18 (1994): 194.
40. Mircea Eliade, ed., *Encyclopedia of Religion*, 16 vols. (New York: Macmillan, 1987).
41. Ordinance no. 1003 of 15 August 1968, issued by the Ministry of Education and Culture. This was the time of the Soviet invasion of Czechoslovakia.
42. Interview, 4 July 1997, Cluj-Napoca.
43. Mary Nell Bryant, "Parliament Library Development Program," *Bulletin of the American Society for Information Science* 19 (April–May 1993): 10.
44. By this law the government hoped to prevent the dissemination of reactionary material.
45. During the thirteen years I worked with the National Library in Bucharest, I cannot recall any instance when efforts were made to purchase a book recommended by a researcher.
46. As of 12 May 1998, the online catalog of the Octavian Goga County Library in Cluj-Napoca provided access to 42,794 titles in 197,903 copies acquired from 1990 to 1997. The online system includes the main library and its sixteen branches.
47. The National Library was one of the libraries where, in the aftermath of the December popular revolt, the staff decided to conduct free elections at the institution and department levels. The outcome was the election of two new directors, the reappointment of some department heads, and the replacement of the politically tainted heads with non-Communist party members.

Leaning to One Side: The Impact of the Cold War on Chinese Library Collections

Priscilla C. Yu

Membership in the Soviet Union-led Communist bloc and the economic embargo imposed by the West led to China's reliance on the Soviet bloc in library development. To spur economic reconstruction and consolidate political power after founding the Communist regime, the Chinese government restructured all libraries to help implement government objectives. The Chinese learned and adopted principles and practices of Soviet librarianship. Russian materials on library science, science, and industry as well as Communist classics were imported or translated into Chinese. The Soviet Union's strong influence on Chinese library collections was demonstrated by analyzing foreign language collections at Peking University Library and the National Library of China (NLC), examining data covering developments primarily in the 1950s and the 1960s. Russian language publications dominated the foreign language collection at Peking University Library from 1953 to 1974. Russian scientific publications outnumbered humanities and social science materials by a ratio of 9 to 1, reflecting China's information needs for its drive toward modernization during its First Five-Year Plan (1953-57). The Russian language collection also predominated over other foreign language materials at the NLC in 1958 and 1959. Besides increased purchasing efforts, the NLC established exchange programs with the Soviet Union's libraries and eventually other countries to acquire costly foreign scientific publications needed for China's economic development. Despite Soviet assistance in library development, the Cold War denied China equal access to all foreign language materials and knowledge, thus hindering China's modernization effort. Chinese libraries can best serve China's developmental goals through the international free and open flow of information.

The Cold War is usually discussed in political and security terms, the division of the world into opposing ideological and political forces and the build-up of massive war machines, including nuclear weapons, by two opposing camps, one led by the United States, the other by the former Soviet Union. One major effect of the Cold War was the division of the globe into regional political-security blocs that communicated and interacted more within blocs; interbloc relations were greatly limited, both by the consequences of the division and by the authorities of the two blocs, with short- and long-term negative repercussions reaching beyond the immediate political-security realm.

A neglected area of inquiry has been the effect of the Cold War on the cultural and intellectual sector, especially library collections and how the erection of political-security blocs limited and prevented their free development in the respective camps. A short-term result was the overdependence on print culture from one primary cultural-political source and the absence of materials from the opposing camp; the long-term consequence, as we have since witnessed, has been the drive by the libraries of the former blocs to acquire the "missing collections."

China and the Cold War

As early as June 1949, Mao Zedong declared, "All Chinese without exception must lean either to the side of imperialism or to the side of socialism. Sitting on the fence will not do . . . Internationally, we belong to the side of the anti-imperialist front headed by the Soviet Union, and so we can turn only to this side for genuine and friendly help, not to the side of the imperialist front." This principle was implemented on 14 February 1950 with the Treaty of Friendship, Alliance, and Mutual Aid between the People's Republic of China and the U.S.S.R.[1] Mao's "lean to one side" policy contributed to heightened U.S. opposition to the new Chinese regime; relations with the United States and the West reached a low point when China intervened in the Korean War in 1950. The event ended any prospects for normal relations between Beijing and Washington. The United States and its allies sought to contain China and enforced a total embargo on trade, seeking thus to totally isolate China.[2]

The effect of the Cold War was evident on Chinese libraries. How did the Cold War affect Chinese library collections? To answer the question, this essay focuses upon foreign language collections at major Chinese university and research libraries, examining data primarily from the 1950s and 1960s. The impact upon China's foreign language collections will be examined against its political-security "leaning to one side" policy, namely, its membership in the then Communist bloc led by the Soviet Union.

Two major academic and research libraries have been chosen for the study, Peking University Library (the premier academic library in China) and the National Library of China (equal to the Library of Congress). Attention will focus on acquisition and collection development of the two libraries. The study is based upon primary Chinese data, secondary sources, and interviews with Chinese librarians, examining sources available and procurable at the time. These will enable us to analyze and understand the challenges and problems faced by academic and research libraries in China during the Cold War.

Libraries in the People's Republic of China, 1949 through the 1960s

When the People's Republic of China was founded in 1949, the new government faced many challenges. China was in a state of chaos economically, politically, and socially. The years of Japanese aggression followed by civil war had destroyed much of the country's industrial, educational, and social base. The new government instantly set up plans for national, social, and economic reconstruction. Libraries and library service played a critical role in achieving stability and unity during this period. To assist in national development, China adopted Russia's experiences, theories, and principles of reconstruction of socialist library service as a model. Library service was transformed into a socialist library service: "The main tasks of the People's Government in its cultural and educational work is to elevate the cultural standard of the people, train personnel for national construction, eradicate all feudalist, compradore-type and Fascist thinking, and foster thoughts of service." As the national economy was gradually restored, the Ministry of Culture took steps to restructure the libraries of the past in order to speed up economic recovery, establish a socialist culture, and consolidate political power. All libraries were replenished with new and old revolutionary publications, in particular, the classic works of Marx, Engels, Lenin, Stalin, and Mao Zedong. Books that were banned included works that opposed the policies and ideology of the party and government as well as works that referred to capitalism (particularly American life), feudalism, idealism, imperialism, and individualism.[3] Library service was to carry out the policy of the party, which was to serve the politics of the proletariat, production, and the workers, peasants, and soldiers.[4] Throughout the country, libraries served two primary objectives: they took inventory of their historical works, and they combed through all "reactionary" publications and removed "fascist," pornographic, and factitious types of literature. As one can see, collection development was connected to the various political objectives; when a policy was declared, books relating to the policy were purchased or banned.[5]

The Soviet Union had a strong influence on the development of libraries in China. During the first half of the 1950s Chinese libraries developed rapidly. The Chinese were interested in establishing an effective library system and sought to learn the operations and practices of librarianship in the Soviet Union. During the early 1950s many works on library science written by Soviet specialists and librarians were translated into Chinese. Many of these works were translated in 1957 and published as *Translations on Library Science*.[6] China adopted many technical aspects of Soviet librarianship. For example, the Chinese classification scheme was based on the four main classes of the 1955 Soviet classification model: Marxism-Leninism, social sciences, natural sciences, and generalia.[7]

Among the newly created libraries, the most successful were the rural and labor libraries. The slogan "Culture going to the mountains and the countryside" was everywhere in order to foster Marxist education and the popularization of socialist culture. The aim of the government was "to elevate the cultural standard of the people, train personnel for national construction, eradicate all feudalist and Fascist thinking and foster thoughts of service to the people." The government threw open the doors to readers; no longer was there admission charged as in the old society, when workers were charged a fee to use the library.[8] The masses were the ruling class, and libraries were organized to serve the workers and peasants who were the ruling class.[9] During the First Five-Year Plan (1953–57), there was great demand for the development of the national economy. This was the time of the 1956 March toward the Sciences movement. During these years there was a surge in the growth of labor union libraries.

By the end of 1956, rural libraries also flourished; it was reported that rural reading rooms had reached 182,960 units, and these reading units enabled laborers and peasants to study current events and policies during the agricultural cooperation period, to elevate their ideological awareness and the standard of their scientific knowledge and production technique.[10] The libraries for the workers were established to help increase productivity by making more science materials available. However, during the Second Five-Year Plan (1958–62), China overextended itself; the Great Leap Forward (1958) proved unrealistic, and Mao's impatience with the rate of development declared an acceleration of national construction, with the result that the national economy suffered a severe reverse. Meanwhile, the Sino-Soviet split developed, and Soviet assistance waned, eventually terminating by the early 1960s. The hope that the Third Five-Year Plan (1966–70) would improve the situation was completely fragmented by the Great Proletarian Cultural Revolution beginning in 1966.

As for the development of major library systems in China, the various ministries held control: the public library system, which included the national, provincial, municipal, county, and cultural center libraries, was under the Ministry of Culture; college and university libraries were under the Ministry of Higher Education; elementary and secondary school libraries were under the Ministry of Education; trade union libraries were under the Trade Union; and special libraries were under appropriate government agencies.[11]

Soviet Influence on Chinese Library Collections

Colleges and universities traditionally have had the best-organized and finest collections of any library system in China. The collections were organized to meet the special needs of the various colleges and universities. In the 1950s, China's educational system, which had been modeled after the Western educational institutions, was succeeded by the Soviet system, including teaching techniques, curricula, and Soviet textbooks and materials.[12] Translations from Russian works on library science flourished, and Soviet librarians were invited to visit China to consult and give lectures.

An important indicator of the impact of China's "leaning to one side" political-security policy upon its libraries can be clearly seen in the foreign language collection development pattern. Soviet influences on collection development were due primarily to Cold War political factors. Beginning in 1952, China secured few Western language materials, due to the strained relations between China, the United States, and other Western countries as a result of the Cold War. It was difficult to find channels through which to buy Western language books, except through third parties such as India, because of the strict embargo act imposed upon China by the West. By the latter half of 1953 fewer Western language books were acquired in comparison to books published by the Soviet Union and Eastern European countries, which were acquired not only through purchase but also through barter arrangements based upon bilateral exchange agreements.[13]

To illustrate the impact of China's reliance upon the Soviet bloc in foreign language collection development, I will examine two major Chinese university and research libraries.

Peking University Library

Peking University is the largest and most comprehensive and prestigious university in China. "Beida," the nickname of Peking University, is also one of the most liberal and progressive institutions of higher learning in the country and has been in the forefront of many reforms and patriotic movements. Peking University was founded in 1898, and the library was first established in 1902 with a collection of over 78,000 volumes.[14] In 1950 the collection totaled over 1 million volumes. By the early 1970s the collection had grown to 2.5 million.[15] Between 1952 and 1974 Peking University Library collected 90,189 volumes in the humanities/social sciences and 77,978 volumes in the sciences.[16] During this period, due to the Cold War, the collection of Western language materials was greatly limited. Russian language sources predominated after 1952.

Soviet influences on collection development were due primarily to political-security factors. Following the outbreak of the Korean War in 1950, there were few purchases of Western language materials, stemming from the increasingly strained relations between China, the United States, and other Western countries. China found it increasingly difficult to find channels through which to secure Western language materials.

Table 1 delineates the Russian language collection by subject held by Peking University Library, beginning in the pre-1953 years through 1991. The acquisition of Russian language materials during the 1953 to 1974 period (the Cold War era) outnumbered all other foreign language materials. It was not until China's warming of relations with the United States and the West beginning in the late 1970s that Russian language acquisitions declined.

It should be noted that prior to 1953, the collection at Peking University Library contained a very limited number of Russian sources. The Russian language collection grew especially during the period of Sino-Soviet friendship, the 1950s through the early 1960s. As Table 1 indicates, during the 1953–74 period, the height of Soviet influence, Russian language sources dominated, ranging from a high of 35 and 50 percent in law and the sciences to a low of 22 and 33 percent in political science and history.

Special attention should be directed to the building of the science collection, as one of China's major goals during the First Five-Year Plan (1953–57) was to secure more scientific materials and find ways to strengthen scientific research in order to increase productivity. As the science collection section of Table 1 shows, there was a strong emphasis on obtaining scientific materials from the Soviets in the 1953–74 period. Indeed, the ratio between books in the humanities and the social sciences and in the sciences and technology was 1 to 9.[17] The greater percentage of Russian scientific items fell in the manufacturing and construction category, since Soviet publications on economic construction and modern technology were heavily sought to aid China's economic development. The collection of Western

TABLE 1
PEKING UNIVERSITY LIBRARY: FOREIGN LANGUAGE
COLLECTIONS BY SUBJECT, PRE-1953 THROUGH 1991

Political Science Collection (Number of volumes)

Language	Pre-1953	1953-74	1975-91
Chinese	6,417 (64%)	2,590 (57%)	5,476 (35%)
Western	2,328 (23%)	522 (11%)	7,018 (46%)
Japanese	1,179 (12%)	434 (10%)	899 (6%)
Russian	73 (1%)	1,020 (22%)	1,975 (13%)

Law Collection (Number of volumes)

Chinese	1,684 (39%)	952 (30%)	3,570 (46%)
Western	2,194 (50%)	856 (27%)	2,493 (32%)
Japanese	474 (11%)	273 (8%)	908 (12%)
Russian		1,125 (35%)	813 (10%)

Economics Collection (Number of volumes)

Chinese	4,772 (40%)	5,424 (45%)	8,630 (40%)
Western	6,106 (52%)	2,617 (22%)	8,863 (41%)
Japanese	690 (6%)	659 (6%)	1,570 (7%)
Russian	216 (2%)	3,217 (27%)	2,561 (12%)

Library and Information Science Collection (Number of volumes)

Chinese	185 (35%)	325 (37%)	901 (52%)
Western	334 (62%)	344 (39%)	704 (41%)
Russian	17 (3%)	212 (24%)	121 (7%)

History Collection (Number of volumes)

Chinese	1,929 (14%)	4,688 (46%)	9,322 (48%)
Western	11,230 (78%)	1,510 (15%)	6,406 (33%)
Japanese	1,156 (8%)	604 (6%)	1,826 (9.5%)
Russian		3,312 (33%)	1,823 (9.5%)

Science Collection (Number of volumes)

Chinese	4,467 (10%)	21,822 (13%)	276,830 (64%)
Western	32,930 (77%)	58,373 (34%)	131,956 (31%)
Japanese	5,504 (13%)	5,278 (3%)	10,628 (2%)
Russian		83,916 (50%)	11,138 (3%)

Source: Shoujing Zhuang, ed., *Beijing Daxue Tushuguan a Guanchan Wenxian Diaocha Pinggu Baogao Ji* (Report on the investigation of the review of the library's holdings, Peking University Library) (Beijing: Peking University Library, November 1992), 81, 90, 118, 141, 228.

materials in the sector was much lower than the Russian during this time. It was not until after the mid-1970s that the Western language collection begin to increase and the limitation removed with regard to the acquisition of the number of science versus social science books.[18]

The impact of the Cold War upon one of China's most prominent academic libraries, Peking University Library, was clear and unambiguous. Due to political-security factors stemming from the Cold War, the Western language materials collection declined while the Russian collection greatly expanded. The disparity between the two collections has been most pronounced in Peking University Library's serial holdings and reference collection; China's "missing collections" are directly attributable to conditions associated with the Cold War.

The National Library of China

The second case study relating to the impact of the Cold War on Chinese libraries examines the National Library of China. I will again focus on the foreign language collections, examining data from the 1950s, during the height of China's "leaning to one side" policy. The National Library of China (hereafter referred to as the NLC) is the leading public research library in China, having the largest and richest collection in the country. Furthermore, the National Library followed a proactive policy of securing foreign language publications, including maintaining a prominent international exchange program with institutions throughout the world.

Historically, the NLC is the successor to the National Library of Peiping, founded in 1929, which was renamed the National Library of China in 1949. At the time, the NLC received a large number of Chinese and foreign materials that had been held by the Japanese-supported puppet government of Wang Qingwei. This was especially the case with Japanese language materials, which numbered in the tens of thousands. During the Second World War, the Japanese had burned many Chinese library collections, though the Japanese collection at the National Library of Peiping remained intact. In 1949 the NLC had a total holding of 1.4 million volumes of books and journals of which 292,162 volumes consisted of foreign language materials; this represented approximately 21 percent of the total collection, as indicated in Table 2.[19] Russian language materials constituted less than 2 percent of the entire foreign language book and periodicals collection.

When the People's Republic of China was established, the mission of the NLC followed along Soviet Lines: "to serve politics,

TABLE 2
NATIONAL LIBRARY OF CHINA: HOLDINGS OF FOREIGN
LANGUAGE MATERIALS, 1949 (NUMBER OF VOLUMES)

General materials in Western Languages	163,126
Books in Japanese	56,565
Books in Russian	4,163
Periodicals in Western Languages	62,382
Periodicals in Japanese	5,926
Total	292,162

Source: Priscilla C. Yu, *Chinese Academic and Research Libraries: Acquisitions, Collections, and Organizations* (Greenwich, Conn.: JAI Press, 1996), 111.

production, workers, peasants, soldiers, and scientific studies."[20] The national policy was to build a productive socialist state with the National Library providing support. As mentioned earlier, the United States and Japan imposed an embargo against China, and, as a result, the NLC's acquisition of U.S. and Western European materials decreased greatly. Meanwhile, China turned toward the Soviet Union and the Eastern European countries for assistance, including library development.

With the introduction of the First Five-Year Plan, China embarked upon a drive toward modernization. A goal was to increase the availability of science materials to increase productivity. By 1956 the March to the Sciences movement had taken hold of the country. There was a definite drive to obtain technical documents and other scientific materials from abroad. It was found that purchase of foreign publications was very costly and difficult; exchange, therefore, played an important role in the acquisition of foreign materials. Especially sought were new Soviet publications on modern technology to aid China's economic development.

During the early 1950s the NLC embarked upon an exchange program with libraries in the Soviet Union, including the Lenin State Library (Moscow), the Library of the Academy of Sciences of the U.S.S.R. (Leningrad), and the Social Science Library of the Academy of Sciences of the U.S.S.R. (Moscow). It is estimated that over a thousand volumes of exchange books were sent each month from the Soviet Union to China. In 1953 the NLC's exchange program partners included fifty-nine institutions in eighteen countries, including the Soviet Union, Poland, Czechoslovakia, Hungary, Romania, Bulgaria, East Germany, Korea, Mongolia, Vietnam, India, Sweden, and Denmark.[21] Toward the latter part of the 1950s, the NLC's international exchange program continued to grow. By 1956 the library had extended exchange relations to 563 institutions in 64 countries, including partners in the Soviet Union, Europe, Asia, Africa, Australia, and South and North America. The NLC received 182,162 books and periodicals on exchange during 1950–56.[22] A greater portion of the publications concerned modern technology, agriculture, and biology, which were indispensable to China's economic development. In 1959 the NLC further increased exchange relations with 749 libraries and educational organizations in 72 countries.[23]

In 1959 an article appeared describing the NLC's exchanges with the Soviet Union:

> The [NLC], China's biggest, received 290,000 books and journals from the Soviet Union in the past ten years, apart from the regular mail of magazines and newspapers. China has sent 306,000 books and journals to the Soviet Union in the same period. The [NLC] has 240,000 Soviet books and magazines as against 4,000 in 1949, the year of Peking's Liberation.
>
> The exchange of books between China and the Soviet Union covers a wide range, including scores, maps, theses for academic degrees, digests, indices, and library reference cards...
>
> The Soviet Union often sends important new works in political economy, the most up-to-date branches of sciences and applied technique and various aspects of culture, education, and arts to help China's large-scale economic construction and scientific research.[24]

Table 3 illustrates the steady increase in the NLC's foreign language collection. As is the case with the major research and comprehensive university libraries of China, the Russian language collection predominated over other Western and foreign language materials. The collection was based upon both a strong international exchange program and increased purchasing efforts.

A Russian visitor to China noted an interesting background to NLC's growing Russian language collection in 1958: "Everywhere we went the people with whom we talked repeatedly pointed out how significant to them was the experience of Soviet libraries, and they expressed gratitude for our help in supplying the Chinese libraries with Soviet publications."[25]

Many tens of thousands of Communist classics, including the works of Marx, Engels, Lenin, and Stalin, were directly imported from Russia or the material was translated into Chinese and published in Beijing and Shanghai. These works were also translated into the

TABLE 3
NATIONAL LIBRARY OF CHINA: GROWTH RATE OF FOREIGN LANGUAGE COLLECTION IN THE 1950s

Year	Language	No. of Volumes	% in Terms of Total Within Each Year
1954	Western languages	28,945	18
	Russian	49,401	32
	Other Asian languages	77,343	50
	Total	155,689	100
1958	Western languages	17,252	30
	Russian	34,007	59
	Other Asian languages	6,358	11
	Total	57,617	100
1959	Western languages	24,851	38
	Russian	30,328	46
	Other Asian languages	10,124	16
	Total	65,303	100

Source: Priscilla C. Yu, *Chinese Academic and Research Libraries: Acquisitions, Collections, and Organizations* (Greenwich, Conn.: JAI Press, 1996), 113.

minority languages, even into languages that had to be provided with written languages where none had existed before.[26] Through 1957, Soviet materials relating to science and industry were translated in great quantities; these translations amounted to 38 percent of the total number of publications published in China for the period.[27] Other books and periodicals were acquired, by purchase, gift, or exchange, from the Soviet Union and distributed to libraries, where they contributed to the development of Russian language collections, including the NLC's collection.

For China, the decade of the 1960s was one of domestic and foreign unrest and turmoil. This was the period of waning relationship with the Soviet Union. In the early 1960s the Soviet Union withdrew all scientific and technical assistance to China, including library development. The ability of China to purchase and/or acquire on exchange the necessary Soviet scientific publications was largely curtailed. To partly rectify the problem, China looked toward Japan and Western Europe for materials in advanced science and technology. There were fewer and fewer foreign contacts. China began a movement toward self-reliance; the populace was discouraged from reading foreign literature, and access to new scientific and technological developments from abroad was restricted.

From the mid-1960s until the mid-1970s, the Cultural Revolution sought to eradicate the old thoughts, old culture, old customs, and old habits of the bourgeois classes. Many libraries in China were destroyed; fortunately, the NLC's collection remained unharmed.[28] In the early 1960s, the NLC was still able to acquire foreign materials, but with the emergence of the Sino-Soviet conflict, acquisition of materials from the Soviet Union all but ceased. Meanwhile, the West continued to impose an embargo on economic relations with China.

Conclusion

This study has examined how the Cold War, through polarizing the world into opposing political-security camps, impacted upon library development in China. Beginning in 1949, China's "leaning to one side" policy resulted in increased U.S. and Western opposition to the new Chinese regime, which had concluded a Treaty of Friendship with the Soviet Union. By the 1950s the United States and other Western powers sought to "contain" China, including enforcing a total embargo on trade and other forms of interaction with China.

A consequence of China's political-security "leaning to one side" policy was the Soviet Union's strong influence upon all sectors of China's development, including libraries. China was eager to modernize and learn the operations and practices of Soviet librarianship. There was a strong desire and need to obtain Soviet publications and possess Russian Communist classics and scientific materials translated into Chinese. Hence, the Soviet Union had a very significant influence on collection development in Chinese libraries.

This study focused on collection patterns in two major libraries in China, examining developments primarily in the 1950s and the 1960s. The two libraries investigated were the National Library of China and the prominent Peking University Library, among the best organized and having the most comprehensive collections of all the library systems in China. It was unmistakably demonstrated that in the context of the Cold War, China's policy of "leaning to one side" affected the foreign language collections of the two libraries. The growth of the Russian language collections and Soviet-related materials was a direct result of China's international political alignment.

In sum, one serious impact of the Cold War on Chinese library development was the denial to China of *equal* access to *all* foreign language materials and knowledge, though China had profited from Soviet assistance and sources. However, China's goal of achieving modernization has yet to be fully realized. Chinese libraries can best serve China's developmental goals through the international free and open flow of information.

Notes

1. Roy C. Macridis, ed., *Foreign Policy in World Politics: States and Regions* (Englewood Cliffs, N.J.: Prentice Hall, 1989), 264.
2. Ibid., 265.
3. John Barclay, *The Seventy-Year Ebb and Flow of Chinese Library and Information Services, May 4, 1919, to the Late 1980s* (Metuchen, N.J.: Scarecrow Press, 1995), 21.
4. "Chinese Communist Library Service in the Past Decade I," *Union Research Service* 19:8 (April 1960): 106-9.
5. Thomas Y. Yeh, "A Profile of Academic Libraries in China," *College & Research Libraries* 46 (November 1985): 500-501.
6. "Chinese Communist Library Service in the Past Decade II," *Union Research Service* 19:10 (May 1960): 149.
7. Polly-Ann Brumley Proett, "A History of Libraries in the People's Republic of China, Including Some Aspects of College and University Library Development, 1949-1974" (Ph.D. diss., George Washington University, 1974), 135.
8. "Chinese Communist Library Service in the Past Decade I," 108-10.
9. Proett, "A History of Libraries in the People's Republic of China," 96.
10. "Chinese Communist Library Service in the Past Decade I," 111-13.
11. K. T. Wu, "Libraries in the People's Republic of China," *Encyclopedia of Library and Information Science*, vol. 4 (New York: Marcel Dekker, 1968), 634.
12. Proett, "A History of Libraries in the People's Republic of China," 114.
13. Fazhen Kan, *A Historical Account of the Foreign Language Collection at the Peking University Library* (Beijing: University of Peking Library, n.d.). Unpublished in Chinese.
14. Priscilla C. Yu, *Chinese Academic and Research Libraries: Acquisitions, Collections, and Organizations* (Greenwich, Conn.: JAI Press, 1997), 12-13.
15. Shoujing Zhuang et al., "Summary Report on the Investigation of the Review of the Holdings of the Peking University Library," in Shoujing Zhuang, ed., *Beijing Daxue Tushuguan a Guanchan Wenxian Diaocha Pinggu Baogao Ji* (Report on the Investigation of the Review of the Library's Holdings, Peking University Library) (Beijing: Peking University Library, November 1992), 7-8. Published on the occasion of the ninetieth anniversary of the university library.
16. Ibid., 9.
17. Yu, *Chinese Academic and Research Libraries*, 20-21.
18. Ibid., 21.
19. Interview with Wenjie Shao, deputy director of the National Library of China, October 1981.
20. Lee-hsia Hsu Ting, "Chinese Libraries during and after the Cultural Revolution," *Journal of Library History* 16 (Spring 1981): 418.

21. "The National Library of Beijing Exchanged Many Books with Foreign Countries in the Past Four Years," *Guangming Ribao*, 24 December 1953: 3.

22. Zhenming Li, "International Exchange of Books and Periodicals in the National Library of Beijing," *Renmin Ribao (People's Daily)*, 8 September 1956: 7.

23. Chi Cheng, "Libraries in China Today," *Libri* 9 (1959): 106.

24. Proett, "A History of Libraries in the People's Republic of China," 137.

25. Ibid., 136.

26. Raymond Nunn, "Libraries and Publishing in Mainland China," *Library Journal*, 1 July 1966: 3331.

27. Ibid., 3332.

28. Ting, "Chinese Libraries during and after the Cultural Revolution," 423.

THE BOOKPLATE

On 1 October 1999 the United States Information Agency (USIA) was abolished, and its programs were integrated into the U.S. Department of State. This action brought full circle a series of reorganizations and administrative changes of the library programs of the U.S. information and cultural programs that started shortly before the United States entered World War II.

The U.S. information program has been an active part of American foreign policy since 1941. Historically, the program began 4 July 1776 with the Declaration of Independence and its "decent respect to the opinion of mankind." Its first official venture, however, was the Committee on Public Information (the Creel Committee), which was established in April 1917, operated during World War I, and was abolished in March 1919, the same year four reading rooms were opened and then closed in Mexico City.

Bookplate courtesy of American Information Resource Center, New Delhi, India.

There were no further developments until 1938, when the Interdepartmental Committee for Scientific and Cultural Cooperation (an advisory group) and the Division of Cultural Cooperation (in the State Department) were set up as the first U.S. bodies concerned with peacetime international information activities. On 16 August 1940 the Office for Coordination of Commercial and Cultural Relations between the American Republics came into being. Then in 1941 three offices—Coordinator of Inter-American Affairs, Facts and Figures, and Coordinator of Information (COI)—were established to report to the American people on the progress of the U.S. defense effort. It was in COI that the present headquarters library started weeks before Pearl Harbor. In the beginning, research specialists prepared reports on specific subjects from basic library materials (books, documents, clippings). Much of this research supported the newly established Voice of America, which went on the air 24 February 1942 from a small, improvised COI studio at 270 Madison Avenue. However, this library operation should not be confused with the agency's overseas library program, which it predates.

The first overseas library began in April 1942 as the Biblioteca Benjamin Franklin at Londres #16, Mexico City, with a grant from the Office of the Coordinator of Inter-American Affairs (CIAA) to the American Library Association. It was part of President Franklin Roosevelt's "Good Neighbor" program in the American Republics. Within the next two years, other libraries opened in places as diverse as London (the first overseas library directly under U.S. government control), Managua, Madrid, Calcutta, Montevideo, and Wellington.

On 13 June 1942 COI was abolished by Executive Order 9182, and its functions, including the libraries, were transferred to the Office of War Information (OWI). OWI was authorized to formulate and carry out, through the use of press, radio, motion picture, and other facilities, information programs designed to provide an intelligent understanding, at home and abroad, of the status and process of the war effort and of the war policies, activities, and aims of the U.S. government.

With the end of World War II, OWI and CIAA were abolished, and their foreign information programs were transferred to the U.S. Department of State. In Germany the U.S. Military Government began opening Information Center (Amerika Häuser) libraries and reading rooms throughout the American zone and in the major cities of the British and French zones. At the same time, Information Center libraries were started under the auspices of U.S. forces in Austria,

Japan, and Korea. The State Department assumed responsibility for these centers when civilian control was restored in each country.

On 1 August 1953, under Reorganization Plan No. 8, the United States Information Agency (USIA) was created as an independent organization within the Executive Branch responsible for the U.S. government's information and cultural programs. Overseas, USIA became the United States Information Service (USIS). Since then, USIS libraries and reading rooms have been opened in virtually every country with which the United States maintains diplomatic relations. Today, there are an estimated 180 worldwide.

The 1989 collapse of the Soviet Union's political system and the domino events that followed, culminating in the end of the Cold War, led to substantial changes in the USIA mission and its programs. Library services for "telling America's story abroad" were replaced by collections that reflected newly emerging democratic processes. In the former Soviet Union, a series of Information Center (Amerika Häuser) libraries, similar to those that began in Germany under the occupation, were reestablished in countries that had to close their libraries due to repressive Communist regimes, especially in Eastern European countries, or begun in places that never had a USIS library such as Tirana, Albania, and Valletta, Malta. In 1994 USIA became part of a reinvention of a government experiment that was initiated by Vice President Al Gore and the Clinton administration. The Agency Library became an Information Resource Center (IRC), and the reference librarians were transferred to five thematic areas: Democracy and Human Rights, Economic Security, Global Issues and Communication, Political Security, and U.S. Society and Values. The overseas library program went to the Office of Geographic Programs with regional divisions: Africa, East Asia, Europe and Newly Independent States, Near East and North Africa, and Western Hemisphere (Latin America and Canada).

In the mid-1990s, in developments parallel to the reinvention in Washington, the USIS libraries evolved into Information Resource Centers (IRCs). Three major factors are given as the impetus for this. First, the changing world political situation upset the global balance as democratic processes replaced Communist regimes. Second, a stronger emphasis on balancing the U.S. budget greatly reduced the funding of U.S. information programs. Third, the explosion of the information age made it possible to get information electronically from commercial databases and the Internet, initiated more access to major U.S. databases, and allowed for extremely sophisticated research that could not be done before. Today, IRCs vary significantly from country to country, but all provide the most current and authoritative information about official U.S. government policies and serve as a primary source of informed commentary on the origin, growth, and development of American social, political, economic, and cultural values and institutions.

References

I want to thank all the IROs who responded to my original message for information, especially Brigitte James and Pierce Sommers (in Berlin) and O. N. Misra and Rebecca McDuff (in New Delhi) for sending the book plates, Mary Boone, and Cynthia Borys.

Gilliam, Bo. "United States Information Agency." In *Bowker Annual*, 44th ed. New Providence, N.J.: R. R. Bowker, 1999. 47–49.

Manning, Martin J. "The Agency Library: Yesterday and Today." *USIA World* (July-August 1984): 12–14.

Martin J. Manning
Economic Security Team (IIP/T/ES),
Office of International Information Programs,
Bureau of Public Diplomacy,
U.S. Department of State

Note on the Bookplates

Most USIS libraries did not have bookplates. Many libraries were too small to purchase bookplates or were no larger than reference centers. Others just didn't feel a need to use them. Those who did used them to identify the book as the property of the U.S. Government ("sell America abroad"), most especially the United States Information Service. I know of no other significance attached to them. I was able to get only two sets of bookplates from overseas libraries: Berlin and New Delhi. Other libraries stopped using their bookplates in the 1980s when funds were cut dramatically for library programs, then discarded the books that had them or transferred their collections to local universities.

New Delhi

The library in New Delhi was one of our earliest; it was established in October 1942 as a reading room when the U.S. information program was in the Office of War Information (OWI), but it was officially opened in April 1943. In September 1944 it was designated a USIS library. The first OWI library in India was opened in September 1942 in Calcutta. There are five different versions (all but one undated but most likely created between 1960 and 1990, when bookplates were still used). All were used in the library in New Delhi. The bookplate with the logo International Communication Agency was used between 1978 and 1982 when this agency existed. The U.S. International Communication Agency was created on 1

April 1978, when the educational exchange program in the U.S. Department of State was transferred to the United States Information Agency (USIA) as a renamed entity, the International Communication Agency. During this period, we continued to use USIS overseas, and this was how our libraries were so designated, but the Washington headquarters kept the new name. In August 1982 the U.S. Congress restored USIA, and things remained like this until USIA was abolished in 1999 and the libraries were incorporated into the State Department. USIS libraries still retain this designation, but it could change at a later date.

The New Delhi library sent me samples of these bookplates:

1. International Communication Agency
American Center Library
New Delhi

2. 1987 American Constitutional Bicentennial
American Center Library
New Delhi

3. United States Information Service
American Center Library
New Delhi

4. American Center Library
New Delhi

5. American Information Resource Center
New Delhi

The plate with the American Constitutional Bicentennial was created for the 1987 observance, which was more popular overseas than in the United States. This bookplate was the last one created, and I don't believe it is used anymore.

Berlin

The American libraries in Germany, subsequently called Amerika Häuser (America Houses), were established after the end of the war in Europe in 1945 by the Office of Military Government, U.S. (OMGUS). Within the next three years, as many as fifty Amerika Häuser, plus an estimated 137 smaller reading rooms, were opened throughout the American, British, and French zones of occupation. In the fall of 1949 the Allied military governments were terminated, and responsibility for the libraries was transferred to the U.S. Department of State, then to USIA in 1953. Before that time, the German program was funded separately from the other U.S. library programs. In early 1952 a fleet of bookmobiles, built in the United States, were bought to carry library services to outlying areas of the country that did not have any library service.

This bookplate, with American Library of Information and the American eagle holding arrows and an olive branch, was used in the 1950s or 1960s in the library in Stuttgart. It was sent to me by the information resource specialist in Berlin, who kept a few of our old Stuttgart books on "long-term loan" as she moved from Bonn to Berlin with the American Embassy. The plate comes from a 1950 edition of a biography of Louisa May Alcott.

Stuttgart opened in January 1946 as an Amerika Haus. Prior to the fall of the Wall in 1989, two libraries were maintained in Berlin. The Amerika Haus in West Berlin opened in November 1945 as a reading room, while its counterpart in East Berlin started in September 1977.

Agency Library (United States International Communication Agency)

This is the only original bookplate I was able to obtain. I used it between 1978 and 1982 when USICA was in existence. After 1982 we stopped using bookplates in the books; instead, we just stamped "THE AGENCY LIBRARY, UNITED STATES INFORMATION AGENCY, WASHINGTON, D.C." in every volume.

The designation "United States International Communication Agency" was a quirky one. Originally, the name of the proposed agency was supposed to be U.S. Agency for International Communication, which was used in the congressional hearings in 1977 that reviewed the merger of the U.S. educational exchange programs in the State Department with USIA. However, when President Carter signed Reorganization Plan No. 1 of 1977, the Carter administration replaced it with USICA instead. This was especially difficult for the USIS libraries as the name, often abbreviated to ICA, came out as CIA in certain languages, leading to all sorts of confusion. Mercifully, USICA only lasted through the Carter years.

274   *The Bookplate*

Agency Library (United States Information Agency)

This bookplate, which is bright yellow with black lettering on the original, was used in the Washington headquarters library from 1954 until 1978. Its colors made it quite distinctive. When United States Information Agency was restored as the agency's name in August 1982, the agency librarian decided to use a stamp instead of bookplates, mostly to save money. With the various weeding projects since then, most of the books in the Agency Library with the yellow and black bookplate have disappeared, but there is still a good selection of volumes in its special collections library, the Public Diplomacy Historical Collection, with this bookplate.

CONTRIBUTORS

Hermina G.B. Anghelescu earned her M.A. in foreign languages and literatures (French and English) from the University of Bucharest (Romania) and her M.L.I.S. and Ph.D. from the Graduate School of Library and Information Science, University of Texas at Austin. Currently, she is assistant professor at the Library and Information Science Program, Wayne State University, Detroit, Michigan. Anghelescu is a member of the editorial board of the *Annual Bibliography of the History of the Printed Book and Libraries—ABHB*, published by the Department of Special Collections of the Royal Library, The Hague, under the auspices of the Committee on Rare and Precious Documents of IFLA. Among her publications are the translation into Romanian of Brooke E. Sheldon's *Leaders in Libraries: Styles and Strategies for Success* (1996); translation and editing of four volumes of conference proceedings (1993, 1996, 1997, 2000); and compilation and coediting of *Libraries & Culture: 25-Year Cumulative Index* (1995). In addition, she has been a contributor to *România*, a series of the *National Bibliography of Romania*, has compiled back-of-the-book indexes, and has published articles, chapters, and dictionary articles as well as book reviews. She has coordinated eight international seminars and workshops in Romania, and she is an Executive Committee member of the IFLA Roundtable for Library History (RTLH). Anghelescu's fellowships include a Fulbright Grant (United States Information Agency), an International Research and Exchanges Board (IREX) grant, an Association of American University Women (AAUW) scholarship, several continuing education fellowships (University of Texas at Austin), and a Summer Continuing Studies Grant awarded by the Shakespeare Institute and the Shakespeare Birthplace Trust–University of Birmingham (UK).

Thierry Crépin holds a Ph.D. in history from Université Paris I. His doctoral dissertation was devoted to the children's press in France that existed between 1934 and 1954. He has studied the penetration of U.S. comic strips in pre– and post–World War II France. He focused his research on the various methods used to generate French-made imitations that had come under attack from teachers of religious and political opinions who eventually, in July 1949, pushed through the French National Assembly a law that regulated children's publications. He recently coedited *On tue à chaque page!* (Paris: Editions du Temps, 1999), a collection of essays on subjects pertaining to the new regulatory laws, including their impact, their short- and long-term effects, and their eventual distortion into a legislation used by the French government to censor publications for adults. Recently, his research has centered on the morality leagues found in pre–World War II France which served as monitors and censors of popular culture.

Oskar Stanislaw Czarnik graduated from Warsaw University Philological Department in 1962. He later acquired a position in the National Library of Warsaw. In 1979 he received his Ph.D. and became an assistant professor at the Institute of Literary Research of the Polish Academy of Sciences of Warsaw. Today he is an associate professor at the Book and Reader Institute of the National Library in Warsaw and an assistant professor in Łódź University's Library Science Department. His publications include *Bibliografia powieści odcinkowych 1918–1926* (Wroclaw: Wydawnictwa Uniwersytetu Wroclawskiego, 1979), a bibliography of serial/column novels published in installments in selected Polish dailies from 1918 to 1926; *Proza artystyczna a prasa codezienna 1918–1926* (Wroclaw: Ossolineum, 1982), artistic prose published in selected Polish dailies from 1918 to 1926; *Między dwoma sierpniami. Polska kultura literacka w latach 1944–1980* (Warszawa: Wiedza Powszechna, 1993), a study of literary culture institutions in Poland and abroad in exile from 1944 to 1980; and *Ideowa I literackie wybory "Robotnika" w latach 1918–1939* (Warszawa: Biblioteka Narodowa, 1996), the cultural policy of the socialist daily *Robotnik* from 1918 to 1939. In addition, Czarnik has written a dozen chapters of various books written by collective authors. He has authored over fifty articles published in scientific and literary journals. His interests include the sociology of literature, literary cultural institutions, cultural policy in totalitarian states, different forms of citizenship, and the history of Polish emigrants and émigrés in the nineteenth and twentieth centuries.

Donald G. Davis, Jr. is a professor of history and LIS and has served in the Graduate School of Library and Information Science, University of Texas at Austin since 1971, after receiving his education at UCLA, UC-Berkeley, and the University of Illinois at Urbana-Champaign. He currently teaches courses on the history of archives, books, and libraries and on collection development in addition to consulting and professional activities around the world. Editor of *Libraries & Culture* (quarterly from the University of Texas Press) since 1977, he has authored or coauthored seven monographs and reference works, including *American Library History: A Comprehensive Guide to the Literature* (1989) and *Encyclopedia of Library History* (1994). He has edited six volumes of conference proceedings and collected papers and published more than 125 articles, chapters, and reports as well as more than 225 book reviews.

Kai Ekholm is a licentiate in philosophy, University of Tampere, the chief librarian at the Jyväskylä University Library, and currently a member of the European Council "New Book Economy" project. He has been an active member of the National Electronic Library–FinELib steering group (1997–99) and is also listed as a member of the National Advisory Committee on the Information Society of Teaching, Research, and Culture, serving since 1997. His special areas of interest are electronic publishing, electronic libraries, and the study of censorship. Additionally, he is considered to be a popular speaker at various seminars and conferences and has written many books and articles on subject matters such as *Hypermedia* with Klaus Oesch (Otava, 1993); *CD-ROM käsikirja* (The CD-ROM handbook) (Otava, 1994); *Tiedon valtatiet ja kinttupolut* (The highways and byways of information), with Ari Haasio and Rami Heinisuo; *Suomen atk-kustannus* (1995); *Kielletyt kirjat* (Banned books) (Library of Parliament, 1996); *Eduskunnan kirjaston tutkimuksia ja selvityksiä,* vol. 3; *Elektronisen viittaamisen opas* (A guide to electronic referencing), with Rami Heinisuo; and *Jyväskylän yliopiston kirjasto* (1996).

Cheng Huanwen is the current director of Zhongshan University Library and professor in the Department of Library and Information Science, Zhongshan University, Guangzhou, China. Before 2000 he was the chair of the Department of Library and Information Science and the associate dean of the School of Information Science and Technology of Zhongshan University. He has actively participated in professional and academic activities and societies. At present, he is an executive member of the Library History Round Table of IFLA, vice-chair of the LIS Research Committee of the Society for Library Science of China, and president of the Library Society of Guangdong Province. His academic achievements in library and information science include five books and more than a hundred articles published at home and abroad. Among his books are the *Selected Works of Book History in China* (1994); *An Introduction to Book Culture in China* (1995); *Information Superhighway–A Way toward Changing Human Life in the 21st Century* (1995); *A Biography of the Father of Library Science Education in China: Samuel T. Y. Seng* (1997); and *A History of Books and Libraries in China* (coauthor, national textbook, 1987). He has won a number of academic and research awards, including the Excellent Faculty Member of Guangdong Province, the Excellent Book of the Ministry of Education of China, and the Best Paper of Guangdong Province.

Contributors

Christine Jenkins is assistant professor at the Graduate School of Library and Information Science at the University of Illinois at Urbana-Champaign. A graduate of Macalester College, she has an M.S. and a Ph.D. from the University of Wisconsin-Madison's School of Library and Information Science, as well as an M.A. in children's literature from Eastern Michigan University. Her background also includes thirteen years as a school media specialist in the Ann Arbor Public Schools. Her research interests include the history of youth services librarianship, young people's texts and reading practices, the children's canon, and intellectual freedom. Her work has appeared in *Libraries & Culture* and in *Reclaiming the American Library Past: Writing the Women In* (Ablex Publishing Corporation, 1996).

Edward Kasinec holds graduate degrees from Columbia University (M.A., 1968, M.Phil., 1979), and Simmons College (M.L.S., 1976). His professional career includes service as reference librarian/archivist for the Harvard University Library and the Ukrainian Research Institute Library (1973–80); librarian for Slavic Collections, University of California, Berkeley, Library (1980–84); and chief, Slavic and Baltic Division, New York Public Library (1984–present). Kasinec has published upward of two hundred articles and books. (For a listing, see I. G. Matveeva and G. V. Mikheeva, "Amerikanskii slavist E. Kazinets i ego osnovnye knigovedcheskie trudy," in *Istoriko-Bibliograficheskie issledovaniia. Sbornik nauchnykh trudov*, vol. 7 [1998], [156]–173.) He has lectured on issues of bibliography and librarianship throughout the world, including at Sapporo University, Hebrew University, and many North American and Russian institutions. He has traveled widely over the last three decades, visiting upward of fifty world capitals in North America, Europe, the Middle East, Asia, the Caribbean, Central America, and Africa. He has served as consultant to programs at the University of Texas, the University of Pennsylvania, St. John's University (Collegeville, Minnesota), Saint Paul's University (Ottawa), the National Library of Canada, the University of California, and the Tolstoy Foundation, and he has been acknowledged in more than 120 publications. He is past chair of the Slavic and East European Section, Association of College and Research Libraries, American Library Association (1978–79); cochair, Bibliography and Documentation Committee, American Association for the Advancement of Slavic Studies (1985–89); and a member of the Society for Textual Scholarship (1992–present), and the Bibliography, Information Retrieval and Documentary Sub-Committee of the Joint Council for Soviet Studies of the American Council of Learned Societies and the Social Science Research Council (1985–present). He has organized numerous symposia and conferences and serves on a number of editorial and advisory committees in the area studies field. Kasinec is the author of six successful grant proposals to the U.S. Department of Education and the National Endowment for the Humanities. He is a member of a number of professional societies and organizations, among them, the Grolier Club.

István Király graduated from the History-Philosophy Faculty of the "Babeş-Bolyai" University, Cluj (Kolozsvár), Romania, in 1976. He received his Ph.D. in philosophy in May 1999. His research and publications concentrate on the fields of the methodology of philosophy, the history of philosophy, and applied philosophy. He has been a librarian at the "Lucian Blaga" Central University Library, Cluj (Kolozsvár), since 1980 and the editor of *Philobiblon, Bulletin of the "Lucian Blaga" Central University Library* since 1995. He has been a lecturer in the Systematic Philosophy Department, Faculty of Philosophy, "Babeş-Bolyai" University, since 1991 and associate professor since 1998. Serving as a researcher-librarian, he focuses his studies on library censorship, library sociology, and the sociology of culture. His major publications include "Teme lukácsiene în 'Istorie şi contiinţa de clasă'" (Lukácsian themes in "History and class conscience"), *Revista de Filosofie a Academiei Române* January–February 1983); "Information und Geheimnis," in *Biblioteca şi Învatamîntul* (Cluj, 1984); "A titok és kategoriális szerkezete" (The secret and its categorical structure), in *Magyar Filozófiai Szemle* (Budapest: Magyar Tudományos Akadémia, 1986); "Le Complot. Serment et secret," in *Politica Hermetica* (Paris: Tome 6, 1992); "Fonds secretes ou fonds interdites? Esquise historiques sur les fonds secretes des Bibliotheques en Roumanie," *Bulletin des Bibliothèques de France* (1994–96); *Fond secret, Fond "S" special. Contributii la istoria fondurilor secrete de biblioteca din România* (Secret library fond, special "S" fond. Contribution to the history of secret library fonds in Romania), in collaboration with Doru Radosav and Ionu Costea (Cluj: Editura Dacia, 1995); *Határ–Hallgatás–Titok* (Limit–silence–secret) (Cluj: Editura Komp-Press, 1996); *Filozófia és Itt-Lét* (Philosophy and presence) (Cluj: Editura Erdélyi Hiradó, 1999); *Fenomenologia existentiala a secretului. Încercare de filosofie aplicata* (The existential phenomenology of the secret. An attempt of applied philosophy) (Piteşti: Editura "Paralela 45," 2000).

Mary Niles Maack has been a faculty member at the University of California at Los Angeles (UCLA) since 1986; currently, she is a professor in the Department of Information Studies. In 1978 Professor Maack earned a doctorate from Columbia University in New York City, and since then she has conducted research on the history of libraries and librarianship in Africa, Europe, and the United States. She spent two years in Senegal and has been a lecturer or consultant in over a dozen other African countries. Her Africanist publications include numerous articles as well as a book entitled *Libraries in Senegal* (published in 1981 by the American Library Association). She also conducted archival and oral history research relating to the first generation of French women to enter librarianship in 1982. She also won the Justin Winsor Award of the ALA Library History Round Table for her paper on that particular topic. In 1982–83 she was named Fulbright lecturer at the Ecole Nationale Supérieure des Bibliothèques in France, and since that time, she has continued her research on topics related to the development of French public library services. Additionally, Maack has begun research on a historical study that will use a biographical approach to analyze and compare the contributions of French, British, and American women who were recognized as library leaders during the period from 1890 to 1945. Her research on gender issues in librarianship includes a book entitled *Aspirations and Mentoring in an Academic Environment* (coauthored with Joanne Passet, Greenwood Press, 1994) as well as articles in journals such as *Libraries & Culture, Library Trends, Library Quarterly,* the *Journal of Library and Information Science Education* and the *Graduate School of Library and Information Science, University of Illinois, Occasional Papers*.

Ilkka Mäkinen graduated in 1980 from the University of Helsinki with an M.A. in comparative literature. In the 1970s and 1980s he worked as a librarian at the Finnish Institute for International Affairs, the Helsinki City Library, and the Library of Parliament in Helsinki. Since the late 1980s he has been working as a researcher and instructor at the Department of Information Studies at the University of Tampere, where he earned his doctorate in 1997. The title of his dissertation is "'The Lending Library Is a Necessity': The Introduction of the Modern 'Desire to Read' into Finland and the Institutions of Reading" (in Finnish with an English summary). In 1997 he became lecturer on the topic of intermediary systems (e.g., libraries) and information sources in the department. He is also a reader in library history. His published articles relate to the subject of Finnish library history in Finnish, Swedish, and English (e.g., in *Libraries & Culture*). In 1999 two of his books were published. The first was an introduction to information studies, and the other was a collection of articles on the history of Finnish public libraries during the twentieth century. His recent research interests include the scholarly exchange in libraries between Finland and the United States since the Second World War;

the history of Finnish libraries; and the history of reading habits during the modern era and the reading societies in northern Europe.

Martin Meyer graduated in 1985 from the Universität Heidelberg, concentrating his thesis on Walter Abish's work. He received his Ph.D. from the Universität Gesamthochschule Kassel in 1992. Between 1986 and 1999 Meyer taught English and American literature in Kassel, holding the position of *wissenschaftlicher Mitarbeiter* in the English Department. His dissertation, "Nachkriegsdeutschland im Spiegel amerikanischer Romane der Besatzungszeit (1945–1955)," was published by Narr (Tübingen) in 1994. It discusses more than twenty novels by American writers in which the setting is postwar Germany (e.g., Thomas Berger's *Crazy in Berlin*). Together with Wolf Kindermann and Gabriele Spengemann, Meyer coedited *Tangenten: Literatur & Geschichte* (Münster: Lit, 1996), a collection of original essays honoring the literary historian Martin Schulze. Having majored in English and political science, Meyer is particularly interested in the role literature played in the political and cultural context of the Cold War years. His publications discussing the function of American literature in Germany after 1945 include *Kay Boyle's Postwar Germany* (1990), *Young Lions in Wasteland* (1995), *Armed Services Editions: Rotationsromane für amerikanische Soldaten* (1996), and *From Armed Services Editions to the Service of Armed Editions?* (2000). Forthcoming are two essays on American literature in Germany in a handbook edited by Detlev Junker at the German Historical Institute in Washington, D.C. (Cambridge University Press). Currently, Meyer is experiencing the vicissitudes of an academic career in today's world: he is currently looking for new employment.

Martine Poulain is the general conservator of the libraries and director of Médiadix, of the University of Paris X, which is the Center for Continuing Education in Librarianship and the IUP. As a sociologist, she has published many works and articles on the sociology of reading, the history of libraries, and the history of censorship. Among her recent publications, she is editor-in-chief of the "La Censure du livre," in *Histoire de l'édition française, 1945–1995* (Paris: Electre-Editions du Cercle de la Librairie, 1998); *Lire en France aujourd'hui* (Paris: Le Cercle de la Librairie, 1993); *La Lecture d'Est en Ouest: regards européens* (Paris: Bibliothèque Publique d'Information, 1993); *Histoire des bibliothèques françaises, 1914–1990* (Paris: Editions du Cercle de la Librairie-Promodis, 1992); *Les Bibliothèques publiques en Europe* (Paris: Editions du Cercle de la Librairie, 1992). In addition, she has held various titles such as president of the Round Table

Research on Reading of IFLA and secretary of the Library History Round Table. She was the coordinator of the conference entitled "Books, Libraries, Reading, and Publishing in the Cold War," organized in Paris in June 1998 by IFLA, Enssib, and Médiadix.

Bernard Pudal is a professor of political science at the University of Montpellier (France) and researcher with the CSU (Culture et Sociétés Urbaines), laboratory of CNRS (Centre National de la Recherche Scientifique), Paris. His work concentrates primarily on Communism and secondarily on reading. He is the author of *Prendre Parti (pour une sociologie historique du Parti Communiste Français, 1920-1980)* (Paris: Presses de la Fondation Nationale des Sciences Politiques). He currently works, in collaboration with Claude Pennetier, researcher at CNRS and editor in chief of *Dictionnaire biographique du Mouvement Ouvrier Français*, on the entry entitled "Le Maitron" on institutional autobiographies from the 1920s to the 1960s. He has published two studies in the journal *Genèses*: "Ecrire son autobiographie, les autobiographies communistes d'institution," 23 (June 1996): 53–75, and "La 'Vérification,'" 23 (June 1996): 145–63. His research concentrates on the relationship of contemporary reading to politics, in addition to the sociohistory of contemporary reading. He recently published, in collaboration with Gérard Mauger and Claude Poliak, *Histoires de lecteurs* (Nathan: Essais et Recherches, 1999), which consists of cross studies of biographical trajectories and reading patterns. He recently published "Le Peuple dans 'Fils du Peuple' de Maurice Thorez," *Sociétés et Représentations* (December 1999): 265–79, in which his interests in the history of Communism and reading intersect.

The late *Pamela Spence Richards* was a professor in the School of Communication, Information, and Library Studies at Rutgers University in New Brunswick, New Jersey, from 1978 until her death in 1999. She received degrees from Harvard and Columbia Universities in Germanic languages and her M.L.S. and D.L.S. in library service from Columbia. Active in a number of professional organizations, her research interests focused on scientific communication channels and the procurement of strategic enemy publications by Axis intelligence and German cartels between 1939 and 1945. Her growing interest in Cold War issues was reflected in her most recent publications. These include her contribution to the 1998 Paris conference on "Books, Libraries, Reading, and Publishing in the Cold War," entitled "Cold War Librarianship: Soviet and American Library Activities in Support of National Foreign Policy, 1946-1991," in this issue of *L&C*. Richards was instrumental in planning and organizing the conference. Another recent article entitled "Soviet-American Library Relations in the 1920s and 1930s: A Study in Mutual Fascination and Distrust," appeared in the *Library Quarterly* 68:4 (October 1998). In addition to her contributions to library journals, Richards served as the editor of a special issue of *Libraries & Culture* (33:1, Winter 1998) on the history of reading and libraries in the United States and Russia, the proceedings of an international conference held in 1996 in Vologda, Russia.

Louise S. Robbins is associate professor and director of the School of Library and Information Studies of the University of Wisconsin-Madison. She has master's degrees in education and library and information studies and received her Ph.D. in library and information studies from the Texas Woman's University in 1991. Her research has focused on the history of censorship and intellectual freedom, especially in libraries. She has authored two books on the topic: *Censorship and the American Library: The American Library Association's Response to Threats to Intellectual Freedom, 1939–1969* (Greenwood, 1996) and the newly published *The Dismissal of Miss Ruth Brown: Civil Rights, Censorship and the American Library* (Oklahoma University Press, 2000). She is pleased that her book is being used in book discussions in Bartlesville, Oklahoma, the book's setting, to open conversations about race. Her articles have appeared in *Library Quarterly*, *Libraries & Culture*, the *Journal of Education for Library and Information Science,* and the *Southwestern Historical Quarterly.* Her 1998 article "'Fighting McCarthyism through Film': A Library Censorship Case Becomes a Storm Center," was recently named winner of the first Donald G. Davis Award for the best article published in library history in the preceding two years. Robbins, who teaches chiefly in the area of government information sources and bibliographic instruction, is a fellow of the University of Wisconsin-Madison Teaching Academy. Her government information sources class recently developed a Web site for the Wisconsin Legislature. With Douglas Zweizig, and others too numerous to mention, Robbins has recently served as advisor to the Governor's Task Force on Privacy. Robbins has lectured at Zhongshan University, Guangzhou, Guangdong Province, P.R.C. She serves on the boards of the Association for Library and Information Science Education and Beta Phi Mu.

Jiřina Šmejkalová graduated from Charles University, Prague, with a degree in Czech literature and linguistics and is currently teaching at the Ustinov Institute for the Study of East and Central Europe,

University of Durham, U.K. She has had teaching and research appointments in Europe and the United States, including Prague, Budapest, Vienna, and Santa Cruz. She is the cofounder and academic board member of the Gender Studies Center, Prague, and is also a member of an expert team of ERICArts. Her research interests include transitions of cultural policies and cultural industries in post-1989 Europe, Czech literary and book history, and questions of gender in post-Communist societies.

Valeria D. Stelmakh is currently a senior researcher at the Russian State Library. In 1957 she graduated from the Moscow Institute of Culture (librarianship), and she earned her Ph.D. in pedagogy at the Leningrad Institute of Culture in 1978. She has held the position of expert in the Department of Culture of the Moscow Magistrate from 1957 to 1965. She was also the senior researcher and head librarian at the Lenin State Library of the U.S.S.R. from 1965 through 1968, when she became the head of the Department of Sociology on Reading and Librarianship at the Lenin State Library from 1968 to 1994. This position led to the title of senior researcher on reading and librarianship at the Department of Sociology at the Russian State Library from 1994 to the present. As an active member of IFLA, she held positions such as founder and chair of the IFLA Round Table on Research in Reading, 1985–91; secretary of the IFLA RTRR, 1991–93; chair of the IFLA RTRR, 1993–95; founder and chair of the IFLA Section on Reading, 1995–97; chair of the IFLA Working Group on Literacy, 1995; and a member of the Standing Committee of the IFLA Section on Reading, 1997–present. In addition, she has been a member of the Working Group on Literacy, 1997, and is an observer of the Section on Library Theory and Research, 1997–present. She has also been a professional coordinator of the following projects at the national level: Books and Reading in the Life of the Small Settlements, 1973; Books and Reading in the Life of the Rural Settlements, 1978; We and Literature, 1991; Public Opinion on the Library, 1992; Book and Reading in the Mirror of Sociology, 1992; Libraries and Reading in Post-Soviet Russia, 1994–95; Reading in the Context of Censorship, 1996; National Idea and National Consciousness in Post-Soviet Russia (based on journalistic and publicistic literary output), 1997; Russia Reads, 1998; Books and Libraries in Contemporary Society, 1999–present. On an international level, her involvements include Reading in the East European Countries, 1975; International Directory of Research Institutes and Groups in Sociology of Books, Libraries and Reading (IFLA project), 1988; Image of the Library (IFLA project), 1993–95; Libraries and Reading in Times of Cultural Change (IFLA project), 1996–97. She is also an editor and compiler of books.

Boris Volodin graduated from the Leningrad State Institute of Culture (now St. Petersburg State University of Culture and Arts) in 1971. From 1971 to 1975 he worked as a member of the library faculty. He then became the librarian at the special library of the Institute of Architecture and worked there from 1975 to 1978. Postgraduate study followed at the Leningrad Institute of Culture (chair of library science) and earned his Ph.D. in 1982. During his studies he was a researcher at the same institution. Since 1980 he has held the following positions: leading researcher (library and information science), National Library of Russia (NLR), present; professor of library history at the High Library School of the NLR, 1993; guest professor (*Gastprofessor*) at the Library and Information School at Stuttgart; research grants in Germany (1998), the United Kingdom (1994), and Poland (1995). He has also been an active participant at international conferences in Austria, Denmark, Germany, Romania, and other countries. Since 1987 he has served as chief editor of the review of the St. Petersburg Library Society, *Peterburgskaya Bibliotechnaya Shkola* (Petersburg Library School). He has authored more than 150 publications in Russian, German, English, French, and other languages, among them "Die Forschungsbibliothek in Russland," *Bibliothek Forschung und Praxis* 22:1 (1998): 111–13; "Russian Library History in a European Context," *Library History* 14:1 (1998): 23–29; "The Scholarly Library at the End of the Twentieth Century," *Libraries & Culture* 33:1 (1998): 120–26. His areas of interest include library history, library and information science, the history of science, and the history of culture.

Priscilla C. Yu is professor of library administration and head of the City Planning and Landscape Architecture Library at the University of Illinois Library, Urbana-Champaign. She received her bachelor's degree at the University of California, Berkeley, and her master's degree at Columbia University. She has served as a research associate at the Center for Chinese Studies, University of California, Berkeley. Her recently published book entitled *Chinese Academic and Research Libraries: Acquisitions, Collections and Organizations* has become a major reference work. Included among her important writings are the "International Gift and Exchange: The Asian Experience," 1981; "Berkeley's Exchange Program: A Case Study," 1982; "National Library of China: The Acquisitions of Foreign Language Materials," 1984; "Taiwan's International Exchange Program: A Study in Cultural Diplomacy," 1985; "Chinese Theories on Collection Development," 1988; "Collection Development of Western Language Materials: Taiwan's National Central Library," 1990; "The Development of Foreign Language Collections at Peking University Library: Problems and Prospects,"

1991; "Chinese University Libraries: The Nanjing Scene," 1993; "Arthur E. Bostwick and Chinese Library Development: A Chapter in International Cooperation," 1998; "Leaning to One Side: The Impact of the Cold War on Chinese Library Collections," to be published in 2001. She has been an active member of and served in a variety of positions in both the American Library Association (ALA) and the Chinese American Librarians Association (CALA), and she is currently serving on the Board of Directors of CALA. Additionally, Yu has been a recipient of many grants for research in China and Taiwan, including those from the Council on Library Resources (Washington, D.C.), the China Exchange Program (UIUC), the Scholar's Travel Fund (UIUC), the Research and Publication Committee Award, (UIUC), and the Research Board (UIUC). She recently was awarded the Chinese American Librarians Association 1999 Distinguished Service Award. Yu serves as a consultant to Peking University Library.

INDEX

This subject index lists information contained in articles, illustrations, and tables. Bibliographic notes are not indexed. Reference to tables are indicated with a "t" following the page number. Page numbers referring to illustrations are italicized. Subject headings are based largely on natural language and are alphabetized word-by-word. The index contains country names that were in use during the Cold War period (e.g. Czechoslovakia, USSR, Yugoslavia, etc.).

Indexes to individual articles were prepared by the students in the Indexing and Abstracting class LIS 8230, Winter 2000, Library and Information Science Program at Wayne State University, Detroit, Michigan, under the supervision of Hermina G.B. Anghelescu. Robert M. Bristow, a student in the Indexing and Abstracting class LIS 8230, Winter 2001, cumulated these indexes and co-edited the final index with Hermina G.B. Anghelescu. The indexers are listed below in alphabetical order of their last name.

Alexa G. Azzopardi
Natalie Bracy-Thomas
David O. Conklin
Andrea M. Coppola
Elizabeth J. Favers
Kristy A. Geier
Pennie J. Howard
Martha E. Joyce
Mary Kickham-Samy
Barbara Koch
Michele P. LaMeau
John Mitchell
Wendy Ng
Jeannette Olbey-Leake
Linda M. Pannuto
Karen Robertson Henry
Rebecca C. Rydzewski
Mary E. Rzepczynski
Amy R. Suchowski
Julia Williford-Sosnowsky

288 Index

A
Academic libraries
  Central University Library,
    Bucharest, Romania, 235, *238,*
    243, 246, 248
  in China, 48t, 254, 257–260, 259t
  Helsinki University Library,
    Finland, 213, 214, 215, 224, 229,
    230t
Africa
  and Cold War, 58–84
  cultural center libraries, 58, 75–80,
    81, 84
  cultural diplomacy, 58–84
  and IFLA, 6
All-Union Book Chamber, Moscow
  and N. M. Sikorsky, 10
Alliance Française
  and cultural centers in Africa, 75–80
  and cultural diplomacy in Africa,
    59, 60–61, 75, 77
  and libraries in Africa, 61, 75–80,
    81, 84
  and the spread of the French
    language, 60–61
American Book Center (ABC) for
  War Devastated Libraries, Inc.
  and Finnish libraries, 213, 215, 219
  and United States Book Exchange,
    Inc., 213
American Book Publishers Council
  (ABPC)
  and Joseph McCarthy, 30, 31, 36
American Information Resource
  Center, New Delhi, India
  bookplate, *267, 267–274, 272, 273,
  274*
American Institute at the University
  of Helsinki
  and Finnish libraries, 224, 226,
    230t
American Library Association (ALA)
  concerns of US libraries in IFLA,
    4–5, 6–7
  and cultural imperialism, 5, 7
  and Finnish libraries, 214, 219
  Intellectual Freedom Committee,
    27, 30, 34

International Relations Office, 214
and libraries in Latin America, 65
Library Bill of Rights, 27
resistance to censorship of
  children literature, 119–128,
  123, 125
Aragon, Louis
  and French Communist Party, 154,
    158
Armed Services Editions (ASE),
  Germany, 162–163, 164
Arrival and Departure (Koestler)
  and *Darkness at Noon,* 173, 174
  and Robert Calmann-Levy, 173,
    174
Asia
  and IFLA, 6
ASLA (Amerikan Suomen Lainan
  Apurahat)
  and academic libraries in Finland,
    211–229, 230t
  and ASLA-Fulbright program,
    211–229, 230t
  and the most favored libraries,
    230t
  significance of, 228–229
  and US Congress, 216–218,
    219–221
Authors
  and censorship in Finland, 51–52
  in Poland, 107, 111, 112
  and self-censorship in USSR, 144

B
Baudrillard, Jean
  on censorship, 55
BBK. *See* Bibliotechno-
  bibiograficheskaia klassifikatsiia
  (BBK)
Bellet, Madeleine
  and comic strips, 134, 140
Bibliotechno-bibiograficheskaia
  klassifikatsiia (BBK), 22, 24. *See
  also* Marxist-Leninist
  classification
Black markets
  and *Darkness at Noon,* 176
  selling of books, USSR, 146–147

Book illustration
 Newbery-Caldecott awards,
 123-128
Book production
 in Germany, 163, 164
 in Poland, 110-112
 in Romania, 240-245
 and Soviet Military
 Administration (SMAD), 165
 in USSR, 144, 145
Book trade
 black market, USSR, 146-147
 and British Council, 63
Bookplates
 United States Information Agency,
 American Information Resource
 Center, New Delhi, India, *267,
 267-272, 271, 272*
 United States Information Agency,
 Germany, 272-274, *273, 274*
Booksellers
 and self-censorship, USSR, 144
Bookstores
 and censorship, Finland, 51-52
 and destruction of books, Poland,
 110
Boorstin, Daniel J.
 on censorship, 11
 as founder of the Center for the
 Book, Library of Congress, vii
British Council
 and book export trade, 63
 and book selection, 72
 and cultural diplomacy in Africa,
 59, 61-65, 71-75, 81, 83, 84
 and cultural propaganda, 62
 and foreign publications, 64
 and libraries, 64, 71-75, 81, 83,
 84
 and Lionel McColvin, 64
 and the Public Library
 Development Scheme, 74
 and Sir Harold Nicolson, 61-62,
 63
Burkhardt, Frederick
 and U.S. National Commission on
 Libraries and Information
 Science, 10

C
Carozzo, Ettore
 and comic strips, 132, 134
 and Librairie Moderne, 132
Cartoonists
 French, 132, 133
 Italian, 132
Catalogs
 of forbidden books in Romania,
 245-246
 at the Lenin State Library,
 Moscow, 22-23
Ceausescu, Nicolae, 239-240, 241
Censorship
 and bookstores, Finland, 51-52
 and the Central Bureau of the
 Press, Publications, and
 Performances Control, Poland,
 106, 107, 108
 of children literature, US, 1946-
 1955, 116-128, *123, 125*
 in Chinese libraries, 255
Controlling Commission, Finland,
 51, 53
 in Czechoslovakia, 87-102
 Daniel J. Boorstin's view on, 11
 Darkness at Noon, 176-177
 distribution of *samizdat* literature
 in USSR, 11-12
 and editors, Poland, 104, 108
 in Finnish libraries, 1944-1946,
 51-56
 and French Communist Party
 (FCP), 152-160
 hermeneutic perspective on, 55-56
 and House Subcommittee on Un-
 American Activities, 199
 and Ministry of Education,
 Finland, 51
 and Ministry of Information and
 Propaganda, Poland, 106, 108,
 111
 in Nazi Germany, 54
 omnicensorship concept, 52, 53
 in Poland, 104, 105-106, 107, 110,
 113, 114
 Polish Committee of National
 Liberation, 105-106

290   Index

and publishers, Finland, 51–52
and publishing houses, Poland, 104
and reading, USSR, 143–151
in Romania, 185–191, 243–246
spetskhran collections at Lenin State Library, Moscow, 21, 53
and Urho Kekkonen, 53
in US, 116–128, *123, 125,* 197–201
Center for Finnish Libraries and book distribution, 215
Center for the Book, Library of Congress, vii, viii, xxiv
Central University Library, Bucharest, Romania, 235, *238,* 243, 246, 248
Children literature
censorship, US, 1946-1955, 116–128, *123, 125*
in France during Cold War, 131–141
China
and IFLA, 6, 47
influence of Western librarianship, 46–49
influences of Soviet librarianship, 43–45, 255–256, 257
influences of US librarianship, 41–43
library collections, 253–265
library science and Du Dingyou, 43
library science and Liu Guojun, 43, 46
library science and Mary Elizabeth Wood, 42
library science and Shen Zhurong, 42–43
National Library of China, 47, 254, 260–264, 261t, 263t
Peking University Library, 254, 257–260, 259t
public and academic libraries, 1949-1990, 48t
segregation of Chinese librarianship from Western librarianship, 45–46
Cold War. *See also* Censorship
and Francophone Africa, 58–84
and IFLA, 1–12
and press for children in France, 131–141
and Soviet librarians, 193–201
and US librarians, 193–201
Comic strips
American, 132, 133, 134, 135, 137, 141
Cino Del Duca, 132, 134, 135
and demoralization of youth, 131, 136
English, 132
Ettore Carozzo, 132, 134
foreign, 131, 136, 138
and Front Patriotique de la Jeunesse, 134
Italian, 132
Madeleine Bellet, 134, 140
Paul Winkler, 132, 133, 134, 135, 141
and Société Parisienne d'Editions, 132
Yugoslavian, 132
Le Comité de Défense de la Littérature at de la Presse pour la Jeunesse (Committee of Defense of Youth Literature and Press)
and regulation of press for children during the Cold War, 131–141
Communist Party of the Soviet Union (CPSU)
and French Communist Party, 159, 160
Controlling Commission, Finland and censorship, 53
Council for Mutual Economic Assistance (Comecon)
and Soviet libraries, 196, 197
Council of Scientific Libraries, Finland
and post-war relief, 225, 226, 229
Cultural center libraries
in Africa, 58, 75–80, 81, 84
Cultural diplomacy
and Alliance Française in Africa, 59, 60–61, 75, 77

and British Council in Africa, 59,
61–65, 71–75, 81, 83, 84
and United States Information
Agency, 67–71, 72, 81, 82, 83, 84
Cultural imperialism
and Lucile M. Morsch, 7
Cultural propaganda
British Council, 62
Czechoslovakia
censorship, 87–102
and IFLA, 4, 7–8
production of *samizdat* literature,
98–99
publishing, 92–102

D
Darkness at Noon (Koestler)
and the black market, 176
and Cold War, 172–180
English edition, 172–173
and French Communist Party, 173,
175, 176
French edition, 173–174
and *Le Zéro et l'infini,* 173
popularity of, 172, 174–176
reaction to, France, 1945-1950,
172–180

F
Fédération Nationale de la Presse
Française
and press for children, 136
Finland
academic libraries, 211–229, 230t
censorship in libraries, 1944-1946,
51–56
German books in academic
libraries, 212
Ministry of Foreign Affairs, 214, 215
US books in academic libraries,
212, 218
Foreign policy
and library activities, US, 193–201
and library activities, USSR,
193–201
France. *See also* Alliance Française
communist intellectuals, 153, 154,
155, 157, 158, 159–160

French Communist Party and
censorship, 152–160
and press for children in France
during Cold War, 131–141
Francis, Frank
and IFLA, 3
French Communist Party (FCP)
and anti-Communist authors, 158
and censorship, 152–160
and *Darkness at Noon* (Koestler),
173, 175, 176
and "heretical" texts, 152–160
and *remise de soi,* 157–159
and Soviet-German Treaty, 156
and the Soviet Union Communist
Party, 159, 160
Fundamental Library on the Social
Sciences, Moscow, 18

G
German Democratic Republic
and IFLA, 4
and West Germany, 166
Germany
Amerika Häuser libraries, 65,
272–274, *273, 274*
Armed Services Editions (ASE),
162–163, 164
book production, 163, 164
censorship during the Nazi period,
54
and German Democratic
Republic, 166
Information Control Division,
Publications Branch, 163, 164
Overseas Edition (OSE), 163, 164
periodicals in, 167
public libraries during the Nazi
period, 54–55
Ghana
libraries, 69, 70, 71, 72, 77, 78, 80,
83, 84
Glavlit
and censorship, Finland, 53
and libraries, USSR, 144, 146
and publishing houses, USSR,
144, 146
and *spetskhran,* 53

Great Britain. *See also* British Council
cultural diplomacy, 58–84
Gross, Elizabeth, 123–128

H
Helsinki University Library, 213, 214, 215, 224, 229, 230t
House Subcommittee on Un-American Activities
and Cold War censorship, 199
Hungary
and IFLA, 4

I
IFLA. *See* International Federation of Library Associations (IFLA)
Illustrators
Newbery-Caldecott awards, 123–128
India
American Information Resource Center, New Dehli, bookplate, *267*, 267–274, *272*, *273*, *274*
and IFLA, 3, 6
Information Center Service (ICS)
and book selection, 66
Information Control Division
and the Publications Branch, Germany, 163, 164
Institute for Scientific Information in the Social Sciences (INION), 18
Institute of Literary Studies of the Polish Academy of Sciences, 108
Intellectual Freedom Committee (IFC), 27–28, 30, 32, 34
Interlibrary loan
and Soviet library science, 205
International Communication Agency American Center Library, New Delhi, India bookplate, *271*
International Federation of Library Associations (IFLA)
and capitalism, 1–12
and Cold War, 1–12
and communism, 1–12
conferences, 1–12
establishment of, 2

and Frank Francis, 3, 5, 6, 8
and Polish Libraries Association, 11–12
Round Table on Library History, xvi, xviii, xx, xxiii
Section on Reading, vii, xx
Soviet influence in, 3–4, 6
and the Soviet invasion of Czechoslovakia, 7–8
and U.S. National Commission on Libraries and Information Science, 10
International Information Adminstration (IIA). *See also* United States Information Agency (USIA)
and Joseph McCarthy, 28, 29, 30, 35
Smith-Mundt Act, 28, 66
Italian Communist Party, 155, 156, 175

J
Japan
and IFLA, 3

K
Kekkonen, Urho
and self-censorship, 53
Kirkegaard, Preban
and IFLA, 3, 5, 8
Koestler, Arthur
and Maurice Merleau-Ponty, 178, 179
Krupskaia, Nadezhda K., 204
Kubow, Stefan
and IFLA, 11
and the Polish Librarians Association, 11

L
Lacy, Dan
and McCarthyism, 28, 30
Lenin, Vladimir I.
views on libraries, 204–205, 206
Lenin State Library, Moscow
catalog, 22–23
censorship, 20, 23–25

collections, 17, 144–150
functions, 16–17
International Exchanges Division, 18
Manuscript Division, 18, 19
Marxist-Leninist classification in, 22, 24
and National Library of China, 261
photocopying in, 21–22
preservation, 20–21
reading rooms, 21, 22
research by foreign scholars, 1971-1972, 17–25
and Soviet library science, 208
spetskhran collections, 21, 53, 144
staffing, 19–20
110th anniversary, 16
Librarians
as censors, 54–55
during Cold War, US, 193–201
during Cold War, USSR, 193–201
and Joseph McCarthy, 27–32
and library research in USSR, 204–209
and self-censorship, USSR, 144
status of in Romania, 236–237
Libraries. *See also* Academic libraries; Public libraries
for children and young people, France, 139
in China, 40–49, 48t, 253–265
closed collections, Romania, 185–191, 243–246
closed collections, USSR, 144, 145, 146, 150
in Finland, 51–56, 211–229, 230t
in Ghana, 69, 70, 71, 72, 77, 78, 80, 83, 84
as instruments of cultural diplomacy in Africa, 58–84
and United States Information Agency, 68–71, 72, 81, 82, 83, 84
in USSR, 16–26, 193–201
Libraries and Reading in Times of Cultural Change conference, Vologda, Russia, vii, xv, xviii, xx, xxi

Library associations. *See also* American Library Association (ALA); International Federation of Library Associations (IFLA)
Library Association of China, 43
Polish Librarians Association, 11–12
in Romania, 237–238
Library History Seminar VI, xviii
Library of Congress
Center for the Book, vii, viii, xxiv
and libraries in Finland, 214
Library of the Institute of Technology, Finland
and post-war relief, 213, 214, 224
Library science
in China, 40–49
in USSR, 204–209
Library science education
in China, 40–49
discontinuation of, Romania, 236
Literary communication
control of, in Poland, 1945-1956, 104–115
Literature
American in Germany during Cold War, 162–171
American translated into German, 163, 168
forbidden, Romania, 189–191, 244–246
forbidden, USSR, 143–151

M
Marxist-Leninist classification
Chinese libraries, 256
Lenin State Library, Moscow, 22
McCarthy, Joseph
and American Book Publishers Council, 30, 31, 33, 36
and Cold War, 27–36, 66–67, 154
and International Information Adminstration, 28, 29, 30, 35
and librarians, 27–32
and US library collections, 27–36, 198, 199
McColvin, Lionel
and British Council, 64

294 Index

Merleau-Ponty, Maurice
  and Arthur Koestler, 178, 179
Mexico
  and IFLA, 3
Ministry of Cooperation and
  Development, France, 80
Ministry of Culture, China, 255, 257
Ministry of Culture, Czechoslovakia,
  96
Ministry of Culture, Poland, 107,
  110, 111
Ministry of Culture, Romania, 206,
  235, 237, 245
Ministry of Culture, USSR, 17, 195,
  xv
Ministry of Education, Finland, 51,
  215, 216
Ministry of Education, Romania,
  236
Ministry of Foreign Affairs, Finland,
  214, 215
Ministry of Information and
  Propaganda, Poland, 106, 108,
  111
Ministry of Security, Poland, 106,
  107
Morsch, Lucile M.
  on role of libraries in cultural
  imperialism, 7

N
National Library of China, 47, 254,
  260–264, 261t, 263t, 264
National Library of Finland, 213
National Library of Romania, 234,
  234, 235, 237, 240, 242, 243
National Library of Russia, 207
Nazism
  and censorship in Germany, 54
  and comic strips, 133
  and libraries, 54
Newbery-Caldecott awards, 123–128
Nicolson, Sir Harold
  and the British Council, 61–62, 63
  1987 American Constitutional
  Bicentennial American Center
  Library, New Delhi, India
  bookplate, *271*

O
Octavian Goga County Library, Cluj-
  Napoca, Romania, 246, 248
Office of Foreign Literature,
  Moscow, 9
Office of Publishing Houses, Printing
  Industry, and Bookselling, 112
Office of War Information (OWI)
  and libraries, 65, 219
Overseas Edition (OSE)
  and Armed Services Editions
  (ASE), Germany, 163, 164
Overseas libraries
  and the freedom to read, 27–36

P
Paper
  supply of in France, 134
  supply of in Poland, 107, 111
Peking University Library, China,
  254, 257–260, 259t
Periodicals
  and censorship, Poland, 107, 108
  and censorship, USSR, 145
  for children in France during Cold
  War, 131–141
  Germany, 167
  of library science, in USSR,
  204–209
Philippines
  and IFLA, 3
Poland
  book production, 1945-1956,
  110–112
  censorship, 104, 105–106, 107,
  110, 113, 114
  Central Bureau of the Press,
  Publications, and Performances
  Control, 106, 107, 108
  Division of Book Collections, 107
  foreign publications, 107, 112
  and IFLA, 4
  libraries, 113
  Ministry of Culture, 107, 110, 111
  Polish Committee of National
  Liberation (PKWN), 105–106
  Polish Writers Union, 108, 109
  reading, 113–115

Stalinism, 113, 114
Polish Committee of National
  Liberation (PKWN)
  and censorship, 105–106
Polish Librarians Association
  and Stefan Kubow, 11–12
Polish Literary Bibliography, 108
Polish United Workers Party Central
  Committee, 106
Political Bureau of the Polish
  Workers Party, 106
Press
  regulation of, Poland, 107
  regulation of, Romania, 240–241
Public libraries
  in Nazi Germany, 54–55
Public Library Development Scheme
  (PLDE)
  and British Council, 74
Publishing
  American Book Publishers
    Council (ABPC), 30
  and censorship, Finland, 51–52
  and censorship, Poland, 104
  in Czechoslovakia, 92–102
  paperback books, Germany,
    162–163, 164
  in Romania, 240–245
  and self-censorship, USSR, 144

R
Radio
  and censorship, Poland, 107
Ranganathan, S. R.
  views on IFLA, 5
Reading
  and censorship, USSR, 143–151
  in Poland, 113–115
Remise de soi (the party spirit)
  and the French Communist Party,
    157–159
Research
  in Soviet libraries, 16–25, 204–209
Richards, Pamela Spence
  festschrift by Betty Turock, xi–xvii
  festschrift by Donald G. Davis, Jr.,
    xiv, xviii–xix, xxiii
  festschrift by John Y. Cole, vii, viii

festschrift by Martine Poulain,
  xxi–xxii
festschrift by Valeria D. Stelmakh,
  xx
picture, ix
Romania
  censorship, 185–191, 243–246
  Central University Library,
    Bucharest, Romania, 235, *238*,
    243, 246, 248
  cultural policies, 240–242
  development of libraries, 233–235,
    234, 237, 238, 241, 242, 244, 247
  and IFLA, 4, 237–238
  image of libraries in society,
    238–240, 247–249
  infrastructure for libraries,
    243–247
  library associations, 237–238
  library collections, 242–243
  library system, 235–236
  Ministry of Culture, 206, 235, 237,
    245
  National Library of Romania, 234,
    234, 235, 237, 240, 242, 243
  Nicolae Ceausescu, 239–240, 241
  Octavian Goga County Library,
    Cluj-Napoca, 246, 248
  publishing, 240–245
  status of librarians, 236–237
Russian State Library, Moscow
  Sector for the Sociology of
    Reading and Librarianship, 146

S
Samizdat literature
  distribution of in USSR, 11–12,
    147–149
  production of in Czechoslovakia,
    98–99
  reading of in USSR, 147–149
Sartre, Jean-Paul
  and communism, 154, 157, 158
Secret
  in Socialist societies, 187–191
Sikorsky, N. M
  and All-Union Book Chamber,
    Moscow, 10

Smith-Mundt Act
  and Congress, 65–66
  and Finland, 218, 219, 220
  and International Information Administration, 28
Société Parisienne d'Editions (SPE)
  and comic strips, 132
South Africa
  and IFLA, 9, 10–11
Soviet Military Administration (SMAD)
  and publishing in Germany, 165
Spetskhran collections
  at Lenin Library, Moscow, 21, 53, 144
Switzerland
  and IFLA, 3

T
Tamizdat literature
  on USSR black market, 146
Theaters
  and censorship, Poland, 107
Translators
  and censorship in Finland, 53

U
UNESCO
  and Cold War rivalry of United States and Soviet Union, 201
  and IFLA, 8, 9, 10
Union de la Jeunesse Républicaine de France (UJRF)
  and Communist comic strips, 134
Union des Vaillants et Vaillantes
  and Communist comic strips, 134
Union of Soviet Socialist Republics Library Council
  and IFLA, 4
United States. *See also* American Library Association (ALA)
  and Amerika Häuser in Germany, 272–273, *273*
  censorship during the McCarthy era, 27–36
  censorship of children literature, 116–128, *123, 125*
  and Finnish libraries, 211–229
  library support of foreign policy, 193–201
Smith-Mundt Act, 28, 65–66, 218, 219, 220
United States Book Exchange, Inc. (USBE)
  and American Book Center for War Devastated Libraries, Inc., 213
United States Department of State Libraries, 199, 200, 201
United States Information Agency, 199, 200
United States Information Agency (USIA)
  Bibliographic Services Division, 70
  bookplates, *267,* 267–274, *271, 272, 273, 274*
  and cultural diplomacy, 67–71, 72, 81, 82, 83, 84, 199, 200
United States Information Services (USIS)
  American Center Library, New Delhi, India, bookplates, *267,* 267–272, *271, 272*
  American Library of Information, Germany, bookplates, 272–274, *273, 274*
US foreign policies and libraries, 199, 200, 201, *267,* 267–274, *271, 272, 273, 274*
USSR
  book production, 144, 145
  censorship and reading, 143–151
  Council for Mutual Economic Assistance (Comecon) and libraries, 196, 197
  foreign policy and library activities, 193–201
  joining IFLA, 4
  Lenin State Library, Moscow, 16–26
  libraries, 16–26, 144, 145, 146, 150, 204–209
  library literature, 206–209
  library research, 204–209, xiv–xv
  library support of foreign policy, 193–201

Ministry of Culture, 17, 195, xv
research in libraries, 1971-1972,
    16-25
Russian State Library, Moscow, 146

W
Wood, Mary Elizabeth, 42
Writers unions
    Poland, 108, 109
    USSR, 145

Y
Yugoslavia
    and IFLA, 4

Z
Le Zéro et l'infini
    and *Darkness at Noon,* 173
Zhurong, Shen, 42-43